HOUGHTON MIFFLIN
Reading
A Legacy of Literacy

Teacher's Edition
Grade 4
Traditions

D1275655

Senior Authors J. David Cooper, John J. Pikulski

Authors Patricia A. Ackerman, Kathryn H. Au, David J. Chard, Gilbert G. Garcia, Claude N. Goldenberg, Marjorie Y. Lipson, Susan E. Page, Shane Templeton, Sheila W. Valencia, MaryEllen Vogt

Consultants Linda H. Butler, Linnea C. Ehri, Carla B. Ford

HOUGHTON MIFFLIN   BOSTON • MORRIS PLAINS, NJ

California • Colorado • Georgia • Illinois • New Jersey • Texas

Credits

Cover Photography
by Tony Scarpetta.

Cover Illustration
by Raul Colón.

Assignment Photography
Parker/Boon Productions
p. 323D

Acknowledgments

Grateful acknowledgment is made for permission to reprint copyrighted material as follows:

Theme 3
"Cinderella" from *Fairy Tales,* illustrated by Eric Kincaid. Text copyright © 1994 by Brimax Books, Ltd. Reprinted by permission of the publisher. All rights reserved.

"Why Raven Stays for the Winter," an Alaskan folk tale retold by Diana C. Conway from the October 1999 issue of *Cricket* magazine. Copyright © 1999 by Diana Conway. Reprinted by permission of Carus Publishing Company.

"Yes, It Really Can Rain Frogs" from *Spencer Christian's World of Wonders: Can It Really Rain Frogs? The World's Strangest Weather Events,* by Spencer Christian and Antonia Felix. Copyright © 1997 by Spencer Christian and Antonia Felix. Reprinted by permission of John Wiley & Sons, Inc.

Student Writing Model Feature

Special thanks to the following teachers whose students' compositions appear as Student Writing Models: **Cindy Cheatwood**, Florida; **Diana Davis**, North Carolina; **Kathy Driscoll**, Massachusetts; **Linda Evers,** Florida; **Heidi Harrison**, Michigan; **Eileen Hoffman**, Massachusetts; **Julia Kraftsow**, Florida; **Bonnie Lewison**, Florida; **Kanetha McCord**, Michigan

Theme 3

That's Amazing!

OBJECTIVES

Reading Strategies monitor/clarify; question; evaluate; phonics/decoding

Comprehension noting details; compare/contrast; fantasy/realism

Decoding Longer Words compound words; words with the suffix *-able;* words with *-ed* or *-ing;* words that begin with *a-* or *be-;* final /ər/, /l/, and /əl/ sounds; consonant digraphs

Vocabulary synonyms; dictionary: spelling table/pronunciation key; dictionary: dividing words into syllables

Spelling compound words; final /ər/ and final /l/ or /əl/; words ending with *-ed* or *-ing*

Grammar action verbs; using exact verbs; main verbs and helping verbs; sentence combining with main verbs and helping verbs; present, past, and future tenses; using the correct tense

Writing an explanation; audience; announcement; ordering important information; summary; paraphrasing; process writing: story

Listening/Speaking/Viewing hold a conversation; compare/contrast texts; announcement

Information and Study Skills story chart; Venn diagrams; real-life reading

Theme 3

That's Amazing!
Literature Resources

Theme Writing Process: A Story

Student Writing Model

My Wish

a story by Javis B.
page 324

Reading-Writing Workshop

A Story

pages 324–325G

Leveled Books

See Cumulative Listing of Leveled Books.

Reader's Library

Very Easy

- One Day in May
- Tattercoat
- The Big Gust

Lessons, pages R2–R7

Theme Paperbacks

Easy

The Story of the Milky Way

by Joseph Bruchac and Gayle Ross

Lesson, page 325I

On Level

Little Oh

by Laura Krauss Melmed

Lesson, page 325K

Challenge

The Real Thief

by William Steig

Lesson, page 325M

 Audiotape and Selection Summary Masters

That's Amazing!
The Stranger
Cendrillon
Heat Wave!

Literature Resources

Grade 4

Theme 3

Bibliography

Books for Independent Reading

Choose books from this list for students to read, outside of class, at least thirty minutes a day.

Key

  Science

 Social Studies

 Multicultural

 Music

 Math

 Classic

Art

Very Easy

Sector 7
by David Wiesner
Houghton 1999 (48p)
This almost wordless book follows the adventures of a boy who creates new shapes for clouds.

June 29, 1999
by David Wiesner
Clarion 1992 (32p) also paper
Holly Evans's science experiment causes giant vegetables to appear all across America.

Secrets from the Dollhouse
by Ann Turner
Harper 2000 (32p)
In a series of poems, Emma, a doll, tells of her family's life.

Swine Lake
by James Marshall
Harper 1999 (40p)
When a lean and hungry wolf stumbles onto a stage of dancing pigs, he is in for a big surprise.

The Best Place
by Susan Meddaugh
Houghton 1999 (32p)
A wolf who loves his screened-in porch suddenly wonders if it is the best place in the world.

Easy

 Gracias the Thanksgiving Turkey
by Joy Cowley
Scholastic 1996 (32p)
Miguel befriends Gracias, who is supposed to be Thanksgiving dinner.

A Day with Wilbur Robinson
by William Joyce
Harper 1990 (32p) also paper
A visitor finds that a day at Wilbur Robinson's house is filled with strange and wonderful adventures.

Dinosaur Bob and His Adventures with the Family Lazardo
by William Joyce
Harper 1995 (48p)
The Lazardo family return from Africa with a dinosaur who becomes a baseball hero.

Hog-Eye
by Susan Meddaugh
Houghton 1995 (32p)
A young piglet, captured by a wolf, uses her smarts to get away and regale her family with her story.

The True Story of the 3 Little Pigs
by Jon Scieszka
Viking 1989 (32p) also paper
A. Wolf, claiming he was framed, wants to set the record straight.
Available in Spanish as *La verdadera historia de los tres cerditos*.

On Level

 Yeh-Shen: A Cinderella Story from China
by Ai-Ling Louie
Putnam 1993 (32p)
A fish helps Yeh-Shen become the bride of the prince.

Squids Will Be Squids
by Jon Scieszka
Viking 1998 (48p)
Both familiar and unfamiliar fables get a zany twist.

Jumanji
by Chris Van Allsburg
Houghton 1981 (32p)
Two children get more than they bargained for in a mysterious jungle-adventure board game.
Also available in Spanish.

The Way Meat Loves Salt
by Nina Jaffe
Holt 1998 (32p)
The author retells a Cinderella story from the Eastern European Jewish tradition.

The Irish Cinderlad
by Shirley Climo
Harper 1996 (32p) also paper
Becan rescues Princess Finola, his future bride.

A Big Cheese for the White House
by Candace Fleming
DK Ink 1999 (32p)
In this strange-but-true story, the citizens of Cheshire, Massachusetts, present Thomas Jefferson with a 1,235-pound cheese.

Cloudy with a Chance of Meatballs
by Judi Barrett
Atheneum 1978 (32p)
Delicious food rains from the sky in the town of Chewandswallow.

My Nine Lives by Clio
by Marjorie Priceman
Atheneum 1998 (48p)
Clio, now in her ninth life, describes all the contributions she's made to civilization.

Black and White
by David Macaulay
Houghton 1990
(32p)
Macaulay tells four stories at once, or is it really just one story?

The Orphan Boy
by Tololwa Mollel
Clarion 1990
(32p)

An old man becomes curious about the mysterious powers of an orphan boy.

The Wreck of the *Zephyr*
by Chris Van Allsburg
Houghton 1983 (32p)
An old sailor relates a very strange story.

Challenge

 James and the Giant Peach
by Roald Dahl
Knopf 1961
(120p) also paper
Inside a peach, James sets off on splendid adventures.

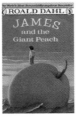 **The Phantom Tollbooth**
by Norton Juster
Random 1961 (256p) also paper
Driving his small electric car through a miniature tollbooth, Milo enters The Lands Beyond.

Poppy
by Avi
Orchard 1995 (160p) also paper

With unfortunate results, Poppy, a deer mouse, defies Mr. Ocax, a great horned owl who rules Dimwood Forest.

Ragweed
by Avi
Avon 1999
(178p)
A young country mouse leaves his family and moves to the city.

Books for Teacher Read Aloud

 The Enormous Egg
by Oliver Butterworth
Little 1956 (188p) also paper
Nate watches over an enormous egg that hatches a triceratops.

 Jouanah: A Hmong Cinderella
by Jewell Reinhart Coburn
Shen's 1996
(32p)
A young Hmong girls finds happiness with the aid of a pair of special shoes.

The King's Equal
by Katherine Paterson
Harper 1992 (64p) also paper
When an arrogant prince sets out to find his equal for a bride, he finds someone much better.

Technology

Computer Software Resources

- **Get Set for Reading CD-ROM**
  That's Amazing!
  Provides background building, vocabulary support, and selection summaries in English and Spanish.

Video Cassettes

- **Over the Moon** *by Rachel Vail. Spoken Arts*
- **Pickles to Pittsburgh** *by Judi Barrett. Live Oak Media*
- **The Borrowers** *by Mary Norton. Media Basics*
- **Cloudy with a Chance of Meatballs** *by Judi Barrett. Media Basics*
- **Tops and Bottoms** *by Janet Stevens. Weston Woods*
- **The Phantom Tollbooth** *by Norton Juster. Media Basics*
- **A Visit with Chris Van Allsburg.** *Houghton*

Audio Cassettes

- **Over the Moon** *by Rachel Vail. Spoken Arts*
- **The Phantom Tollbooth** *by Norton Juster. HarperAudio*
- **Jumanji** *by Chris Van Allsburg. Houghton*
- **The Wreck of the Zephyr** *by Chris Van Allsburg. Houghton*
- **James and the Giant Peach** *by Roald Dahl. HarperAudio*
- **Cloudy with a Chance of Meatballs** *by Judi Barrett. Kimbo Educational*
- **Many Moons** *by James Thurber. HarperAudio*
- **Poppy and Rye** *by Avi. Recorded Books*
- **Pickles to Pittsburgh** *by Judi Barrett. Live Oak Media*
- **Audiotapes for *That's Amazing!*** *Houghton Mifflin Company*

Technology Resources addresses are on page R28.

Education Place
www.eduplace.com *Log on to Education Place for more activities relating to* That's Amazing!

Book Adventure
www.bookadventure.org *This Internet reading incentive program provides thousands of titles for students to read.*

Theme 3

Theme at a Glance

Theme Concept: *Fantastic tales ranging from the mysterious to the hilarious*

☑ **Indicates Tested Skills**
See page 292G for assessment options.

Anthology Selection 1:
The Stranger
Poetry Link

Anthology Selection 2:
Cendrillon
Dance Link

Anthology Selection 3:
Heat Wave!
Science Link

Theme Resources

Reading		Word Work
Comprehension Skills and Strategies	**Information and Study Skills**	**Decoding Longer Words** Structural Analysis/Phonics
☑ Noting Details, *299D, 307, 323A* **Visual Literacy:** Point of View, *303;* **Comprehension:** Cause and Effect, *305;* Drawing Conclusions, *315;* **Genre:** Fantasy, *313;* Poetry, *322;* How to Read a Poem, *320* Spiral Review, *323Q* **Strategy Focus:** Monitor/Clarify, *299C, 304, 314*	Story Chart, *323C*	☑ Structural Analysis: Compound Words, *323E* **Phonics:** Words That Begin with *a-* or *be-*, *323F* Spiral Review, *323R*
☑ Compare and Contrast, *327D, 333, 357A* **Genre:** Fairy Tales, *331;* **Comprehension:** Fantasy and Realism, *347;* Noting Details, *349;* **Writer's Craft:** Point of View, *335* ☑ Strategy Focus: Question, *327C, 332, 344*	How to Read a Time Line, *356* Recording Information on a Venn Diagram, *357C*	☑ Structural Analysis: Words with the Suffix *-able*, *357E* **Phonics:** Final /ər/, /l/, and /əl/ Sounds, *357F*
☑ Fantasy and Realism, *359D, 365, 381A* **Genre:** Tall Tales, *363;* **Comprehension:** Compare and Contrast, *369;* Story Structure, *371;* **Visual Literacy:** Artist's Style, *375* Spiral Review, *381Q* **Strategy Focus:** Evaluate, *359C, 364, 372*	How to Read a Diagram, *380* ☑ Real-Life Reading, *381C*	☑ Structural Analysis: Words Ending with *-ed* or *-ing*, *381E* **Phonics:** Consonant Digraphs, *381F*
Reteaching: Comprehension, R8, R10, R12 **Challenge/Extension: Comprehension,** R9, R11, R13		**Reteaching: Structural Analysis,** R14, R16, R18

Test Preparation
Taking Tests: Writing a Personal Response
- Anthology, *382*
- Teacher's Edition, *382*
- Practice Book, *205–206*

Spelling
Additional Lessons:
- Frequently Misspelled Words
- Spelling Review/Assessment

THEME 3: That's Amazing!

Pacing	Multi–age Classroom	Technology 
• This theme is designed to take approximately 4 to 6 weeks, depending on your students' needs.	**Related themes—** • **Grade 3** *Incredible Stories* • **Grade 5:** *Animal Encounters*	**Education Place: www.eduplace.com** Log on to Education Place for more activities relating to *That's Amazing!* **Lesson Planner CD-ROM** Customize your planning with the Lesson Planner.

Spelling	Vocabulary Skills, Vocabulary Expansion	Writing & Language			Cross-Curricular
		Grammar, Usage, and Mechanics	**Writing**	**Listening/ Speaking/Viewing**	**Content Area**
☑ Spelling: Compound Words, *323G*	☑ Synonyms, *323I* **Scientific Terms:** Weather Words, *323J*	☑ Action Verbs, *323K*	An Explanation, *323M* Audience, *323N*	Hold a Conversation, *323O*	**Responding:** Math, Art, Internet, *319* **Theme Resources:** *R26–R27*
☑ Spelling: Final /ər/ and Final /l/ or /əl/, *357G*	☑ Dictionary: Spelling Table/Pronunciation Key, *357I* Types of Clothing, *357J*	☑ Main Verbs and Helping Verbs, *357K* **Spiral Review,** *357Q*	Writing an Announcement, *357M* Ordering Important Information, *357N* **Spiral Review,** *357R*	Compare and Contrast Texts, *357O*	**Responding:** Social Studies, Viewing, Internet, *355* **Theme Resources:** *R26–R27*
☑ Spelling: Words Ending with *-ed* or *-ing*, *381G*	☑ Dictionary: Dividing Words into Syllables, *381I* **Scientific Terms:** Climate Words, *381J* **Spiral Review,** *381R*	☑ Present, Past, and Future Tenses, *381K*	Writing a Summary, *381M* ☑ Paraphrasing, *381N*	Listen to and Make an Announcement, *381O*	**Responding:** Science, Listening and Speaking, Internet, *379* **Theme Resources:** *R26–R27*
		Reteaching: Grammar, *R20–R22*	**Writing Activities,** *R23–R25*		**Cross-Curricular Activities,** *R26–R27*

• Teacher's Edition, *325F, 383*
• Practice Book, *172–174, 207–209*

Reading-Writing Workshop: A Story
• Anthology: Student Writing Model, *324–325*
• Practice Book, *170, 171*

• Teacher's Edition, *324–325G*
  Writing Process
  Developing Plot, Character, and Setting
  Writing Dialogue
  Using Possessives

Planning for Assessment

Use these resources to meet your assessment needs. For additional information, see the **Teacher's Assessment Handbook**.

Diagnostic Planning

Baseline Group Test

Phonics/Decoding Screening Test

Lexia Quick Phonics Assessment CD-ROM

Continue to monitor students' progress in order to plan your class and individual instruction. Conduct individual retesting with students you have concerns about, using the assessments below as appropriate. Check individual students' oral reading fluency, using the **Leveled Reading Passages** or other texts (see the Theme Assessment Wrap-Up or the **Teacher's Assessment Handbook**, page 25) several times during the year.

Baseline Group Test
- Indicates the amount of reading support individual students will need

Houghton Mifflin Phonics/Decoding Screening Test
- Assesses a student's use of phonics to decode and spell one- to three-syllable words

Lexia Quick Phonics Assessment CD-ROM
- Identifies students who need more help with phonics

Leveled Reading Passages Assessment Kit
- Can be used to determine reading level and instructional needs

Theme Skills Test
- Various subtests can be used as a pretest to find which skills students know prior to instruction and to plan levels of support for meeting individual needs.

Ongoing Informal Assessment

Comprehension Checks

Selection Tests

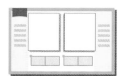

Reading-Writing Workshop

Day-to-day informal measurement of your students' progress should be performed as an integral part of your instructional plan. Your observations, recorded on checklists and in anecdotal records, will complement the informal measures listed below.

Comprehension
- Selection Comprehension Checks, **Practice Book,** pp. 157, 177, 192
- Selection Tests, **Teacher's Resource Blackline Masters**

Writing
- Reading-Writing Workshop: Story, pp. 324–325G
- Other student writing samples for portfolios

Observation Checklist

Ongoing Informal Assessment *continued*

Other Informal Assessment

- Diagnostic Checks, pp. 309, 317, 323B, 323F, 323L, 339, 353, 357B, 357F, 357L, 367, 377, 381B, 381F, 381L, R3, R5, R7–R8, R10, R12, R14, R16, R18, R20–R22
- Student Self-Assessment, pp. 319, 325G, 355, 379
- Reading Fluency, p. 383A
- Observation Checklist, **Teacher's Resource Blackline Masters**

Integrated Theme Test

Theme Skills Test

End-of-Theme Assessment

Use the following formal assessments to help you measure student progress in attaining the theme's instructional goals.

Integrated Theme Test

- Tests in a format that reflects instruction
- Tests comprehension strategies and skills, word skills, spelling, grammar, and writing

Theme Skills Test

- Tests discrete skills: comprehension skills, word skills, spelling, grammar, writing, and information and study skills

Benchmark Progress Test

Periodic Progress Assessment

Periodically throughout the year, evaluate your students' progress compared to other students at the same grade level.

Benchmark Progress Test

- Assesses overall student progress in reading and writing, two to four times a year

Assessment Management

Learner Profile™ CD-ROM by Sunburst Technology

Learner Profile™ CD-ROM

- Records students' achievement of instructional goals
- Has companion software, **Learner Profile to Go™,** that allows you to record student information on a handheld computer device

Theme Resources

Houghton Mifflin Reading includes a wide variety of resources for meeting the needs of all students. The chart below indicates features and components of the program and the students for whom they are appropriate.

Universal Access: Reaching All Students

	On Level Students	English Language Learners	Challenge Students	Extra Support Students	Inclusion/ Special Needs
Anthology					
Get Set to Read	★	★	○	★	★
Content Links	★	★	★		★
Education Place	★	○	★	○	★
Student Writing Model	★	★	○	★	★
Taking Tests	★	★	○	★	★
Audiotape	○	★		★	★
Teacher's Edition					
Teacher Read Aloud	★	★	○	★	★
Universal Access notes		★	★	★	★
Theme Resources	★	★	★	★	★
Selection Summaries	○	★		★	★
Theme Project	★	○	★	○	○
Reading-Writing Workshop	★	★	★	★	★
Practice Book	★	★	★	★	★
Leveled Books					
Reader's Library Very Easy	○	○		★	★
Theme Paperback Easy		★		★	★
Theme Paperback On Level	★		○		
Theme Paperback Challenge	○	○	★		
Literature Resources	★	○	★	○	○
* **Challenge Handbook**	○	○	★		
* **Extra Support Handbook**		○		★	★

* **See Universal Access Plans, pp. 297B—297C, 326E—326F, 358E—358F**

KEY: ★ = highly appropriate
○ = appropriate

	On Level Students	English Language Learners	Challenge Students	Extra Support Students	Inclusion/ Special Needs
* Classroom Management Handbook	★	★	★	★	○
* Handbook for English Language Learners		★		○	○
Home/Community Connections	★	★	★	★	★

Technology

	On Level Students	English Language Learners	Challenge Students	Extra Support Students	Inclusion/ Special Needs
Education Place	★	○	★	○	○
Get Set for Reading CD-ROM	★	★	○	★	★
Lexia Quick Phonics Assessment CD-ROM				★	★
Lexia Phonics CD-ROM: Intermediate Intervention				★	★
Published by Sunburst Technology*					
• Tenth Planet®: Vowels: Short & Long	★	★	○	★	★
• Tenth Planet®: Blends and Digraphs	★	★	○	★	○
• Tenth Planet®: Word Parts	○	○	★	○	
• Reading Who? Reading You!	○	○	★	○	
• EasyBook Deluxe	★	★		○	○
• Writer's Resource Library	★	★	○	○	○
• Media Weaver™ (Sunburst/Humanities Software)	★	★	★	○	

Launching the Theme
for *That's Amazing!*

Theme **3**

That's Amazing!

If sunlight fell like snowflakes,
gleaming yellow and so bright,
we could build a sunman,
we could have a sunball fight . . .

from "Sunflakes" by Frank Asch

Olive Trees with Yellow Sky and Sun
by Vincent van Gogh ▶

292

➤ Using the Theme Opener

Read aloud the theme title and poem on Anthology page 292. Explain that this is a part of a longer poem. Use the following suggestions to prompt discussion:

- Name some things you think are amazing. Are these things real or imaginary? What makes them amazing?
- What makes the painting *Olive Trees with Yellow Sky and Sun* look like something you would not see in nature? Do you like that about the painting? Why or why not? (colors, everything is wavy, shadows don't follow trees, paintbrush strokes)
- What is realistic in the poem? What makes it fantastic? (The poem tells about snowflakes, a real thing. The fantastic part is that the sunshine is treated like snow.)
- What kinds of stories do you think will be in *That's Amazing!*? (stories that combine the real and the fantastic, such as fairy tales and tall tales)

Multi-age Classroom

Related Themes:

Grade 5 . . . Animal Encounters

Grade 4 . . . That's Amazing!

Grade 3 . . . Incredible Stories

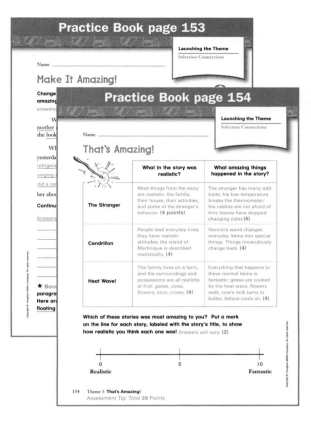

▶ Theme Connections

Introduce Selection Connections on **Practice Book** pages 153–154. Have students do the first page. Explain that students will add to the second page after each selection and at the end of the theme to build their understanding of *That's Amazing!*

⭐ **Connecting/Comparing** questions in Responding (Anthology pages 318, 354, 378) help students focus on relationships among selections and to the theme overall.

Fantasy Writing Project

✏️ **Writing** Using the stanza from "Sunflakes" as an example, have students compose their own amazing poems, possibly starting with the word *if.* Suggest they begin with something realistic, such as snow, rain, or flowers, and then brainstorm a list of ideas of what might happen *if . . . .* They should incorporate these ideas into their poem.

Challenge Have students write a *whopper*—a make-believe tale about something that supposedly happened to them. Encourage them to mix realistic elements with fantasy, and to add illustrations if they wish. Review some of the elements that might make for a good whopper:

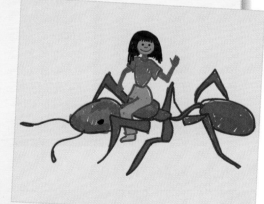

- exaggerated details
- setting, characters, a problem, or events that couldn't exist in real life
- many realistic details
- telling the story as though it were true

Technology

Education Place

www.eduplace.com

Log on to **Education Place** for more activities relating to *That's Amazing!*

Lesson Planner CD-ROM

Customize your planning for *That's Amazing!* with the Lesson Planner.

Home Connection

Send home the theme letter for *That's Amazing!* to introduce the theme and suggest home activities. See **Teacher's Resource Blackline Masters**.

For other suggestions relating to *That's Amazing!*, see **Home/Community Connections**.

The Stranger
Different texts for different purposes

Anthology: Main Selection
Purposes

- strategy focus: monitor/clarify
- comprehension skill: noting details
- vocabulary development
- critical thinking, discussion

Genre: Fantasy

Characters and events that could occur in real life combine with those that could not.

 Awards

- *New York Times* Best Illustrated Books of the Year
- *American Bookseller* Pick of the Lists
- Kentucky Bluegrass Award

Selection Summary
The Baileys take in an injured stranger. The man doesn't speak or seem to know who he is, but strange cold drafts seem to follow him, and the autumn comes to a halt. Even so, the stranger becomes part of the family—until he suddenly realizes he must go. But he does return every fall.

Teacher's Edition: Read Aloud

Purposes

- listening comprehension: noting details
- vocabulary development
- critical thinking, discussion

Anthology: Get Set to Read

Purposes

- background building: autumn
- developing key vocabulary

Anthology: Content Link

Purposes

- content reading: poetry
- skill: how to read a poem
- critical thinking, discussion

Leveled Books and Resources

Use these resources to ensure that students read, outside of class, at least thirty minutes a day. See also Cumulative Listing of Leveled Books.

Reader's Library

Very Easy

One Day in May
by **Kitty Colton**

(Also available on blackline masters)

Purposes
- fluency practice in below-level text
- alternate reading for students reading significantly below grade level
- strategy application: monitor/clarify
- comprehension skill application: noting details
- below-level independent reading

Lesson Support
- Lesson Plan, page R2
- Alternate application for Comprehension Skill lesson on noting details, page 323A
- Reteaching for Comprehension Skill: noting details, page R8

Selection Summary Masters

The Stranger
Teacher's Resource Blackline Masters

Audiotape

The Stranger
Audiotape for
That's Amazing!

Reaching All Students
Inclusion Strategy

Significantly Below-level Readers

Students reading so far below level that they cannot read *The Stranger* even with the suggested Extra Support should still participate with the class whenever possible.

- Include them in the Teacher Read Aloud (p. 298A) and Preparing to Read (pp. 299A–299D).
- Have them listen to *The Stranger* on the audiotape for *That's Amazing!* and read the Selection Summary while others read Segment 1 of the selection.
- Have them read "One Day in May" in the Reader's Library collection for *That's Amazing!* while others read Segment 2 of *The Stranger*.
- Have all students participate in Wrapping Up Segment 2 (p. 317) and Responding (p. 318).

Theme Paperbacks

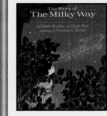

Easy

The Story of the Milky Way
by **Joseph Bruchac** and **Gayle Ross**

Lesson, TE page 325I

On Level

Little Oh
by **Laura Krauss Melmed**

Lesson, TE page 325K

Challenge

The Real Thief
by **William Steig**

Lesson, TE page 325M

Technology

Get Set for Reading CD-ROM
The Stranger

Provides background building, vocabulary support, and selection summaries in English and Spanish.

Education Place
www.eduplace.com

Log on to Education Place for more activities relating to *The Stranger*.

Book Adventure
www.bookadventure.org

This Internet reading incentive program provides thousands of titles for students to read.

Daily Lesson Plans

Instructional Goals	Day 1	Day 2
Reading (60–80 minutes) *Strategy Focus:* Monitor/Clarify ✓ *Comprehension Skill:* Noting Details *Comprehension Skill Review:* Cause and Effect; Drawing Conclusions *Information and Study Skills:* Story Chart	**Teacher Read Aloud** *Why Raven Stays for the Winter, 298A* **Preparing to Read The Stranger** • Get Set: Background and Vocabulary, *299A* • Key Vocabulary, *299B; **Practice Book**, 155* • Strategy/Skill Preview, *299C* Detail Map, ***Practice Book***, *156* **Reading Segment 1** *The Stranger, 300–309* • Supporting Comprehension • Strategy Focus, *304* **Wrapping Up Segment 1,** *309*	**Reading Segment 2** The Stranger, *310–317* • Supporting Comprehension • Strategy Focus, *314* **Wrapping Up Segment 2,** *317* **Responding** • Comprehension Questions: Think About the Selection, *318* • Comprehension Check, ***Practice Book***, *157* **Rereading/Revisiting the Text** • Comprehension: Noting Details, *307*
Word Work (30–40 minutes) ✓ *Spelling:* Compound Words *Decoding Longer Words:* ✓ *Structural Analysis:* Compound Words *Phonics:* Words That Begin with *a-* or *be-* ✓ *Vocabulary:* Synonyms	**Spelling** • Pretest, *323G* • Instruction: Compound Words, *323G* • Take-Home Word List, ***Practice Book: Handbook***	**Decoding Longer Words Instruction** • Structural Analysis: Compound Words, *323E* • *Practice Book, 160* **Spelling** • *Practice Book, 161*
Writing & Language (30–40 minutes) ✓ *Grammar:* Action Verbs *Writing:* An Explanation; Audience *Listening/Speaking/Viewing:* Hold a Conversation	**Daily Language Practice,** *323L* **Grammar Instruction** • Action Verbs, *323K* ✏ **Writing** • Journal Writing, *301*	**Daily Language Practice,** *323L* **Grammar Instruction** • *Practice Book, 165* ✏ **Writing Instruction** • Journal Writing, *310* • An Explanation, *323M* • *Practice Book, 168*

✓ = tested skills

Teacher's Notes

 Leveled Books, pp. 325H–325N
 For reading outside of class and homework

Technology

Lesson Planner CD-ROM
Customize your planning with the Lesson Planner.

Day 3

Rereading/Revisiting the Text
- Visual Literacy: Point of View, *303*
- Genre: Fantasy, *313*

Comprehension Skill Instruction
- Noting Details, *323A*
- *Practice Book, 158–159*

Phonics Instruction
- Words That Begin with *a-* or *be-*, *323F*

Spelling
- *Practice Book, 162*

Daily Language Practice, *323L*

Grammar Instruction
- Be Specific!, *323K*

✎ **Writing**
- Describing: Write a Character Sketch, *318*

Day 4

Comprehension Skill Instruction
- Reteaching Noting Details with Reader's Library, *R8*

Reading the Poetry Link
- "Autumn Poems," *320–323*
- Genre: Poetry, *322*

Information and Study Skills Instruction
- Story Chart, *323C*

Decoding Longer Words
- Reteaching Structural Analysis: Compound Words, *R14*
- Challenge/Extension Activities, *R15*

Spelling
- Turning Leaves, *323H*
- *Practice Book, 163*

Vocabulary Skill Instruction
- Synonyms, *323I*
- *Practice Book, 164*

Daily Language Practice, *323L*

Grammar
- Reteaching, *R20*
- *Practice Book, 166*

✎ **Writing**
- Audience, *323N*
- *Practice Book, 169*

Listening/Speaking/Viewing
- Hold a Conversation, *323O*

Day 5

Rereading/Revisiting the Text:
Comprehension Review Skill Instruction
- Cause and Effect, *305*
- Drawing Conclusions, *315*

Rereading for Fluency
The Stranger, 300–317

Activity Choices
- Responding Activities, *318*
- Challenge/Extension, *R9*
- Cross-Curricular Activities, *R26–R27*

Spiral Review, *323Q*

Vocabulary Expansion
- Scientific Terms: Weather Words, *323J*

Spelling
- Posttest, *323H*

Spiral Review, *323R*

Daily Language Practice, *323L*

Grammar
- Using Exact Verbs, *323L*
- *Practice Book, 167*

✎ **Writing**
- Writing Activities, *R23–R25*
- Sharing Students' Writing: Author's Chair

✎ **Reading-Writing Workshop: Story, pp. 324–325G**

See Universal Access Planning Chart on the following pages.

Universal Access Plans
for Reaching All Learners

Grouping for Instruction

	Day 1	**Day 2**
30–45 minutes		
With the Teacher **Extra Support** **Teach**—Use Extra Support Handbook	**Preteach** Compound Words **Preview** Selection, Segment 1 ■ Extra Support Handbook pp. 98–99	**Preteach** Noting Details **Preview** Selection, Segment 2 ■ Extra Support Handbook pp. 100–101
Working Independently **On Level** Use Classroom Management Handbook **Challenge** Use Challenge Handbook **English Language Learners** Use Classroom Management Handbook or Challenge Handbook	**Independent Activities** For each group, assign appropriate activities—your own or those in the handbooks listed below. Then get students started on their independent work. ■ Classroom Management Handbook pp. 36–37 ■ Challenge Handbook pp. 22–23	See plan for Day 1 **Monitor** Answer questions, if necessary.
30–45 minutes		
With the Teacher **English Language Learners** **Teach**—Use Handbook for English Language Learners	**Preteach** Seasons **Preteach** Get Set to Read; Selection, Segment 1 **Preteach** Structural Analysis: Compound Words ■ Handbook for ELL pp. 102–103	**Preteach** Temperature **Preteach** Selection, Segment 2 **Reteach** Grammar: Action Verbs ■ Handbook for ELL pp. 104–105
Working Independently **On Level** Use Classroom Management Handbook **Challenge** Use Challenge Handbook **Extra Support** Use Classroom Management Handbook	**Independent Activities** Students can continue their assigned activities, or you can assign new activities from the handbooks below. ■ Classroom Management Handbook pp. 36–37 ■ Challenge Handbook pp. 22–23	See plan for Day 1 **Monitor** Partner Extra Support students, if needed.

Independent Activities

Classroom Management Handbook
- Daily Activities
- Grouping
- Management

Resources for Reaching All Learners

Extra Support Handbook
- Daily Lessons
- Preteaching and Reteaching
- Skill Support

Handbook for English Language Learners
- Daily Lessons
- Language Development
- Skill Support

Challenge Handbook
- Independent Activities
- Instructional Support

Day 3	**Day 4**	**Day 5**
Reteach Compound Words **Review** Selection ■ Extra Support Handbook　　pp. 102–103	**Reteach** Action Verbs **Preview** *One Day in May* ■ Extra Support Handbook　　pp. 104–105	**Reteach** Noting Details **Revisit** Selection and *One Day in May* ■ Extra Support Handbook　　pp. 106–107
See plan for Day 1	See plan for Day 1	See plan for Day 1
Check in Reinforce instruction, if needed.	**Check in** Regroup English learners, if needed.	**Build confidence** Reinforce successful independent work.
Preteach Weather Words **Preteach** Vocabulary: Synonyms ■ Handbook for ELL　　pp. 106–107	**Preteach** Animals **Reteach** Selection Summary and Review **Reteach** Grammar: Action Verbs ■ Handbook for ELL　　pp. 108–109	**Preteach** Directions **Reteach** Writing: Audience ■ Handbook for ELL　　pp. 110–111
See plan for Day 1	See plan for Day 1	See plan for Day 1
Check in Reinforce instruction, if needed.	**Monitor** How well are challenge projects progressing?	**Share work** Allow students time to share work.

OBJECTIVES

Students listen to the selection for important or entertaining details.

▶ Activate Prior Knowledge

Connecting to the Theme Tell students that you are going to read aloud an Alaskan folktale about why the raven stays through the winter rather than flying south like other birds.

Help students connect the selection with what they know, using these suggestions:

■ Have students discuss what they know about animals that migrate south in winter.

■ Ask students to describe other folktales they are familiar with.

Teacher Read Aloud

Listening Comprehension: Noting Details

Why Raven Stays for the Winter
An Alaskan Folk Tale

retold by Diana C. Conway

An eager raven tries to fly south for the winter in this tale from Cricket.

1 Why do you think the author uses the phrase "in the month of yellow leaves"?
(Sample answer: The detail "yellow leaves" in this phrase tells the reader that it is fall. The author might have used this phrase instead of naming a month to make the folktale seem timeless or very old.)

Winter in Alaska is a time of few birds. Yet you can always spot Raven, black as a chunk of burnt firewood, hopping about in the snow. Why doesn't Raven leave for the winter as the ducks, geese, and songbirds do? This is what the old ones told me when I was a child.

In the month of yellow leaves, many **1** birds gathered at Coho Marsh to eat their fill before the long journey south.

Raven flew out of the forest and circled over the marsh. Aha! What was this he saw? A noisy party in progress, and nobody had invited him. He cocked his head first left, then right, checking out the company. Duck, duck, goose: <u>pintails</u>, <u>mallards</u>, <u>widgeons</u>, <u>teals</u>, and great flocks of Canada geese.

All these birds and more waited at Coho Marsh for the north wind to come and carry them away. They ate as they waited and gabbled as they ate.

"What fun!" said Raven.

He tucked in his wings and tumbled down on a clump of marsh grass. Nearby, Pintail fed on underwater roots.

"What's up, Pintail?" croaked Raven.

What was up was Pintail's tail, straight up in the air, but her head was down in the water. She couldn't hear a word Raven said, so of course she didn't answer.

"Well, if that's how you feel ...," said Raven.

He shrugged his wings and took four hops to the side.

"Teal," he croaked, "what's new?"

2 What was new was Teal's feathered parka, all snazzy red and green. He was so busy admiring himself in the water that he didn't bother to answer.

"Well, if that's how you feel ...," said Raven.

He flapped his wings and landed with a great splash in the mud next to a long-necked Canada goose.

"What's happening, Goose?" he croaked.

"Flying south, flying south," said Goose.

"Are we?" said Raven. "Oh, goody. I just love to travel."

"Not you, Raven," said Canada Goose. "It's too long a journey for you."

"Ha!" answered Raven. "I'm twice the flier you are. If *you're* flying south, *I'm* flying south."

2 What does the author mean when she says "feathered parka"?
(Sample answer: Teal's "feathered parka" refers to his bright red and green feathers. A parka is a hooded coat used in very cold areas, so saying "feathered parka" is like saying "feathered coat.")

Listening Comprehension: ✓ Noting Details

Tell students that details can explain ideas, give information, and reveal characters' feelings. Point out that an author can use details to illustrate an object or to describe a situation. Details can also give clues about an author's viewpoint or a character's feelings.

Use the questions in the margin to help assess students' understanding as you read. Reread sections for clarification if necessary.

Teacher's Note

Tip for Read Alouds Review the story before reading it aloud. Look for details and repeated phrases you might want to emphasize. Use different voices for different characters' speech.

Reaching All Students
English Language Learners

Ask students if they have ever noticed birds flying south in the chevron (V) formation. Discuss the identities of the "old ones" and the narrator, and preview the names of the various birds in the story.

(**Teacher Read Aloud,** *continued*)

Just then the north wind began to blow. The birds stood up on tiptoe and stretched their wings far out to each side. One by one they took off into the sky—pintails, mallards, widgeons, teals, and great flocks of Canada geese. Oh yes, and one shiny black raven.

"Look at me!" croaked Raven to Goose. "I can fly circles around you." And so he did. He raced ahead, turned back, and looped around again and again.

"Slow down," said Goose. "We have a long way to go."

"Slow down?" said Raven. "Not me. Why, I'm only just beginning." He turned somersaults in the air. "Can you do this, Goose?" he taunted.

Goose didn't answer. She flapped her wings steadily up and down and saved her breath for flying.

Raven flew halfway to the sun, then dived like a spear toward the ground. "How about this, Goose?"

Still Goose didn't answer. She just flapped her wings and flew on.

3 "Don't you know how to have fun?" said Raven as he did a perfect roll from front to back and right side up again.

But Goose just kept flying steadily south all day long.

In the month of yellow leaves, the days are already short. As the sun went to bed and the moon awoke, Raven flew up beside Goose. He gasped for air between words.

"Isn't—it—time—to—rest?" he asked.

3 How does Raven fly differently from Goose? (Sample answer: Raven does tricks while Goose flies steadily; Raven flies quickly while Goose flies at one speed; Raven talks while Goose saves her breath for flying.)

"Rest?" said Goose. "Go fly some circles, Raven. Dive to earth; roll on your back."

Raven huffed and puffed. "But it's night! Only owls fly at night."

"There's a fine moon to light our way," **4** said Goose. "And excuse me, but it's my turn to lead." Off she flew to the head of the flock, leaving Raven behind.

He tried to keep up with her, but his wings grew heavier with each beat. At last he settled to earth and watched the others disappear across the moon—pintails and mallards, widgeons and teals, and great flocks of Canada geese.

That is why, when the flyaway birds have long since left for warmer places, you'll still see Raven hopping in the snow. "What's up? What's new? What's happening?" he croaks, just to keep his voice ready for when his friends come home.

4 What does this paragraph tell you about Goose? (Sample answer: Goose is very responsible. After flying steadily to avoid wasting energy, she now takes her turn leading the flock.)

> **Discussion**

Summarize After reading the story, discuss parts that students found particularly interesting or entertaining. Then ask them to summarize the selection.

Listening Comprehension:
✓ **Noting Details** Have students discuss how the author uses details in this folktale. Reread small sections of the story that show a lot of detail. Ask students to suggest other ways the author could have written those sections.

Personal Response Ask students to think about why Raven doesn't fly south for the winter. Have them suggest other ways to tell the story, giving different reasons why Raven might stay for winter.

★ **Connecting/Comparing** Ask students what makes this an amazing story.

THE STRANGER

Technology

Get Set for Reading CD-ROM

The Stranger
Provides background building, vocabulary support, and selection summaries in English and Spanish.

Preparing to Read

▶ **Using *Get Set* for Background and Vocabulary**

Connecting to the Theme Tell students that the title of this theme is "That's Amazing!" They will read three stories that tell about wondrous people and events. In *The Stranger* they will meet a man who is more than what he appears.

Talk about signs of autumn you expect to see as summer ends. Then use the Get Set to Read on pages 298–299 to learn about that season.

■ Ask a student to read aloud "When the Leaves Fall."

■ Have volunteers read aloud and discuss other events that occur in autumn.

■ Ask students to define the boldfaced Key Vocabulary words: *autumn, draft, mercury, thermometers, frost, etched,* and *timid.* Have students use these words as they talk about this season.

Get Set to Read

The Stranger

Background and Vocabulary

When the Leaves Fall

Autumn is the season that comes between summer and winter. In much of North America, autumn weather begins in late September and lasts until late November. The days grow shorter and the nights get cooler. You might start to feel a cold draft from an open window. The mercury in outdoor thermometers begins to fall, and in the morning you will sometimes find lines of frost etched on leaves and windows. Read *The Stranger* to find out about an autumn that doesn't quite follow the rules.

◀ Animals that are normally timid leave their homes to gather food for the winter.

▲ Some birds fly south to spend the winter in warmer climates.

◀ Autumn is also called *fall,* because this is when the leaves on many trees turn bright colors and then fall to the ground.

▲ Autumn is also when apples, pumpkins, and other crops are harvested.

298   299

Reaching All Students

English Language Learners

With students, create a list of things that can be expected to happen during a fall season that "follows the rules." Draw from the passage on page 298. If possible, have visuals of the four seasons available.

Vocabulary

▶ Developing Key Vocabulary

Use **Transparency 3–1** to introduce Key Vocabulary from *The Stranger*.

■ Model how to identify clues for the meaning of the word *autumn*.

■ For each remaining sentence, ask students to locate clues for the meaning of each Key Vocabulary word.

Remind students that it's helpful to use the Phonics/Decoding Strategy when they read. For students who need more help with decoding, use the review below.

Practice/Homework **Practice Book** page 155.

Strategy Review
Phonics/Decoding

Modeling Write this sentence from *The Stranger* on the board, and point to *formation*.

> High above them a flock of geese, in perfect V <u>formation</u>, flew south.

Think Aloud

First I notice the shorter word for. *I also see the t-i-o-n ending that sounds like /shun/ as in the word* definition. *I'm not sure if the letter a in the middle is short or long, so I'll try both when I blend all the sounds together. / for•MA•shun / or / for•MAY•shun / The second way sounds like a word I've heard before. I've seen birds flying in a V shape in the sky, so maybe* formation *means "shape." Since I'm not sure, I'll look it up in the dictionary.*

Skill Finder • Decoding Longer Words, pp. 323E–323F

Key Concept
changing seasons

Key Vocabulary

autumn: the season after summer

draft: a flow of air

etched: made a design by cutting lines

frost: very thin covering of ice

mercury: silvery white metal used in thermometers

peculiar: unusual, strange or odd

thermometer: an instrument that measures temperature

timid: easily frightened; shy

See Vocabulary notes on pages 302, 306, 308, 310, 312, 314 and 316 for additional words to preview.

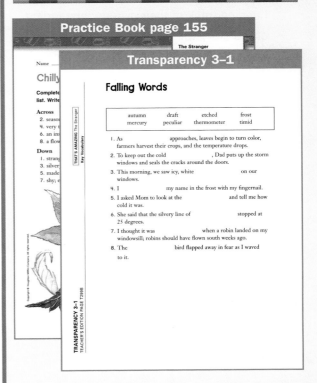

Practice Book page 155

The Stranger

Name

Chilly

Complete
list. Writ

Across
2. seaso
4. very
6. an ins
8. a flow

Down
1. strang
3. silver
5. made
7. shy; e

Transparency 3–1

Falling Words

| autumn | draft | etched | frost |
| mercury | peculiar | thermometer | timid |

1. As _____ approaches, leaves begin to turn color, farmers harvest their crops, and the temperature drops.

2. To keep out the cold _____, Dad puts up the storm windows and seals the cracks around the doors.

3. This morning, we saw icy, white _____ on our windows.

4. I _____ my name in the frost with my fingernail.

5. I asked Mom to look at the _____ and tell me how cold it was.

6. She said that the silvery line of _____ stopped at 25 degrees.

7. I thought it was _____ when a robin landed on my windowsill; robins should have flown south weeks ago.

8. The _____ bird flapped away in fear as I waved to it.

Preparing to Read (299B)

Reading Strategy

When a mysterious stranger arrives at the Baileys' house, unusual things begin to happen. **Monitor** your reading. If something doesn't make sense, reread to **clarify**.

▶ **Strategy Focus:**
Monitor/Clarify

Strategy Focus

When a mysterious stranger arrives at the Baileys' house, unusual things begin to happen. **Monitor** your reading. If something doesn't make sense, reread to **clarify**.

Teacher's Note

Strategy/Skill Connection For a better understanding of *The Stranger*, students can use the

• Monitor/Clarify Strategy

• Noting Details Comprehension Skill

Keeping track of their own understanding of the story will allow students to notice the way details bring a story to life, which will increase their enjoyment of reading.

As students complete their Detail Maps for *The Stranger* (**Practice Book** page 156 and **Transparency 3–2**), they can use their answers to understand how details help the reader "see" the story.

Have students turn to page 301 as you read aloud the selection's title and author. Allow time for students to skim the selection and look at the pictures, telling them to consider the Monitor/Clarify strategy as they do. Then ask students to share ideas about the story that they hope to clarify as they read.

Teacher Modeling Tell students that monitoring and clarifying are ways of making sure that you are following the story and understanding what you read. This involves identifying what you don't understand and then rereading or reading ahead to find the answer. Then model the strategy.

Think Aloud

Looking at the pictures, I don't understand how the stranger got to the house. I'll look for the answer as I read. I may even have to reread pieces of the story to clarify this problem.

In their journals, have students write two ideas they don't understand about the story. Then tell the students that summarizing the story and asking questions about it are good ways to monitor their understanding.

Comprehension Skill

✓ **Comprehension Skill Focus:**
Noting Details

Detail Map Explain that students will focus on Noting Details as they read *The Stranger*. To develop and practice the skill, students will complete a Detail Map to see how the author describes the stranger and the weather. Display **Transparency 3–2**, and demonstrate how to use the graphic organizer.

- Ask a student to read aloud the first paragraph on page 306. Ask someone to offer the phrase from the story that describes the stranger's appearance.

- Have someone read the top center oval on the Detail Map. Model how to complete the first oval on the Detail Map with the correct phrase.

- Ask students to complete the first oval on **Practice Book** page 156 with the same answer.

- Have students complete the remaining ovals as they read. Monitor their work or have students check each other's maps.

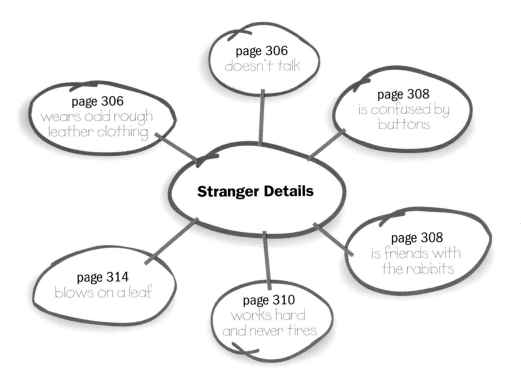

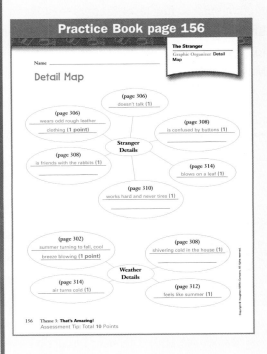

Focus Questions

Have students turn to Responding on page 318. Read the questions aloud and tell students to keep them in mind as they read *The Stranger*.

Preparing to Read (299D)

Reading

Beginning of Segment 1: *pages 300–309*

Options for Reading

▶ **Reading in Segments** Students can read *The Stranger* in two segments (pages 300–309 and 310–317) or in its entirety.

▶ **Deciding About Support** Looking for clues to the stranger's identity will keep readers alert as they read this fantasy.

■ Because of the simple vocabulary and sequential plot most students should be able to follow On-Level reading instruction.

■ Students who have difficulty "reading between the lines" and making inferences may need Extra Support.

■ Significantly below-level readers may listen to the Audiotape and read the Selection Summary for *The Stranger,* and then read "One Day in May" in the **Reader's Library.**

▶ **Universal Access** Use the notes at the bottom of the pages.

MEET THE AUTHOR AND ILLUSTRATOR
Chris Van Allsburg

If you've read books by Chris Van Allsburg before, you know that he writes mysterious stories that leave a lot for you to figure out. To help you, he provides clues throughout each book. In order to find the clues, you must read the story and look at all the pictures very carefully. What things seem strange to you in *The Stranger*? What explanations can you find in the author's words and illustrations to explain these mysteries?

Van Allsburg says that his stories usually start out as simple pictures or ideas. "It almost seems like a discovery, as if the story was always there," he says. "The few elements I start out with are actually clues. If I figure out what they mean, I can discover the story that's waiting." It takes him about seven months to write and draw a book, from start to finish.

Other books: *The Polar Express, Jumanji, The Mysteries of Harris Burdick, Just a Dream*

 **Internet**

Find out more about Chris Van Allsburg by visiting Education Place. **www.eduplace.com/kids**

300

 MEETING INDIVIDUAL NEEDS

Classroom Management

On Level
Reading Card 2

While Reading: Detail Map (**Practice Book** page 156); Literature Discussion (p. 308, Reading Card 2); generate questions

After Reading: Literature Discussion (page 316); Wrapping Up Segment 1 (page 309) and Segment 2 (page 317)

Challenge
Reading Cards 1–3

While Reading: Detail Map (**Practice Book** page 156); Mood (p. 305, Reading Card 1); Allegory (p. 315, Reading Card 3)

After Reading: Literature Discussion (page 316); Wrapping Up Segment 1 (page 309) and Segment 2 (page 317)

English Language Learners

Intermediate and Advanced Fluency Have partners read together. Each pair can write a one-sentence prediction of what will come after reading each page.

For English language learners at other proficiency levels, use the **Handbook for English Language Learners.**

Selection 1

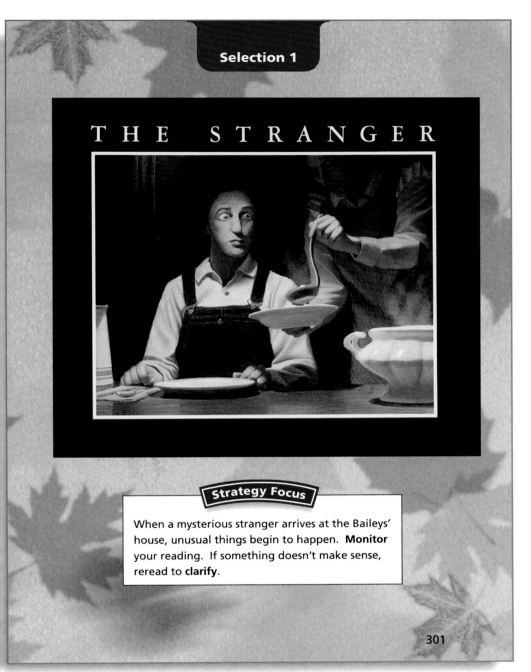

THE STRANGER

Strategy Focus

When a mysterious stranger arrives at the Baileys' house, unusual things begin to happen. **Monitor** your reading. If something doesn't make sense, reread to **clarify**.

301

Reading Segment 1

pages 300–309

Purpose Setting As students read have them monitor their understanding as unusual things begin to happen and the stranger begins to seem to be more than just a typical man. If something doesn't make sense, students should clarify their understanding by rereading or reading ahead.

 Journal Writing Students can record any information that provides clues to the identity of the stranger.

Reinforcing Comprehension and Strategies

- Remind students to use Monitor/Clarify and other strategies as they read and to add to their Detail Map (**Practice Book** page 156).

- Use the Strategy Focus notes on pages 304 and 314 to reinforce the Monitor/Clarify strategy.

- Use Supporting Comprehension questions beginning on page 302 to help students develop higher-level understanding of the text.

Extra Support: Previewing the Text

Before each segment, preview the text, using the notes below and on page 310. **While** reading, model strategies (pages 303, 313, and 314). **After** reading, review each segment (page 308 and 316) before students join the Wrapping Up discussion.

pages 302–303 In what kind of place is this story set?

pages 304–305 What do you think happened to the man in the road?

pages 306–307 The farmer brings the man home, but he seems to have lost his memory. What kinds of problems might this cause?

pages 308–309 What would you think if you saw a man petting a wild rabbit?

▶ Supporting Comprehension

1 What words provide information as to when the story takes place? *(when summer turns to fall)*

2 How has the author set up some suspense as this page ends? *(We don't know what the farmer has hit.)*

Vocabulary *(page 302)*
jammed: to push suddenly or hard

---

1   It was the time of year Farmer Bailey liked best, when summer turned to fall. He whistled as he drove along. A cool breeze blew across his face through the truck's open window. Then it happened. There was a loud "thump." Mr. Bailey jammed on his brakes. "Oh

2 no!" he thought. "I've hit a deer."

302

Reaching All Students
English Language Learners

Vocabulary Building

Preteach the following vocabulary so that students can evaluate unusual occurrences as they read: *stranger, mysterious, unusual* (p. 301), *confused* (p. 308), *peculiar* (p. 312), *terribly* (p. 314), and *surround* (p. 316). Explain the meanings, and use each word in a sentence. Write the sentence on the board, and discuss the part of speech.

303

Revisiting the Text

Visual Literacy Lesson
Point of View

OBJECTIVES

Students identify different points of view in illustrations.

Tell students that point of view is the angle from which a viewer sees a scene. The artist Chris Van Allsburg is known for the unusual points of view he incorporates into his illustrations. An unusual point of view can add drama to an illustration. It can help the artist to express a certain mood.

Have students determine the point of view in the illustration on page 303. Where does the viewer seem to be located? (high on a hill) This viewpoint provides a peaceful and relaxing mood to begin the story.

As students read, have them notice how the artist uses point of view to draw them into the scenes and create different moods.

Reaching All Students

Extra Support

Strategy Modeling

Monitor/Clarify Use this example to model the strategy.

There are a lot of clues to the sort of story this is going to be on this page. Some important things I learn include the time of year, the name of a main character, and a major event. If I miss anything or don't quite understand what has happened, I can reread the page or read on to see whether my confusion is cleared up.

▶ Strategy Focus: Monitor/Clarify

Teacher/Student Modeling Explain that reading a fantasy requires certain active reading techniques. Among them is the strategy Monitor/Clarify, which helps readers make sure they are understanding the material before they get too bogged down and confused. Readers might monitor their understanding of page 304 by asking themselves: "What is happening? Why is it happening?" They could then clarify anything they don't understand by rereading or reading ahead.

Ask students to read page 304 silently, and to ask themselves as they read whether there is anything they don't understand. Discuss any confusion they have, and show them how to move backward or forward in the text to clear up their confusion.

▶ Supporting Comprehension

3 In the first sentence how does the author set up suspense? (It seems like the man lying in the road might be dead.)

4 Does the stranger act as you would expect? (No; it isn't normal to try to run away after being hit by a truck.)

5 How does the farmer show his sensible nature? (He takes the stranger's arm and puts him in his truck.)

3 But it wasn't a deer the farmer found lying in the road, it was a man. Mr. Bailey knelt down beside the still figure, fearing the worst. **4** Then, suddenly, the man opened his eyes. He looked up with terror and jumped to his feet. He tried to run off, lost his balance, and fell down. He got up again, but this time the farmer took his arm and **5** helped him to the truck.

128

304

305

Spiral Review

Comprehension Skill Lesson
Cause and Effect

OBJECTIVES

Students identify the relationships between causes and effects.

Remind students that a cause is the reason an event happens and an effect is the result of that cause. Readers can ask questions to identify causes and effects:

- Why did it happen? (to determine a cause)

- What happened? (to determine an effect)

- Sometimes, clue words help signal cause-effect relationships. Possible clue words include *because, so, since,* and *as a result.*

Have students use the text on pages 302–305 to complete these cause-effect chains.

CAUSE	EFFECT
1. Farmer Bailey heard a loud thump while driving.	1. As a result, he *jammed on his brakes.*
2. Mr. Bailey saw a man lying in the road,	2. so he *knelt beside him fearing the worst.*
3. The man tried to run off a second time,	3. so the farmer *took the stranger's arm and helped him to his truck.*

 Skill Finder

- **Instruction,** Theme 5, pp. 555A–555B

- **Reteaching,** Theme 5, p. R8

- **Review,** Th. 1, p. 37; Th. 2, p. 237; Th. 6

UNIVERSAL ACCESS

Reaching All Students

Challenge

Reading Card 1

Mood

Explain that mood is the feeling created in the reader by a story or passage. Mood may be created by the author's word choice, the setting of the story, or story events and details. When the farmer hits something with his truck, the mood turns dark as he realizes that he hit a man.

Have students come up with a word that describes the mood of the story when these events occurred.

1. There was a loud "thump." 2. But it wasn't a deer..., it was a man. 3. He looked up with terror and jumped to his feet.

▶ Supporting Comprehension

6 How does the illustration place you in Katy's shoes? (It gives the reader the same point of view as Katy when she's peeking through the door to try to see the stranger.)

7 How does the author establish the oddness of the stranger? (with details about his odd clothing and his inability to talk)

8 The broken thermometer is a strange detail. What do you think it means? (Answers will vary.)

Vocabulary *(page 306)*

thermometer: an instrument for measuring temperature

mercury: a silvery white metal used in thermometers

Cross-Curricular Connection

Science Memory loss, or amnesia, rarely happens and usually results from shock, brain injury, or severe illness. The loss may be temporary, as in some cases when a person receives a blow to the head. In the case of diseases such as Alzheimer's, memory loss is progressive and permanent.

---

6   Mr. Bailey drove home. He helped the stranger inside, where Mrs. Bailey made him comfortable on the parlor sofa. Katy, their daughter, peeked into the room. The man on the sofa was dressed in odd rough leather clothing. She heard her father whisper "... must be some kind of hermit ... sort of fellow who lives alone in the woods." The stranger didn't seem to understand the questions Mr. Bailey asked **7** him. "I don't think," whispered Mrs. Bailey, "he knows how to talk."

   Mr. Bailey called the doctor, who came and listened to the stranger's heart, felt his bones, looked in his eyes, and took his temperature. He decided the man had lost his memory. There was a bump on the back of his head. "In a few days," the doctor said, "he should remember who he is and where he's from." Mrs. Bailey stopped the doctor as he left the house. He'd forgotten his <u>thermometer</u>. "Oh, you can throw that out," he answered. "It's broken, the <u>mercury</u> is stuck at **8** the bottom."

306

Reaching All Students

English Language Learners

Draw a diagram of a mercury thermometer on the chalk board or ask a student to describe one. Talk about the parts of the thermometer and label the diagram accordingly. Remind students that the level of mercury indicates the temperature and that the two things are not the same, even though the term *mercury* is often used as a metaphor for *temperature*.

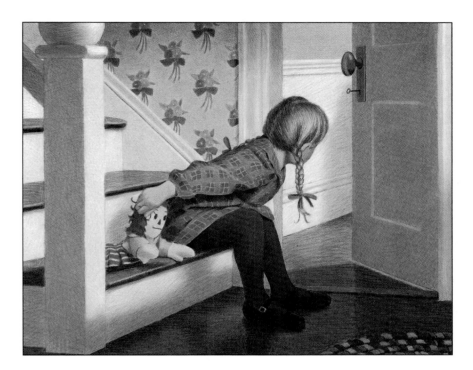

307

Tested Skill

Comprehension Skill Lesson
Noting Details

OBJECTIVES

Students note important details about the story characters, events, and setting.

Remind students that details are important to a story because they help readers

- understand characters and events

- evaluate the characters

- picture the story setting

Have someone read aloud the second paragraph on page 306. Ask students to list details that give information about what the doctor did before making a diagnosis. (listened to the stranger's heart, felt his bones, looked in his eyes, took his temperature)

Have students go back to the first paragraph on page 306. Ask them to fill in details on a chart to support this main idea: The stranger is mysterious.

The stranger is mysterious

odd, rough leather clothing

looks like some kind of hermit

didn't seem to understand
questions

seems to have broken the
thermometer

Skill Finder

- **Instruction,**
  pp. 323A–323B

- **Reteaching,** p. R8

- **Review,** Th. 2, p. 201;
  Th. 3, p. 349; Th. 6, p. 637

▶ Supporting Comprehension

9 How does this detail about the cold draft fit in with the detail about the broken thermometer? (Both make it seem that the stranger is somehow connected with cold air.)

10 Think about the author's intended audience. Why do you think he so often tells what Katy sees? (to give the story a child's viewpoint to appeal to young readers)

11 The rabbits seem to know something that the Baileys do not. What do you think they know? (possibly the identity of the stranger)

Vocabulary *(page 308)*

fascinated: greatly interested

draft: a flow of air

> Mr. Bailey lent the stranger some clean clothes. The fellow seemed confused about buttonholes and buttons. In the evening he joined the Baileys for dinner. The steam that rose from the hot food fascinated him. He watched Katy take a spoonful of soup and blow
> **9** gently across it. Then he did exactly the same. Mrs. Bailey shivered. "Brrr," she said. "There's a draft in here tonight."
>
> The next morning Katy watched the stranger from her bedroom window. He walked across the yard, toward two rabbits. Instead of
> **10** running into the woods, the rabbits took a hop in his direction. He picked one of them up and stroked its ears, then set it down. The
> **11** rabbits hopped away, then stopped and looked back, as if they expected the stranger to follow.

308

Reaching All Students
Extra Support

Segment 1: Review

Before students join the whole class for Wrapping Up on page 309, have them

- check predictions
- take turns modeling Monitor/Clarify and other strategies they used
- add to **Transparency 3–2**, check and revise their Detail Map on **Practice Book** page 156, and use it to summarize

---

Reaching All Students
On Level   Challenge

Reading Card 2

Literature Discussion

In mixed-ability groups of five or six, students can discuss their own questions and the discussion prompts on Reading Card 2.

- Imagine you were describing this story to someone who hadn't read it. What descriptive words would you use?
- How would you feel if this particular stranger were staying at your house? Why?

Wrapping Up Segment 1

pages 300–309

First, provide Extra Support for students who need it (page 308). Then bring all students together.

■ **Review Predictions/Purpose** Discuss ways students monitored their reading and clarified confusing parts.

■ **Model Strategies** Refer students to the **Strategies Poster** and have them take turns modeling Monitor/Clarify and other strategies they used as they read. Provide models if needed (page 303).

■ **Share Group Discussions** Have students share their questions and literature discussions.

■ **Summarize** Have students use the transparency and their Detail Maps to summarize main ideas and details in the story so far.

Comprehension/Critical Thinking

1 What is the stranger's problem? What might happen when he solves it? (He can't remember who he is; he might leave.) **Predicting Outcomes**

2 Was it wise of the Baileys to welcome the stranger into their home? (Answers will vary.) **Making Judgments**

End of Segment 1:
pages 300–309

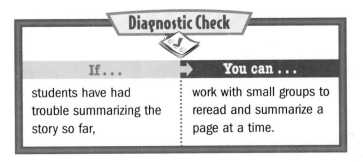

Diagnostic Check

If . . .	You can . . .
students have had trouble summarizing the story so far,	work with small groups to reread and summarize a page at a time.

Beginning of Segment 2: *pages 310–317*

Reading Segment 2
pages 310–317

Purpose Setting Have students summarize the story so far and continue to monitor and clarify their reading during Segment 2. Have students use new details to check their previous prediction about the stranger's identity and revise it if necessary.

 Journal Writing Students can add additional details they uncover that help in determining the stranger's identity.

Vocabulary *(page 310)*
hypnotized: put into a trance or dazed condition

When Katy's father went into the fields that day, the stranger shyly tagged along. Mr. Bailey gave him a pitchfork and, with a little practice, he learned to use it well. They worked hard. Occasionally Mr. Bailey would have to stop and rest. But the stranger never tired. He didn't even sweat.

That evening Katy sat with the stranger, watching the setting sun. High above them a flock of geese, in perfect V formation, flew south on the trip that they made every fall. The stranger could not take his eyes off the birds. He stared at them like a man who'd been hypnotized.

310

 Reaching All Students
Extra Support: Previewing the Text

Before reading Segment 2, preview the text, using the notes below. **While** reading, model strategies (pages 312 and 314). **After** reading, review the segment (page 316) before students join the Wrapping Up discussion.

pages 310–311 What does this illustration tell you about the family's acceptance of the stranger?

pages 312–313 Compare the trees in the distance with those close by. Why do you notice?

pages 314–315 The stranger has finally figured out who he is.

pages 316–317 This picture shows the Baileys alone again. Where do you suppose the stranger has gone?

311

Reading

▶ Supporting Comprehension

12 What detail does the author use to show that Farmer Bailey is wrong about his identification of the stranger as a hermit? (He is happy around people.)

13 Why does the author use the word *couldn't* instead of *wouldn't* in the phrase "as if the seasons couldn't change"? (to plant the idea that the seasons are being prevented from changing)

14 Trees in full leaf aren't usually thought of as "drab and ugly." Why does the author use these words? (to show how uncomfortable the stranger is with summer)

Vocabulary *(page 312)*

timid: easily frightened; shy

peculiar: unusual or odd

autumn: the season after summer

Cross-Curricular Connection

Science All leaves contain yellow pigments. Trees rich in sugar have leaves that contain red pigments if exposed to sunlight. These pigments are covered up by the green pigments of chlorophyll, which is manufactured in the leaves during the growing season. In late summer, a firm layer of cells called the *separation layer* forms where the leaf joins the stem. At the same time, the manufacture of chlorophyll stops. As the green in the leaves vanishes, the other colors become visible. The separation layer holds the leaf in place until wind breaks the leaf loose, and it falls to the ground.

---

12 Two weeks passed and the stranger still could not remember who he was. But the Baileys didn't mind. They liked having the stranger around. He had become one of the family. Day by day he'd grown less <u>timid</u>. "He seems so happy to be around us," Mr. Bailey said to his wife. "It's hard to believe he's a hermit."

13 Another week passed. Farmer Bailey could not help noticing how <u>peculiar</u> the weather had been. Not long ago it seemed that <u>autumn</u> was just around the corner. But now it still felt like summer, as if the seasons couldn't change. The warm days made the pumpkins grow larger than ever. The leaves on the trees were as green as they'd been three weeks before.

One day the stranger climbed the highest hill on the Bailey farm. He looked to the north and saw a puzzling sight. The trees in the distance were bright red and orange. But the trees to the south, like those round the Baileys', were nothing but shades of green.

14 They seemed so drab and ugly to the stranger. It would be much better, he thought, if all trees could be red and orange.

312

 Reaching All Students
Extra Support

Strategy Modeling

Monitor/Clarify If students need help modeling the strategy, use this example to model it for them.

I'm not sure when the weather started seeming peculiar. I know it probably has something to do with the arrival of the stranger. To find out, I'll go back and reread, looking for references to the weather or the changing seasons.

313

Genre Skill Lesson
Fantasy

OBJECTIVES

Students identify elements of fantasy in the selection.

Tell students that fantasy is a form of literature that features unlikely or impossible characters, settings, and/or events. Fantasy may involve magic, as in many fairy tales and folktales. Ghost stories are a form of fantasy, and so is most science fiction.

Ask students to brainstorm a list of elements that make *The Stranger* a fantasy. Suggest that they use questions like the ones below to help them determine where the story crosses the line between fiction and fantasy.

1. Which characters are realistic? Which have unlikely or impossible traits?

2. In what ways is the setting realistic? What about the setting seems unlikely or impossible?

3. Which events could really happen? Which events could never happen?

Reaching All Students

English Language Learners

As they read or reread, have students look for the following plurals and possessives in the story: *the Baileys* (308), *the Baileys'* (312), *the stranger's* (314), and *the tree's* (314). Have volunteers read the sentences aloud. Write the phrases on the board. Use the sentences from the selection and some student-generated suggestions about the selection to teach or reteach possessives.

▷ **Strategy Focus:**
Monitor/Clarify

Student Modeling Have students model the strategy by asking themselves if there's anything they don't understand on page 314. They should read ahead or reread what came before to clarify what's happening.

▷ **Supporting Comprehension**

15 What do you suppose happened to the leaf the stranger blew on? Why do you think the author doesn't tell you? (It turned red or yellow; the author wants readers to figure out the stranger's identity for themselves.)

16 Are you surprised that the air turned cold and the leaves changed as the stranger left? Why or why not? (No; he is clearly connected to the changing of the seasons.)

Vocabulary *(page 314)*
trembling: shaking

The stranger's feelings grew stronger the next day. He couldn't look at a tree's green leaves without sensing that something was terribly wrong. The more he thought about it, the more upset he became, until finally he could think of nothing else. He ran to a tree **15** and pulled off a leaf. He held it in a <u>trembling</u> hand and, without thinking, blew on it with all his might.

At dinner that evening the stranger appeared dressed in his old leather clothes. By the tears in his eyes the Baileys could tell that their friend had decided to leave. He hugged them all once, then dashed out the door. The Baileys hurried outside to wave good-bye, but the stranger had disappeared. The air had turned cold, and the leaves on **16** the trees were no longer green.

314

Reaching All Students
Extra Support

Strategy Modeling

Phonics/Decoding Use this example to model the strategy.

In disappeared, *I notice the prefix* dis-. *I also see an* -ed *ending. I'll split the middle part between the double p's. I'll say* / ap / *and the shorter word* pear *as in the fruit. If I put it all together, the word is* / dihs•ap•pair•ed /. *That doesn't sound right. Let me look at the sentence again. Oh, they couldn't wave good-bye because the stranger had* / dihs•uh•PEERD /.

Reaching All Students
English Language Learners

Before reading page 316, pause and ask students why they think the stranger blew on the leaf (p. 314). Challenge students to find another instance in the story when the stranger blows on something. Ask students: *Who did the stranger learn this technique from? What does the stranger expect to happen when he blows on the leaf?*

315

Comprehension Skill
Drawing Conclusions

OBJECTIVES

Students draw conclusions from story details.

Explain that authors do not always say everything they want their readers to know. Sometimes, readers must draw conclusions from story details to figure out what the author does not explain directly.

Display the following equation, and use it to model how to draw conclusions. Point out how "adding up" the details on pages 306–315 can help readers conclude the identity of the stranger. Have the class work together to provide details for the equation, then add them up to draw a conclusion about the stranger's identity.

> The stranger was dressed oddly. **+** The stranger could not speak or use buttons. **+** The doctor's thermometer broke when used on the stranger. **+** Rabbits seemed to like the stranger. **+** The stranger blew on soup and caused a cold draft. **+ ? = ?**

Have small groups create a similar equation that shows the details and conclusion that can be drawn about the following: How would you describe the Bailey Family?

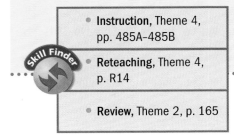

- **Instruction,** Theme 4, pp. 485A–485B
- **Reteaching,** Theme 4, p. R14
- **Review,** Theme 2, p. 165

Skill Finder

Reaching All Students

Challenge

Reading Card 3

Allegory

An allegory is a story with more than one level of meaning. Often an allegory tells a simple story on its face but has a deeper meaning— perhaps a message or moral—underneath. In allegories, authors may give their characters names that reflect their abstract identities; for example, *Death, Hope,* or *Big Brother.*

Ask students to write a paragraph explaining what *The Stranger* teaches us about the impossibility of holding back the passage of time. Ask them to give the stranger a name that represents his true identity.

▶ Supporting Comprehension

17 How does the author show that time has passed since the stranger first arrived? (with the phrase *every autumn since the stranger's visit*)

18 Why do you suppose the colors at the Bailey farm are the brightest around? (The stranger loves colorful leaves, and he provides his friends with the brightest ones possible.)

19 Does it make sense that the stranger's message would be *etched in frost*? Why? (Yes; the stranger would leave his message in a natural way that let the Baileys know he had been there, and for him, frost is natural.)

Vocabulary *(page 316)*

etched: made a design by cutting lines

frost: very thin covering of ice

---

17 Every autumn since the stranger's visit, the same thing happens at the Bailey farm. The trees that surround it stay green for a week **18** after the trees to the north have turned. Then overnight they change their color to the brightest of any tree around. And <u>etched</u> in <u>frost</u> on **19** the farmhouse windows are words that say simply, "See you next fall."

316

Reaching All Students
Extra Support

Segment 2 Review

Before students join in Wrapping Up on page 317, have them:

- review and discuss the accuracy of their predictions
- take turns modeling the reading strategies they used
- complete **Transparency 3–2** and their Detail Maps
- summarize the whole story

Reaching All Students
On Level   Challenge

Literature Discussion

Have small groups of students discuss the story, using their own questions or the questions in Think About the Selection on Anthology page 318.

**End of
Segment 2:**
pages 310–317

 Reaching All Students
English Language Learners

Work with students to develop a sequence of unusual events in the selection. Have students skim the selection looking for incidents involving the stranger and the temperature. Use student suggestions and direction for sequence, listing all unusual events on the board. Use the sequence of events to resolve any confusion students may have about the selection.

Wrapping Up Segment 2
pages 310–317

Provide Extra Support for students who need it (page 316). Then bring all students together.

- **Review Predictions/Purpose** Have students review whether their predictions were accurate and explain why or why not. Then discuss places in their reading where students needed to stop and clarify what was happening in the selection.

- **Model Strategies** Have students take turns modeling the Monitor/Clarify strategy and discuss where they used the strategy as they read. Provide models if needed (pages 303 and 312).

- **Share Group Discussions** Have students discuss how they feel about the dilemma faced by the stranger.

- **Summarize** Have students use their Detail Maps to discuss the author's purpose in writing the story.

Comprehension/Critical Thinking

1. Why do you think the stranger stayed as long as he did? (Answers will vary.) **Drawing Conclusions**

2. Do you think the stranger will continue to visit the Bailey family each year? Why? (Answers will vary.) **Predicting Outcomes**

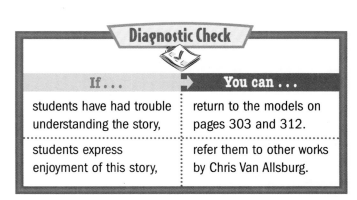

Diagnostic Check

If . . .	You can . . .
students have had trouble understanding the story,	return to the models on pages 303 and 312.
students express enjoyment of this story,	refer them to other works by Chris Van Allsburg.

Responding

▶ Think About the Selection

Discuss or Write Have students discuss or write their answers. Sample answers are provided; accept reasonable responses that are supported with evidence from the story.

1 **Making Judgments** The family is warm, trusting, and caring. Mr. Bailey brings the stranger home. The family lets him stay as long as he wants, gives him clothes, and treats him like family.

2 **Noting Details** The stranger doesn't speak and can't use buttons. When the stranger blows on his soup, he creates a cold draft. He seems to have a special relationship with rabbits.

3 **Making Inferences** It should be fall on the the farm but it is still summer. The birds have flown south and the trees to the north of the Bailey farm have turned their fall colors.

4 **Drawing Conclusions** The stranger might be Fall, Winter, or possibly Jack Frost. Some possible clues: the mercury of the thermometer gets stuck at the bottom after taking the stranger's temperature; there's a draft when he blows on his soup; the leaves don't turn colors while he's visiting; the message written in frost.

5 **Making Inferences** Since the stranger must leave in order for the season to change, there would be a nice long summer.

6 **Connecting/Comparing** Noting Details The author describes the stranger's unusual behavior (silence, unfamiliar with farm life and work, relationship with animals) but never explains it. The illustrations emphasize his feelings toward nature.

Responding

Think About the Selection

1. What is the Bailey family like? Use details from the story to support your description.

2. What are the first few clues that tell you that something is unusual about the stranger?

3. The stranger feels that something is "terribly wrong" when he sees green leaves on the trees. What do you think is wrong?

4. Who do you think the stranger is? List three clues that help you guess his identity.

5. If the stranger stayed for a while in the area where you live, what effect do you think he would have on the climate?

6. **Connecting/Comparing** What does Chris Van Allsburg do to make this story mysterious and amazing? Look at both the words and the illustrations.

Write a Character Sketch

The stranger is an unusual person. Write a character sketch of him so that someone who has not read this story will understand what he is like.

Tips
- To get started, look for details in the story and the illustrations.
- Include what the stranger looks like and how he acts.

318

Reaching All Students
English Language Learners

Beginning/Preproduction Point out that the stranger and Katy are the only characters whose faces we see. Compare the illustration of Katy and the stranger with that of Mr. and Mrs. Bailey.

Early Production and Speech Emergence In small groups have students look for clues that link the stranger with cold.

Intermediate and Advanced Fluency Ask small groups to describe the change of the seasons in northern climates. If students are not familiar with the seasons, they can find photos to describe the changes.

MATH

Find the Average Temperature

Use a thermometer and some math to find the average temperature for a week where you live. Find each day's average temperature for seven days in a row. Write the temperatures in a notebook. When you have seven readings, find the average temperature for that week.

Bonus Use a newspaper to find the average temperature for another city during the same week. Calculate how much hotter or colder that city was than where you live.

ART

Draw a Picture

Where do you think the stranger goes after he leaves the Baileys' farmhouse? Make a drawing of the stranger in the place where he stays next or lives during the rest of the year. You might want to draw a picture that is somewhat mysterious, like the ones Chris Van Allsburg draws.

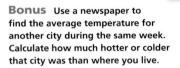

Post a Review

Would you like to share your opinion of *The Stranger* with other students on the Internet? Write a review of the book and post it on Education Place. **www.eduplace.com/kids**

319

 Personal Response

Invite volunteers to share their personal responses to *The Stranger*. As an alternative, ask students to write in their journals how they might have reacted if the stranger had moved into their homes.

▶ **Comprehension Check**

Assign **Practice Book** page 157 to assess students' understanding of the selection.

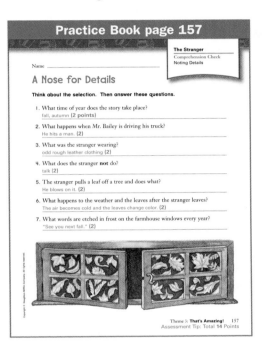

Practice Book page 157

The Stranger
Comprehension Check
Noting Details

Name _____

A Nose for Details

Think about the selection. Then answer these questions.

1. What time of year does the story take place?
   fall, autumn (2 points)
2. What happens when Mr. Bailey is driving his truck?
   He hits a man. (2)
3. What was the stranger wearing?
   odd rough leather clothing (2)
4. What does the stranger **not** do?
   talk (2)
5. The stranger pulls a leaf off a tree and does what?
   He blows on it. (2)
6. What happens to the weather and the leaves after the stranger leaves?
   The air becomes cold and the leaves change color. (2)
7. What words are etched in frost on the farmhouse windows every year?
   "See you next fall." (2)

Theme 3: **That's Amazing!** 157
Assessment Tip: Total **14** Points

 End-of-Selection Assessment

Selection Test Use the test in the **Teacher's Resource Blackline Masters** to assess selection comprehension and vocabulary.

Student Self-Assessment Have students assess their reading with additional questions such as

- What parts of this selection were difficult for me? Why?

- What strategies helped me understand the story?

- Would I recommend this story to my friends and family? Why?

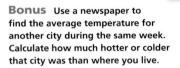
Reaching All Students

English Language Learners

Have students work in small mixed groups to create word webs about the stranger. Students should refer to the illustrations and the text to include what they learn about the stranger from his actions and expressions. Later, students can draw on the word web as they write their character descriptions.

Poetry Link

pages 320–323

▶ Skill: How to Read a Poem

Read aloud the titles of the poems. Explain that these poems all deal with the topic of autumn. Have selected students explain in their own words how poetry differs from other writing forms. Since a poem is a unique form of writing, students should read these selections differently than they would a short story. Explain that a poem is a form of writing creatively describing a person, place, feeling, or event—often in rhyme. Point out that reading poetry requires a careful approach to reading. Then review the tips in the left column on page 320:

- Students should **read** the poems several times. Reading the poems aloud will give the class a better sense of the meter.

- Instruct readers to **look** or **listen** for patterns such as rhythm, repetition and rhyme. Ask them to focus on the poet's specific word choices.

- Finally, students should **reread** each poem. Ask them to stop and **think** about the idea the poet is trying to express. Have them discuss how each poem makes them feel.

Vocabulary *(pages 320–321)*

spiraling: twirling in a circular pattern

main: power

bide: to wait around

Poetry Link

Skill: How to Read a Poem

- Read the poem several times. Try reading it aloud.

- Listen for the words that **rhyme**.

- Listen for a **rhythm**, and try to tap out the beats.

- Look at the words to see if they form a **picture** on the page.

- Finally, reread the poem. Try to picture what the poet is describing. Also, think about the meaning of the poem.

Autumn Poems

Fall Wind

I scarcely felt a breath of air;
I didn't hear a sound,
But one small leaf came spiraling
In circles to the ground.

And then the wind began to rise.
I felt it on my face.
It blew my jacket out behind
And made the white clouds race.

It seized the branches of the trees
And shook with might and main.
The leaves poured down upon the earth
Like drops of colored rain.

by Margaret Hillert

        going out of my way
        to crunch them as I walk;
        first leaves of autumn

by Lee Gurga

320

Reaching All Students

Classroom Management

All Students

Reading Poetry Some students may benefit from having the poems read aloud. Have all students complete the Sensory Details Chart, Genre Lesson, and Comprehension Check activities. For students having difficulty discovering a poem's inherent sense of meter, encourage them to tap out the natural rhythm as they read aloud. Initially, you may need to guide them.

Falling Leaves

Some glide,
Some slide,
And some bide their time.

Some hurl,
Some twirl,
And some whirl and climb.

Some slip,
Some zip,
And some dip and play.

Falling leaves
Depart their trees
In every sort of way.

by Lucinda A. Cave

321

▶ Sensory Details Chart

Tell students that many poems appeal to the senses of sight, hearing, touch, smell, or taste. Ask them to complete this chart as they read. Demonstrate by completing the following chart together on the board for the first poem, "Fall Wind."

Sight	Hearing	Touch	Smell	Taste
• leaf spiraling • drops of colored rain	• didn't hear a sound	• scarcely felt a breath of air • felt it on my face		

Have students complete their own Sensory Details Charts for selected poems throughout the Link. Students may find the chart works better for certain poems than for others.

Purpose Setting As students read the other poems in the Link, have them look for images that appeal to the senses and are specific to the autumn theme. Suggest that they use Evaluate and other strategies to monitor their own feelings about the poems.

Reaching All Students
Extra Support

Reading Free Verse

Even students who have little trouble with the rhythmic and rhyming poems in this Link may find "Moon of Falling Leaves" difficult. Explain that this kind of poetry is designed to follow the patterns of normal speech. The poem is written in sentences; only the line breaks tell us that it is really a poem. Ask students to work in pairs to read "Moon of Falling Leaves" aloud to each other until they are comfortable with the pattern and meaning of the poem.

Poetry Link continued

pages 320–323

pages 320–323

Revisiting the Text

Genre Lesson
Poetry

OBJECTIVES

Students identify examples of poetic devices.

Explain that poets use many different poetic devices to make a poem that paints clear images in the reader's mind. To do this a poet may:

- play with the meanings of words

- use interesting sound combinations

- create vivid mental images with words

- create rhymes that may be either subtle (internal) or obvious

- establish sound patterns by repeating specific letter sounds (alliteration)

- suspend certain rules common to other forms of writing (poetic license)

- strategically use specific words which illicit special kinds of feelings

Have students identify examples of each of the above devices in the Link. Discuss alternative methods a poet might use to make a poem.

Vocabulary *(page 322)*

padded: muffled

windswept: windy or gusty

Canada Geese

Padded drum
of beating wings
fills the steel gray sky.
See them sketching, stretching skyward.
Hear their lonely cry. See them in the windswept
autumn. Hear them call
goodbye.

by Kristine O'Connell George

migrating geese
one falls farther and farther
behind

by Charles Dickson

322

Reaching All Students

English Language Learners

Say to students: *It is time to talk about rhyme.* Ask a volunteer to identify the rhyme in what you just said. Write *time* and *rhyme* on the board and point out that words don't have to be close in spelling to rhyme. Ask volunteers to come up with more examples of rhyming words. List their ideas on the board.

Moon of Falling Leaves

Long ago, the trees were told
they must stay awake
seven days and nights,
but only the cedar,
the pine and the spruce
stayed awake until
that seventh night.
The reward they were given
was to always be green,
while all the other trees
must shed their leaves.

So, each autumn, the leaves
of the sleeping trees fall.
They cover the floor
of our woodlands with colors
as bright as the flowers
that come with the spring.
The leaves return the strength
of one more year's growth
to the earth.

This journey
the leaves are taking
is part of that great circle
which holds us all close to the earth.

by Joseph Bruchac and Jonathan London
based on a traditional Cherokee story
of the Tenth Moon

323

▶ ## Comprehension Check

Sensory Details Chart Have students share the various columns on their sensory details charts by reading them aloud. Ask them to identify the poems that best appealed to their senses. Write selected answers on the board.

Comprehension/Critical Thinking Ask students to use their charts and the selection to answer these questions.

1. Both "Fall Wind" and "Falling Leaves" deal with the movement of leaves in autumn. What strong verbs do the poets use to describe that movement? (*spiraling, poured; glide, slide, bide, hurl, twirl, whirl, climb, slip, zip, dip, play*) **Noting Details**

2. Whom do you picture as the speaker in the poem by Lee Gurga? Explain. (Possibly a child— someone young would be more likely to go out of his way to crunch leaves.) **Drawing Conclusions**

3. What is "that great circle" about which the poet writes in "Moon of Falling Leaves"? (the circle of birth and death; the circle of the seasons) **Making Inferences**

4. **Connecting/Comparing** In *The Stranger,* the stranger is "hypnotized" by a flock of geese flying south. How does the poem "Canada Geese" reflect the mood of that scene? (It reflects the stranger's loneliness and loss.) **Compare and Contrast**

Reaching All Students
Challenge

Writing

Have students choose the poem they like best. After discussing the merits of their selections, instruct them to write an original poem about their favorite season. Review the poetic devices explained in the Genre Lesson on page 322. Have selected students share their poems with the class. You may choose to have the class complete Sensory Details Charts as they listen.

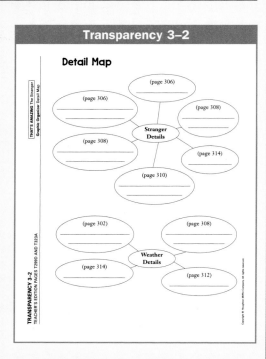

Transparency 3–2

Detail Map

Practice Book page 156

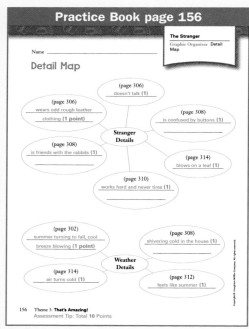

Comprehension Skills

 Noting Details

▶ **Teach**

Review with the students the details used to describe the stranger and the weather in *The Stranger*. Use **Transparency 3–2** to discuss

■ how details allow the reader to see, hear, and feel

■ why some details are more important than others

Students may refer to the selection and to **Practice Book** page 156.

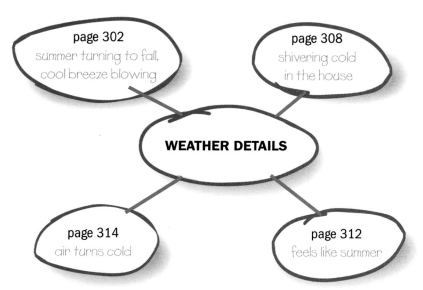

Modeling Tell students that once they have identified details it is necessary to decide which ones are important and less important. Figuring out which ones to focus on will allow them to better understand meanings that the author is trying to convey. Ask a student to read aloud the second paragraph on page 306. Have students think about the detail of the broken thermometer as you think aloud.

Think Aloud

Though the doctor says the thermometer is broken like it's no big deal, I think this detail is important. I've never heard of a thermometer's mercury being stuck. It either works or it's broken into pieces. It has no moving parts that can break. I think that the stranger had something to do with this because the doctor just examined him. I'm not sure why the thermometer isn't working, but it's important because it makes the stranger even more mysterious.

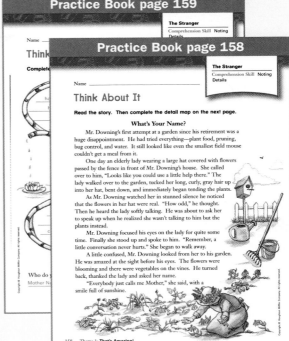

Practice Book page 159

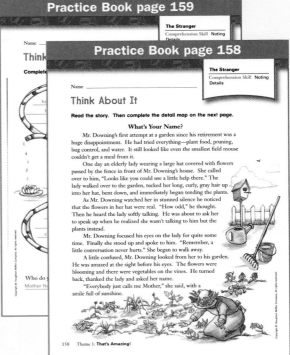

Practice Book page 158

The Stranger

Comprehension Skill Noting Details

Name _____

Think About It

Read the story. Then complete the detail map on the next page.

What's Your Name?

Mr. Downing's first attempt at a garden since his retirement was a huge disappointment. He had tried everything—plant food, pruning, bug control, and water. It still looked like even the smallest field mouse couldn't get a meal from it.

One day an elderly lady wearing a large hat covered with flowers passed by the fence in front of Mr. Downing's house. She called over to him, "Looks like you could use a little help there." The lady walked over to the garden, tucked her long, curly, gray hair up into her hat, bent down, and immediately began tending the plants.

As Mr. Downing watched her in stunned silence he noticed that the flowers in her hat were real. "How odd," he thought. Then he heard the lady softly talking. He was about to ask her to speak up when he realized she wasn't talking to him but the plants instead.

Mr. Downing focused his eyes on the lady for quite some time. Finally she stood up and spoke to him. "Remember, a little conversation never hurts." She began to walk away.

A little confused, Mr. Downing looked from her to his garden. He was amazed at the sight before his eyes. The flowers were blooming and there were vegetables on the vines. He turned back, thanked the lady and asked her name.

"Everybody just calls me Mother," she said, with a smile full of sunshine.

158   Theme 3: **That's Amazing!**

▶ **Practice**

Have pairs of students decide which details about Mr. Bailey on pages 302–310 are important to understanding what he is like. Tell students to list all the details first, then decide about the importance. They should record their thoughts in a chart like the one below.

MR. BAILEY

	Details	Important Details (Accept reasonably varied answers.)
page 302	whistles as he drives Autumn is his favorite season.	(none.)
page 304	kneels down by man in road helps injured man into truck	kneels down by man in road helps injured man into truck

What makes some of these important? (Accept reasonably varied answers.)
(The important details are the ones that show me the kind of person Mr. Bailey is. By having him help out the stranger, the author shows me that Mr. Bailey is a kind and caring person.)

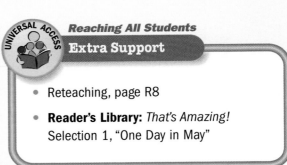

Reaching All Students
Extra Support

- Reteaching, page R8
- **Reader's Library:** *That's Amazing!* Selection 1, "One Day in May"

▶ **Apply**

Use **Practice Book** pages 158–159 to diagnose whether students need Reteaching. Students who do not need Reteaching may work on Challenge/Extension Activities, page R9. Students who need Extra Support may apply the skill to an easier text using **Reader's Library** selection "One Day in May" and its Responding activity.

Skill Finder

• Revisiting, p. 307	• Review, Th. 2, p. 201; Th. 3, p. 349; Th. 6, p. 637	• Reteaching, p. R8

Diagnostic Check

If . . .	→ You can . . .
students need extra help noting details,	use the Reteaching Lesson on page R8.
students have successfully met the lesson objectives,	have them do the Challenge/Extension Activities on page R9.

Students

- learn how to fill in a story chart
- practice identifying main characters, conflict, main events, and conflict resolution

---

Transparency 3–3

Story Chart for *The Stranger*

Main Characters
Farmer Bailey
The Stranger

Problems

Events
- Farmer Bailey hits a young man with his truck.
- The man doesn't seem to talk or know about ordinary things.
- The stranger stays with the family for three weeks. During that time, trees stay green and the weather doesn't get colder, even though it is fall.
- The stranger gets upset that the leaves haven't turned color.
- When the stranger goes away, the weather immediately gets colder and the leaves turn.
- Every year, fall comes a week late to the Bailey farm. Someone writes "See you next fall" in frost on a window.

Resolution

TRANSPARENCY 3–3
TEACHER'S EDITION PAGE T323C

THAT'S AMAZING! *The Stranger*
Information and Study Skills Story Chart

Copyright © Houghton Mifflin Company. All rights reserved.

Information & Study Skills
Story Chart

▶ Teach

Have selected students briefly retell a favorite fairy tale. Point out that although various stories have different details, they have certain features in common. These features include main characters who have a problem or a conflict with someone or something and story events that tell how the characters deal with the problem or conflict. Many stories end with the problem or conflict being solved. This part of the story is called the resolution. Explain that students can more easily understand the stories they read if they identify these features individually. A story chart is one very helpful way to do this.

Display **Transparency 3–3** and identify it as a story chart. Have students read the headings aloud and discuss how they correspond to the features of a story. Use the transparency to model how to identify the features of the story, *The Stranger*.

Model Have students turn to the first page of *The Stranger* and use the story as a reference while you fill in the first three sections of the story chart. Leave the final section, *resolution*, for students to do as Practice.

Think Aloud

The two main characters in The Stranger *are Farmer Bailey and the stranger, a young man whom he hits with his truck. I'll write their names in the first section of the story chart. Now, what problems do these characters have? And which problem is the most important one in the story? First, I'll list the important events in the story.* (Recount the story events shown on the transparency.) *From these events, I can see that the most important problem is that fall isn't coming to the Bailey farm, even though it should have arrived by now. Another problem, though not as important, is that the stranger does not know who he is. So, I'll write these in the second box. Next, I'll need to determine how all this is sorted out in the end. I'll write the resolution in the last box ...*

▶ Practice

Have students reread pages 314–317 of *The Stranger*. Tell them to pay attention to the pictures as well as the words. Then discuss how the problem of the story is resolved. You may wish to prompt them by asking the following questions:

- What happens when the stranger leaves?

- Why do you think fall comes suddenly?

- What happens every fall after this one?

- Who do you think the stranger really is?

Work with students to decide how to fill in the last box on the story chart and do so as a class.

▶ Apply

Have students work in small groups and choose a favorite story, television program, or movie to analyze. Distribute blank copies of the story chart to each group or

ask them to copy a blank story chart on a piece of paper. Then have students fill in the story chart together. Have groups share their results with the class. Point out that story charts are a good way to summarize a story for listeners.

Word Work

DAY 1	• Spelling Pretest • Spelling Instruction
DAY 2	• Structural Analysis Instruction • Spelling Practice
DAY 3	• Phonics Instruction • Spelling Practice
DAY 4	• Structural Analysis Reteaching • Vocabulary Skill Instruction • Spelling Game
DAY 5	• Expanding Your Vocabulary • Spelling Test

OBJECTIVES

Students

• identify and read compound words

• read words that begin with *a-* or *be-*

• use the Phonics/Decoding strategy to decode longer words

• learn academic language: **compound word**

 **Teacher's Note**

The relationship between the meaning of a compound word and the meaning of its word parts will not always be clear. For example, a butterfly doesn't look like butter, and a strawberry doesn't look or taste like straw.

Decoding Longer Words

 *Structural Analysis:*
Compound Words **Spelling Connection**

▶ Teach

Write this sentence on the board:

Explain that *bedroom* is a compound word, a word formed from two or more shorter words. Circle *bed* and *room* and explain that the word

Katy watched the stranger from her bedroom window.

bedroom means "room with a bed." Point out that in this compound word the shorter words run together with no space. The shorter words can also be separated by a space (*high school*) or joined together by a hyphen (*weather-beaten*). Tell students that they can look in a dictionary to see whether a compound word is written as one word, includes a space, or is joined by a hyphen. Have students review the Phonics/Decoding strategy.

Modeling Display the following sentence and model how to decode *pitchfork*: *Mr. Bailey gave the stranger a* <u>*pitchfork*</u>.

Think Aloud

I see the shorter word pitch. *When I cover it, I see another word I know,* fork. *It's a compound word. Pitch means "to throw" and a fork is a tool you eat with. I know on farms people sometimes use a tool that's shaped like a big fork to lift and throw hay. Maybe that's called a pitchfork. That makes sense in the sentence.*

▶ Practice

Have students copy these words from the board: *buttonholes; good-bye; overnight; weather vane; well-mannered.* Tell students to circle the shorter words within each compound word, decode it, and give its meaning.

▶ Apply

Have students complete **Practice Book** page 160.

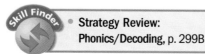 • Strategy Review: Phonics/Decoding, p. 299B | • Reteaching, p. R14

Phonics

Words That Begin with a- or be-

▶ Teach

Tell students that understanding words that begin with *a-* and *be-* can help them use the Phonics/Decoding strategy to decode unfamiliar words. Explain that

- in two-syllable words, the unstressed /ə/ sound at the beginning of a word may be spelled *a*
- in two-syllable words, the unstressed /bĭ/ sound may be spelled *be*

Modeling Display this sentence and model how to decode *became: The more he thought about it, the more upset he became.*

Think Aloud

I know that the b-e spelling pattern can make the unaccented /bih/ sound at the beginning of a word. Next I see a shorter word I know, came. When I put both parts together, I say /bih•KAYM/. I know that word and it makes sense.

▶ Practice

Write these phrases on the board and have students copy the underlined words: *because he was hurt; across the yard; any tree around; before he disappeared.*

Have students circle the *a-* and *be-* beginnings, and then decode each word. Call on individuals to model their answers at the board.

▶ Apply

Tell students to decode the following words from *The Stranger* and discuss their meanings: *along,* page 302; *beside,* page 304; *alone,* page 306; *believe,* page 312; *another,* page 312.

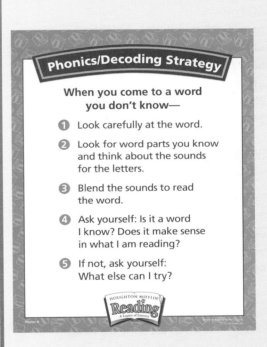

Practice Book page 160

The Stranger
Structural Analysis
Compound Words

Name _____

Compound Challenge

Write the compound word that matches each clue. Then write the circled letters in order at the bottom of the page to spell a word that describes the Stranger.

1. carousel m e r r y - g o - r o u n d (1 point)
2. a yard at the back of a house b a c k y a r d (1)
3. the first meal of the day b r e a k f a s t (1)
4. light coming from stars s t a r l i g h t (1)
5. Saturday and Sunday w e e k e n d (1)
6. a truck used by firefighters f i r e e n g i n e (1)
7. a bank shaped like a pig p i g g y b a n k (1)
8. a coat worn to protect against rain r a i n c o a t (1)
9. a house for a dog d o g h o u s e (1)
10. a walk on the side of a road s i d e w a l k (1)

A word to describe the Stranger:
m y s t e r i o u s (2)

160 Theme 3: **That's Amazing!**
Assessment Tip: Total **12 Points**

Phonics/Decoding Strategy

When you come to a word you don't know—

1. Look carefully at the word.
2. Look for word parts you know and think about the sounds for the letters.
3. Blend the sounds to read the word.
4. Ask yourself: Is it a word I know? Does it make sense in what I am reading?
5. If not, ask yourself: What else can I try?

HOUGHTON MIFFLIN
Reading
A Legacy of Literacy

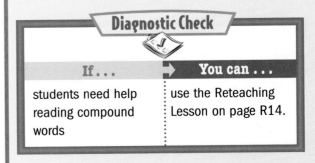

Diagnostic Check

If . . .	→ You can . . .
students need help reading compound words	use the Reteaching Lesson on page R14.

Decoding Longer Words 323F

Word Work

Spelling
 **Compound Words**

Spelling Words

Basic Words

railroad*	fireplace
airport*	ourselves
seat belt	all right*
everywhere*	forever*
homesick*	breakfast
understand*	whenever*
background*	everything*
anything*	meanwhile
ninety-nine	afternoon*
already*	make-believe*

Review Words

inside*
outside*
birthday*
baseball
sometimes*

Challenge Words

landmark
nationwide
postscript
motorcycle
handkerchief*

Forms of these words appear in the literature.

 **Reaching All Students**

Extra Support

Basic Word List You may want to use only the left column of Basic Words with students who need extra support.

323G **THEME 3: That's Amazing!**

Day 1 Teaching the Principle

Pretest Use the Day 5 Test sentences. Say each underlined word, read the sentence, and then repeat the word. Have students write only the underlined word.

Teach Write *railroad, ninety-nine,* and *seat belt* in separate columns on the board. Point to and say each word and have students repeat it. Explain that each word is a compound word, a word made up of two (or sometimes more) smaller words. Ask students to help you identify the smaller words in each compound. Point out that some compound words are written as one word, some as a hyphenated word, and some as separate words.

Add the column heads *One Word, Hyphenated Word,* and *Separate Words* above their respective examples on the board. Then write each remaining Basic Word in the appropriate column, say it, and have students repeat it. When you present *already,* explain that this word is different because an *l* was dropped when *all* and *ready* were joined to form the compound.

Practice/Homework Assign **Practice Book** page 417. Tell students to use this Take-Home Word List to study the words they missed on the Pretest.

Day 2 Reviewing the Principle

Practice/Homework Review the spelling principle and assign **Practice Book** page 161.

Day 3 Vocabulary

Word Origins Tell students that language is constantly changing, and that new words are created to keep up with the latest trends and technology. Write *railroad, airport, seat belt,* and *motorcycle* on the board. Ask students to speculate on when and why these words came into being. (Responses will vary.)

Next, list the Basic Words on the board. Have students use each word orally in a sentence. (Sentences will vary.)

Practice/Homework For spelling practice, assign **Practice Book** page 162.

Day 4   Turning Leaves

Have students work in groups of five, and give each group a spelling word list. Ask each group to cut out 25 construction-paper leaves and to write a meaning or clue for a different Basic or Review Word on one side of each leaf. Students then mix up the leaves and stack them facedown. They also turn the spelling list facedown.

To play, players take turns turning over a leaf and then naming and spelling the word that fits the clue. If a word is spelled correctly, the player keeps the leaf. If not, the leaf is placed at the bottom of the stack. The player with the most leaves at the end of the game wins.

Practice/Homework For proofreading and writing practice, assign **Practice Book** page 163.

Day 5   Spelling Assessment

Test Say each underlined word, read the sentence, and then repeat the word. Have students write only the underlined word.

Basic Words

1. The <u>railroad</u> has miles of train tracks.
2. His plane left the <u>airport</u> at noon.
3. Everyone in our car wears a <u>seat belt</u>.
4. It was cold <u>everywhere</u> we went.
5. I felt <u>homesick</u> on my trip.
6. Did you <u>understand</u> the lesson?
7. Trees fill the <u>background</u> in this picture.
8. Can I have <u>anything</u> I want?
9. She can count to <u>ninety-nine</u>.
10. Is it <u>already</u> time to leave?
11. The <u>fireplace</u> kept the room warm.
12. We taught <u>ourselves</u> the game.
13. Was the boat <u>all right</u> after the storm?
14. Pat and I will be friends <u>forever</u>.
15. He ate two eggs for <u>breakfast</u>.
16. The cat comes <u>whenever</u> I call her.
17. I liked <u>everything</u> I bought.
18. The children hid behind the hedge <u>meanwhile</u>.
19. The best time at the beach is the <u>afternoon</u>.
20. The child has a <u>make-believe</u> friend.

Challenge Words

21. The train went by a <u>landmark</u>.
22. They travel <u>nationwide</u> by plane.
23. She wrote a <u>postscript</u>.
24. Would you like a ride on my <u>motorcycle</u>?
25. He lost the <u>handkerchief</u>.

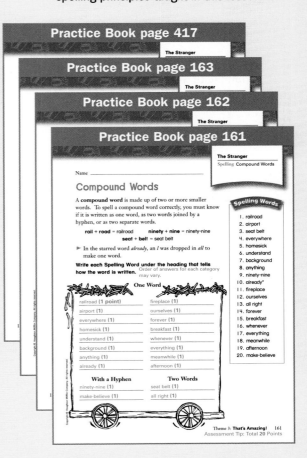

Technology

Spelling Spree!™

Students may use the **Spelling Spree!™** for extra practice with the spelling principles taught in this lesson.

Practice Book page 417

Practice Book page 163

Practice Book page 162

Practice Book page 161

Compound Words

A **compound word** is made up of two or more smaller words. To spell a compound word correctly, you must know if it is written as one word, as two words joined by a hyphen, or as two separate words.

rail + road = railroad   ninety + nine = ninety-nine
seat + belt = seat belt

▶ In the starred word *already*, an *l* was dropped in *all* to make one word.

Write each Spelling Word under the heading that tells how the word is written. Order of answers for each category may vary.

Spelling Words
1. railroad
2. airport
3. seat belt
4. everywhere
5. homesick
6. understand
7. background
8. anything
9. ninety-nine
10. already*
11. fireplace
12. ourselves
13. all right
14. forever
15. breakfast
16. whenever
17. everything
18. meanwhile
19. afternoon
20. make-believe

One Word

railroad (1 point)   fireplace (1)
airport (1)   ourselves (1)
everywhere (1)   forever (1)
homesick (1)   breakfast (1)
understand (1)   whenever (1)
background (1)   everything (1)
anything (1)   meanwhile (1)
already (1)   afternoon (1)

With a Hyphen   **Two Words**
ninety-nine (1)   seat belt (1)
make-believe (1)   all right (1)

Theme 3: **That's Amazing!**   161
Assessment Tip: Total **20** Points

···· **Houghton Mifflin Spelling and Vocabulary** ····
Correlated instruction and practice, pp. 84, 146

Reaching All Students
Challenge

Challenge Word Practice Students can make rebus puzzles for the Challenge Words. Then they can exchange papers and solve one another's puzzles by writing the Challenge Words.

Practice Book page 164

Transparency 3–4

What Is a Synonym?

A **synonym** is a word that means the same or nearly the same thing as another word.

	1	2	3
Word	found	look	odd
Synonym	discovered	gaze	strange

Match the word in column 1 to its synonym in column 2.

Word	Synonym
4. shy	fear
5. trip	couch
6. terror	timid
7. sofa	journey

Give a synonym for the underlined word.

8. Occasionally, Mr. Bailey would have to <u>stop</u> and rest.

9. That <u>evening</u>, Katy and the stranger watched the setting sun.

10. He <u>stared</u> at the trees, puzzled.

11. The green trees seemed <u>drab</u> and ugly to the stranger.

12. The more he thought about it, the more <u>upset</u> he became.

Vocabulary Skills

✓ *Vocabulary: Synonyms*

▶ Teach

Display **Transparency 3–4,** blocking out all but the definition of *synonym.* Read the definition to the class. Explain that synonyms often come in pairs, and the word in each synonym pair expresses the same, or nearly the same, meaning.

Then uncover sample synonym pairs 1 through 3 on the transparency. Read aloud each pair. Explain the meaning of each word in the pair and how the meanings are similar. Then read aloud the following sentences as examples:

Mr. Bailey found the stranger in the road.
Mr. Bailey discovered the stranger in the road.

The stranger stopped to look at the beautiful autumn leaves.
The stranger stopped to gaze at the beautiful autumn leaves.

It was odd that fall had not come.
It was strange that fall had not come.

Modeling Now display the last portion of the transparency, which shows synonym pairs 4 through 7 in two columns. Point out the first word in column 1, *shy.* Model how to find its synonym, *timid,* in column 2. Draw a line linking the two words.

Think Aloud

I know that shy *means nervous or fearful of others. For example, some wild animals are shy around people. They hide until the people are gone. Looking at the words in column 2, the one closest to this meaning is* timid. *This tells me that* timid *is a synonym of* shy.

▶ Practice

In pairs or small groups, have students match the remaining synonym word pairs. As they identify the pairs, draw lines linking the words in each pair. Have students provide model sentences using the words in each pair.

Display items 8 through 12 at the bottom of the transparency. Each sentence contains an underlined word. Have students substitute a synonym using the sentence context. Then have students discuss which word they prefer in the sentence and why.

▶ Apply

Have students complete **Practice Book** page 164.

Expanding Your Vocabulary
Scientific Terms: Weather Words

In the selection, words such as *frost* and *breeze* give clues to the stranger's mysterious influence on the weather. Explain that *meteorologists* (people who study the weather) use specialized words to describe and forecast the weather, such as *north* and *radar*. As a class, create a word web that shows technical vocabulary related to the weather, similar to the following:

Have students suggest other weather words and add the words to the web.

Challenge/Extension Activities, p. R15

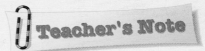

Homophones Explain that English has many *homophones,* words that are pronounced the same but have different spellings and meanings. Point out that in the beginning of the selection, Mr. Bailey thinks he has hit a *deer,* a large animal. The word *deer* is often confused with its homophone, *dear,* which means "beloved or cherished." Ask students to define each of the following homophone pairs and use them in a sentence. Answers are in parentheses.

peek (look at quickly)

peak (top of a hill or mountain)

seem (appear)

seam (stitches binding two pieces of cloth)

sight (a view)

site (location)

weather (daily atmospheric conditions)

whether (a word used to present two alternatives)

·· **Houghton Mifflin Spelling and Vocabulary** ···
Correlated instruction and practice, pp. 73, 166

Reaching All Students
English Language Learners

Review clue words that can signal a cause-effect relationship, such as *because, since, so,* and *as a result.* Incorporating these terms into students' monitor/clarify reading strategy will help them to see the pattern of unusual occurrences in the selection.

Writing and Language Instruction	
DAY 1	• Daily Language Practice • Grammar Instruction • Journal Writing
DAY 2	• Daily Language Practice • Writing an Explanation • Journal Writing • Grammar Practice
DAY 3	• Daily Language Practice • Grammar Instruction • Write a Character Sketch
DAY 4	• Daily Language Practice • Listening/Speaking/Viewing • Writing: Improving Your Writing • Grammar Practice
DAY 5	• Daily Language Practice • Grammar: Improving Your Writing

OBJECTIVES

Students

• identify action verbs

• give examples of action verbs

• proofread and correct sentences with grammar and spelling errors

• use exact verbs in sentences to improve writing

• learn academic language: **action verb**

Wacky Web Tales

Students may use the **Wacky Web Tales** floppy disk to create humorous stories and review parts of speech.

Grammar Skills

 Action Verbs

Day 1

Display the chart on **Transparency 3–5**. Identify the action verb in each of the three sentences at the top of the transparency. Then go over the following definition:

■ An action verb is a word that shows action.

Ask students to look at *The Stranger* to find examples of action verbs and to share the examples they find. Tell students to copy the numbered sentences on **Transparency 3–5** on a separate sheet of paper. Have students underline the action verbs in the sentences to identify them. Then have them correct the Day 1 Daily Language Practice sentences on **Transparency 3–7**.

Day 2

Practice/Homework Have students correct the Day 2 Daily Language Practice sentences. Then assign **Practice Book** page 165.

Day 3 Be Specific!

Divide the class into two teams. Have each team choose one member to act as moderator. The moderators choose an area such as sports, farm life, gardening, or biking, for example. Play begins as a member of the first team names an action verb in the category chosen by the moderators. Then a member of the second team must make up a sentence using that verb. If the player succeeds, the second team gets a chance to name an action verb. If the player fails to come up with a sentence, then the first team gets a point and another chance to name an action verb. After five verbs have been named, the moderators pick a new category and the teams must think of action verbs in that category. Play continues until every student has had a chance to name a verb or create a sentence.

Then have students correct the Day 3 Daily Language Practice sentences.

Day 4

Practice/Homework Have students correct the Day 4 Daily Language Practice sentences. Assign **Practice Book** page 166.

Day 5 — Improving Your Writing

Using Exact Verbs: Tell students that good writers use exact verbs that name specific actions instead of vague, general verbs. Display the sentences on **Transparency 3–6**.

Ask volunteers to go to the board and rewrite the sentences by substituting an exact verb for the general verb or phrase in parentheses.

Have students review a piece of their own writing to see if they can improve it by making sure that they have used exact verbs.

Practice/Homework Have students correct the Day 5 Daily Language Practice sentences. Then assign **Practice Book** page 167.

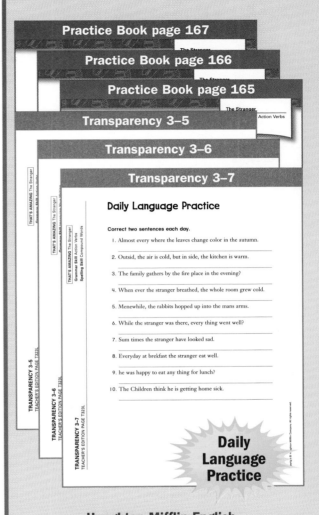

Practice Book page 167

Practice Book page 166

Practice Book page 165

Transparency 3–5

Transparency 3–6

Transparency 3–7

Daily Language Practice

Correct two sentences each day.

1. Almost every where the leaves change color in the autumn.
2. Outsid, the air is cold, but in side, the kitchen is warm.
3. The family gathers by the fire place in the evening?
4. When ever the stranger breathed, the whole room grew cold.
5. Menewhile, the rabbits hopped up into the mans arms.
6. While the stranger was there, every thing went well?
7. Sum times the stranger have looked sad.
8. Everyday at brekfast the stranger eat well.
9. he was happy to eat any thing for lunch?
10. The Children think he is getting home sick.

Daily Language Practice

········· **Houghton Mifflin English** ···········
Correlated instruction and practice, pp. 96–97, 118

Diagnostic Check

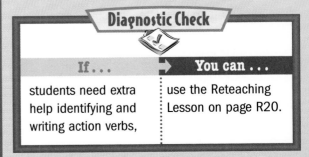

If . . .	You can . . .
students need extra help identifying and writing action verbs,	use the Reteaching Lesson on page R20.

Writing Skills
An Explanation

▶ Teach

Explain to students that an explanation tells why or how something happens. An explanation usually begins with a topic sentence. The other sentences in a paragraph of explanation give reasons or facts to support the topic sentence. In an explanation that tells why something happens, the reasons or facts are often arranged in order of importance. In an explanation that tells how something happens, the reasons or facts are often arranged in time order.

▶ Practice

Display **Transparency 3–8.** Have students read the model paragraph. Ask:

■ **What is being explained?** (why leaves change from green to yellow, orange, and red in autumn)

■ **Which sentence tells the reader what this explanation is about?** (The green leaves of summer turn yellow, orange, and red in autumn.)

■ **What do the other sentences in the paragraph do?** (The other sentences support the topic sentence, giving reasons and facts that explain why leaves turn color.)

■ **Does this paragraph explain why or how something happens?** (why)

■ **How are the supporting details organized?** (in order of importance)

Discuss with students the guidelines for writing an explanation.

Transparency 3–8

Writing an Explanation

Transparency 3–9

Audience

Writers are always aware of their audience.

• Formal writing is for reports, presentations, and other school assignments.

Formal: Leaves are green because of a substance called chlorophyll. Chlorophyll makes food for the tree. Two-thirds of the color of leaves comes from chlorophyll.

• Informal writing is for friendly letters, postcards, or e-mails between friends.

Informal: I love how green everything is in May. When I look out my window, I can see green for miles!

Look at each of the following topics. Make a formal statement about each topic, as if you were reporting it to a group of people you didn't know. Then make an informal statement as if you were sending an e-mail to a friend.

fall colors
frost on the window
heating the house in the winter
ice melting
spring buds on trees

Penmanship

 Teacher's Resource Disk:
Penmanship Blackline Masters

Use these masters to model correct letter formation, size, and spacing and to give students practice writing legibly in cursive.

Guidelines for
Writing an Explanation

• An explanation begins with a topic sentence.
• The sentences that follow the topic sentence should give reasons or facts to support the topic sentence.
• In an explanation that tells *why* something happens, the reasons or facts should be stated in order of importance from most to least.
• In an explanation that tells *how* something happens, the steps should be stated in time order.

▶ Apply

Have students write a paragraph that explains why or how something happens. Remind students to begin their explanations with a topic sentence. Discuss the best way to organize the supporting sentences in a paragraph that explains why (order of importance from most to least), or how (time order). Students can use **Practice Book** page 168 to help them plan and organize their writing. Create a Did You Know? bulletin board display with students' final products.

Improving Your Writing
Audience

Teach Remind students that when they write, they are writing for an audience. That audience may be a teacher who is grading a report or someone scoring a test. The audience may be a friend to whom you are writing a letter, postcard, or e-mail. The vocabulary and sentence structure for your audience may be formal, as for a class assignment, or informal, as when you write to a friend.

Practice Explain that the paragraph on **Transparency 3–8** is an example of formal writing that might be found in an encyclopedia or in a science book. To model how to change formal writing to informal and informal writing to formal, display **Transparency 3–9.**

Have students read the examples of formal and informal writing at the top of the transparency. Discuss the differences in the choice of vocabulary. Point out that slang and pop culture references are not appropriate in formal writing for school, but are acceptable for an informal audience of friends or peers.

Have students practice transforming formal sentences to informal and informal sentences to formal ones.

Apply Assign **Practice Book** page 169. Then have students review their own paragraphs of explanation. Have them change any informal vocabulary or phrases or sentences to more formal language suitable for this writing assignment.

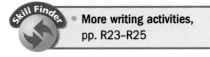
More writing activities, pp. R23–R25

Technology

The Writer's Resource Library

Students may use this set of reference tools as they work on their own writing.

©Sunburst Technology Corporation, a Houghton Mifflin Company. All Rights Reserved.

Type to Learn™

Students may use **Type to Learn™** to learn proper keyboarding technique.

©Sunburst Technology Corporation, a Houghton Mifflin Company. All Rights Reserved.

Portfolio Opportunity

Save students' paragraphs of explanation as samples of their writing development.

·········· **Houghton Mifflin English** ··········
Correlated instruction and practice, pp. 359–364

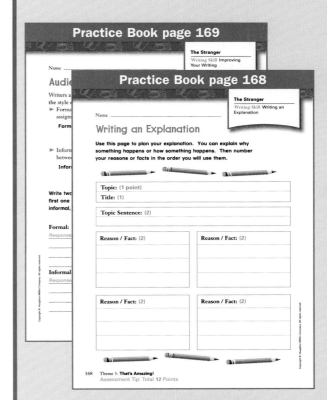

Practice Book page 169

Practice Book page 168

The Stranger
Writing Skill Writing an Explanation

Name _____

Writing an Explanation

Use this page to plan your explanation. You can explain why something happens or how something happens. Then number your reasons or facts in the order you will use them.

Topic: (1 point)
Title: (1)

Topic Sentence: (2)

Reason / Fact: (2)	Reason / Fact: (2)

Reason / Fact: (2)	Reason / Fact: (2)

168   Theme 3: **That's Amazing!**
Assessment Tip: Total **12** Points

Listening/Speaking/Viewing

Hold a Conversation

Students

- generate guidelines for holding a conversation
- role-play conversations and evaluate them according to guidelines

▶ Teach

Ask students to recall recent conversations that they have had with classmates, friends, or relatives. Remind them of the important role that conversation plays in people's daily communication. Then ask students to generate ideas about what makes a good conversation and how people can converse effectively. Be sure students understand that listening skills are as important as speaking skills in all conversations. Work with students to brainstorm a list of guidelines for holding an effective conversation. Help students elicit the following points:

- ■ Keep in mind that the purpose of a conversation is to gain understanding and to share thoughts. The purpose of a conversation never is to have a contest.

- ■ Concentrate on listening to the other person instead of focusing on what you want to say. Make sure that you are listening, not just waiting for your turn to talk.

- ■ Pay attention to the facial expressions and behavior of the other person. See if what the person says matches how he or she looks.

- ■ Ask questions if you do not understand what someone has said.

- ■ Let others know that you understand what they have said.

Tell students that a person with good communication skills keeps all of these guidelines in mind when holding a conversation. Encourage students to think of their daily conversations as opportunities to practice these skills.

Reaching All Students

English Language Learners

In order to participate in conversations, English language learners will benefit from practicing the request that someone repeat or clarify, speak more slowly, or spell a name. Have more proficient students role-play conversations that include such requests so that less proficient learners can observe. Then switch partners and have all students practice.

▶ Practice

Divide students into small groups. In each small group, designate one student to role-play a student who is new to the neighborhood or community. Have students role-play a conversation with the "new" student. Monitor students' conversations to see if they are following the guidelines. Evaluate student mastery by assessing whether they listen as well as speak, ask questions, and exchange meaningful information.

▶ Apply

Have students role-play a conversation that might take place between two of the characters in *The Stranger*. In each conversation, one student might recount something interesting about the mysterious stranger, and the other student might react. Or, one student might converse with the stranger by asking questions or making comments and the other student might role-play what the stranger would say in response. Have the other members of the class evaluate each conversation according to the guidelines.

Improving Listening and Speaking Skills

Share the following additional conversation skills tips with students:

- Concentrate on the ideas and information that others have to offer. Do not think of a conversation merely as a chance to express just your ideas.

- Look at the person who is speaking. Use facial expressions or gestures to show that you are interested.

- Use questions to encourage others to offer their ideas or to recount their experiences.

- Always let others finish what they have to say before you begin speaking in a conversation. It is impolite to interrupt another person who is speaking.

- Allow others to express their opinions freely. Try to keep an open mind even if you disagree.

Skill Reminder

Adverbs; Using Exact Adverbs

Remind students that adverbs are words that describe verbs. They tell *how, when,* or *where* an action happens. Point out that most adverbs that tell *how* end with *-ly,* as in *bravely* and *slowly.*

Write these adverbs from *The Stranger* on the board: *suddenly, shyly, gently.* Have students use them in sentences.

Taught: *Grade 3, Theme 6*
Reviewed: *Grade 4, Theme 2*

Spiral Review

Comprehension: *Story Structure*

▷ **Review**

Review what students have learned about story structure.

- Story structure includes main characters, setting, and plot.
- Plot is often referred to as a problem and its resolution.
- The climax of the plot is the point at which the problem is most severe.

Write the headings for the following chart on the chalkboard. Then together with the class fill in the story elements of *The Stranger.*

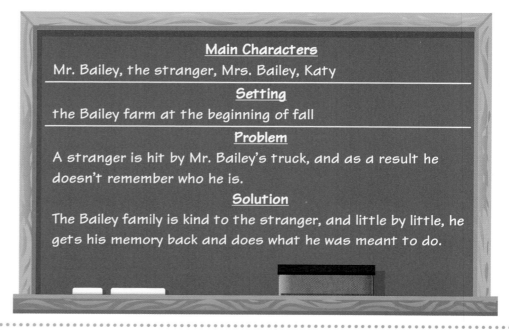

Main Characters
Mr. Bailey, the stranger, Mrs. Bailey, Katy

Setting
the Bailey farm at the beginning of fall

Problem
A stranger is hit by Mr. Bailey's truck, and as a result he doesn't remember who he is.

Solution
The Bailey family is kind to the stranger, and little by little, he gets his memory back and does what he was meant to do.

▷ **Apply**

Divide the class into four groups to discuss how the outcome of *The Stranger* might be different if one of the story elements changed. Assign one of these suggestions to each group: *the stranger is an old man; the story takes place in an apartment building in a city; the Baileys are unfriendly to the stranger; when the stranger blows on the leaf, it changes to snow.* Ask group members to identify the story element that has changed and to write a new solution for *The Stranger* based on their discussion.

Story Structure Grade 4, Theme 1, p. 57A

Structural Analysis: *Word Roots* tele, rupt; *Word Roots* sign, spect

▷ Review

Review the word roots *tele, rupt, sign,* and *spect* with students.

- A word root is a word part that has meaning but cannot stand alone.

- *Tele* is a word root that means "distance" or "over a distance," as in *telephone*.

- *Rupt* is a word root that means "break," as in *interrupt*.

- *Sign* is a word root that means "a sign or mark," as in *signal*.

- *Spect* is a word root that means "to look at," as in *inspect*.

Write this sentence on the board and read it to the class:

Every fall, the neighbors enjoyed the <u>spectacle</u> of the Bailey's bright trees.

Underline *spectacle* and ask students to find the root. Then circle *spect*, pronounce the word, and tell the class it means "a remarkable sight." Next, draw a word web for *spect* and work with students to think of words that have this root. Add the words to the web and discuss their meanings. (Sample answers are given.)

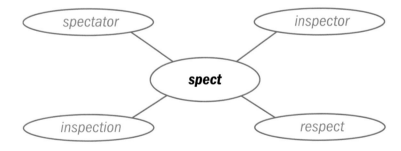

▷ Apply

Have pairs of students work together to complete a word web like the one above for the roots *tele* or *sign*. Assign one word root to half of the pairs and the other word root to the rest. When pairs have finished their word webs, have them list the words on the board and read them to the class. Then challenge pairs to use each of their words in a sentence. (Sample words: telephone, telegram, telescope, television, signature, design, assignment, signify, resignation)

- **Word Roots *tele, rupt*** Grade 4, Theme 1, p. 133E
- **Word Roots *sign, spect*** Grade 4, Theme 2, p. 215E

Skill Reminder

Writing Dates and Times

Review writing dates and times with students.

- A comma is added between the day and the year when writing a date, as in *July 4, 1776.*

- When writing time, add *a.m.* for times between midnight and noon and *p.m.* for times between noon and midnight.

Write the following on the board:

I was born on (month) (day) (year).

The last class ended at 2:15 (after noon).

Have students copy and correctly complete the sentences with the information called for in parentheses. Remind them to add a comma where it is needed.

Taught: *Grade 3, Theme 5*
Reviewed: *Grade 4, Theme 2*

Reading-Writing Workshop

Story

What Makes a Great Story? Review with students these characteristics of a story.

A story tells about a true or fictional experience. A story has a main character. A story has a beginning, a middle, and an end.

When you write a story, remember to

- introduce your characters and setting at the beginning of the story

- develop a plot that has a definite beginning, middle, and end

- tell the story's sequence of events in a meaningful order

- use an engaging voice and dialogue to make the story come alive

- write an ending that resolves the story's conflict in a satisfying way

Have students read the Student Writing Model. Then discuss with them what the student writer did to make his writing interesting to read.

A Story

A story tells about a true or fictional experience. It has a main character, and has a beginning, a middle, and an end. Use this student's writing as a model when you write a story of your own.

> **Dialogue** helps make **characters** come to life.

> Readers want to know the **setting** of a story right away.

> A good story has a **problem** that needs to be solved.

My Wish

Shirley yelled, "Get ready for bed!"
Javis said, "Yes, ma'am."

Javis climbed into his bunkbed. When he got into his bed, he saw someone who looked like a fairy godmother. She told him that she was his godmother, and that her name was Jamie. She exclaimed, "What would you like as a wish, little boy?"

Now Javis was a short little boy, about three feet tall. He thought a lot, and then he said, "I wish to be ten feet tall." The fairy godmother waved her wand, and Javis fell asleep.

The next morning Javis woke up and he was ten feet tall. He was gigantic, huge, tall, and strong all put together.

When he went in to brush his teeth he didn't see his toothbrush. He looked all over but still didn't see it. It was too small to use! By this time he had messed up the whole bathroom.

324

 Skill Finder

Theme Writing Skills	Theme Grammar Skills
• Audience, p. 323N	• Using Exact Verbs, p. 323L
• Ordering Important Information, p. 357N	• Sentence Combining with Main Verbs and Helping Verbs, p. 357L
• Paraphrasing, p. 381N	• Using the Correct Tense, p. 381L

Of course all that noise woke up his parents. When they saw him, they were worried and rushed him to the doctor. Javis couldn't fit into the car, so his parents drove and he walked. He stepped on many cars but didn't feel a thing.

When they got to the doctor's office, Javis reached out to shake hands. The doctor saw Javis's belt buckle, and he immediately fell unconscious.

When the doctor woke up, he said Javis had a disease. It was called "tallest." So Javis's parents took him to a specialist.

The specialist decided to put Javis in a shrinking machine. He stayed there for one hour. When he came out, the only thing big was his head, so they put him back in. Then Javis was back to normal. So, if you ever get a free wish, wish for something that won't cause problems.

> **Details** should be exact, never vague.

> A good story ends with a **resolution** to its problem.

Meet the Author

Javis B.
Grade: four
State: Florida
Hobbies: drawing, basketball, and singing
What he'd like to be when he grows up: a church worker

Reading as a Writer

1 Who is the story's main character? (Javis)

2 How does the author set the plot into motion? (Javis goes to bed, and a fairy godmother grants him a wish.)

3 How does the author use dialogue to get the story off to a fast start? (Javis speaks to his mother; Javis wishes to be 10 feet tall.)

4 What problem or conflict did the main character of the story have? How does he solve this problem? (Javis's problem is that he becomes too tall. He solves this problem by being shrunk.)

Skill Finder

Theme Spelling Skills

- **Compound Words**, p. 323G
- **Final /ər/ and Final /l/ or /əl/**, p. 357G
- **Words with -ed or -ing**, p. 381G

Workshop Focus Skills

- **Developing Plot, Character, and Setting**, p. 325C
- **Writing Dialogue**, p. 325D
- **Using Possessives**, p. 325E
- **Frequently Misspelled Words**, p. 325F

Reading-Writing Workshop

Story,
continued

·········· **Houghton Mifflin English** ··········
Correlated instruction and practice, pp. 297–316

Technology

Type to Learn™

Students may use **Type to Learn™** to learn proper keyboarding technique.

©*Sunburst Technology Corporation, a Houghton Mifflin Company. All Rights Reserved.*

The Writer's Resource Library

Students may use this set of reference tools as they work on their own writing.

©*Sunburst Technology Corporation, a Houghton Mifflin Company. All Rights Reserved.*

Choosing a Topic

Tell students they are going to write their own stories. Have students answer these questions, either in a writing journal or on a sheet of paper:

- Whom do you see as the audience of your story: friends? other fourth-grade students? both adults and children?

- What is the purpose of your story: to make people laugh? to send a chill down your audience's spine? simply to tell a story?

- How do you plan to publish your story? Will you make it into a booklet? Will you read it aloud? Will you display it on a bulletin board?

Have students write at least three ideas for their own stories. Offer these prompts if students are having trouble getting started.

- Think of a good name for the main character of your story. What will this character be like?

- Main characters in stories usually face a problem or conflict that they must solve. What problem or conflict will your main character face?

- Add a new twist to a story you are already familiar with. Change the characters, setting, and other elements of the story.

Have students work with a partner or in small groups to decide which topic would be the best one to write about.

> **Tips for**
> ## Getting Started
> - Think of a name and traits for your main character.
> - Think of a situation that you have been in that seemed like a story.
> - Think of a problem that your character faces.
> - Write a one-sentence summary of your story.

Organizing and Planning

Review the three parts of a story, with a description of each component.

- **Beginning** The beginning introduces the characters, puts them in a setting, and tells about a problem or conflict that they face.

- **Middle** The middle shows the efforts characters make to work out the problem or conflict.

- **Ending** The ending tells how the problem or conflict is resolved.

Inform students that a successful story has a clear sequence of events. It starts out with an attention-grabbing beginning, it takes the reader through a series of related events, and it ties things up in the end. The beginning grabs the readers' attention and makes them want to find out more about the characters and their problem. The middle expands on the problem and shows how the characters go about solving it. The ending resolves the problem in an interesting way, often showing how the characters have changed or grown.

Have students sketch out three different plans for their stories. Then have them choose the one they like the best. Use **Transparency RWW3–1** to help students map out their stories.

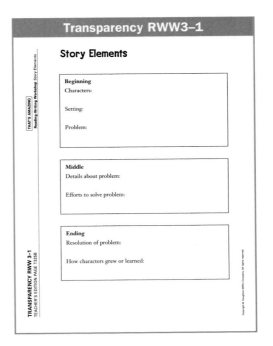

Tips for
Organizing a Story

- Start with a strong idea about your story's main events.
- Work out plot details ahead of time.
- Tell your events in a sequence that will make sense to the reader.

Story,
continued

PREWRITING   **DRAFTING**   REVISING   PROOFREADING   PUBLISHING

Focus Skill

Developing Plot, Character, and Setting

Transparency RWW3–2

Developing Plot, Characters, and Setting

Plot
Problem or conflict:_____
_____
Efforts to resolve problem:_____
_____
Final resolution of problem:_____
_____
_____

Main Character
Appearance:_____
_____
Likes and dislikes:_____
_____
Behavior:_____
_____
Feelings and thoughts:_____
_____

Setting
Country or state:_____
City or town:_____
Time period:_____
Local sights and sounds:_____

Tell students that good writers plan and develop their story's plot, characters, and setting. Discuss examples from stories they've read of exciting plots, interesting characters, and memorable settings. Then go over these main points about how to create a well-developed story.

■ Create a main character or characters for the story. Present a problem or conflict for the main character to solve.

■ Outline the main events of the plot. Think of any clues or twists you want to include.

■ Think about the setting for the story. Include important details to make the time and place of the story come alive.

Use **Transparency RWW3–2** to model sketching out ideas for plot, character, and setting with the students. Then distribute copies of Transparency RWW3–2 for students to use to plan their stories.

Tips for
Developing Plot, Character, and Setting

• Start with a main character and move on to other characters.
• Use your characters to develop a plot.
• Keep the setting in mind as you develop characters and plot.

Writing Dialogue

Remind students that good writers use dialogue to make their stories come alive. Go over the functions of dialogue in a story:

- Dialogue gives characters a distinctive personal style.

- Dialogue lets characters voice their feelings and motivations.

- Dialogue moves the plot forward.

Display **Transparency RWW3–3.** Have volunteers read both forms of the first paragraph. Refer students to the characteristics of effective dialogue.

- The speaker is identified and quotation marks are used.

- Speech is direct and has a natural rhythm.

- Speakers may not always talk in full sentences.

- Dialogue helps move the plot forward.

Have students revise the other paragraphs by including dialogue. Remind students to include dialogue to make their own story characters vivid and colorful.

Tips for
Writing Dialogue

- Use quotation marks and identify each speaker.
- Always capitalize the first word of a quotation.
- Use a comma to separate a quotation from the words that tell who is speaking. If a quotation comes first in a sentence, put a comma (or question mark or exclamation point) inside the last quotation marks. See the Student Writing Model and Transparency RWW3–3 for examples.
- Dialogue should have a natural rhythm.
- Write your dialogue the way people talk.

Transparency RWW3–3

Writing Dialogue

No Dialogue Version	Dialogue Version
Molly asked her brother if he planned on going to the Fall Fiesta. Simon said he planned to go. Molly felt something was wrong. Finally Simon told her he didn't know how to dance.	"Are you going to the Fall Fiesta?" Molly asked. "I suppose so," Simon said. "What's wrong?" Molly asked. "Oh nothing," he said. "It's just that I don't know how to dance."

No Dialogue Version	Dialogue Version
Molly suggested that she teach Simon how to dance. But Simon thought that was ridiculous. She didn't know how to dance either. So Molly suggested that they teach each other how to dance.	

No Dialogue Version	Dialogue Version
Molly found a "How to Dance" book. It was not so hard after all, Simon felt. Molly was proud of him; he had taught himself to dance well. Simon agreed. But he said that he never could have done it without Molly's help.	

TRANSPARENCY RWW 3–3
TEACHER'S EDITION PAGE T325D

Story, *continued*

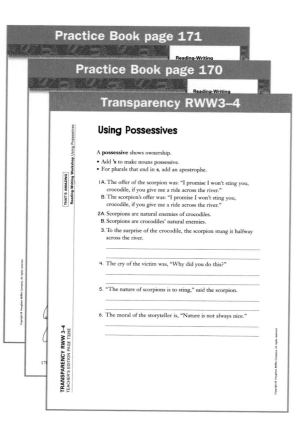

Practice Book page 171

Practice Book page 170

Transparency RWW3–4

Using Possessives

A **possessive** shows ownership.
• Add 's to make nouns possessive.
• For plurals that end in **s**, add an apostrophe.

1A. The offer of the scorpion was: "I promise I won't sting you, crocodile, if you give me a ride across the river."
B. The scorpion's offer was: "I promise I won't sting you, crocodile, if you give me a ride across the river."

2A. Scorpions are natural enemies of crocodiles.
B. Scorpions are crocodiles' natural enemies.

3. To the surprise of the crocodile, the scorpion stung it halfway across the river.

4. The cry of the victim was, "Why did you do this?"

5. "The nature of scorpions is to sting," said the scorpion.

6. The moral of the storyteller is, "Nature is not always nice."

Revising

Have students evaluate their finished drafts, using Revising Your Story on **Practice Book** page 170. Students may want to evaluate their drafts with a partner in a Writing Conference.

Once students have evaluated and discussed their drafts, have them go back and revise any parts they feel still need work.

Improving Your Writing
GRAMMAR LINK ➤ Using Possessives

Remind students that using possessives can streamline their writing and make it smoother and more efficient. Review the use of possessives.

A **possessive** shows ownership.

■ Add 's to make nouns possessive.

■ For plurals that end in *s,* add an apostrophe.

Using **Transparency RWW3–4,** model using possessives to shorten sentences. Have volunteers read the first two pairs of sentences aloud. Point out how the use of possessives shortens and streamlines each sentence.

Have students rewrite the remaining sentences, using possessives.

Assign **Practice Book** page 171. After they have completed the Practice Book page, have students look at their stories to see if they can improve them by using possessives.

Proofreading

Have students proofread their papers carefully to correct any capitalization, punctuation, and spelling errors. Students can use the chart on **Practice Book** page 433 to help them with their proofreading marks.

Practice Book

Spelling Practice: pp. 172–174
Take-Home Word List: p. 417

5-Day Spelling Plan

See p. 323G

Improving Your Writing

Spelling Connection **Frequently Misspelled Words**

Write the Spelling Words on the board or distribute the Take-Home Word List on **Practice Book** page 417. Read the words aloud, and have students repeat them. Help students identify the part of the word likely to be misspelled.

Spelling Assessment

Pretest

1. I finished my movie script <u>tonight</u>.
2. The <u>whole</u> thing took six months.
3. I worked at my job <u>while</u> I wrote it.
4. I <u>could</u> not get anyone to read it.
5. I think it's the best script in the <u>world</u>.
6. I started <u>writing</u> it in the summer.
7. I tried to <u>build</u> on my experiences.
8. I showed it to friends at <u>school</u>.
9. I <u>finished</u> it just last week.
10. I'm sending it out this <u>morning</u>.
11. An agent is <u>coming</u> to see me.
12. I <u>stopped</u> having doubts.
13. My script is <u>getting</u> a real look.
14. I hope everything <u>goes</u> well.
15. Perhaps I'm <u>going</u> to be famous!

Test: Use the Pretest sentences.

Challenge Words

16. Nothing <u>happened</u> to my script.
17. I <u>received</u> no feedback.
18. I don't <u>believe</u> anyone read it.
19. I had better not <u>quit</u> my job.
20. I'm not <u>quite</u> sure what to do.

Challenge Word Practice

Have students create a crossword puzzle, using the Challenge Words.

Spelling Words

tonight	stopped
whole	getting
while	goes
could	going
world	
writing	**Challenge Words**
build	happened
school	received
finished	believe
morning	quit
coming	quite

Story,
continued

Publishing and Evaluating

Have students make a final copy of their stories. Remind them to use good penmanship. Then tell students to look at the publishing ideas list they made when they were choosing a topic for their stories. Tell them to decide if that's still the way they would like to share their writing. If students need help deciding how to share the stories they have written, here are some additional suggestions:

■ Perform your story as part of a read-aloud festival.

■ Submit your story to a magazine.

The Scoring Rubric is based on the criteria in this workshop and reflects the criteria students used in Revising Your Story on **Practice Book** page 170. A six-point rubric can be found in the **Teacher's Assessment Handbook.**

Penmanship

Teacher's Resource Disk:
Penmanship Blackline Masters

Use these masters to model correct letter formation, size, and spacing and to give students practice writing legibly in cursive.

Portfolio Opportunity

Save students' final copies of their stories as examples of their writing development.

Student Self-Assessment

- What was the strongest part of your story?

- What part of your story did your readers like best?

- Which do you think you handled best—the plot of your story, its characters, or its setting? Explain why.

- How effective was the dialogue in your story? Explain.

- What would you change in your story if you had the chance to start all over again?

- What did you learn from writing this story that will help you with the next thing that you write?

Scoring Rubric

4

The story meets all major evaluation criteria. It has an effective beginning, middle, and ending. The story has a convincing setting, a creative plot, and characters who come alive in the reader's mind. Dialogue is used effectively. There are a variety of sentence types and very few usage, mechanics, or spelling errors.

3

The main idea is good. The sequence is adequately developed, but the beginning or ending could be stronger. The story's characters, plot, and setting could be more fully developed. There are a variety of sentence types, but the writer could have used more dialogue. There are some usage, mechanics, and spelling errors.

2

The story meets the criteria minimally. The characters, plot, and setting are not well developed, and the organization is weak. Dialogue is ineffective. Possessives are used incorrectly, and there are several usage, mechanics, and spelling errors.

1

The work does not meet the standards for a story. The paper has little or no sense of organization and few details. There is no sentence variety, and serious errors interfere with comprehension.

Using Leveled Books

Paperbacks for *That's Amazing!*

Leveled **Theme Paperbacks** provide varying levels of reading difficulty—Easy, On Level, and Challenge—to meet all students' needs.

Options for Reading
Students may

■ begin reading the Theme Paperbacks at the start of the theme, after the class has read the first Anthology selection, or at any point in the theme;

■ read the books at their levels independently or with appropriate teacher support;

■ finish an Easy or On Level book before the completion of the theme and move on to the next difficulty level;

■ move to an easier book if appropriate, based on your observation. If a student is struggling with the Easy book, have that student read the Very Easy Reader's Library book for this theme.

Theme Paperbacks

Easy	On Level	Challenge

See **Cumulative Listing of Leveled Books.**

Reader's Library   Very Easy

Reader's Library books offer stories related by skill and topic to the Anthology stories at a difficulty level approximately two grades below grade level.

Reader's Library

Literature Resources

Literature Resources, Grade 4

The Story of the Milky Way

retold by Joseph Bruchac and Gayle Ross

Easy

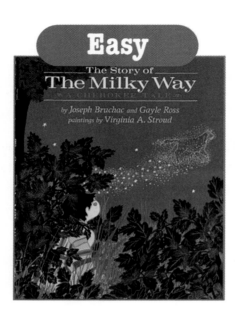

The Story of
The Milky Way
A CHEROKEE TALE
by Joseph Bruchac and Gayle Ross
paintings by Virginia A. Stroud

Selection Summary

The Cherokee legend *The Story of the Milky Way* tells of the origin of the Milky Way. In the legend, a Cherokee couple finds their cornmeal is being stolen. With the help of the village's wise woman, the thief—a giant spirit dog—is driven into the sky. As the cornmeal falls from the dog's mouth, it leaves behind a starry path that is now known as the Milky Way.

Key Vocabulary

grind, p. 6: to crush into bits or powder

eerie, p. 15: strange and frightening

beloved, p. 16: a person who is dearly loved

form, p. 21: shape

band, p. 29: a thin strip

 Preparing to Read

Building Background Point out to students that ancient peoples told many myths and legends to help them understand things they couldn't explain. For example, many Native American legends explain the appearance of stars in the sky. Describe, or ask students to describe, the appearance and location of the Milky Way. Encourage students to look carefully at the illustrations before they begin reading.

Developing Key Vocabulary Preview with students the Key Vocabulary words listed at the left for each segment of the book, pages 1–19 and pages 20–30. Point out and explain the Cherokee names "Grandmother Sun," "Beloved Woman," and "Elder Brother Moon."

 Previewing the Text

The *Story of the Milky Way* may be read in two segments, pages 1–19 and pages 20–30. Suggest that students read the author notes and examine the illustrations before they begin reading the story. Have students use decoding strategies and context clues to unlock the meaning of unknown words or phrases. Encourage students to restate the story in their own words at the end of each segment.

Supporting the Reading

pages 1–19

■ **Why does the author begin the story by saying, "This is what the old people told me when I was a child"?** (The author wants the reader to understand that the story has been handed down from one generation to another.)

■ **Explain to students the meaning of the phrase *dropped by a handspan*. Point out that the expression refers to a hand with fingers spread apart and is used to measure how much cornmeal is missing from the bin.**

■ **Why is corn an important crop for the villagers?** (They can grind it into cornmeal to make bread, which will help keep them from starving during the winter months.)

- **What is happening to the elderly couple's cornmeal?** (It is being stolen at night.)

- **What makes the boy believe that what he saw was real?** (In the morning, he sees the scattered cornmeal and tracks of the giant dog.)

- **Why are the villagers willing to do what the Beloved Woman asks of them?** (They obey because she is an old and wise leader. They think her plan will solve the problem.)

pages 20–30

- **How do the villagers react when they see the dog?** (They are frightened because it is so big, but Beloved Woman reassures them.)

- **What does the dog do when the villagers make noise and chase it?** (It runs and leaps into the sky in fear.)

- **Help students with the pronunciation and meaning of the Cherokee words** *Gil'liutsun stanun'yi.*

- **Why does the author end the story with "That is how the Milky Way came to be"?** (The author wants to make it clear that the legend explains how this formation was created.)

▶ Responding

Encourage students to think about why people tell such legends and tales about nature and to share similar tales they may know. Ask student to discuss their reading strategies. Finally, have students discuss and summarize the main events of this book.

Activity Have students work in groups to create a series of drawings that summarize the major events of the legend. Have each group use their drawings to retell the legend.

Reaching All Students

English Language Learners

Be sure students understand the words used to describe the noises made to frighten the dog *(Thum-thum, shissh-shissh)* and the reference to "the Thunderer when he speaks."

 **Little Oh**

by Laura Krauss Melmed

On Level

Selection Summary

In the fiction book *Little Oh,* a lonely woman creates an origami doll that comes to life. The woman thinks of the doll as her daughter. When the doll girl is separated from her mother, she has many adventures, but she longs to be back with her mother. At last, through the kindness of a man and his son, Little Oh is reunited with her mother and the four become a family.

Key Vocabulary

origami, p. 1: the Japanese art of folding paper into shapes such as flowers or birds

kimono, p. 1: a long, loose robe with wide sleeves and a broad sash worn by the Japanese as an outer garment

supple, p. 5: easily bent or folded

loped, p. 10: ran with a long, easy stride

serenade, p. 15: a musical performance given to honor or express love for someone

▶ **Preparing to Read**

Building Background Ask students to share any information they have about origami and its country of origin, Japan. Be sure students understand that origami is an art form. If possible, show them an example of origami. As students read, encourage them to make predictions about what will happen to Little Oh.

Developing Key Vocabulary Preview with students the Key Vocabulary words listed at the left for each segment of the book, pages 1–11 and pages 12–30. Explain that a lacquer box is varnished and glossy.

▶ **Previewing the Text**

Little Oh may be read in its entirety or in two segments, pages 1–11 and pages 12–30. Ask students to look through the illustrations before they begin reading. Encourage them to make inferences about Little Oh and her behavior as they read. Tell students to be ready to explain whether they think this story could happen in real life.

▶ **Supporting the Reading**

pages 1–11

■ **Why does the author set the scene with a mother telling her son a story?** (The author wants the reader to understand that the story may not be something that could happen in real life.)

■ **What surprises the woman the morning after she makes the origami paper doll?** (The origami girl she made came alive overnight.)

■ **Explain that the phrase** *supple as a sapling* **means "bending and moving as easily as a young tree."**

■ **How are the mother and Little Oh alike and how are they different?** (Alike: They love each other and enjoy spending time with one another. Different: The mother is more cautious and is satisfied to stay at home. Little Oh is impatient and wants to have adventures.)

■ **Why does Little Oh fall out of her mother's basket?** (She doesn't heed her mother's warning and peeks out of the basket, drawing the attention of a mischievous dog that knocks her out of the basket. His chase forces her to flee down the river.)

pages 12–30

■ **Explain that the word** *crockery* **means "earthenware."**

■ **What do the crane and Little Oh share?** (They are both lonely. They share memories of their loved ones and spend a pleasant time together.)

■ **How are Little Oh and her mother similar to the boy and his father?** (Neither adult has a spouse and neither child has a second parent or a sibling to play with.)

■ **Which parts of the story could happen in real life? Which parts could not?** (Could happen: a woman could make an origami doll and could become friendly with neighbors. Could not happen: an origami doll couldn't come to life or survive the situations in which Little Oh finds herself.)

■ **Why does the author say, "And now my telling's over, though the story is far from done"?** (The author wants the reader to understand that the family will be together for a long time to come.)

▶ Responding

Lead a discussion in which students identify the facts and fantasy of this story. Have students discuss their inferences and predictions about Little Oh. Encourage students to discuss their reactions to the end of the book. Finally, have students discuss and summarize the main events of the story.

Reaching All Students

English Language Learners

Be sure that students understand the descriptive language used in the story, including *skip over the stones like the little brook, pink tongue lolling, rocks poked up like bony knees,* and *tree-frog serenade.* Also point out the idiomatic expressions *fast asleep* and *passed away.*

The Real Thief

by William Steig

Challenge

THE REAL THIEF
WILLIAM STEIG

Is Gawain's goose really cooked?

Selection Summary

The animal story *The Real Thief* takes place in a make-believe animal kingdom. It is a story about friendship, trust, and discovering the things in life that bring true happiness.

Key Vocabulary

unpretentious, p. 3: modest, not showy

obsequious, p. 10: overly willing to serve

circumstantial, p. 24: not of primary importance; incidental

nabob, p. 28: a person of wealth or prominence

salver, p. 32: a serving tray

restitution, p. 36: restoration of something to its rightful owner; compensation for loss or damage

assuage, p. 40: to make less burdensome or painful

vindicated, p. 52: cleared of blame

aftermath, 58: result; the period following a disastrous event

 Preparing to Read

Building Background Ask students if they know other stories in which animals assume human personalities and characteristics. Point out that these stories often have a moral, or a lesson. Before students begin to read *The Real Thief*, encourage them to reread any passages that may be difficult.

Developing Key Vocabulary Encourage students to use illustrations and context clues to unlock word meanings. Preview the Key Vocabulary words listed at the left for each segment of the book, pages 1–21, pages 23–41, and pages 43–58.

 Previewing the Text

The Real Thief may be read in three segments, pages 1–21, pages 23–41, and pages 43–58. Have students read the title, look through the illustrations, and mark off the three segments of the book before they begin reading. Encourage students to stop regularly and formulate questions about the characters' reactions and motivations. Tell students that they should be reading to find the answers to these questions.

Supporting the Reading

pages 1–21

- **What does Gawain discover?** (He discovers that twenty-nine rubies have disappeared from the king's treasure house. He quickly reports this to the king.)

- **What actions do the king and Gawain take?** (The king questions the other three guards, the locks are checked by experts, and Gawain redoubles his efforts to watch everyone and everything with great care.)

- Explain to students that the word *scrutinize* means to examine or look closely with great care. Explain that the Latin phrase *Quod erat demonstrandum* on page 10 means "thus it was demonstrated." This term is often used in mathematics.

- **Why does the author say, on page 20, that Gawain stared at his feet because "They, at least, seemed real"?** (The author is emphasizing that Gawain can't believe what is happening to him, almost as if he is dreaming.)

pages 23–41

■ **Why does Derek steal the treasures?** (When he sees all the beautiful things in the treasure house, he becomes envious and takes things to make his house more beautiful.)

■ **What happens to Derek after he begins to steal?** (He feels more important and starts to put on airs. He denies to himself that he is a thief. He becomes more lonely because he cannot share his secret with anyone.)

■ **How does Derek try to prove Gawain's innocence?** (He starts stealing again. With Gawain gone, people will know that he was not the thief. Derek then puts the treasures back.)

■ **Why does the author say, on page 41, "The pall of gloom that hung over the whole kingdom hung thickest over [Derek]"?** (While everyone is saddened over what has happened, Derek also feels responsible and guilty.)

pages 43–58

■ Explain to students that a *fugitive* is someone who runs from the law and that a *recluse* is one who withdraws from the world to live in seclusion.

■ **Describe Gawain's reaction when he hears Derek's confession.** (Gawain feels happy to be vindicated but angry at what has happened and at the betrayal of his friends. He longs for his old life and feels pity for Derek.)

■ **In your own words, retell the ending of the story.** (Derek and Gawain return to town and are given a party. Gawain's friends ask for his forgiveness. Gawain is appointed Royal Architect and builds an opera house. Derek closes up the chink in the treasury.)

▶ Responding

Encourage students to share their reactions to the actions and emotions of the main characters—the king, Gawain, and Derek. Ask students what, if anything, they would change about the ending. Then ask them what the moral of this story might be. Have students discuss the reading strategies they used. Finally, have students discuss and summarize the main events of this book.

Bonus Ask students how a detective might have identified the real thief before Gawain was arrested and convicted.

Reaching All Students
English Language Learners

Be sure students understand the references to the noun *rushes,* beginning on page 44. Use the illustration on page 45 to show what this plant looks like. Explain to students that they are probably more familiar with *rushes* as a verb, and have students give some examples of its correct use as a verb.

Cendrillon
Different texts for different purposes

Anthology: Main Selection
Purposes

- strategy focus: question
- comprehension skill: compare/contrast
- vocabulary development
- critical thinking, discussion

Genre: Fairy Tale

A fantasy story that has been retold through generations and in many cultures.

 Award

★ **Americas Award Honorable Mention**

Selection Summary
This Cinderella story is narrated by Cendrillon's godmother, who has a magic wand. She and Cendrillon go to the ball, but when the princely Paul later arrives with the slipper, Cendrillon refuses a magical change back into her beautiful clothes. Paul loves her for herself, and they wed.

Teacher's Edition: Read Aloud

Purposes
- listening comprehension: compare/contrast
- vocabulary development
- critical thinking, discussion

Anthology: Get Set to Read

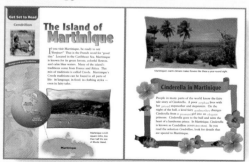

Purposes
- background building: Martinique
- developing key vocabulary

Anthology: Content Link

Purposes
- content reading: dance
- skill: how to read a time line
- critical thinking, discussion

Leveled Books and Resources

Use these resources to ensure that students read, outside of class, at least thirty minutes a day.
See also Cumulative Listing of Leveled Books.

Reader's Library

Very Easy

Tattercoat
by **Susan Delaney**

(Also available on
blackline masters)

Purposes

- fluency practice in below-level text
- alternate reading for students reading significantly below grade level
- strategy application: question
- comprehension skill application: compare/contrast
- below-level independent reading

Lesson Support

- Lesson Plan, page R4
- Alternate application for Comprehension Skill lesson on compare/contrast, page 357A
- Reteaching for Comprehension Skill: compare/contrast, page R10

Selection Summary Masters

Cendrillon
Teacher's Resource Blackline Masters

Audiotape

Cendrillon
Audiotape for
That's Amazing!

Reaching All Students
Inclusion Strategy

UNIVERSAL ACCESS

Significantly Below-level Readers

Students reading so far below level that they cannot read *Cendrillon* even with the suggested Extra Support should still participate with the class whenever possible.

- Include them in the Teacher Read Aloud (p. 326G) and Preparing to Read (pp. 327A–327D).

- Have them listen to *Cendrillon* on the audiotape for *That's Amazing!* and read the Selection Summary while others read Segment 1 of the selection.

- Have them read "Tattercoat" in the Reader's Library collection for *That's Amazing!* while others read Segment 2 of *Cendrillon.*

- Have all students participate in Wrapping Up Segment 2 (p. 353) and Responding (p. 354).

Theme Paperbacks

Easy

The Story of the Milky Way
by **Joseph Bruchac** and
Gayle Ross

Lesson, TE page 325I

On Level

Little Oh
by **Laura Krauss Melmed**

Lesson, TE page 325K

Challenge

The Real Thief
by **William Steig**

Lesson, TE page 325M

Technology

Get Set for Reading CD-ROM
Cendrillon

Provides background building, vocabulary support, and selection summaries in English and Spanish.

Education Place
www.eduplace.com

Log on to Education Place for more activities relating to *Cendrillon.*

Book Adventure
www.bookadventure.org

This Internet reading incentive program provides thousands of titles for students to read.

Daily Lesson Plans

Instructional Goals	Day 1	Day 2

Reading
60–80 minutes

- ✓ *Strategy Focus:* Question
- ✓ *Comprehension Skill:* Compare and Contrast

Comprehension Skill Review: Fantasy and Realism; Noting Details

Information and Study Skills: Recording Information on a Venn Diagram

Day 1

Teacher Read Aloud
Cinderella, 326G

Preparing to Read *Cendrillon*
- Get Set, *327A*
- Key Vocabulary, *327B*
  Selection Vocabulary, *Practice Book, 175*
- Strategy/Skill Preview, *327C*
  Venn Diagram, *Practice Book, 176*

Reading Segment 1 *Cendrillon, 328–339*
- Supporting Comprehension
- Strategy Focus, *332*

Wrapping Up Segment 1, *339*

Day 2

Reading Segment 2
Cendrillon, 340–353
- Supporting Comprehension
- Strategy Focus, *344*

Wrapping Up Segment 2, *353*

Responding
- Comprehension Questions: Think About the Selection, *354*
- Comprehension Check, *Practice Book, 177*

Rereading/Revisiting the Text
- Comprehension: Compare and Contrast, *333*

Word Work
30–40 minutes

- ✓ *Spelling:* Final /ər/, Final /l/ or /əl/

Decoding Longer Words:

- ✓ *Structural Analysis:* Words with the Suffix *-able*

Phonics: Final /ər/, /l/, and /əl/ Sounds

- ✓ *Vocabulary:* Spelling Table/ Pronunciation Key

Day 1

Spelling
- Pretest, *357G*
- Instruction: Final /ər/ and Final /l/ or /əl/, *357G*
- Take-Home Word List, *Practice Book: Handbook*

Day 2

Decoding Longer Words Instruction
- Structural Analysis: Words with the Suffix *-able, 357E*
- *Practice Book, 180*

Spelling
- *Practice Book, 181*

Writing & Language
30–40 minutes

- ✓ *Grammar:* Main Verbs and Helping Verbs

Writing: Writing an Announcement; Ordering Important Information

Listening/Speaking/Viewing: Compare and Contrast Texts

Day 1

Daily Language Practice, *357L*

Grammar Instruction
- Main Verbs and Helping Verbs, *357K*

 Writing
- Journal Writing, *329*

Day 2

Daily Language Practice, *357L*

Grammar Instruction
- *Practice Book, 185*

 Writing Instruction
- Journal Writing, *340*
- Writing an Announcement, *357M*
- *Practice Book, 188*

Teacher's Notes

THEME 3: That's Amazing!   ✓ = tested skills

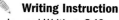 **Leveled Books, pp. 325H–325N**
For reading outside of class and homework

Technology

Lesson Planner CD-ROM
Customize your planning with the Lesson Planner.

Day 3

Rereading/Revisiting the Text
- Genre: Fairy Tales, *331*
- Writer's Craft: Point of View, *335*

Comprehension Skill Instruction
- Compare and Contrast, *357A*
- *Practice Book, 178–179*

Phonics Instruction
- Final /ər/, /l/, and /əl/ Sounds, *357F*

Spelling
- *Practice Book, 182*

Daily Language Practice, *357L*

Grammar Instruction
- Helping a Verb, *357K*

✏ **Writing**
- Narrating: Write Another Scene, *354*

Day 4

Comprehension Skill Instruction
- Reteaching Compare and Contrast with Reader's Library, *R10*

Reading the Dance Link
- "Let's Have a Ball!," *356–357*

Information and Study Skills Instruction
- Recording Information on a Venn Diagram, *357C*

Decoding Longer Words
- Reteaching Structural Analysis: Words with the Suffix *-able, R16*
- Challenge/Extension Activities, *R17*

Spelling
- Some Final Business, *357H*
- *Practice Book, 183*

Vocabulary Skill Instruction
- Dictionary: Spelling Table/Pronunciation Key, *357I*
- *Practice Book, 184*

Daily Language Practice, *357L*
Grammar
- Reteaching, *R21*
- *Practice Book, 186*

✏ **Writing**
- Ordering Important Information, *357N*
- *Practice Book, 189*

Listening/Speaking/Viewing
- Compare and Contrast Texts, *357O*

Day 5

Rereading/Revisiting the Text: Comprehension Review Skill Instruction
- Fantasy and Realism, *347*
- Noting Details, *349*

Rereading for Fluency
Cendrillon, 328–353

Activity Choices
- Responding Activities, *354*
- Challenge/Extension Activities, *R11*
- Cross-Curricular Activities, *R26–R27*

Vocabulary Expansion
- Types of Clothing, *357J*

Spelling
- Posttest, *357H*

Daily Language Practice, *357L*

Grammar
- Sentence Combining, *357L*
- *Practice Book, 187*

Spiral Review, *357Q*

✏ **Writing**
- Writing Activities, *R23–R25*
- Sharing Students' Writing: Author's Chair

Spiral Review, *357R*

✏ **Reading-Writing Workshop: Story, pp. 324–325G**

See Universal Access Planning Chart on the following pages.

Universal Access Plans
for Reaching All Learners

Grouping for Instruction

	Day 1	**Day 2**
30–45 minutes		

With the Teacher

Extra Support
Teach—Use Extra Support Handbook

	Day 1	**Day 2**
	Preteach Words with the Suffix *-able* **Preview** Selection, Segment 1 ■ Extra Support Handbook　　　　pp. 108–109	**Preteach** Compare and Contrast **Preview** Selection, Segment 1 ■ Extra Support Handbook　　　　pp. 110–111

Working Independently

On Level
Use Classroom Management Handbook

Challenge
Use Challenge Handbook

English Language Learners
Use Classroom Management Handbook or Challenge Handbook

Day 1	**Day 2**
Independent Activities For each group, assign appropriate activities—your own or those in the handbooks listed below. Then get students started on their independent work. ■ Classroom Management Handbook　　pp. 40–41 ■ Challenge Handbook　　　　　　　pp. 24–25	See plan for Day 1 **Monitor** Answer questions, if necessary.

30–45 minutes

With the Teacher

English Language Learners
Teach—Use Handbook for English Language Learners

Day 1	**Day 2**
Preteach Landforms **Preteach** Get Set to Read; Selection, Segment 1 **Preteach** Structural Analysis: Words with the Suffix *-able* ■ Handbook for ELL　　　　　　pp. 112–113	**Preteach** Bodies of Water **Preteach** Selection, Segment 2 **Reteach** Grammar: Main Verbs and Helping Verbs ■ Handbook for ELL　　　　　　pp. 114–115

Working Independently

On Level
Use Classroom Management Handbook

Challenge
Use Challenge Handbook

Extra Support
Use Classroom Management Handbook

Day 1	**Day 2**
Independent Activities Students can continue their assigned activities, or you can assign new activities from the handbooks below. ■ Classroom Management Handbook　　pp. 40–41 ■ Challenge Handbook　　　　　　　pp. 24–25	See plan for Day 1 **Monitor** Partner Extra Support students, if needed.

Independent Activities

Classroom Management Handbook

- Daily Activities
- Grouping
- Management

Resources for Reaching All Learners

Extra Support Handbook

- Daily Lessons
- Preteaching and Reteaching
- Skill Support

Handbook for English Language Learners

- Daily Lessons
- Language Development
- Skill Support

Challenge Handbook

- Independent Activities
- Instructional Support

Day 3

Reteach The Suffix -able
Review Selection

◼ Extra Support Handbook   pp. 112–113

See plan for Day 1

Check in
Reinforce instruction, if needed.

Preteach Telling Time
Preteach Vocabulary/Dictionary: Spelling Table/Pronunciation Key

◼ Handbook for ELL   pp. 116–117

See plan for Day 1

Check in
Reinforce instruction, if needed.

Day 4

Reteach Main Verbs and Helping Verbs
Preview *Tattercoat*

◼ Extra Support Handbook   pp. 114–115

See plan for Day 1

Check in
Regroup English learners, if needed.

Preteach Fruits
Reteach Selection Summary and Review
Reteach Grammar: Main Verbs and Helping Verbs

◼ Handbook for ELL   pp. 118–119

See plan for Day 1

Monitor
How well are challenge projects progressing?

Day 5

Reteach Compare and Contrast
Revisit Selection and *Tattercoat*

◼ Extra Support Handbook   pp. 116–117

See plan for Day 1

Build confidence
Reinforce successful independent work.

Preteach Colors
Reteach Writing: Ordering Important Information

◼ Handbook for ELL   pp. 120–121

See plan for Day 1

Share work
Allow students time to share work.

Teacher Read Aloud

Listening Comprehension:
✓ Compare and Contrast

Cinderella

Reading Instruction

DAY 1	• Teacher Read Aloud • Preparing to Read • Reading the Selection, Segment 1
DAY 2	• Reading the Selection, Segment 2 • Responding
DAY 3	• Revisiting the Text • Comprehension Skill Instruction
DAY 4	• Comprehension Skill Reteaching • Reading the Content Link • Information and Study Skills Instruction
DAY 5	• Comprehension Skill Review • Activity Choices

OBJECTIVES

Students listen to the selection to identify elements that are alike and different.

▶ Activate Prior Knowledge

Connecting to the Theme Help students connect the selection with what they know, using this suggestion:

■ Ask students to give a brief summary of the story *Cinderella*.

Reaching All Students

English Language Learners

Find out what students know about *Cinderella* and about fairy tales in general. For students familiar with the story, ask what the tale is called in their language. Instruct students to listen carefully to learn who calls on Cinderella to try on the glass slipper so they can later make their own comparisons between *Cinderella* and *Cendrillon*.

This story is one of many versions of the traditional Cinderella tale.

1 How is Cinderella different from her stepsisters? (Sample answer: Cinderella has to work hard, while her stepsisters just boss her around.)

Cinderella lived in a big house. She was always busy. Her two stepsisters made her work hard.

"Cinderella! Sweep the floor!"
"Cinderella! Wash the dishes!"
"Make the beds!"
"Clean the windows!"
Cinderella's work was never done. **1**
Her stepsisters spent half the day telling Cinderella what to do. They spent the other half trying to make themselves pretty.

"Cinderella! Brush my hair!"
"Cinderella! Tie my bow!"
"Powder my nose!"
"Fasten my buttons!"
One day a letter arrived at the house. "There is to be a ball at the palace. We are invited!" shouted the stepsisters.

"Am I invited?" asked Cinderella.

"Even if you are, you cannot go," said her stepsisters. "You will be too busy getting us ready."

The day of the ball came. The stepsisters kept Cinderella very busy indeed. There was so much to do. Poor Cinderella did not know what to do first.

At last, the stepsisters had gone and the house was quiet. Cinderella sat by the fire and began to cry. "If only I could go to the ball," she wept.

"You SHALL go to the ball," said a voice behind her.

Cinderella jumped up in surprise. She thought she was alone in the house.

"Who ... who are you?" she gasped.

"I am your Fairy Godmother," said the stranger. "I have come to get you ready for the ball."

"Bring me a pumpkin," said the Fairy Godmother. She turned the pumpkin into a coach.

"Bring me four white mice," said the Fairy Godmother. She turned the mice into four white horses.

"Bring me three lizards," said the Fairy Godmother. They became a coach-driver and two footmen.

"I cannot go to the ball dressed in rags," said Cinderella sadly.

The Fairy Godmother waved her magic wand once more. Cinderella's rags turned into a beautiful ballgown. Her bare feet were covered with dainty glass slippers.

"Now you are ready for the ball," said the Fairy Godmother. "But first, a warning. You must leave before the clock strikes twelve. At twelve everything will change back again."

"I will remember," said Cinderella. "Thank you, dear Fairy Godmother."

Listening Comprehension: ✓ Compare and Contrast

Explain to students that to compare is to find similarities, and to contrast is to find differences. Point out that comparing and contrasting details in a story can help a reader understand the characters, plot, and setting.

Use the questions in the margin to help assess students' understanding as you read. Also use the questions as stopping places to reread for clarification if necessary.

Teacher's Note

Tip for Read Alouds Review the story before reading to students. You might want to use similar voices for both stepsisters to show how much they are alike, and a different voice for Cinderella to show how different she is from her stepsisters.

(Teacher Read Aloud, continued**)**

Cinderella danced all night with the Prince. Her stepsisters saw her, but they did not know it was Cinderella. They thought she was a princess.

2 Cinderella was so happy she forgot all about the Fairy Godmother's warning. Then the palace clock began to strike the chimes of midnight. One ... two ... three ...

"I must go!" cried Cinderella and she ran from the palace.

"Stop! Stop!" cried the Prince.

Cinderella did not hear him. As she ran down the palace steps she lost one of her glass slippers. ... ten ... eleven ... TWELVE!!!

The beautiful gown turned into rags. The coach turned into a pumpkin. The mice and the lizards ran away.

The Prince found her glass slipper lying on the palace steps. He called to a footman. "Take this slipper and find its owner. I will marry the girl it fits."

The footman traveled all over the kingdom with the slipper. It fitted no one. At last he came to the house where Cinderella lived.

"Let me try it!" said one of the stepsisters. She snatched the slipper from the footman. "Look!" she cried "A perfect fit."

"No it is not!" shouted the other stepsister. "Your heel is hanging out. Give it to me!" She snatched the glass slipper.

It didn't fit her either, though she tried to pretend that it did.

"Is there anyone else in the house who should try the slipper?" asked the footman.

"No!" said both stepsisters together.

"Yes there is," said their father. "Cinderella has not tried it yet."

---

2 How is Cinderella different at the ball? How is she the same?

(Sample answer: Different: Before the ball, Cinderella was wearing rags. At the ball, no one recognized her because she was wearing a beautiful ballgown and slippers. The same: Cinderella is the same person at the ball as she was before the ball. Only her clothing has changed, not her physical appearance or her personality.)

3 "The Prince would never marry HER!" laughed the stepsisters.

"The Prince said everyone must try the slipper," said the footman.

It fitted Cinderella perfectly. Her stepsisters were so surprised they fainted.

The stepsisters still looked surprised when the Prince and Cinderella were married.

3 How are the two stepsisters alike? (Sample answer: The two stepsisters think, talk, and act alike. They do not even have names, and you can't always tell which one of them is speaking. They often speak in unison.)

▶ **Discussion**

Summarize After reading, discuss the parts of the story that students found most interesting. Then ask them to summarize the selection.

Listening Comprehension:
✓ **Compare and Contrast** Write these headings on the board: *Compare, Contrast.* Have students suggest elements from the story that can be either compared or contrasted with each other. Write their suggestions under the appropriate heading.

Personal Response Ask students to evaluate the personal characteristics of the Prince.

★ **Connecting/Comparing** Have students compare and contrast the stranger's presence at the Bailey's farm with Cinderella's presence at the ball.

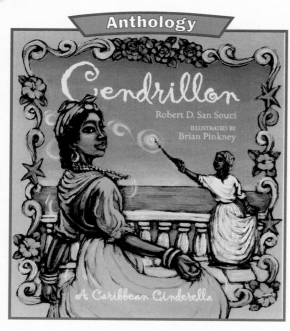

Technology

Get Set for Reading CD-ROM

Cendrillon

Provides background building, vocabulary support, and selection summaries in English and Spanish.

Preparing to Read

▶ Using *Get Set* for Background and Vocabulary

Connecting to the Theme Remind students that this theme is about amazing stories. They just read a story about a mysterious stranger. Now they will read *Cendrillon*, a familiar and enchanting tale.

Discuss with students the geography of the Caribbean. Then use the Get Set to Read on pages 326–327 to learn about a particular Caribbean island.

- Ask a student to read aloud "The Island of Martinique."

- Go over the pictures of the island, asking a student to read the captions. Discuss how this area might affect what they know about the tale of Cinderella.

- Ask students to define the boldfaced Key Vocabulary: *orphan, proud, godmother, peasant,* and *elegant*. Have students use these words as they discuss the tale of Cinderella.

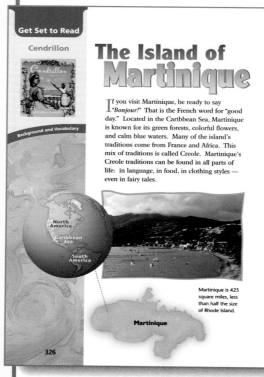

Get Set to Read

Cendrillon

Background and Vocabulary

The Island of Martinique

If you visit Martinique, be ready to say "*Bonjour!*" That is the French word for "good day." Located in the Caribbean Sea, Martinique is known for its green forests, colorful flowers, and calm blue waters. Many of the island's traditions come from France and Africa. This mix of traditions is called Creole. Martinique's Creole traditions can be found in all parts of life: in language, in food, in clothing styles — even in fairy tales.

Martinique is 425 square miles, less than half the size of Rhode Island.

Martinique

326

Martinique's warm climate makes flowers like these a year-round sight.

Cinderella in Martinique

People in many parts of the world know the fairy tale story of Cinderella. A poor orphan lives with her proud stepmother and stepsisters. On the night of the ball, a kind fairy godmother changes Cinderella from a peasant girl into an elegant princess. Cinderella goes to the ball and wins the heart of a handsome prince. In Martinique, Cinderella is known as Cendrillon [SOHN-dree-yhon]. As you read the selection *Cendrillon*, look for details that are special to Martinique.

327

UNIVERSAL ACCESS

Reaching All Students

English Language Learners

Help students locate Martinique, France, and Africa on a map. Point out that Martinique is an island that is far away from France and Africa. Discuss the photographs on pages 326–327, and encourage students to make observations.

Vocabulary

▶ Developing Key Vocabulary

Use **Transparency 3–10** to introduce Key Vocabulary from *Cendrillon*.

■ Ask a student to provide the appropriate letter for the word *crossly*. Model how to locate clues to the meaning of this word in the sentences that follow.

■ For each remaining word, ask students to give the correct letter and then have them locate clues to the meaning of each Key Vocabulary word in the sentences.

Remind students that it's helpful to use the Phonics/Decoding Strategy when they read. For students who need more help with decoding, use the review below.

Practice/Homework Practice Book page 175.

Strategy Review
Phonics/Decoding

Modeling Write this sentence from *Cendrillon* on the board, and point to *blistered*.

Her hands were
blistered and red.

Think Aloud

I see the letters bl, *which probably sound the way they do in words like* blood *and* black. *Next are the letters* is. *When I blend* bl *and* is, *I see that the first part probably sounds like /blihs / because a vowel followed by a consonant usually has a short sound. The next part might sound like / ter /, and I see an -ed ending. / blihs•ter•ehd /. I know. The word is / BLIHS•terd /. That makes sense because it also says her hands are red. If she was working hard, it could cause blisters and make her hands sore and red.*

Skill Finder • Decoding Longer Words, pp. 357E–357F

Key Concept
the Cinderella story

Key Vocabulary

crossly: in a grumpy or grouchy way

elegant: marked by good taste; graceful

godmother: a woman who acts as a child's parent

orphan: a child whose parents are dead

peasant: relating to a poor farm worker

proud: thinking too highly of oneself

See Vocabulary notes on pages 332, 334, 336, 338, 340, 348, and 350 for additional words to preview.

Practice Book page 175

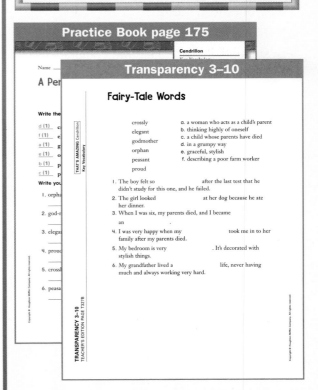

Transparency 3–10

Fairy-Tale Words

crossly	a. a woman who acts as a child's parent
elegant	b. thinking highly of oneself
godmother	c. a child whose parents have died
orphan	d. in a grumpy way
peasant	e. graceful, stylish
proud	f. describing a poor farm worker

1. The boy felt so _____ after the last test that he didn't study for this one, and he failed.
2. The girl looked _____ at her dog because he ate her dinner.
3. When I was six, my parents died, and I became an _____
4. I was very happy when my _____ took me in to her family after my parents died.
5. My bedroom is very _____. It's decorated with stylish things.
6. My grandfather lived a _____ life, never having much and always working very hard.

Reading Strategy

Strategy Focus

This version of the Cinderella story takes place in Martinique. As you read, think of **questions** to ask about how the setting affects the story.

✓ **Strategy Focus:**
Question

Teacher's Note

Strategy/Skill Connection For a better understanding of *Cendrillon*, students can use the

- Question Strategy
- Compare and Contrast Comprehension Skill

Thinking about questions to ask helps students monitor their own comprehension and allows them to make more advanced comparisons in the story. Doing this will help students to become more active readers.

As students complete their *Cendrillon* Venn Diagram (**Practice Book** page 176 and **Transparency 3–11**), they can use their answers to better understand the characters.

Have students turn to page 329 as you read aloud the selection's title and author. Allow time for students to skim the selection and look at the pictures. Ask students to compare and contrast silently what they see with their memory of Cinderella's tale.

Teacher Modeling Explain to students that formulating questions as they read is a good way of making sure they understand the story. Then model the strategy.

Think Aloud

I know that this story is similar to the tale of Cinderella. This makes me think of questions I can ask my classmates when we are done reading: What is Cendrillon's carriage made out of? Does she have two evil stepsisters?

Have students write in their journals another question they have based on the illustrations and their knowledge of Cinderella. Tell them that they may ask their classmates the questions when they complete the reading. Remind students also to use their other reading strategies as they read the selection.

Comprehension Skill

Comprehension Skill Focus:
Compare and Contrast

Venn Diagram Explain that students will focus on comparing and contrasting as they read *Cendrillon*. To develop and practice the skill, students will complete a Venn diagram to compare and contrast two characters. Display **Transparency 3–11**, and demonstrate how to use the graphic organizer.

- Ask someone to read aloud the last paragraph on page 331 and the first paragraph on page 332.

- Ask a student to provide a piece of information about both Cendrillon and Vitaline from those paragraphs. Model how to write in the first pieces of information in each part of the diagram, explaining how you had to draw the conclusion that they have the same father.

- Have students fill in the same information on **Practice Book** page 176.

- Have students complete the diagram as they read and tell them it may be necessary to draw conclusions or make inferences in order to fill in the chart. Monitor their work or have them check each other's diagrams.

Graphic Organizer: Venn Diagram

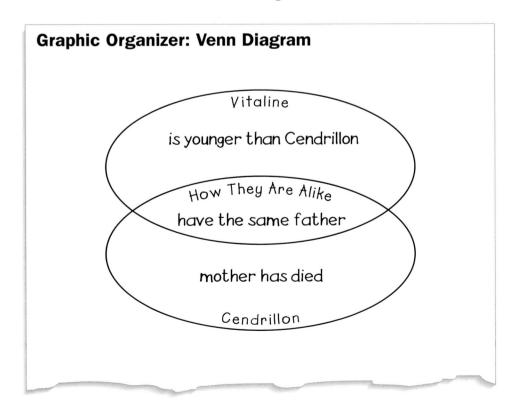

Focus Questions

Have students turn to Responding on page 354. Read the questions aloud and tell students to keep them in mind as they read *Cendrillon*.

Beginning of Segment 1: pages 328–339

Options for Reading

▶ **Reading in Segments** Students can read *Cendrillon* in two segments (pages 328–339 and 340–353) or in its entirety.

▶ **Deciding About Support** Students should enjoy this regional retelling of the famous French fairy tale.

- The familiar story line should enable most students to follow On-Level instruction.

- Students who are distracted by foreign words may need Extra Support.

- Significantly below-level readers may listen to the Audiotape and read the Selection Summary for *Cendrillon*, and then read "Tattercoat" in the **Reader's Library**.

▶ **Universal Access** Use the notes at the bottom of the pages.

MEET THE AUTHOR

Robert D. San Souci

Robert D. San Souci likes to tell old stories with a new twist. Whenever he retells a folktale, he researches the history of the country to make sure that all his details will be accurate. Even when it's a tale that's hundreds of years old, San Souci gets ideas from the modern world. He likes to ride the bus just to hear how ordinary people talk!

MEET THE ILLUSTRATOR

Brian Pinkney

Illustrator Brian Pinkney gets totally involved in his subjects. When he illustrated a book on ballet, he took dance lessons. When he wrote and illustrated a book about a boy who plays drums, he used his own experience playing drums. Pinkney illustrates in a style called scratchboard. He scratches lines into a board coated with a special black paint over white clay. The lines in the white clay show the picture he's drawn.

Other books by the team of Robert D. San Souci and Brian Pinkney: *Sukey and the Mermaid, Cut from the Same Cloth*

 **Internet**

To learn more about the author and the illustrator, visit Education Place. **www.eduplace.com/kids**

328

 Reaching All Students

Classroom Management

On Level
Reading Card 5

While Reading: Venn diagram (**Practice Book** page 176); Literature Discussion (p. 338, Reading Card 5); generate questions

After Reading: Literature Discussion (page 352); Wrapping Up Segment 1 (page 339) and Segment 2 (page 353)

Challenge
Reading Cards 4–6

While Reading: Venn diagram (**Practice Book** page 176); Heroine (p. 333, Card 4); Fairy Tale Objects (p. 344, Card 6)

After Reading: Literature Discussion (page 352); Wrapping Up Segment 1 (page 339) and Segment 2 (page 353)

English Language Learners

Intermediate and Advanced Fluency This selection will be challenging for most English language learners. Have students follow along as you read aloud or play the audiotape. For English language learners at other proficiency levels, use the **Handbook for English Language Learners**.

Selection 2

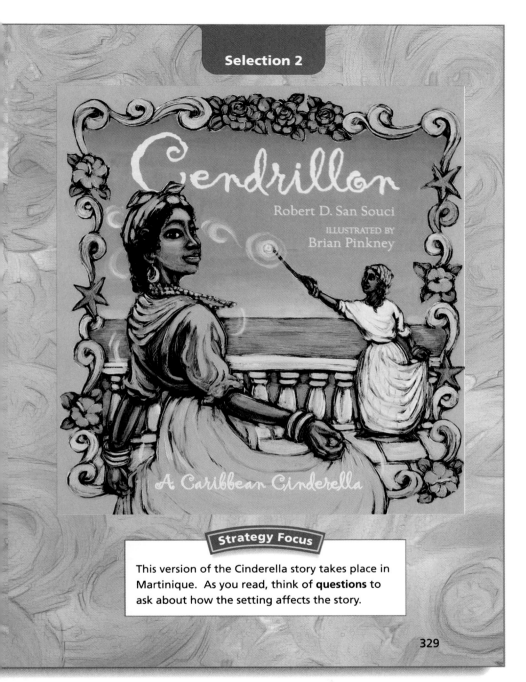

Cendrillon

Robert D. San Souci

ILLUSTRATED BY
Brian Pinkney

A Caribbean Cinderella

Strategy Focus

This version of the Cinderella story takes place in Martinique. As you read, think of **questions** to ask about how the setting affects the story.

329

Reading Segment 1
pages 328–339

Purpose Setting Remind students that this is a regional retelling of a famous fairy tale. As they read, have students think of questions about the setting and think about how this story varies from the more familiar version of Cinderella.

Journal Writing Students can record their questions about the setting and list differences from the more familiar Cinderella story.

Reinforcing Comprehension and Strategies

■ Remind students to use Question and other strategies as they read and to add to their Venn diagrams (**Practice Book** page 176).

■ Use the Strategy Focus notes on pages 331 and 343 to reinforce the Question strategy.

■ Use Supporting Comprehension questions beginning on page 330 to help students develop higher-level understanding of the text.

Extra Support: Previewing the Text

Before each segment, preview the text, using the notes below and on page 340. **While** reading, model strategies (pages 331, 343, and 345). **After** reading, review each segment (pages 338 and 352) before students join the Wrapping Up discussion.

pages 330–333 What do the illustrations tell you about the setting of the story?

pages 334–335 Cendrillon is doing laundry by the river with her godmother. They are discussing the ball.

pages 336–337 What can you tell about Cendrillon's stepmother from this illustration?

pages 338–339 Cendrillon is dressed for the ball. How does her clothing differ from her everyday clothing?

▶ ## Supporting Comprehension

1 What details does the author provide about the limitations of the narrator's magic wand? (The wand's magic lasts only a short time and can only be used to help someone she loves.)

2 How does the narrator's kind nature lead her to become Cendrillon's godmother? (She takes care of Cendrillon's sickly mother for many years.)

3 What does the author mean when he describes Cendrillon's stepmother as *"puffed up proud"*? (She thinks too highly of herself without good reason)

Vocabulary *(page 331)*

orphan: a child whose parents are dead

godmother: a woman who acts as a child's parent

proud: thinking too highly of oneself

You may *think* you know this story I am going to tell you, but you have not heard it for true. I was there. So I will tell you the truth of it. Now.

330

Reaching All Students

English Language Learners

Vocabulary Building

Pause at the end of page 331. Explain that a *godparent* is chosen by a baby's parents to sponsor that baby during its christening, and that godparents and godchildren are often special to one another. Ask volunteers to tell the class about their godparents. Say that a *christening* is a ceremony in which new babies become members of their parents' church. Explain *wand of mahogany.*

I live on a green-green island in the so-blue Mer des Antilles [MEHR de-ZON-teeyl], the Caribbean Sea. Long ago, when I was a child, my family was poor. When my mother died, she left me only one thing: a wand of mahogany. "Three taps will change one thing into another," my mother had whispered. "But only for a short time. And the magic must be used to help someone you love." **1**

Of what use was this to an <u>orphan</u> like me, who every day struggled to find shelter and fill her belly? I could not use the wand. I had no one to love and no one who loved me.

When I grew up, I worked as a *blanchisseuse* [blahn-SHEEZ-seuz], a washerwoman, scrubbing other people's sheets and shirts at the riverside. Drying them in the sun.

One woman I worked for was kind. I often nursed her, for she was always sickly, poor creature. In thanks, she made me the *nannin'* [non-NIHN], <u>godmother</u>, of her baby girl, Cendrillon [SOHN-dree-yhon]. When I held that *bébé* [BEEYH-beeyh] in my arms on her christening day, I felt such love! And I saw love returned from her sweet brown eyes. **2**

Alas! Cendrillon's mamma died soon after this. Then her papa, Monsieur [MOHN-sur], married again. Madame Prospèrine [Pros-SPER-in] was a cold woman, and puffed-up <u>proud</u> because her grandfather had come from France. **3**

331

Strategy Modeling

Question If students need help modeling the strategy, use this example to model it for them:

By paying close attention to the details on this page, I can think of questions I might ask someone else who has read the story: Why couldn't the narrator use the wand when she was young? What role did the narrator play in Cendrillon's mother's life?

Genre Lesson
Fairy Tales

OBJECTIVES

Students identify elements of fairy tales in the selection.

Tell students that folktales are stories that are passed down orally from generation to generation. A *fairy tale* is a particular kind of folktale. "Cinderella" is one such tale, first collected in 1697 by the French author Charles Perrault in a book called *Mother Goose Tales*. Like the other stories in that collection, which include "The Sleeping Beauty," "Tom Thumb," and "Puss-in-Boots," "Cinderella" is a tale of magic. Tales of magic might feature fairies, giants, impossible tasks, and other such occurrences.

Explain that a typical fairy tale follows this pattern:

Introduction

| characters | setting | problem |

↓

Development

Problem grows and reaches a climax.

↓

Conclusion

Problem is solved.
Everyone lives happily ever after.

Have students identify the characters, setting, and problem and the element of magic as introduced on page 331. As they read, ask them to locate the development and conclusion of the story and to look for the uses of magic that are typical of fairy tales.

Strategy Focus: Question

Teacher/Student Modeling Remind students that their goal is to become active, involved readers. Active readers can use the Question strategy to make sure that they understand the author's main points. Page 333 might lead to these questions that a reader might ask another reader: How does Cendrillon's stepmother treat her? How does the narrator fit into the stepmother's world?

Ask students to read page 334 and to formulate a question for other students based on what they read.

Supporting Comprehension

4 What does the detail about Cendrillon's hands tell us? (She works very hard.)

5 How does the author foreshadow what is to come? (The author hints that the narrator will in fact find a way to help Cendrillon.)

Vocabulary *(pages 332–333)*

peasant: relating to a poor farm worker

hollow: false or meaningless

When a new daughter, Vitaline [VEE-tah-LEEN], was born, Madame gave a christening party for her rich friends. What a feast it was!

Madame and the other fine ladies were dressed in satin and velvet, all the colors of the rainbow. They laughed at my worn white skirts and peasant's way of speaking.

4 Pretty Cendrillon came and kissed me. "*Bonjou*' [BOH-zhew], *Nannin*'." She gave me a cup of punch. Her hands were blistered and red.

 Reaching All Students

English Language Learners

Nannin' makes herself seem familiar to her readers. Discuss the godmother's storytelling style, the *you* and *I* references, the personal details of her difficult childhood, and her love for the infant Cendrillon. Point out that the godmother, as narrator, introduces and concludes the story by explaining her qualifications and purpose.

"*Pauv' ti* [pov tee] *Cendrillon*, poor little child!" I cried. "What have you done to yourself?"

She shrugged. "My father's wife works me like a serving-girl."

"And Monsieur allows this?"

Sighing, she said, "He fears Madame. But I am strong. The work hurts my hands but not my heart."

"Someday, I will find a way to help." Even as I spoke them, my words sounded <u>hollow</u>. What could I — a poor washerwoman — do for my dearest?

5

Challenge

Reading Card
4

Heroine

Tell students that a *heroine* is a female character whose actions are especially admirable or inspiring. Heroines must usually overcome enemies or escape terrible difficulties against great odds. Although they may have help, it is clear that they deserve to win based on their inner goodness.

As students read, have them chart those qualities that make Cendrillon a true heroine.

Revisiting the Text

Comprehension Skill Lesson
Compare and Contrast

Tested Skill

OBJECTIVES

Students compare and contrast details within the selection.

Tell students that when they think about how things are alike, they compare them. When they think about how things are different, they contrast them. By comparing and contrasting details in a story, students can better understand what they read.

Ask students to locate details on page 332 that show how Madame and the fine ladies in her home contrast with the narrator. Help them use the details to complete a Venn diagram like this:

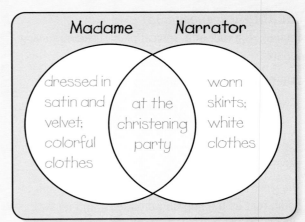

Madame   Narrator

dressed in satin and velvet; colorful clothes — at the christening party — worn skirts; white clothes

Skill Finder

- **Instruction,** pp. 357A–357B
- **Reteaching,** page R10
- **Review,** Th. 2, p. 193; Th. 3, p. 369; Th. 4; Th. 5

▶ Supporting Comprehension

6 How does the author contrast Cendrillon's behavior on this day with her normal behavior? (Whereas she is usually happy and sunny, today she does not smile at all.)

7 Do the details the author gives about Cendrillon match Mamma's opinion of her? (No; she obviously works very hard.)

8 How does Cendrillon's description of Paul compare with the narrator's description of Cendrillon herself? (She, too, is kind and good-looking.)

Vocabulary *(page 335)*

manioc: the root of a tropical plant, used in making pudding

pallet: a narrow, hard mattress

 Word Study

The word *fete* (or *fête,* in Parisian French) is from the same root as the English words *feast* and *festival.* Other related words students might look up in the dictionary are *festoon* and *festive.*

When she was older, Cendrillon would come to the river each morning to do the family's laundry. Her sweet "*Bonjou'*" was music. Her smile was sunshine even when clouds hid the sun. We knelt beside the other *blanchisseuses* and talked and sang and laughed as we scrubbed the clothes. Cendrillon seemed so happy, I wished that I could always see her so.

Nothing was easy for her at home. Madame and spoiled Vitaline ate dainties. Cendrillon often had only a handful of <u>manioc</u> flour and tail ends of codfish. All day she worked. At night she slept on a hard straw <u>pallet</u>.

Then, one day, she came sad-faced to the river. No singing or joking would make her smile. I asked, "What troubles you so, my child?" **6**

"There is a ball tonight, but I am not to go," she said, looking so miserable, my heart nearly snapped in two. "Vitaline and Mamma will go. But Mamma says I am lazy." **7**

"Does it mean so much to you, this ball?"

"Oh, yes, *Nannin'*!" she cried. "It is a birthday *fet'* [FET] for Paul, Monsieur Thibault's [TEE-bowlz] son. He is so handsome and well spoken, he is like a prince. Yet he is kind." **8**

"Do not cry, dear one," I said, hugging her. "Tonight you will go to the ball."

"For true?"

"Upon my soul, I promise this," I said. Though I was fearful of risking so much when I had no plan.

But her smile lightened my heart. As she gathered up her laundry, I heard her singing.

335

Writer's Craft Lesson
Point of View

OBJECTIVES

Students identify point of view in the selection.

Remind students that point of view in art is the angle from which a viewer sees a scene. Similarly, point of view in literature is the angle from which a reader connects to the story as provided by the narrator, or the person who tells the story.

Have students identify the narrator of the story. (the laundress, Cendrillon's godmother) Demonstrate with examples from page 335 that this narrator sees things only from her own limited point of view. She doesn't know Cendrillon's thoughts but she can tell her feelings from her actions and words. Point out that the author's choice of a narrator who is part of the story makes the story more personal and draws the reader in.

Discuss how the story would change if it were told by an omniscient, all-knowing narrator in the third person.

Reading

▶ Supporting Comprehension

9 The author has already told you about this wand. Are you surprised that it comes into use now? Why? (No; it is clear that magic is needed to help Cendrillon.)

10 How does the author show Madame's and Vitaline's attitude toward Cendrillon? (by showing them ordering her around and yelling at her)

11 What does the term *good riddance* tell you about the narrator's point of view? (She doesn't like Cendrillon's family.)

Vocabulary *(page 336)*

riddance: removal of something unwanted

Long after she left, I sat watching the river. *How am I to keep my promise?* I asked myself. Then, as the day grew late, I began to think what I must do.

9 It was dark when I reached home, took my mother's wand from the shelf, and hurried to my sweet Cendrillon.

What a hubble-bubble at the house! Cendrillon's papa stood on the porch, holding his gold watch, while the coachman waited beside the family carriage. "We are late," Monsieur said, as if the fault belonged to me. Inside, Madame and Vitaline were shouting, **10** "Cendrillon, find my shoulder-scarf!" "Cendrillon, comb my hair!" I helped arrange Madame's gown, while Cendrillon combed Vitaline's hair.

11 Finally they were off, away. Good <u>riddance</u>!

336

Reaching All Students

English Language Learners

As you read aloud page 336, ask students to listen for clues to Nannin's attitude toward Cendrillon's family. Then ask students to share what they have observed. Challenge students to find other statements that reveal Nannin's attitude toward Cendrillon's family.

337

Reaching All Students

English Language Learners

Pronunciation

Find out if any students are speakers of French or Creole. Encourage those students to help you and their classmates with pronunciation of the Creole throughout the selection.

Reading

▶ Supporting Comprehension

12 How does the author show Cendrillon's trusting nature as she responds to her godmother? (Even though she has doubts, she does what her nannin' tells her.)

13 How do the details about what things are changed into what other things help to set this story in a particular place? (The author names regional plants and animals.)

14 What does the author mean by the line *It was enough to hurt my eyes to look at my darling*? (Cendrillon was so splendid she dazzled the eyes.)

Vocabulary *(page 339)*

gilded: covered with a layer of gold

agoutis: rodents that dig in the ground

elegant: marked by good taste; graceful

338

 Reaching All Students
Extra Support

Segment 1: Review

Before students join the whole class for Wrapping Up on page 339, have them

- check predictions
- take turns modeling Question and other strategies they used
- add to **Transparency 3–11**, check and revise their Venn diagram on **Practice Book** page 176, and use it to summarize

 Reaching All Students
On Level   Challenge

Reading Card 5

Literature Discussion

In mixed-ability groups of five or six, students can discuss their own questions and the discussion prompts on Reading Card 5.

- Is Cendrillon a true heroine? Why do you think so?
- Think of other versions of this story you have read. What makes this version new and unusual? Do you like it?

Upon the instant, I told Cendrillon, "Now *you* will go to the ball."

"But I have no carriage," she protested. "I have no gown."

"Go into the garden and pick a *fruit à pain* [FREE-ya pan]," I said.

The child looked at me as if she thought, *My poor* nannin' *has gone mad.* But she found a big, round breadfruit.   **12**

I tapped this three times — *to, to, to!* — with my wand, and it became a <u>gilded</u> coach.

So far so good!

Cendrillon gasped, but I told her, "Do not waste your breath on questions; we still have much to do."

To, to, to! Six *agoutis* [ah-GOO-teez] in a cage became six splendid carriage horses. *To, to, to!* Five brown field lizards became five tall   **13** footmen. *To, to, to!* A plump *manicou* [MAN-ee-coo] was changed to a coachman.

Then I tapped Cendrillon. Her poor calico dress was changed to a trailing gown of sky-blue velvet. Upon her head sat a turban just as blue, pinned with a *tremblant* [TRHEM-blahn], pin of gold. She had a silk shoulder-scarf of pale rose, rings in her ears, bracelets, and a necklace of four strands of gold beads, bigger than peas.

Upon her feet were <u>elegant</u> pink slippers, embroidered with roses.   **14** It was enough to hurt my eyes to look at my darling.

End of Segment 1: *pages 328–339*

Wrapping Up Segment 1
pages 328–339

First, provide Extra Support for students who need it (page 338). Then bring all students together.

■ **Review Predictions/Purpose** Discuss the questions that students have come up with while reading Segment 1. Compare and contrast this story with more familiar versions of Cinderella.

■ **Model Strategies** Refer students to the **Strategies Poster** and have them take turns modeling Question and other strategies they used as they read. Provide models if needed (page 331).

■ **Share Group Discussion** Have students share their questions and literature discussions.

■ **Summarize** Have students use the transparency and their Venn diagrams to make important comparisons and contrasts and summarize the story so far.

Comprehension/Critical Thinking

1 **What is Cendrillon's problem? How is her god-mother helping her?** (She wants to go to the ball but her stepmother will not let her; her godmother is going to use magic so Cendrillon can go to the ball.)
Problem Solving and Decision Making

2 **Is the story of Cinderella a universal story—one that can appeal to people from many different cultures? Why do you think so?** (Answers will vary.)
Making Judgments

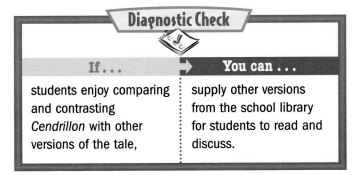

Diagnostic Check	
If . . .	**You can . . .**
students enjoy comparing and contrasting *Cendrillon* with other versions of the tale,	supply other versions from the school library for students to read and discuss.

Reading

Reading Segment 2
pages 340–353

Purpose Setting Review the story so far and remind students to think of questions as they read. Have students pay attention to details that make *Cendrillon* a unique version of the Cinderella fairy tale.

Journal Writing Students can record any details that make *Cendrillon* a unique story, or any questions that they think of.

Vocabulary *(page 340)*

<u>shift:</u> a loose-fitting dress

<u>chaperone:</u> to go with a young woman when she is out in public with a young man

---

Finally, I turned my washerwoman's <u>shift</u> into a fine red dress. I would <u>chaperone</u> Cendrillon, as suited a proper young lady.

Away we went, over the bridge, through the town, along the shore to the *granmaison* [grahn-MAY-zohn] of Monsieur Thibault.

Just before we stepped down from our carriage, I warned Cendrillon, "The magic lasts only a short time. We must leave before the midnight bell is rung."

"Yes, *Nannin'*," she promised.

340

Reaching All Students

Extra Support: Previewing the Text

Before reading Segment 2, preview the text, using the notes below. **While** reading, model strategies (pages 343 and 345). **After** reading, review the segment (page 352) before students join the Wrapping Up discussion.

pages 340–343 How does this setting contrast with Cendrillon's ordinary life?

pages 344–347 At midnight, the magic ends. How does the contrast in these illustrations show this change?

pages 348–351 Paul tries the slipper on the foot of every girl on the island. Whom do you think it will fit?

pages 352–353 Many fairy tales end with the words "They lived happily ever after." How does this illustration hint at that happy ending?

341

▶ Supporting Comprehension

15 This is the second time France has been mentioned in the story. What does it mean to "come from France" in this community? (Someone who comes from France is believed to be of better breeding and quality than someone born on the island.)

16 What is the author saying about Cendrillon's stepmother and stepsister and their concern with appearances? (They can't see beyond the surface to find the real Cendrillon under the pretty gown.)

17 Why does the author include the detail that there was chocolate sherbet at the party? (Sherbet is probably a rare delicacy, at least as far as the narrator is concerned, so it proves that the party was very fancy indeed.)

> **Vocabulary** *(page 342)*
> <u>crossly:</u> in a grumpy or grouchy way

 Cross-Curricular Connection

Social Studies The social caste system in *Cendrillon* stems from the history of Martinique. Discovered in 1502 by Columbus, the island was settled in the 1600s by the French, who killed off the native Indians and brought in African slaves. The difference in status between the French settlers and their slaves leads Cendrillon's stepmother and others to believe that being from France is superior to being from the island.

What a grand entrance Cendrillon made! All eyes turned toward her and could not turn away. I heard whispers all around: "Who is that pretty girl?" "Look how fine her clothes are!" "Did she come from France?"

15

Even Cendrillon's stepmother and sister did not recognize the two of us, though they peered crossly at us.

16

Then Paul, his eyes blazing with love, asked her to dance. And he refused to dance with any other. I know. I watched as I ate. Oh, what fine food I helped myself to, as I watched the handsome couple. Even chocolate sherbet.

17

343

Strategy Modeling

Question If students need help modeling the strategy, use this example to model it for them.

One interesting question I might ask another reader after reading page 343 is this: Why doesn't anyone recognize Cendrillon?

Strategy Focus: Question

Student Modeling Have students model the strategy by coming up with questions they might ask a fellow reader about the material on pages 344–345. Remind them that asking questions of this sort helps them focus on the main ideas and details of the story.

▶ Supporting Comprehension

18 How does the narrator show her point of view toward her goddaughter in this first paragraph?

(She is happy when Cendrillon is happy.)

19 Why is the detail of the lost slipper important?

(It gives Paul a way to find Cendrillon.)

344

 **Reaching All Students**
Challenge

Reading Card
6

Fairy Tale Objects

It's worthwhile questioning why Cendrillon's slipper doesn't vanish along with her ball gown and carriage at the stroke of midnight—the answer being that the slipper is just a special object whose purpose is to bring Cendrillon together with her prince and end her struggles forever. Ask students to read one of the classic tales below and to write a paragraph describing the role of the special object(s) in the tale.

"The Magic Porridge Pot"   "Jack and the Beanstalk"

"The Sleeping Beauty"   "The Twelve Dancing Princesses"

Cendrillon was so happy, and I was happy seeing her so, that we forgot to mark the time. Suddenly, I heard distant bells strike the first chime of midnight.

18

Astonishing all with my rudeness, I grabbed Cendrillon's hand and cried, "It is nearly midnight! We must go!"

For a moment, I feared she would not obey. Then she turned, and we ran toward the door.

Paul cried, "Wait! I do not even know your name!"

He ran after us, but guests and servants, confused by such running and shouting, blocked his way. As it was, we barely escaped to our carriage because Cendrillon stumbled on the stair. She had to leave behind one embroidered slipper.

19

345

Reaching All Students

Extra Support

Strategy Modeling

Phonics/Decoding Use this example to model the strategy.

First I'll try splitting the word commotion *between the double m's. The first part might say* / kuhm /. *Now I see recognize the shorter word* motion. *When I put the parts together, I say* / kuhm•moh•shun /. *Oh, the word is* / kuh•MOH•shun /. *I think a commotion is when there's a lot of noise and confusion. That makes sense in the sentence.*

▶ **Supporting Comprehension**

20 What does the author mean by *the twelfth stroke*? (the last chiming of the clock at midnight)

21 How does the author show that the magic spell has ended? (The carriage is a breadfruit, the horses are agoutis, and the footmen and coachman are lizards and a manicou.)

22 How does the author show Cendrillon's despair? (She refers to *a happiness I will never know again.*)

Off we sped into the night as I counted the chimes. And the moment I heard the twelfth stroke, we found ourselves in the dusty road, beside a smashed breadfruit. Around us, *agoutis* and lizards and a fat *manicou* scurried into the brush.

We walked home like two ragged washerwomen. Our fine clothes were gone — all except Cendrillon's one pink slipper.

She took it off, saying, "I will keep this to remind me of this wonderful night and a happiness I will never know again."

"But," I said, "I will help you visit Paul again."

20
21
22

347

Using Illustrations

Before you read page 347, remind students to use illustrations to help them figure out unfamiliar vocabulary. After you read, pause and ask what they think breadfruit, *agoutis,* and *manicou* might be. Students can point to the objects and animals in the art.

Revisiting the Text

Spiral Review

Comprehension Skill Lesson
Fantasy and Realism

OBJECTIVES

Students classify events as fantasy or realism.

Write these sentences on the board.

> 1. Cendrillon held a fat lizard in her hand.
> 2. The lizard opened his mouth and spoke to her.

Have students indicate which sentence tells about an event that could happen in real life and which one tells about an event that could never happen. Label the first sentence *realism* and the second *fantasy*. Discuss students' reasoning for their choices.

Explain that fairy tales are a mixture of realism and fantasy. The inclusion of events that could never happen in real life make fairy tales particularly entertaining. The inclusion of events that are realistic help readers relate to the characters in the story.

Draw this chart on the board and have students help you complete it with events from the story.

Event/Detail	Fantasy (F) or Realism (R)	How I Know

Skill Finder
- **Instruction,** Theme 3, pp. 381A–381B
- **Reteaching,** Theme 3 p. R12
- **Review,** Theme 4, p. 399

▶ Supporting Comprehension

23 The narrator fears that she cannot give Cendrillon the gift of a love that will change her life. How has the narrator's own love for Cendrillon already changed the girl's life? (She has treated Cendrillon kindly when no one else did, and she has given her a wonderful night.)

24 How does the narrator's point of view differ from Madame's and Vitaline's? Why do you think this is so? (Because the narrator loves her goddaughter, she sees that Cendrillon is suffering, whereas they think she's being lazy.)

25 How does the narrator show her attitude toward Vitaline and her mother? (She makes fun of Vitaline's big feet.)

Vocabulary *(page 349)*
commotion: noisy activity

348

She shook her head. "I see now that it was not Cendrillon he fell in love with," she said. "He was under the spell of your wand. When the magic goes, the love, too, will fade from his eyes."

"Alas!" I said. "My plans have come to nothing. I cannot give you the gift of a love that would change your life for true."

"Dear Godmother," she said, kissing my cheek, "you gave me this night. It is enough." **23**

I did not see Cendrillon at the river the next day. When I called at the house, I found she was in bed. Madame and Vitaline said she was being lazy. But I saw she was sick with a broken heart. I stroked her brow for a good long time — until I heard a great commotion. **24**

When I looked for the cause, I found that Paul had arrived. He was followed by a footman carrying Cendrillon's lost pink slipper on a satin pillow.

To Madame and Vitaline, he explained, "I am searching for the lovely stranger who was at the *fet'* last night. This is her slipper. I am asking all unmarried young women on the island to try it on. I will wed the one whose foot it fits."

From the doorway I heard Madame say, "My pretty daughter is the only unmarried girl in the house."

Then Vitaline and her mamma tried to force the girl's big foot, with toes like sausages, into the slipper. Such grunting and groaning you never heard! So eager were they, I feared they would destroy the slipper.

"If you cut off those big toes," I called out, "it would be a fine fit." **25**
Madame screeched, "Go away, old woman!"

And I did. Straight back to Cendrillon's room I marched.

349

Comprehension Skill Lesson
Noting Details

OBJECTIVES

Students identify details that explain, give information, or convey feelings.

Remind students that main ideas are the most important ideas an author is trying to get across to the reader. Main ideas are supported by *details* that explain ideas, give specific information, or convey feelings.

Ask students to locate details on page 349 that support the idea that Vitaline and her mother are not nice people. As a class, complete a chart similar to the one below that supports the fact that Vitaline and her mother are not nice. Then add a word after each detail to more completely describe Vitaline and Madame.

Vitaline and Madame
think Cendrillon is being lazy (insensitive)
claim that Vitaline is the only unmarried girl in the house (liars)
try to force Vitaline's foot into the slipper (desperate)

Skill Finder

- **Instruction**, Th. 1; Th. 3, pp. 323A–323B
- **Reteaching**, Theme 1, p. R16; Theme 3, p. R8
- **Review**, Theme 2, p. 201; Theme 6, p. 637

▶ Supporting Comprehension

26 What does the author mean by *the battle of the slipper*? (Vitaline's and Madame's desperate attempt to cram Vitaline's toes into the shoe)

27 Why doesn't Cendrillon want to appear before Paul as she did at the ball? (She is afraid he loves her only in her enchanted form; she wants him to see her as she is.)

28 How does Paul prove that he is worthy of Cendrillon? (He loves her as she really is.)

Vocabulary *(page 350)*

charged: directed or ordered

hesitation: doubt or delay

"Now, child, if you love me," I charged her, "do this one thing for me: Go out into the hall."

She drew a shawl around her cotton shift. Barefoot, she went into the hall, where panting Madame and sobbing Vitaline had given up the battle of the slipper. But just as Paul was turning to go, I tapped Cendrillon — *to, to, to!* — with my wand. To the astonishment of all, she appeared as she had at the ball.

"No, Godmother dear," she said. "No more spells."

With a sigh, I touched her again, and she was as before, in her shift and shawl.

Without hesitation, Paul knelt before her. Gently he placed the slipper on her foot. Then he said, "You are as beautiful this minute as you were last night." And everyone in the room could see the true-love in his eyes.

351

352

▶ Supporting Comprehension

29 Why does the author compare Cendrillon's wedding to that of the king and queen of France? (In Cendrillon's world, French nobles are considered the highest form of civilization, so for her wedding to be better means that it was unbelievably grand.)

30 What does this list—*"ate and danced and sang and ate again"*—tell you about the wedding? (It went on and on and was very merry.)

31 How does the narrator remind the reader that this is her story to tell? (by pointing out that she was there to witness everything and left only to tell the tale)

Reaching All Students

Extra Support

Segment 2 Review

Before students join in Wrapping Up on page 353, have them:

- review their purpose

- take turns modeling the reading strategies they used

- complete **Transparency 3–11** and their Venn diagrams

- summarize the whole story

Reaching All Students

On Level   Challenge

Literature Discussion

Have small groups of students discuss the story, using their own questions or the questions in Think About the Selection on Anthology page 354.

Cendrillon and Paul were married soon after this. Even the king and queen of France never had such a wedding! The guests ate and danced and sang and ate again for three days.

I know because I was there. I danced the *gwo-kā* [gwoh-KAH] and ate nine helpings of chocolate sherbet and came away only to tell you this tale.

29

30

31

End of Segment 2:
pages 340–353

Wrapping Up Segment 2
pages 340–353

Provide Extra Support for students who need it (page 352). Then bring all students together.

- **Review Predictions/Purpose** Have students discuss the questions they formulated while reading.

- **Model Strategies** Have students take turns modeling Question and discuss where they used the strategy as they read. Provide models if needed (pages 331 and 343).

- **Share Group Discussions** Have students compare and contrast this version with other versions of the Cinderella story.

- **Summarize** Have students use their Venn diagrams to make important comparisons and contrasts and summarize the story.

Comprehension/Critical Thinking

1. Are Cendrillon and Paul a good match? Explain your answer. (Answers will vary.) **Making Judgments**

2. What does this story teach us about basing our opinions on appearances? (It's important to look deeper and see things as they really are.) **Author's Viewpoint**

Reaching All Students
English Language Learners

Reread the references to France on pages 331, 343, and 353. Ask students to describe the impressions of France that Nannin's narrator provides. Have students discuss what they have learned about France and Martinique from this story.

Diagnostic Check

If...	You can...
students have difficulty comparing and contrasting,	return to the minilesson on page 333 and comprehension questions on pages 334 and 352.
students summarize the story accurately and well,	make sure they have the opportunity to share their summaries.

Responding

▶ Think About the Selection

Discuss or Write Have students discuss or write their answers. Sample answers are provided; accept reasonable responses that are supported with evidence from the story.

1 **Drawing Conclusions** Madame and Vitaline were very surprised. They were also angry and jealous.

2 **Fantasy and Realism** In real life there is poverty and children can lose their mothers; people fall in love. The amazing power of the magic wand is pure fantasy. It could not happen in real life.

3 **Making Inferences** She wants Paul to see her as she really is and to love her for herself rather than for her fine clothes.

4 **Predicting Outcomes** She would not have been in a rush and lost her slipper. Paul would have had nothing to search with.

5 **Making Inferences** People all over the world like to see goodness rewarded and triumphant.

6 ⭐ **Connecting/Comparing** Compare and Contrast Answers will vary. Students might suggest that some of the strange events in *The Stranger* might have scientific explanations while the magic in *Cendrillon* is utterly unreal.

Responding

Think About the Selection

1. How do you think Madame and Vitaline felt when they found out that Cendrillon was the mysterious guest at the ball?

2. Which events in the story could happen in real life? Which amazing events could never happen in real life?

3. Why does Cendrillon want to wear her own clothes when Paul puts the slipper on her foot?

4. How would this story have been different if Cendrillon had left the ball on time?

5. Many countries have versions of the Cinderella story. Why do you think this story is so popular all over the world?

6. **Connecting/Comparing** Which story do you think is more amazing, *Cendrillon* or *The Stranger*? Give reasons for your answer.

 Narrating

Write Another Scene

How would *Cendrillon* be different if it were told by another character, such as the stepmother or Paul? Choose one scene from the story. Then pick a different character to narrate the events of that scene. Write the scene from that character's point of view.

Tips
- Start your story with "Now let me tell you what happened . . ."
- Tell only what that character would know about events.

354

 **Reaching All Students**
English Language Learners

Beginning and Preproduction Have students offer suggestions of events that make this story amazing. Guide the responses with questions about sequence.

Early Production and Speech Emergence Students can tell a partner about favorite parts of the *Cendrillon* version of the *Cinderella* fairy tale.

Intermediate and Advanced Fluency In small groups, have students compare *Cendrillon* and *Cinderella*.

Social Studies

Make a Travel Brochure

If you were going to Cendrillon's island home, what would you see there? Make a travel brochure of Martinique. Look in the selection and in the Get Set to Read on pages 326–327 for details about Martinique to include in your brochure.

Viewing

Watch a Movie Version

View one of the many film or television versions of *Cinderella*. Then, in a small group, discuss how the movie compares to the story *Cendrillon*. Which version do you like better? Why?

An animated version of *Cinderella*

Send an E-postcard

Now that you've read two selections in this theme, send an e-postcard about these amazing stories to a friend. You'll find a postcard at Education Place.

www.eduplace.com/kids

355

Personal Response

Invite volunteers to share their personal responses to *Cendrillon*. As an alternative, ask students to write in their journals about some of the differences between life in the United States and that in Martinique.

Comprehension Check

Assign **Practice Book** page 177 to assess students' understanding of the selection.

Reaching All Students
English Language Learners

Have students choose a character from whose point of view they would like to retell a scene. Those students who have chosen the same character should work in a group to create a word web for that character.

End-of-Selection Assessment

Selection Test Use the test in the **Teacher's Resource Blackline Masters** to assess selection comprehension and vocabulary.

Student Self-Assessment Have students assess their reading with additional questions such as

- What parts of this selection were difficult for me? Why?

- What strategies helped me understand the story?

- Would I recommend this story to my friends? Why?

Dance Link

pages 356–357

▶ ## Skill: How to Read a Time Line

Read the title of the link and the introductory paragraph aloud. Direct students' attention to the time line. Explain that a time line is a tool that quickly explains the way many events have unfolded over time and that it can help students understand cause-and-effect relationships. Before having students independently read the time line, review the points in the left column on page 356.

■ First, students should read the title of the time line in order to understand its topic.

■ To fully grasp the range of time being addressed, instruct students to read the first and last dates shown on the time line. (It spans approximately 400 years.)

■ Make sure students understand that a time line is meant to be read from left to right. The earliest date appears all the way to the left and builds chronologically, culminating at the entry farthest on the right. Each empty space between entries represents the passage of time.

Vocabulary *(page 356)*

ballroom: a dance hall, often very grand in style

Direct students to read the captions below each point on the time line to learn about the history of ballroom dance.

Dance Link

Skill: How to Read a Time Line

● Read the **title** to see what the time line is about.

● Look for **dates** and notice the **time span** each section of the time line shows.

● Scan the time line from left to right. The earlier **events** will be on the left. The later events will be on the right.

Let's Have a BALL!

Fantastic balls like the one in *Cendrillon* aren't just in fairy tales. In real life, people still go to fancy parties like balls. Guests wear their most formal clothing. And what type of dancing do they do? <u>Ballroom</u> dancing, of course!

The History of Ballroom Dance

1600s   1700s

One of the first ballroom dances, the **minuet**, was popular in Europe in the **1600s**. Dancers stood in two lines. They moved along the floor in an *S* or *Z* pattern, joining hands at different parts in the dance.

People first danced the **waltz** in Germany during the **1700s**. With its gliding steps and graceful turns, it quickly became popular all over the world.

The graceful minuet was a favorite among the lords and ladies of Europe.

356

Reaching All Students

Classroom Management

All Students

Reading a Time Line Direct all students to take part in How to Read a Time Line, time line reading, and Comprehension Check activities. To ensure that students requiring Extra Support can follow the time line, write these dance names on index cards and mix them up. Make sure students can place the names in chronological order: *minuet, waltz, fox trot, tango.*

These professional dancers perform an elegant tango.

Guests loved to waltz at balls like this one, held by the Skidmore Guard in the 1870s.

Dancers had to be quick on their feet for the lively fox trot.

1800s   1900s   2000s

The waltz stayed popular throughout the **1800s**. Some of the best-loved waltz music was written in that century. You may even have ice-skated to "The Skaters' Waltz."

The **fox trot** was a favorite ballroom dance of the **1900s**. The dance was named after Harry Fox, a famous performer who used to trot across the stage! At that time, Latin American dances such as the **rumba** and the **tango** became popular too.

Today, you can still see guests waltzing at weddings or doing the **tango** on televised dance contests. Hundreds of years after the first dancers twirled across the floor, ballroom dancing is as popular as ever.

357

▶ Comprehension Check

Comprehension/Critical Thinking Ask students to read aloud the parts of the selection that support their answers.

1 How does the origin of the minuet differ from the origin of the waltz? (The minuet was first danced in the 1600s; the waltz became popular in the 1700s.) **Compare and Contrast**

2 What do the fox trot, the rumba, and the tango have in common? (All are popular ballroom dances of the 1900s.) **Noting Details**

3 Would you expect ballroom dancing to be popular 100 years from now? Why or why not? (Yes; it has been popular for 400 years.) **Predicting Outcomes**

4 After reading the time line, which dance would you say was the most popular over the course of time? (The waltz. It has entries for two centuries and is mentioned as still being contemporary.) **Drawing Conclusions**

5 **Connecting/Comparing** The story of Cinderella was first written down in the late 1600s. Which dance would have been popular in Cinderella's time? (minuet) **Noting Details**

Reaching All Students

English Language Learners

Explain to students that this time line covers many years because the time increments are centuries. Show students the current century. Guide students so that they can locate the century they were born in on this time line.

OBJECTIVES

Students

- compare details to see how characters and events are alike

- contrast details to see how characters and events differ

- learn academic language: **compare, contrast**

Practice Book page 176

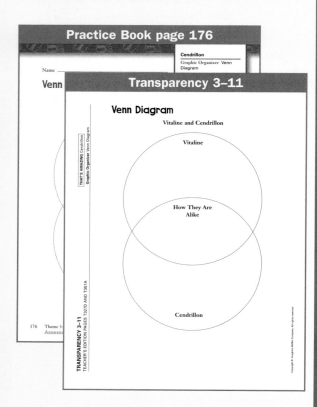

Comprehension Skills
✓ Compare and Contrast

▶ **Teach**

Tell students that comparisons show similarities among characters and events and contrasts show the differences. Explain that by comparing information to something you already know, it becomes easier to remember and understand the new information. Use **Transparency 3–11** to discuss

- the similarities between Vitaline and Cendrillon

- the differences between Vitaline and Cendrillon

- how it is easier to remember something about one when compared to the other

Students may refer to the selection and to **Practice Book** page 176.

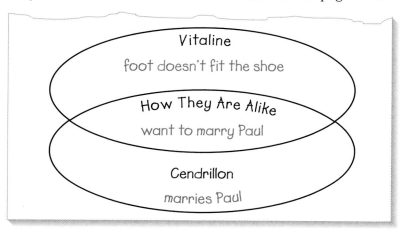

Modeling Remind students that when they explain how two things are alike they are comparing them and when they explain how two things are different they are contrasting them. Tell students that this allows them to better understand what they are reading, especially if they have a question about something. Ask a student to read aloud the first paragraph on page 353. Then use the Think Aloud.

Think Aloud

I don't understand why the author mentions the king and queen of France in this paragraph. But if I compare this to the section we read about the island the story is set on, I see that this island has many pieces of French culture. The author must be referring to that in this paragraph. By comparing what I didn't know to what I've already learned, I now understand the story better.

Explain that sometimes a reader needs to make comparisons outside of the story in order to understand it.

▶ Practice

Choose a version of Cinderella to read to the students. Have students help you fill out a story map on the board like the one below for that version. Ask students to work in pairs to create their own story maps of *Cendrillon* for comparison.

	Cinderella	**Cendrillon**
Characters	Cinderella, godmother, stepmother, two stepsisters, prince	
Setting	Europe	
Plot Outline	Cinderella works hard. Her stepsisters are invited to the prince's ball. Her godmother turns a pumpkin into a carriage. Cinderella wears glass slippers to the ball. She leaves a slipper at the ball.	
Resolution	The prince fits the slipper to Cinderella's foot. The prince and Cinderella marry.	

Have the class share their charts and discuss how comparing the two helps them better understand the stories and even the cultures in which the stories were told.

▶ Apply

Use **Practice Book** pages 178–179 to diagnose whether students need Reteaching. Students who do not need Reteaching may work on Challenge/Extension Activities, page R11. Students who need Extra Support may apply the skill to an easier text using the **Reader's Library** selection "Tattercoat" and its Responding activity.

Skill Finder		
• Revisiting, p. 333	• Review, Th. 2, p. 193; Th. 3, p. 369; Th. 4, p. 495; Th. 5	• Reteaching, p. R10

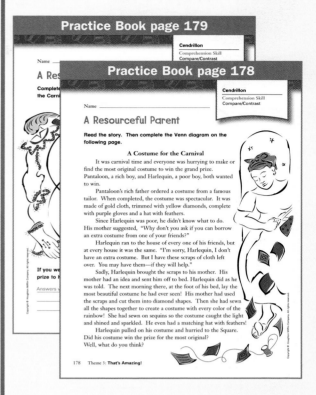
Practice Book page 178

Name _____

Cendrillon
Comprehension Skill
Compare/Contrast

A Resourceful Parent

Read the story. Then complete the Venn diagram on the following page.

A Costume for the Carnival

It was carnival time and everyone was hurrying to make or find the most original costume to win the grand prize. Pantaloon, a rich boy, and Harlequin, a poor boy, both wanted to win.

Pantaloon's rich father ordered a costume from a famous tailor. When completed, the costume was spectacular. It was made of gold cloth, trimmed with yellow diamonds, complete with purple gloves and a hat with feathers.

Since Harlequin was poor, he didn't know what to do. His mother suggested, "Why don't you ask if you can borrow an extra costume from one of your friends?"

Harlequin ran to the house of every one of his friends, but at every house it was the same. "I'm sorry, Harlequin, I don't have an extra costume. But I have these scraps of cloth left over. You may have them—if they will help."

Sadly, Harlequin brought the scraps to his mother. His mother had an idea and sent him off to bed. Harlequin did as he was told. The next morning there, at the foot of his bed, lay the most beautiful costume he had ever seen! His mother had used the scraps and cut them into diamond shapes. Then she had sewn all the shapes together to create a costume with every color of the rainbow! She had sewn on sequins so the costume caught the light and shined and sparkled. He even had a matching hat with feathers!

Harlequin pulled on his costume and hurried to the Square. Did his costume win the prize for the most original? Well, what do you think?

178 Theme 3: **That's Amazing!**

Reaching All Students

Extra Support

- Reteaching, page R10

- **Reader's Library:** *That's Amazing!* Selection 1, "Tattercoat"

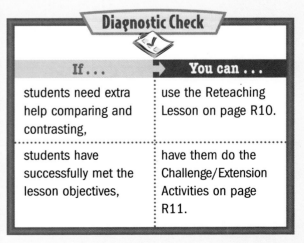

Diagnostic Check

If . . .	You can . . .
students need extra help comparing and contrasting,	use the Reteaching Lesson on page R10.
students have successfully met the lesson objectives,	have them do the Challenge/Extension Activities on page R11.

Comprehension Skills (357B)

OBJECTIVES

Students

- learn how to use a Venn diagram to compare and contrast

- apply Venn diagram skills to differentiate between two versions of a folktale

- learn academic language: **Venn diagram**

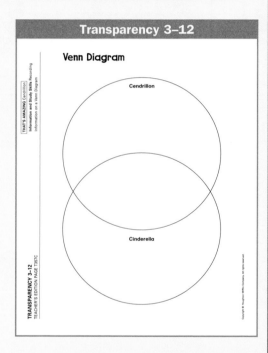

Transparency 3–12

Venn Diagram

Cendrillon

Cinderella

Information & Study Skills

Recording Information on a Venn Diagram

▶ Teach

Tell students that a Venn diagram is a visual way of comparing and contrasting information between two things. (If you wish, tell students that the diagram is named after the person who invented it, John Venn.) A Venn diagram shows, at a glance, how two things are alike and different.

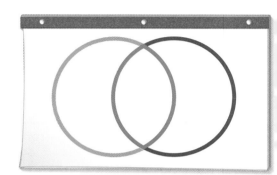

Display **Transparency 3–12**, or draw a large Venn diagram on the board. Point out that a Venn diagram consists of two circles that, to varying degrees, overlap. The center, or overlapping portion, represents what the two items have in common. The two, nonoverlapping portions of each circle represent how the two items being compared are different, or unique from the other. The degree to which the two circles overlap is dependent on how much the two items have in common. For instance, two items with a great deal in common would have a much larger overlapping area than two extremely dissimilar items.

Tell students that they are going to use the Venn diagram to compare the story they have read called *Cendrillon* to the version of the Cinderella story with which they are most familiar. Remind students that there are many versions of the Cinderella folktale all over the world. The main events of the story are usually very similar, but the setting, some of the characters, and the details vary widely from country to country.

Model Begin by having students review a version of the folktale with which they will be most familiar, such as the Cinderella tale featured in the Teacher Read Aloud (pages 326E–326F). Students will use this version as a basis of comparison with *Cendrillon*. Demonstrate for students how to compare and contrast the two stories using a Venn diagram.

Think Aloud

The heading in the top circle says Cendrillon *and the heading in the bottom circle says* Cinderella. *After comparing the two, it is clear that the basic story of* Cendrillon *is the same as that of* Cinderella. *The events of each story are basically the same. The center, or overlapping part, of the two circles is for things that are* **the same** *in the two stories, so I will write in this overlapping part: "Main events of story are the same." Now I will write ways in which the two stories are* **different**. *I can think of one important difference.* Cendrillon *takes place on the island of Martinique in the Caribbean. The story of* Cinderella *takes place somewhere in Europe. In the top circle under* Cendrillon *I will write "takes place in Martinique." In the bottom circle under* Cinderella, *I will write "takes place in Europe."*

▶ Practice

Have students find further similarities and differences between the two stories and incorporate them into a more detailed Venn diagram. Have them take turns demonstrating how to interpret the completed Venn diagram. You may wish to have them draw conclusions by writing a short paragraph articulating the primary differences and similarities between the stories.

▶ Apply

Have students discuss why a Venn diagram is a good way to differentiate between two things. Then, have them use Venn diagrams to analyze other forms of writing, such as comparable selections or Links within an Anthology theme, or other reading materials you may have on hand. You may choose to extend the analysis of the folktale genre by having students read yet another version of the Cinderella tale.

Word Work Instructions

DAY 1	• Spelling Pretest • Spelling Instruction
DAY 2	• Structural Analysis Instruction • Spelling Practice
DAY 3	• Phonics Instruction • Spelling Practice
DAY 4	• Structural Analysis Reteaching • Vocabulary Skill Instruction • Spelling Game
DAY 5	• Expanding Your Vocabulary • Spelling Test

OBJECTIVES

Students

- read words with the suffix *-able*

- read words with the final / ər /, / l /, or / əl / sound

- use the Phonics/Decoding strategy to decode longer words

Teacher's Note

Tell students that when adding the suffix *-able* to a word, the spelling of the base word may change. If the base word contains a short vowel and ends in a silent *e*, such as *love,* the *e* is dropped when adding *-able*. Write these sentences on the board: *Is that slipper comfortable on your foot? Is this mystery solvable? From the moment she was born, Cendrillon was lovable.* Have students identify the words containing a suffix and tell how each was formed.

Decoding Longer Words

 Structural Analysis: Words with the Suffix -able

▶ Teach

Write this sentence on the board: *Cendrillon hoped the pink slipper was not breakable.* Circle *-able* in *breakable* and explain that it is a word formed by adding the suffix *-able* to the base word *break.* Tell students that the suffix *-able* means "able to be." On the board, write: *breakable = able to break.* Have students give examples of other words that are formed by adding *-able* to a word. (*accept/acceptable, change/changeable, wear/wearable*)

Have students review the Phonics/Decoding strategy. Explain that this strategy will help them to decode longer words with the suffix *-able.*

Modeling Display the following sentence and model how to decode *enjoyable: The ball was so enjoyable, Cendrillon forgot the time.*

Think Aloud

I see the suffix -able *at the end of this word. When I cover it, I see the base word* enjoy. *I know if you enjoy something you have a good time. Since the suffix* -able *means "able to be" the word* enjoyable *probably means "able to be enjoyed." That makes sense in the sentence: Cendrillon forgot the time because she was having such a good time.*

▶ Practice

Write these phrases on the board and have students copy the underlined words: *readable handwriting, valuable gifts, washable gown, comfortable shoes.* Have students work in pairs to decode the words and give their meanings. Then ask individuals to come to the board to model for the class.

▶ Apply

Have students complete **Practice Book** page 180.

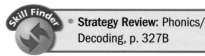

	Strategy Review: Phonics/ Decoding, p. 327B	• Reteaching, page R16

Phonics Spelling Connection

Final / ər /, / l /, and / əl / sounds

▶ Teach

Tell students that understanding the final sounds in *shower* and *middle* can help them use the Phonics/Decoding strategy to decode unfamiliar words.

- The spelling patterns *er, or,* and *ar* can have the final / ər / sound in a two-syllable word.

- The spelling patterns *el, al,* and *le* can have the final / l / or / əl / sound in a two-syllable word.

Modeling Display this sentence and model how to decode *struggled: The poor girl struggled to find food.*

Think Aloud

The s-t-r spelling reminds me of the word stripe. I also notice a double consonant pattern, so I'll try splitting the word between the two g's. I think the first syllable has a short vowel sound because the single vowel u is followed by a consonant sound, /struhg/. I know the l-e spelling pattern can have the /əl/ sound as in the word middle. In this word, the second syllable probably sounds like /guhld/. I've got it. The word is /STRUHG•uhld/. She had to work really hard to find food.

▶ Practice

Have students copy the underlined words from the board:

> *Cendrillon could settle for just a memory. "Don't bother me, old woman!" screeched Vitaline. She had a silk shoulder-scarf of pale rose. I watched the handsome couple.*

Have students work in pairs to circle the final / ər /, / l / and / əl / patterns and decode each word. Call on individuals to model at the board.

▶ Apply

Tell students to decode the following phrases: *travel by carriage; a crystal bracelet; looked in the mirror; a poor beggar; another day of work; enter the ballroom; a gentle girl.*

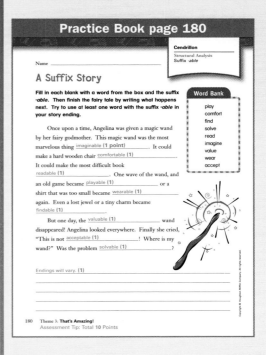

Practice Book page 180

A Suffix Story

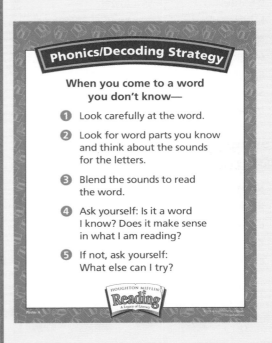

Phonics/Decoding Strategy

When you come to a word you don't know—

1. Look carefully at the word.

2. Look for word parts you know and think about the sounds for the letters.

3. Blend the sounds to read the word.

4. Ask yourself: Is it a word I know? Does it make sense in what I am reading?

5. If not, ask yourself: What else can I try?

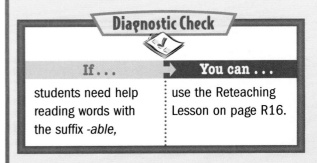

Diagnostic Check

If...	You can ...
students need help reading words with the suffix *-able,*	use the Reteaching Lesson on page R16.

Decoding Longer Words (357F)

OBJECTIVES

Students write spelling words that have final /ər/, /l/, or /əl/ sounds.

Spelling Words

Basic Words

harbor	medal
final*	collar
middle	proper*
weather	towel
labor	beggar
model	battle*
chapter	trouble*
special	shower
sugar	uncle
bottle	doctor

Review Words	Challenge Words
neighbor	shoulder*
little*	decimal
dollar	trifle
daughter*	solar
circle	cancel

Forms of these words appear in the literature.

Reaching All Students
Extra Support

Basic Word List You may want to use only the left column of Basic Words with students who need extra support.

Spelling

✓ Final /ər/ and Final /l/ or /əl/

Day 1 Teaching the Principle

Pretest Use the Day 5 Test sentences. Say each underlined word, read the sentence, and then repeat the word. Have students write only the underlined word.

Teach Write *weather, harbor,* and *sugar* on the board. Have the class say each word after you. Tell students that each word has two syllables, and that the final syllable ends with a weak vowel sound, called the schwa, + r. Underline the final /ər/ pattern in each word and point out that *er, or,* and *ar* are three common patterns for spelling final /ər/ sounds.

Add *model, final,* and *middle* to the board; have students say each word after you. Explain that each two-syllable word has the final /l/ or /əl/ sounds. Underline each word's final /əl/ pattern and point out that *el, al,* and *le* are common spellings for final /l/ or /əl/. Say each remaining Basic Word as you write it on the board and have students repeat it. Select students to underline the final /ər/, /l/, or /əl/ sounds in the words.

Practice/Homework Assign **Practice Book** page 417. Tell students to use this Take-Home Word List to study the words they missed on the Pretest.

Day 2 Reviewing the Principle

Practice/Homework Review the spelling principle and assign **Practice Book** page 181.

Day 3 Vocabulary

Multiple-Meaning Words Write these sentences on the board and discuss the different meanings of *model:*

Then have students choose one of these words: *harbor, collar, trouble, shower, doctor.* Tell students to find two dictionary meanings for their chosen word, write a sentence for each meaning, and share their sentences with the class. (Sentences will vary.)

> He will <u>model</u> the coat at the fashion show.
>
> She built a <u>model</u> out of cardboard.

Next, list the Basic Words on the board. Have students use each word orally in a sentence. (Sentences will vary.)

Practice/Homework For spelling practice, assign **Practice Book** page 182.

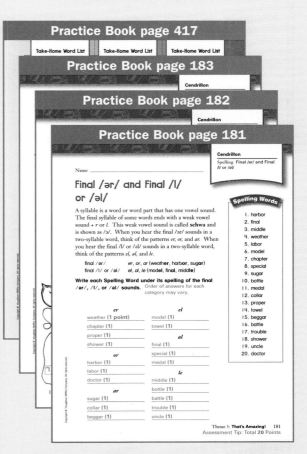

Practice Book page 417

Take-Home Word List | Take-Home Word List | Take-Home Word List

Practice Book page 183

Cendrillon

Practice Book page 182

Cendrillon

Practice Book page 181

Cendrillon

Spelling: Final /ər/ and Final /l/ or /əl/

Name _____

Final /ər/ and Final /l/ or /əl/

A syllable is a word or word part that has one vowel sound. The final syllable of some words ends with a weak vowel sound + *r* or *l*. This weak vowel sound is called **schwa** and is shown as /ə/. When you hear the final /ər/ sounds in a two-syllable word, think of the patterns *er, or,* and *ar*. When you hear the final /l/ or /əl/ sounds in a two-syllable word, think of the patterns *el, al,* and *le.*

final /ər/   er, or, ar (weather, harbor, sugar)
final /l/ or /əl/   el, al, le (model, final, middle)

Write each Spelling Word under its spelling of the final /ər/, /l/, or /əl/ sounds. Order of answers for each category may vary.

er		**el**
weather (1 point)		model (1)
chapter (1)		towel (1)
proper (1)		**al**
shower (1)		final (1)
or		special (1)
harbor (1)		medal (1)
labor (1)		**le**
doctor (1)		middle (1)
ar		bottle (1)
sugar (1)		battle (1)
collar (1)		trouble (1)
beggar (1)		uncle (1)

Spelling Words

1. harbor
2. final
3. middle
4. weather
5. labor
6. model
7. chapter
8. special
9. sugar
10. bottle
11. medal
12. collar
13. proper
14. towel
15. beggar
16. battle
17. trouble
18. shower
19. uncle
20. doctor

Theme 3: **That's Amazing!** 181
Assessment Tip: Total **20** Points

Day 4   Some Final Business

Ask students to form groups of three: two players and a caller. Give each group a set of letter tiles or cards, and have the groups make pattern cards for these patterns: *er, or, ar, el, al, le.* Supply the caller with a list of Basic and Review Words. Then explain these game rules:

The caller says a list word. Player 1 uses individual letter tiles or cards and a pattern card to spell the word. The caller checks the word's spelling. If it is correct, Player 1 earns a point. If it is misspelled, the caller can use the word again later. Play then passes to Player 2. After both players have had a chance to spell a word, one player and the caller switch roles. The student with the highest score after all words have been spelled wins.

Practice/Homework For proofreading and writing practice, assign **Practice Book** page 183.

Day 5   Spelling Assessment

Test Say each underlined word, read the sentence, and then repeat the word. Have students write only the underlined word.

Basic Words

1. Was the boat safe in the <u>harbor</u>?

2. The <u>final</u> game ends our baseball season.

3. We are in the <u>middle</u> of the story.

4. In the summer our <u>weather</u> is hot.

5. We put hours of <u>labor</u> into the garden.

6. I built a <u>model</u> airplane.

7. Read the first <u>chapter</u> in your book.

8. I have two pencils and a <u>special</u> pen.

9. We do not want juice with <u>sugar</u>.

10. Did you drink your <u>bottle</u> of water?

11. The best runner won a <u>medal</u>.

12. The <u>collar</u> of your shirt is dirty.

13. Is this the <u>proper</u> way to hit a ball?

14. I dried my hands on the <u>towel</u>.

15. At dinner our dog acts like a <u>beggar</u>.

16. Two armies fought in a <u>battle</u>.

17. That loud noise could mean car <u>trouble</u>.

18. A little <u>shower</u> will water the flowers.

19. My dad's brother is my <u>uncle</u>.

20. Please call the <u>doctor</u> for the sick child.

Challenge Words

21. She hurt her <u>shoulder</u> in the game.

22. Put a <u>decimal</u> point here.

23. I added a <u>trifle</u> of salt.

24. The <u>solar</u> heat warmed us.

25. Please <u>cancel</u> my order.

Reaching All Students
Challenge

Challenge Word Practice Ask students to write five sentences, each telling one thing they would do if they had a magic wand. Tell students to use a different Challenge Word in each sentence.

OBJECTIVES

Students

- identify a pronunciation key
- understand how to use a pronunciation key
- learn academic language: **spelling table, pronunciation key**

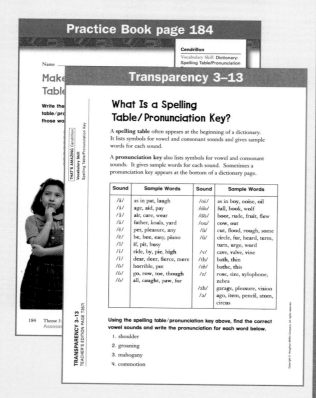

Vocabulary Skills

✓ Dictionary: Spelling Table/Pronunciation Key

▶ Teach

Display **Transparency 3–13,** blocking out all but the definitions of *spelling table* and *pronunciation key*. Read aloud the definitions to the class. Explain that we often can't tell what a word sounds like just by looking at the letters, because the same letter is often pronounced differently in different words. Similarly, we often can't tell how to spell a word just by hearing it. Tell students that a spelling table/pronunciation key can help them decide how a word is pronounced or spelled.

Uncover the spelling table/pronunciation key. Point out the symbol /ă/ and read aloud the sample words: *pat, laugh.* Explain that these two words have the same *a* sound but are spelled differently.

Modeling Point out the /ə/ symbol. Explain that this special symbol is pronounced *schwa,* and that it stands for soft "uh" sound heard in many words. A *schwa* represents the vowel sound of the syllables that are not stressed at all. Read aloud the five examples in the lower left column of the chart, stressing the schwa sound in each word.

Then point out the two-letter symbols /th/ and /zh/ on the transparency. Identify these as *digraphs* and explain that the two joined letters act as a team to produce a single sound. Read aloud each word to the class and stress the sounds in each word.

On the board, write the word *midnight.* Model for students how to write the correct pronunciation of the word *midnight* using the spelling table/pronunciation key.

Think Aloud

If I look at the sample words, I can find other words that sound like parts of midnight. *I'll try the first half of the word,* mid. *The* i *sound is the same as* if, pit, *and* busy. *The symbol for this is* /ĭ/. *So* mid *looks like* m/ĭ/d. *Now let me look at the second part of the word,* night. *The* i *sound in this word sounds the same as* ride, by, pie, *and* high. *The symbol for this is* /ī/, *so* night *looks like* n/ī/t. *The stress is on the first syllable,* mid. *So the pronunciation of* midnight *would be* m/ĭ/d' n/ī/t.

▶ Practice

Display questions 1 through 4 on the transparency. In pairs or small groups, have students write down the correct pronunciation for each word. Have students share their work with the class and explain how they used the spelling table/pronunciation key to learn how to say the words correctly.

▶ Apply

Have students complete **Practice Book** page 184.

Expanding Your Vocabulary
Types of Clothing

Explain that in the selection, the author uses many different words to describe types of clothing, such as *skirt* and *shawl.* Create a word web similar to the following:

Have students work with partners to find other clothing words in the selection and from their own knowledge. Add these words to the web.

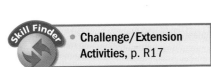
Challenge/Extension Activities, p. R17

📎 Teacher's Note

Words from French Point out that the author of *Cendrillon* uses many French Creole words to give a sense of the setting. Explain that some of the French Creole words in the story are close in sound and meaning to English words because they share the same roots. Have students look in the selection to find French Creole words that are similar in sound and meaning to the following English words. The answers are given in parentheses.

baby, an infant *(bébé)*

fete or **festival,** a large party *(fet')*

mansion, a large home *(granmaison)*

••• **Houghton Mifflin Spelling and Vocabulary** •••
Correlated instruction and practice, pp. 50, 74, 98, 277–278, 315

Reaching All Students
English Language Learners

Focus on the vocabulary that English language learners may encounter again. Write the following words on the board: *hollow, riddance, gilded, chaperone, charged, hesitation.* Pronounce, point to each syllable, and have students repeat. Underline the *ch* in *chaperone* and compare the pronunciation with the *ch* in *charged.* Remind students that they came across this less common *ch* sound in *chandelier* in *Finding the Titanic.*

Writing and Language Instruction

DAY 1	• Daily Language Practice • Grammar Instruction • Journal Writing
DAY 2	• Daily Language Practice • Writing an Announcement • Journal Writing • Grammar Practice
DAY 3	• Daily Language Practice • Grammar Instruction • Write Another Version
DAY 4	• Daily Language Practice • Listening/Speaking/Viewing • Writing: Improving Your Writing • Grammar Practice
DAY 5	• Daily Language Practice • Grammar: Improving Your Writing

OBJECTIVES

Students

- identify main verbs and helping verbs

- give examples of main verbs and helping verbs

- proofread and correct sentences with grammar and spelling errors

- combine sentences using main verbs and helping verbs to improve writing

- learn academic language: **main verb, helping verb**

Wacky Web Tales

Students may use the **Wacky Web Tales** floppy disk to create humorous stories and review parts of speech.

Grammar Skills

 Main Verbs and Helping Verbs

Day 1

Display the sentences at the top of **Transparency 3–14**.

Underline the main verb and circle the helping verb in each sentence. Then go over the following definitions:

- When a verb has more than one word, the main verb shows the action.

- A helping verb works with the main verb. The verbs *has* and *have* help other verbs to show past time.

Ask students to look at *Cendrillon* to find examples of main verbs and helping verbs and to share the examples they find. Tell students to copy the numbered sentences at the bottom of **Transparency 3–14**, on a separate sheet of paper. Have students underline the main verb and circle the helping verb in each sentence. Then have them correct the Day 1 Daily Language Practice sentences on **Transparency 3–16**.

Day 2

Practice/Homework Have students correct the Day 2 Daily Language Practice sentences. Then assign **Practice Book** page 185.

Day 3   Helping a Verb

Divide the class into an even number of small groups. Ask each group to come up with four action verbs that can be main verbs. Then assign pairs of groups to play the game together. One group in each pair names an action verb. The other group must then give a sentence that uses the main verb plus a helping verb. Suggest that students restrict themselves to the helping verbs *will, has,* and *have.* (Example: *help, The woman has helped Cendrillon.*) For each sentence that is correct, the group gets one point and then gets to suggest a verb. If a team fails to come up with a correct sentence, the other group gets the point, and gets another chance to suggest a verb. Play continues until every group has played with every other group once. Then have students correct the Day 3 Daily Language Practice sentences.

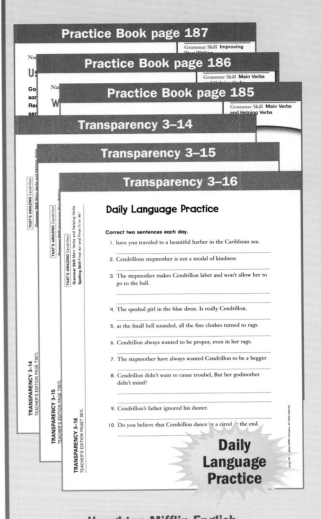

Practice Book page 187

Practice Book page 186

Practice Book page 185

Transparency 3–14

Transparency 3–15

Transparency 3–16

Daily Language Practice

Correct two sentences each day.

1. have you traveled to a beautiful harber in the Caribbean sea.

2. Cendrillons stepmother is not a modal of kindness

3. The stepmother makes Cendrillon laber and won't allow her to go to the ball.

4. The speshul girl in the blue dress. Is really Cendrillon.

5. as the finall bell sounded, all the fine clothes turned to rags.

6. Cendrillon always wanted to be propor, even in her rags.

7. The stepmother have always wanted Cendrillon to be a begger

8. Cendrillon didn't want to cause troubel, But her godmother didn't mind?

9. Cendrillon's father ignored his dauter.

10. Do you believe that Cendrillon dance in a circel at the end.

Daily Language Practice

Day 4

Practice/Homework Have students correct the Day 4 Daily Language Practice sentences. Assign **Practice Book** page 186.

Day 5   Improving Your Writing

Sentence Combining with Main Verbs and Helping Verbs Tell students that good writers often combine two sentences with the same subject and different main verbs by using helping verbs. Display the sentences on **Transparency 3–15**.

Then ask volunteers to go to the board and rewrite each group of two sentences as one by combining the main verbs in the two sentences. Tell students to use the same subject with only one helping verb. Have students review a piece of their own writing to see if they can improve it by combining sentences using helping verbs and main verbs.

Practice/Homework Have students correct the Day 5 Daily Language Practice sentences. Then assign **Practice Book** page 187.

·········· **Houghton Mifflin English** ··········

Correlated instruction and practice, pp. 98–99

Diagnostic Check

If...	You can ...
students need extra help identifying main verbs and helping verbs,	use the Reeaching Lesson on page R21.

Writing Skills

Writing an Announcement

▶ Teach

There are several opportunities in *Cendrillon* for announcements, such as Vitaline's birth, the ball, and Cendrillon and Paul's wedding. Other occasions for announcements include a concert, fair, or sporting event. Explain that an announcement presents important information about something that has happened or will happen.

▶ Practice

Display **Transparency 3–17.** Have students read a possible birth announcement. Ask questions such as: *Who are the parents? When was Vitaline born? Where was she born? What other information is included?*

You might use a graphic organizer like the following one to record the information in the announcement.

Who?	What?	Where?	When?	Why?	How?
Monsieur and Madame Prosperine	birth of their daughter, Vitaline	Martinique General Hospital	November 5	Vitaline is named for Madame's grand-mother.	delivered by Dr. Davide

Discuss with students the guidelines for writing an announcement.

Guidelines for
Writing an Announcement

- Have a clear purpose for writing an announcement.
- Write down all the important information.
- Include dates, times, places, and costs or fees if appropriate. Be exact and specific.
- Include a few interesting details.
- Use friendly language that your audience will understand.

Transparency 3–17

Writing an Announcement

Transparency 3–18

Ordering Important Information

- When writing an announcement, first decide what information is most important. Put that information first.
- Put other information in order of importance from most important to least important.
- Be sure your announcement includes all the necessary information that answers some or all of these questions: who, what, where, when, why, how.

Announcement

It will be a fancy-dress costume ball.
The ball will be given at the Hotel Martinique.
The celebration will begin at 7:00 P.M., and end promptly at 1:00 A.M.
Monsieur and Madame Thibault will hold a celebration ball.
Please come dressed as your favorite fictional character.
The ball is for their son, Paul, on the occasion of his 18th birthday.

1. What information should be first?
2. What information should be second? Third?
3. What information is missing?
4. Where should the missing information go?

Penmanship

 Teacher's Resource Disk: Penmanship Blackline Masters

Use these masters to model correct letter formation, size, and spacing and to give students practice writing legibly in cursive.

▶ Apply

Assign **Practice Book** page 188. Have students use it to write an announcement about a birth, wedding, concert, fair, parade, or other special event. Remind students to include all the important information, including what the event or occasion is, when, where, how, why, and who. Use friendly language that will appeal to your audience and add a few interesting details to the announcement.

Improving Your Writing
Ordering Important Information

Teach Remind students that announcements are like short news items. Tell them that the most important information is always first. The details that follow are in order of importance from most to least. In a birth announcement, the most important information is who gave birth, followed by the baby's gender. The information that follows that may include the baby's birth weight and length, name, and the hospital or facility where the baby was born. For an announcement about a parade, the most important information is when.

Practice To model how to order important information, display **Transparency 3–18.** Have students read the possible announcement. Discuss the order of information in the announcement. Ask students to identify the sentence that should be first. Then have them order the rest of the information. As students put the information in order of importance, they should notice that an important piece of information is missing from the announcement. (the date) Have them suggest where in the announcement the missing information should go. (after or before *where*)

Apply Assign **Practice Book** page 189. Then have students review their announcements for order of information from most to least important. Have students exchange announcements with a partner. Let partners proofread each other's announcements to be sure no important information is missing.

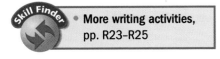
Skill Finder • More writing activities, pp. R23–R25

Technology

The Writer's Resource Library

Students may use this set of reference tools as they work on their own writing.

©Sunburst Technology Corporation, a Houghton Mifflin Company. All Rights Reserved.

Type to Learn™

Students may use **Type to Learn™** to learn proper keyboarding technique.

©Sunburst Technology Corporation, a Houghton Mifflin Company. All Rights Reserved.

Portfolio Opportunity

Save students' announcements as samples of their writing development.

⋯⋯⋯ **Houghton Mifflin English** ⋯⋯⋯
Correlated instruction and practice, p. 99

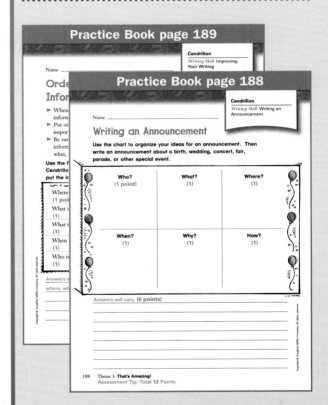

Practice Book page 189

Cendrillon
Writing Skill Improving Your Writing

Name _____

Orde
Infor

▶ When
inform
▶ Put ot
impor
▶ Be sur
inform
what,

Use the
Cendrillon
put the in

Practice Book page 188

Cendrillon
Writing Skill Writing an Announcement

Name _____

Writing an Announcement

Use the chart to organize your ideas for an announcement. Then write an announcement about a birth, wedding, concert, fair, parade, or other special event.

Who? (1 point)	What? (1)	Where? (1)
When? (1)	Why? (1)	How? (1)

Answers will vary. **(6 points)**

188 Theme 3: **That's Amazing!**
Assessment Tip: Total **12 Points**

Writing Skills (357N)

Listening/Speaking/Viewing
Compare and Contrast Texts

▶ **Teach**

Discuss with students how appreciating a good story may involve comparing it with other stories, or with other versions of the same story. Have them recall that *Cendrillon* is a version of the familiar story of Cinderella, but with a different setting and with certain details about the story events and characters changed. Explain to students that good readers often compare and contrast story details. They stop and ask themselves questions such as the following:

■ How does this version of the story compare with the version you know? Are the story events different or similar? What do I think of the differences?

■ How do the characters in this version differ from the characters in the traditional version? How are they similar? What do I think of the differences?

■ How does the setting of this version differ from the setting of the traditional version? What do I think of the differences?

Locate a copy of the traditional Cinderella story in the library and read it aloud to students. Then have students compare and contrast it with *Cendrillon*. Use prompts such as those that follow. Chart students' responses.

■ One version takes place in Europe. What is the setting of the other version?

■ In one version the heroine's godmother is a fairy. What is she in the other?

■ In one version the coach is made from a pumpkin. What is it made from in the other?

■ In one version the ball is given by a prince. Who gives the ball in the other?

■ In one version the heroine's slipper is made of glass. What is it made of in the other?

Reaching All Students
English Language Learners

Have students work in small mixed groups to compare and contrast *Cinderella* and *Cendrillon*. Show students how to begin with a two-columned chart that looks point by point at the two stories. Guide students in comparing characters, setting, and other story elements. Model responding to questions, such as *How do the characters differ?*

Ask students what they think of each difference between the two versions. Does it improve the story? Does it fit better with the changed setting? Does it give the reader a new understanding of events or characters?

▶ Practice

Have small groups of students create a Venn diagram to compare and contrast the traditional Cinderella story with *Cendrillon*. Their diagrams should list which features are common to both versions, which ones exist only in the traditional version, and which ones exist only in *Cendrillon*.

▶ Apply

Ask the same small groups to focus on the character of Cendrillon. Ask them to list all the ways in which she is the same as, or differs from, the traditional Cinderella. Students should think about where Cendrillon lives, what she wears, the work she does, what she eats, and the like. Have groups share their lists with the class.

Improving Listening and Speaking Skills

Share with students the following tips for comparing and contrasting texts:

- As you read a story, ask yourself, "How is this story the same as or different from other stories that I have read? Are the story events similar? What are the differences?"

- As you read about a character, ask yourself, "Does this character remind me of a character from another story that I have read? What are the similarities? What are the differences?"

- When you compare and contrast characters and story events, ask yourself, "What do I think about any similarities or differences? What do they tell me about the characters and events in each story?"

Skill Reminder

Noting Details; Taking Notes

Review with students that writing story details on note cards will help them to organize and remember information. Remind them that when noting details they must distinguish between important and less important details. Read this passage from *Cendrillon* (page 335):

Cendrillon often had only a handful of manioc flour and tail ends of codfish. All day she worked. At night she slept on a hard straw pallet.

Ask students: Which details from this passage would you record on a note card? (Cendrillon worked all day and didn't have much to eat.)

Then ask: Name some less important details from the passage. (Cendrillon ate manioc and codfish ends; she slept on a hard pallet.)

Taught: *Grade 4, Theme 1*
Reviewed: *Grade 4, Theme 2*

Spiral Review

Grammar: *Common and Proper Nouns, Singular and Plural Nouns*

➤ Review

Review what students have learned about common and proper nouns, and singular and plural nouns:

- A common noun names any person, place, or thing. *(girl, park, shell)*

- A proper noun names a particular person, place, or thing. A proper noun begins with a capital letter and may consist of more than one word. *(Caribbean Sea)*

- A singular noun names one person, place, or thing. *(that gown)*

- A plural noun names more than one person, place, or thing. *(two gowns)* To form the plural of most nouns, add *-s* to the singular noun. *(bracelet, bracelets)*

- To form the plural of a singular noun ending in *s, x, ch, or sh,* add *-es* to the singular noun. *(coach, coaches)*

- To form the plural of a singular noun ending in a consonant and *y,* change the *y* to *i* and add *-es. (baby, babies)*

- Some singular nouns have special plural forms. *(tooth, teeth)* Some nouns have the same form for singular and plural. *(one sheep, three sheep)*

➤ Apply

Have students form teams of three to find nouns in *Cendrillon.* Explain that teams will have five minutes to find and list as many nouns as possible. One team member should list singular common nouns, another plural common nouns, and the third proper nouns. Each student should label his or her list and search for only that type of noun. Explain that singular common nouns are worth 1 point, plural common nouns 2 points, and proper nouns 3 points. Tell them that a word will not count if it is written incorrectly or included on the wrong list. After the five minutes are up, teams should display their lists for checking. The team with the most points wins.

- **Common Nouns** Grade 4, Theme 1, p. 133K
- **Proper Nouns** Grade 4, Theme 2, p. 181K
- **Singular and Plural Nouns** Grade 4, Theme 2, p. 215K
- **More Plural Nouns** Grade 4, Theme 2, p. 245K

Writing: *Using Commas in Dates and Places*

▶ Review

Review using commas in dates and places with students.

- In dates, a comma is added between the day and year, as in *March 15, 1993.*

- A comma is also added after the year if the date appears in a sentence in any position except at the end, as in *Magda was born on March 15, 1993, in Maine.*

- In place names, a comma is added between the town or city and the state, as in *Bangor, Maine.*

- A comma is also added after the state if the two place names appear together in a sentence in any position except at the end. Write the following example on the chalkboard:

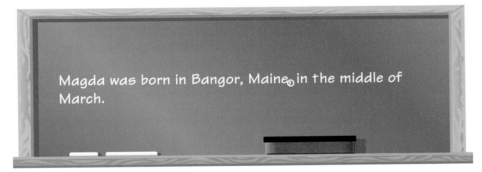

Magda was born in Bangor, Maine, in the middle of March.

Write these sentences on the board and have students insert commas where they are needed in the dates and place names:

Magda wrote a version of the Cinderella story on June 22 2002. (June 22, 2002)

She sent her story to a magazine in Boston Massachusetts. (Boston, Massachusetts)

The editor replied on August 1 2002 and said he liked her story. (August 1, 2002,)

▶ Apply

Have students work in pairs to write five sentences that include dates and places. Ask them to leave out the commas. Then have pairs exchange papers and correct the sentences by adding the missing commas. When pairs have finished, have them exchange papers again to check the work.

Using Commas in Dates and Places Grade 4, Theme 1, p. 133N

Skill Reminder

Alphabetical Order; Guide Words; Using a Thesaurus

Review with students that the guide words at the top of a dictionary page are the first and last entry words on that page. All of the other entries on the page fall in alphabetical order between the two guide words. Write the guide words *scheme/score, shaggy/share,* and *sheet/ship* on the board. Have students tell under which set of guide words the word *sherbet* would fall. (sheet/ship)

Remind students that a thesaurus is a book of synonyms. It helps a writer find a word with just the right shade of meaning. Have students use a thesaurus to find synonyms for the word *elegant,* as in *elegant pink slippers.* (fancy, stylish, grand, fine)

Taught: *Grade 4, Theme 1*
Reviewed: *Grade 4, Theme 2*

Heat Wave!
Different texts for different purposes

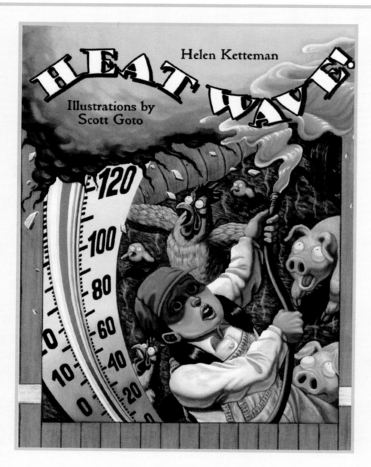

Helen Ketteman

Illustrations by Scott Goto

Anthology: Main Selection

Purposes

- strategy focus: evaluate
- comprehension skill: fantasy/realism
- vocabulary development
- critical thinking, discussion

Genre: Tall Tale

Characters with exaggerated qualities and abilities perform fantastic feats.

Selection Summary

A fantastic heat wave hits a Kansas farm, roasting the geese, popping the corn in the fields, and causing other distressing events. The farm girl tries a few clever ways to get rid of it, and finally succeeds when she plants iceberg lettuce.

Teacher's Edition: Read Aloud

Purposes

- listening comprehension: fantasy/realism
- vocabulary development
- critical thinking, discussion

Anthology: Get Set to Read

Purposes

- background building: heat wave
- developing key vocabulary

Anthology: Content Link

Purposes

- content reading: science
- skill: how to read a diagram
- critical thinking, discussion

Leveled Books and Resources

Use these resources to ensure that students read, outside of class, at least thirty minutes a day. See also Cumulative Listing of Leveled Books.

Reader's Library

Very Easy

One Big Gust
by **Andrew Clements**

(Also available on blackline masters)

Purposes

- fluency practice in below-level text
- alternate reading for students reading significantly below grade level
- strategy application: evaluate
- comprehension skill application: fantasy/realism
- below-level independent reading

Lesson Support

- Lesson Plan, page R6
- Alternate application for Comprehension Skill lesson on fantasy/realism, page 381A
- Reteaching for Comprehension Skill: fantasy/realism, page R12

Selection Summary Masters

Heat Wave!
Teacher's Resource Blackline Masters

Audiotape

Heat Wave!
Audiotape for
That's Amazing!

Theme Paperbacks

Easy

The Story of the Milky Way
by **Joseph Bruchac** and **Gayle Ross**

Lesson, TE page 325I

On Level

Little Oh
by **Laura Krauss Melmed**

Lesson, TE page 325K

Challenge

The Real Thief
by **William Steig**

Lesson, TE page 325M

UNIVERSAL ACCESS
Reaching All Students
Inclusion Strategy

Significantly Below-level Readers

Students reading so far below level that they cannot read *Heat Wave!* even with the suggested Extra Support should still participate with the class whenever possible.

- Include them in the Teacher Read Aloud (p. 358G) and Preparing to Read (pp. 359A–359D).
- Have them listen to *Heat Wave!* on the audiotape for *That's Amazing!* and read the Selection Summary while others read Segment 1 of the selection.
- Have them read "One Big Gust" in the Reader's Library collection for *That's Amazing!* while others read Segment 2 of *Heat Wave!*.
- Have all students participate in Wrapping Up Segment 2 (p. 377) and Responding (p. 378).

Technology

Get Set for Reading CD-ROM
Heat Wave!

Provides background building, vocabulary support, and selection summaries in English and Spanish.

Education Place
www.eduplace.com

Log on to Education Place for more activities relating to *Heat Wave!*.

Book Adventure
www.bookadventure.org

This Internet reading incentive program provides thousands of titles for students to read.

Daily Lesson Plans

Instructional Goals	Day 1	Day 2

Reading
60–80 minutes

Strategy Focus: Evaluate

✓ **Comprehension Skill:** Fantasy and Realism

Comprehension Skill Review: Compare and Contrast; Story Structure

✓ **Information and Study Skills:** Real-life Reading

Day 1

Teacher Read Aloud
Yes, It Really Can Rain Frogs!, 358G

Preparing to Read *Heat Wave!*
- Get Set, *359A*
- Key Vocabulary, *359B; Practice Book, 190*
- Strategy/Skill Preview, *359C*
  Fantasy/Realism Chart, *Practice Book, 191*

Reading Segment 1, *Heat Wave!, 360–367*
- Supporting Comprehension
- Strategy Focus, *364*

Wrapping Up Segment 1, *367*

Day 2

Reading Segment 2
Heat Wave!, 368–377
- Supporting Comprehension
- Strategy Focus, *372*

Wrapping Up Segment 2, *377*

Responding
- Comprehension Questions: Think About the Selection, *378*
- Comprehension Check, *Practice Book, 192*

Rereading/Revisiting the Text
- Comprehension: Fantasy and Realism, *365*

Word Work
30–40 minutes

✓ **Spelling:** Words Ending with *-ed* or *-ing*

Decoding Longer Words:

✓ **Structural Analysis:** Words Ending with *-ed* or *-ing*

Phonics: Consonant Digraphs

✓ **Vocabulary:** Dictionary: Dividing Words into Syllables

Day 1

Spelling
- Pretest, *381G*
- Instruction: Words Ending with *-ed* or *-ing*, *381G*
- Take-Home Word List, ***Practice Book: Handbook***

Day 2

Decoding Longer Words Instruction
- Structural Analysis: Words Ending with *-ed* or *-ing*, *381E*
- *Practice Book, 195*

Spelling
- *Practice Book, 196*

Writing & Language
30–40 minutes

✓ **Grammar:** Present, Past, and Future Tenses

✓ **Writing:** Writing a Summary; Paraphrasing

Listening/Speaking/Viewing: Listen to and Make an Announcement

Day 1

Daily Language Practice, *381L*

Grammar Instruction
- Present, Past, and Future Tenses, *381K*

 Writing
- Journal Writing, *361*

Day 2

Daily Language Practice, *381L*

Grammar Instruction
- *Practice Book, 200*

 Writing Instruction
- Journal Writing, *368*
- Writing a Summary, *381M*
- *Practice Book, 203*

Teacher's Notes

Leveled Books, pp. 325H–325N
For reading outside of class and homework

Technology

Lesson Planner CD-ROM
Customize your planning with the Lesson Planner.

Day 3

Rereading/Revisiting the Text
- Genre: Tall Tales, *363*
- Visual Literacy: Artist's Style, *375*

Comprehension Skill Instruction
- Fantasy and Realism, *381A*
- *Practice Book, 193–194*

Phonics Instruction
- Consonant Digraphs, *381F*

Spelling
- *Practice Book, 197*

Daily Language Practice, *381L*

Grammar Instruction
- Tense Times, *381L*

Writing
- Narrating: Write a Sequel, *378*

Day 4

Comprehension Skill Instruction
- Reteaching Fantasy/Realism with Reader's Library, *R12*

Reading the Science Link
- "Constructing a Straw Thermometer," *380–381*

Information and Study Skills Instruction
- Real-life Reading, *381C*

Decoding Longer Words
- Reteaching Structural Analysis: Words Ending with *-ed* or *-ing, R18*
- Challenge/Extension Activities, *R19*

Spelling
- Grab Bag Spelling, *381H*
- *Practice Book, 198*

Vocabulary Skill Instruction
- Dictionary: Dividing Words into Syllables, *381I*
- *Practice Book, 199*

Daily Language Practice, *381L*

Grammar
- Reteaching, *R22*
- *Practice Book, 201*

Writing
- Paraphrasing, *381N*
- *Practice Book, 204*

Listening/Speaking/Viewing
- Listen to and Make an Announcement, *381O*

Day 5

Rereading/Revisiting the Text:
Comprehension Review Skill Instruction
- Compare and Contrast, *369*
- Story Structure, *371*

Rereading for Fluency
Heat Wave!, 360–377

Activity Choices
- Responding Activities, *378*
- Challenge/Extension, *R13*
- Cross-Curricular Activities, *R26–R27*

Spiral Review, *381Q*

Vocabulary Expansion
- Scientific Terms: Climate Words, *381J*

Spelling
- Posttest, *381H*

Spiral Review, *381R*

Daily Language Practice, *381L*

Grammar
- Using the Correct Tense, *381L*
- *Practice Book, 202*

Writing
- Writing Activities, *R23–R25*
- Sharing Students' Writing: Author's Chair

Reading-Writing Workshop: Story, pp. 324–325G

See Universal Access Planning Chart on the following pages.

Universal Access Plans
for Reaching All Learners

Grouping for Instruction

	Day 1	**Day 2**
30–45 minutes		
With the Teacher **Extra Support** **Teach**—Use Extra Support Handbook	**Preteach** Words with *-ed* or *-ing* **Preview** Selection, Segment 1 ◼ Extra Support Handbook pp. 118–119	**Preteach** Fantasy and Realism **Preview** Selection, Segment 2 ◼ Extra Support Handbook pp. 120–121
Working Independently **On Level** Use Classroom Management Handbook **Challenge** Use Challenge Handbook **English Language Learners** Use Classroom Management Handbook or Challenge Handbook	**Independent Activities** For each group, assign appropriate activities—your own or those in the handbooks listed below. Then get students started on their independent work. ◼ Classroom Management Handbook pp. 44–45 ◼ Challenge Handbook pp. 26–27	**See plan for Day 1** **Monitor** Answer questions, if necessary.
30–45 minutes		
With the Teacher **English Language Learners** **Teach**—Use Handbook for English Language Learners	**Preteach** Heat **Preteach** Get Set to Read; Selection, Segment 1 **Preteach** Structural Analysis: Words with *-ed* or *-ing* ◼ Handbook for ELL pp. 122–123	**Preteach** Snacks **Preteach** Selection, Segment 2 **Reteach** Grammar: Present, Past, and Future Tenses ◼ Handbook for ELL pp. 124–125
Working Independently **On Level** Use Classroom Management Handbook **Challenge** Use Challenge Handbook **Extra Support** Use Classroom Management Handbook	**Independent Activities** Students can continue their assigned activities, or you can assign new activities from the handbooks below. ◼ Classroom Management Handbook pp. 44–45 ◼ Challenge Handbook pp. 26–27	**See plan for Day 1** **Monitor** Partner Extra Support students, if needed.

Independent Activities

Classroom Management Handbook
- Daily Activities
- Grouping
- Management

Resources for Reaching All Learners

Extra Support Handbook
- Daily Lessons
- Preteaching and Reteaching
- Skill Support

Handbook for English Language Learners
- Daily Lessons
- Language Development
- Skill Support

Challenge Handbook
- Independent Activities
- Instructional Support

Day 3

Reteach Words with -ed or -ing
Review Selection
- Extra Support Handbook   pp. 122–123

See plan for Day 1

Check in
Reinforce instruction, if needed.

Preteach Midwestern States
Preteach Vocabulary/Dictionary: Dividing Words into Syllables
- Handbook for ELL   pp. 126–127

See plan for Day 1

Check in
Reinforce instruction, if needed.

Day 4

Reteach Present, Past, and Future Tenses
Preview *The Big Gust*
- Extra Support Handbook   pp. 124–125

See plan for Day 1

Check in
Regroup English learners, if needed.

Preteach Making Bread
Reteach Selection Summary and Review
Reteach Grammar: Present, Past, and Future Tenses
- Handbook for ELL   pp. 128–129

See plan for Day 1

Monitor
How well are challenge projects progressing?

Day 5

Reteach Fantasy and Realism
Revisit Selection and *The Big Gust*
- Extra Support Handbook   pp. 126–127

See plan for Day 1

Build confidence
Reinforce successful independent work.

Preteach Salads
Reteach Writing: Paraphrasing
- Handbook for ELL   pp. 130–131

See plan for Day 1

Share work
Allow students time to share work.

Reading Instruction

DAY 1	• Teacher Read Aloud • Preparing to Read • Reading the Selection, Segment 1
DAY 2	• Reading the Selection, Segment 2 • Responding
DAY 3	• Revisiting the Text • Comprehension Skill Instruction
DAY 4	• Comprehension Skill Reteaching • Reading the Content Link • Information and Study Skills Instruction
DAY 5	• Comprehension Skill Review • Activity Choices

OBJECTIVES

Students listen to the selection to identify elements of fantasy and realism.

▶ **Activate Prior Knowledge**

Connecting to the Theme Use these suggestions to help students connect the selection with what they know:

■ Ask students whether they think this will be a fantasy or a realistic selection. Why?

■ Have students discuss odd weather events they have heard about or experienced.

Reaching All Students

English Language Learners

Preview the names of the strange rains and animals *(frogs, snails, clams, snakes)*. Ask an English-speaking volunteer to help explain the expression "it's raining cats and dogs" and clarify the references to Garfield and Lassie.

Teacher Read Aloud

✓ Listening Comprehension: Fantasy and Realism

Yes, It Can Really Rain Frogs! Rain of All Sorts

by Spencer Christian and Antonia Felix

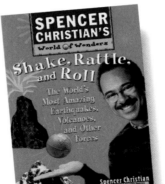

This article explains why frogs and other strange things sometimes fall from the sky.

1 Do you think this might be a fantasy or a real event? Explain your answer. (Sample answers: This might be a fantasy, because fish do not fall from the sky; this sounds like a fantasy but it might be a real event, because the author includes names and dates. There might be a realistic explanation for fish falling from the sky.)

J ust before eight o'clock one Thursday morning in October 1947, a man named A. D. Bajkov and his wife were having breakfast at a restaurant in Marksville, Louisiana, when the waitress came over to their table and made an odd announcement: "Fish are falling from the sky!"

Mr. and Mrs. Bajkov rushed outside to see what all the excitement was about. Sure enough, covering the streets, roofs, and yards, and hanging in the trees of the small town were thousands of fresh fish, flapping about in the morning fog.

When we say "It's raining cats and dogs," we don't mean that Garfields and Lassies are falling from the sky—it's just an expression we use to describe heavy rain. But it really did rain fish on that morning in 1947. How could this happen?

Raining Snakes, Frogs, and Fish

No one has ever observed snakes, frogs, fish, or other animals being carried up into the skies. The only logical explanation for these strange rains, however, is that the culprits are tornadoes, columns of air that drop down from storm clouds and twirl at very high speed, or waterspouts, tornadoes that touch down on water instead of land. There are numerous accounts of tornadoes picking up trucks, automobiles, farm equipment, even entire houses, and depositing them elsewhere.

2 Large waterspouts have been reported picking up objects as big as a 5-ton houseboat, so it makes sense that they could pick up small creatures like fish and frogs. Once aloft, the living debris could be carried tens, perhaps hundreds, of miles by powerful winds before plummeting to Earth in the downdrafts of a thunderstorm, or dropped when the wind died down.

2 How can snakes, frogs, and fish really fall from the sky?
(Sample answer: Tornadoes and water-spouts can pick up large objects such as a houseboat. Frogs and fish could be picked up and then dropped down like rain.)

Listening Comprehension:
✓ Fantasy and Realism

Explain to students that fantasy involves events that could not happen in real life. Realism involves things that could happen or that have happened. Point out that authors can also use different techniques to help the reader know whether a story is fantasy or realistic.

Use the questions in the margin to assess students' understanding as you read. Reread for clarification as needed.

There have also been accounts in ancient writings of red, yellow, and milk-white downpours, sometimes described as rains of blood or milk. These rains were probably colored by small particles of dust or plant pollen that had been blown great distances. The Sahara Desert contains areas of reddish iron dust picked up by desert whirlwinds, and in some areas red algae grows so quickly after a storm that it seems as if it fell from the sky. Yellow rains result when certain tree pollens are blown upwards. And gray volcanic ash blown into the sky mixes with water to form a white rain that looks like milk.

Some of History's Weirdest, Wackiest, and Totally Bizarre Rains

Eighteen hundred years ago, two towns in Greece experienced a rain of frogs so thick, the ground was completely covered with heaps of the slippery, slimy creatures! Unable to walk the streets or find a water supply that wasn't packed with frogs, most people left town and never came back!

Snails fell with a slow, whirling motion during a light rain shower over Chester, Pennsylvania, in 1869, and a similar report of hundreds of thousands of snails falling from the sky came from Algiers in 1953.

A boy who was walking in the rain in Yuma, Arizona, in 1941 was hit on the shoulder by a falling clam.

Live, dark brown snakes, from 12 to 18 inches long, covered the ground after a torrential rain on Memphis, Tennessee, on December 15, 1876.

Near Dubuque, Iowa, in 1882, a hailstone **3** containing two live frogs fell to the ground. After the ice melted, the frogs hopped away!

3 What clues tell you that these events really occurred? (Sample answer: The title says that these events occurred in history; the author provides dates and locations for each event.)

▶ **Discussion**

Summarize After reading, discuss parts of the selection that students may have found confusing or especially interesting. Then ask them to summarize the selection.

Listening Comprehension:
✓ **Fantasy and Realism** Have students list real events from the selection that they would normally think were fantasy. Write their responses on the board.

Personal Response Ask students what they would do if they had to tell about something real that would normally seem impossible.

★ **Connecting/Comparing** Have students compare the events described in this selection with the events in *Cendrillon*.

Anthology

HEAT WAVE!

Helen Ketteman

Illustrations by
Scott Goto

Technology

Get Set for Reading CD-ROM

Heat Wave!

Provides background building, vocabulary support, and selection summaries in English and Spanish.

Preparing to Read

▶ Using *Get Set* for Background and Vocabulary

Connecting to the Theme Remind students that the stories in this theme all deal with extraordinary and incredible events. In the previous selection, students read about a Caribbean Cinderella and her amazing good fortune. Now they will read *Heat Wave!*, a tall tale about how a Kansas farm girl's quick thinking ends an amazing heat wave. Discuss with students the effects a heat wave may have. Use the Get Set to Read on pages 358–359 to introduce some information on real heat waves.

■ Have a volunteer read aloud "What Is a Heat Wave?"

■ Go over the pictures, having someone read aloud the captions. Discuss the characteristics of a heat wave and what can be done to survive one.

■ Ask students to define the boldfaced Key Vocabulary words: *temperature, singe, horizon,* and *affected.* Have students use each word to discuss a heat wave.

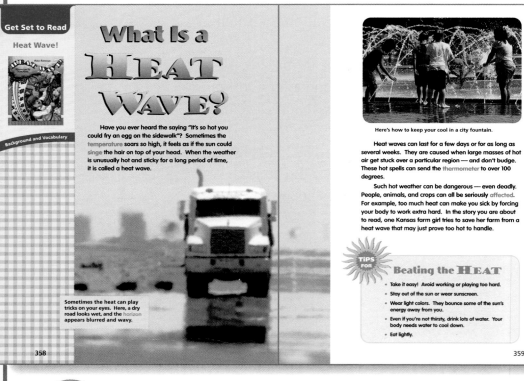

Get Set to Read

Heat Wave!

Background and Vocabulary

What Is a HEAT WAVE?

Have you ever heard the saying "It's so hot you could fry an egg on the sidewalk"? Sometimes the temperature soars so high, it feels as if the sun could singe the hair on top of your head. When the weather is unusually hot and sticky for a long period of time, it is called a heat wave.

Sometimes the heat can play tricks on your eyes. Here, a dry road looks wet, and the horizon appears blurred and wavy.

Here's how to keep your cool in a city fountain.

Heat waves can last for a few days or for as long as several weeks. They are caused when large masses of hot air get stuck over a particular region — and don't budge. These hot spells can send the thermometer to over 100 degrees.

Such hot weather can be dangerous — even deadly. People, animals, and crops can all be seriously affected. For example, too much heat can make you sick by forcing your body to work extra hard. In the story you are about to read, one Kansas farm girl tries to save her farm from a heat wave that may just prove too hot to handle.

TIPS FOR

Beating the HEAT

• Take it easy! Avoid working or playing too hard.
• Stay out of the sun or wear sunscreen.
• Wear light colors. They bounce some of the sun's energy away from you.
• Even if you're not thirsty, drink lots of water. Your body needs water to cool down.
• Eat lightly.

358

359

Reaching All Students

English Language Learners

Explain *heat wave;* discuss heat waves students have experienced. Ask students how they kept cool. Point out the similar spelling and rhyme in *beat* and *heat* on page 359. List key vocabulary. Ask students to determine the entry words for *affected* and *miscalculated.*

Vocabulary

▶ Developing Key Vocabulary

Use **Transparency 3–19** to introduce weather-related words from *Heat Wave!*

- Model how to figure out that *horizon* goes in the first blank by studying the sentence's context for clues.

- For each remaining blank, ask students to use clues from the context to decide which word best fits. Have students explain their reasoning.

Remind students that it's helpful to use the Phonics/Decoding Strategy when they read. For students who need more help with decoding, use the review below.

Practice/Homework Practice Book page 190.

Strategy Review
Phonics/Decoding

Modeling Write this sentence from *Heat Wave!* on the board, and point to *crinkled*.

> I saw a big old clump of <u>crinkled</u>, yellow air rolling across the sky.

Think Aloud

When I read the letters from left to right, I see the shorter word led. The first part probably sounds like /krihnk/. /krihnk•led/ That's definitely not a word I've heard before! I know the le spelling sometimes makes the /uhl/ sound at the end of a word like middle. /krihnk•uhld/ I know that word. /KRING•kuhld/ means sort of wrinkled. That makes sense.

> **Decoding Longer Words,** pp. 381E–381F

Key Concept
heat waves

Key Vocabulary

<u>affected</u>: caused a change in

<u>horizon</u>: line along which the earth and sky seem to meet

<u>miscalculated</u>: figured incorrectly

<u>singe</u>: to burn slightly

<u>temperature</u>: measure of heat or coldness

<u>weather vane</u>: movable pointer that shows wind direction

See Vocabulary notes on pages 362, 364, 366, 368, 370, 372, and 374 for additional words to preview.

Practice Book page 190

Transparency 3–19

Heat Words

| affected | horizon | miscalculated |
| singe | temperature | weather vane |

When you look out at the _____, you can sometimes see weather coming from far away. If you see storm clouds in the distance, looking at a _____ to see in which direction the wind is blowing can let you know if the storm is heading your way. Sometimes a storm can bring a big change in the _____, making it cold very fast. Other times, how hot or cold it is outside is barely _____ by a storm.

Have you ever _____ how hot or cold it would be during the day? You probably got stuck wearing too many clothes or not enough clothes. Neither way is very comfortable. You can feel as if the heat is about to warm, or even _____, your skin, or you can feel your fingertips begin to freeze.

It's always good to be aware of the weather so you don't get caught unprepared.

Teacher's Note

Strategy/Skill Connection For a better understanding of *Heat Wave!*, students can use the

- Evaluate Strategy
- Fantasy and Realism Comprehension Skill

Understanding which parts of a story are fantasy and which are real will allow students to better evaluate how well the author tells it.

As students complete their *Heat Wave!* Fantasy/Realism Chart (**Practice Book** page 191 and **Transparency 3–20**), they can use their answers to evaluate how well the author has succeeded at making this story funny and incredible.

Reading Strategy

▶ **Strategy Focus:**
Evaluate

Strategy Focus

What amazing things happen when a heat wave strikes a Kansas farm? **Evaluate** how the author and the illustrator make this story funny and incredible.

Have students turn to Anthology page 360 as you read aloud the selection's title and author. Ask someone to read the Strategy Focus. Give students a moment to read silently page 361, telling them to think about the Evaluate strategy. Then ask students to evaluate how the author and illustrator make the opening of the story both funny and incredible. Record their responses.

Teacher Modeling Review with students how to evaluate what they read. Tell them to pay attention to the fantastic and realistic details in the story as they evaluate. Then model the strategy.

Think Aloud

After reading this first page, I can tell that this story is probably going to be funny. The author describes geese being plucked, stuffed, and roasted, which can happen. But that can't happen by simply flying in hot weather. Combining fantasy with reality makes this part of the story funny. The author has done a very good job so far.

Tell students that asking questions about the story and using other reading strategies may help them better evaluate if the author has succeeded in telling a funny and incredible tale.

Comprehension Skill

✓ Comprehension Skill Focus:
Fantasy and Realism

Fantasy/Realism Chart Explain that as students read *Heat Wave!*, they will focus on fantasy and realism. To develop this skill, students will examine story details, deciding which ones are made up and which ones can really happen. They will record their thoughts on a fantasy/realism chart. Display **Transparency 3–20** and demonstrate how to use the graphic organizer.

- Return to page 361 and ask someone to read it aloud.

- Ask one student to offer an example of fantasy on this page and another student to provide an example of realism.

- Model how to record the answers in the chart. Have students copy these answers onto **Practice Book** page 191.

- Ask students to complete their charts as they read. Direct students to find one example of both fantasy and realism on the pages indicated and remind them that their answers may vary a bit. Monitor their work, or have students check each other's charts.

Page	Story Detail (accept varied answers)	Fantasy (F)/Realism (R)
361	Geese are plucked, stuffed, and roasted.	R
	Geese are cooked in the sky.	F
367	Milk is churned into butter.	R
	Cows' jumping causes the milk to become butter.	F

Transparency 3–20

Fantasy/Realism Chart

Page	Story Detail	Fantasy (F)/Realism (R)
361		
367		
368		
371		
375		

THAT'S AMAZING Heat Wave!
Graphic Organizer Fantasy/Realism Chart
TRANSPARENCY 3–20
TEACHER'S EDITION PAGES T359D AND T361A
Copyright © Houghton Mifflin Company. All rights reserved.

Practice Book page 191

Name _____

Heat Wave!
Graphic Organizer
Fantasy/Realism Chart

Fantasy/Realism Chart

Page	Story Detail (accept varied answers)	Fantasy (F)/Realism (R)
361	Geese are plucked, stuffed, and roasted. / Geese are cooked in the sky. (2 points)	R / F (1 point)
367	Milk is churned into butter. / Cows jumping causes the milk to become butter. (2)	R / F (1)
368	Getting oats wet makes oatmeal. / Oatmeal makes fine glue. (2)	R / F (1)
371	Adding water to flour and yeast makes dough. / The rising dough picks up the tractor and the mule. (2)	R / F (1)
375	They plant lettuce seeds and lettuce grows. / Lettuce grows as soon as the seeds hit the dirt. (2)	R / F (1)

Theme 3: **That's Amazing!** 191
Assessment Tip: Total **15 Points**

Focus Questions

Have students turn to Responding on page 378. Read the questions aloud and tell students to keep them in mind as they read *Heat Wave!*

Reading

Selection 3

Options for Reading

▶ **Reading in Segments** Students can read *Heat Wave!* in two segments (pages 360–367 and 368–377) or in its entirety.

▶ **Deciding About Support** Far-out humor in text and illustrations make this story fun to read.

■ Straightforward narration and detail-rich illustrations will enable most students to follow On Level reading instruction.

■ Students unfamiliar with the exaggeration, nonsense, and jokes common to tall tales may have trouble getting into the story. These students will benefit from Extra Support.

■ Significantly below-level readers can listen to the Audiotape and read the Selection Summary for *Heat Wave!* and then read "The Big Gust" in the **Reader's Library**.

▶ **Universal Access** Use the notes at the bottom of the pages.

Helen Ketteman

Illustrations by Scott Goto

Strategy Focus

What amazing things happen when a heat wave strikes a Kansas farm? **Evaluate** how the author and the illustrator make this story funny and incredible.

360

Reaching All Students

Classroom Management

On Level

Reading Card 8

While Reading: Fantasy/Realism Chart (**Practice Book** page 191); Literature Discussion (p. 366, Reading Card 8); generate questions

After Reading: Literature Discussion (page 376); Wrapping Up Segment 1 (page 367) and Segment 2 (page 377)

Challenge

Reading Cards 7–9

While Reading: Fantasy/Realism Chart (**Practice Book** page 191); Character's Perspective (p. 365, Reading Card 7); Double-Meaning Words (p. 375, Reading Card 9)

After Reading: Literature Discussion (page 376); Wrapping Up Segment 1 (page 367) and Segment 2 (page 377)

English Language Learners

Intermediate and Advanced Fluency Read this selection as a group with students reading a paragraph aloud, in turn. As students listen, they can try to figure out new vocabulary from the context and illustrations. For students at other levels, use the **Handbook for English Language Learners.**

My big brother, Hank, used to tease me that girls couldn't be farmers. But he sure changed his tune the day the Heat Wave hit.

I was feeding the chickens when I heard a loud roar. I looked out across the <u>horizon</u> and saw a big old <u>clump</u> of <u>crinkled</u>, yellow air rolling across the sky. A flock of geese flew in one side and came out the other side plucked, stuffed, and roasted.

361

Reading Segment 1
pages 360–367

Purpose Setting As students read have them evaluate why the story is fun and note how the exaggerated illustrations add to the overall enjoyment of this tall tale.

 Journal Writing Students can evaluate and record if and why they feel the author has succeeded in entertaining the readers of *Heat Wave!*

Reinforcing Comprehension and Strategies

- Remind students to use Evaluate and other strategies as they read and to add to their Fantasy/Realism Chart (**Practice Book** page 191).

- Use the Strategy Focus note on page 363 to reinforce the Evaluate strategy.

- Use Supporting Comprehension questions beginning on page 362 to help students develop higher-level understanding of the text.

Extra Support: Previewing the Text

Before each segment, preview the text, using the notes below and on page 368. **While** reading, model strategies (pages 363, 372, and 375). **After** reading, review each segment (pages 367 and 377) before students join the Wrapping Up discussion.

page 361 The heat wave is beginning. The geese fly into the heat wave and come out of it cooked!

pages 362–363 What details does the author use here to make certain the reader knows this is a tall tale?

pages 364–365 If there is a heat wave, why does the hound dog turn blue and freeze?

pages 366–367 Somehow the narrator and her family can handle the heat enough to milk cows and shovel popcorn. Does this seem realistic to you?

▶ Supporting Comprehension

1 Why does the narrator holler for Ma and Pa and Hank? (because she wants them to see the "heat wave" and the strange thing that happened to the geese)

2 How does the author continue to show that this is no ordinary heat wave? (by having the mercury blast out of the thermometer and the flowers crawl under the porch by their roots)

3 How would you describe the expression on the girl's face in the illustration? (possible answers: amazed, puzzled, not believing her eyes)

Vocabulary (*pages 361 and 363*)

horizon: line along which the earth and the sky seem to meet

clump: a group of things close together

crinkled: wrinkled

mercury: a silvery-white metal that is liquid at room temperature; used in thermometers

---

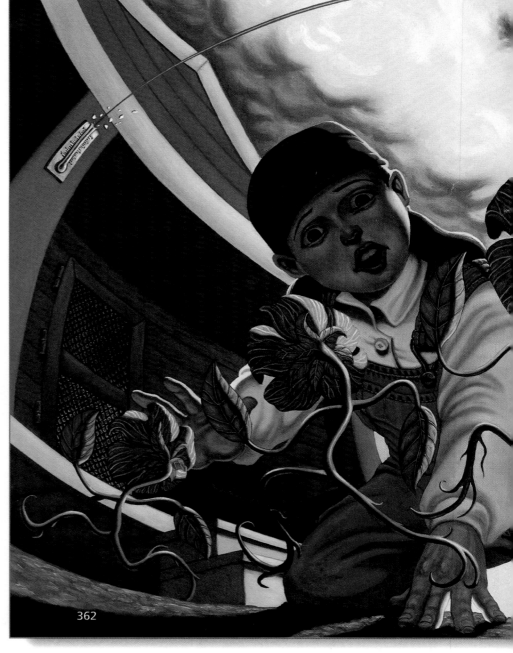

362

 Reaching All Students
English Language Learners

Point out the capital letters on *Heat Wave*. Compare this to a proper name; suggest that students think of the Heat Wave as a character in the story. Say: *As you read, think about the ways the author makes heat seem like a person.* Then have students do a picture walk of the selection.

I hollered for Ma and Pa and Hank, but before they got outside, the Heat Wave hit. The <u>mercury</u> blasted out of the porch thermometer like a rocket. Ma's flowers pulled themselves up by their roots and crawled under the porch looking for shade.

118

363

Reaching All Students
Extra Support

Strategy Modeling

Evaluate If students are having difficulty modeling the strategy, use this example to model it for them.

So far, this story seems crazy. It is hilarious when the geese get cooked in the heat wave and I love the look on the chickens' faces! I think the author has done a good job of making me want to keep reading.

Revisiting the Text

Genre Lesson
Tall Tales

OBJECTIVES

Students identify elements of tall tales in the selection.

Explain the characteristics of tall tales:

- A tall tale is the form of folktale most often tied to the American frontier. Different areas of the country have their own local tall tales.

- There may be some realistic story elements, and a story may be presented as though it were true. But humor often results from the use of *hyperbole*, a figure of speech in which exaggeration is used for effect. Also, the contrast between straightforward narrative and fantastic story elements helps to emphasize the humor.

- Characters are usually "larger than life." Some tall tales are based on made-up exploits of real heroes, such as Annie Oakley. In that sense, they overlap with legends. Other times, characters are made up and could not exist in real life, for example, Paul Bunyan.

- Details of settings are sometimes realistic, but often such things as weather, a mountain to drill through, or the origin of a river are the very point of a tall tale.

Have students look for and point out details of plot, characterization, and setting (including the illustrations) in *Heat Wave!* that make it a tall tale. In small groups discuss how the story might be different if it were written and illustrated as realistic fiction.

Reading

► Strategy Focus: Evaluate

Teacher/Student Modeling Explain that good readers evaluate what they read by asking themselves how they think and feel about a selection. Suggest that one question they might ask themselves about the story so far is "In the author's efforts to entertain and provide humor, does she make the story too ridiculous?" (Possible answer: No. The author creates a fantasy world, but one situation leads to another with its own logic.)

► Supporting Comprehension

4 Why do you think the narrator and her family don't try to unsnag the Heat Wave from the weather vane? (There was time enough only to try to save the harvest and it would probably be far too hot for them to get nearer.)

5 How does the author show that the narrator is starting to show she's quick-thinking? (She is the one who helps thaw out the frozen hound dog.)

Vocabulary *(page 365)*

snagged: caught on something sticking out

weather vane: a movable pointer that shows which way the wind is blowing

harvest: gathering in of crops

blizzard: a long, heavy snowstorm

364

Reaching All Students

English Language Learners

Action Verbs

Ask students to find examples of the many action verbs throughout the story. These include *crinkled* (p. 361), *hollered* (p. 363), *snagged* (p. 365), *raced, hopping, scrubbed, churned* (p. 367), and *dog-paddled* (p. 368). Discuss meanings and have students act out the verbs to show their understanding.

By the time everybody ran outside, the Heat Wave had gotten <u>snagged</u> on the barn's <u>weather vane</u>. It was near <u>harvest</u> time, so we raced to the cornfield to save what we could. But by the time we got there, it was already too late. The corn had started popping. It looked like a <u>blizzard</u> had hit. One of our old hound dogs turned blue and froze when he saw it. I wrapped him in a blanket, and he thawed out okay.

4

5

365

Reaching All Students
Challenge

Reading Card 7

Character's Perspective

The story is told from the perspective—or point of view—of the nameless narrator. Have students consider how the story might be different if told by a third-person narrator or by one of the other characters in the story.

Have students keep in mind

- the features of a tall tale (as described on page 363)
- the idea of a different "voice" for a different narrator

Revisiting the Text

Tested Skill

Comprehension Skill Lesson
Fantasy and Realism

OBJECTIVES

Students tell why a story detail could happen in real life or, if not, why it can exist only in fantasy.

Tell students not to believe everything they read! Write these two sentences on the board.

> Ma's flowers pulled themselves up by their roots and crawled under the porch looking for shade.
>
> Ma's flowers wilted in the heat and fell over.

Point out that the first sentence is fantasy because it could not happen in real life. Explain that most fantasy contains some details that could exist in real life, such as the roots in the first sentence. Ask students if *Heat Wave!* is a fantasy or a realistic story. Have students list four events or details from the story so far, identify each as realistic or fantastic, and explain how they know, using a chart such as this:

Event/Detail	Fantasy (F) or Realism (R)	How I Know

Remind students that the organizer above is similar to the Fantasy/Realism Chart they are using while they read.

Skill Finder

- **Instruction,** pp. 381A–381B
- **Reteaching,** p. R12
- **Review,** Theme 3, p. 347; Theme 4, p. 399

Reading

▶ Supporting Comprehension

6 Why do you think the author tells about the cows now? (to set up the joke of putting butter on the popcorn)

7 How do the narrator's actions connect with what she did before? (By coming up with the solution for the popcorn, she shows quick thinking just as she did with the hound.)

8 Does it make sense that people are at the drive-in movie in the middle of the day in a heat wave? Why did the author include this? (No; this is an excellent example of the nonsense that runs through the story.)

Vocabulary *(page 367)*

commotion: noisy confusion

pasture: land used for animals to graze (eat grass)

churned: stirred or shook greatly

366

 Reaching All Students
Extra Support

Segment 1: Review

Before students join the whole class for Wrapping Up on page 367, have them

- review their purpose
- take turns modeling the Evaluate strategy and any other strategies they used
- add to **Transparency 3–20**, check and revise their Fantasy/Realism Chart on **Practice Book** page 191, and use it to summarize

 Reaching All Students
On Level   Challenge

Reading Card
8

Literature Discussion

In mixed-ability groups of five or six, students can discuss their own questions and the discussion prompts on Reading Card 8.

- Would you enjoy this story as much without the illustrations? Can you imagine a different style of illustration for the story?
- How might a tall tale about a heat wave where you live be similar to this one, and how might it be different?

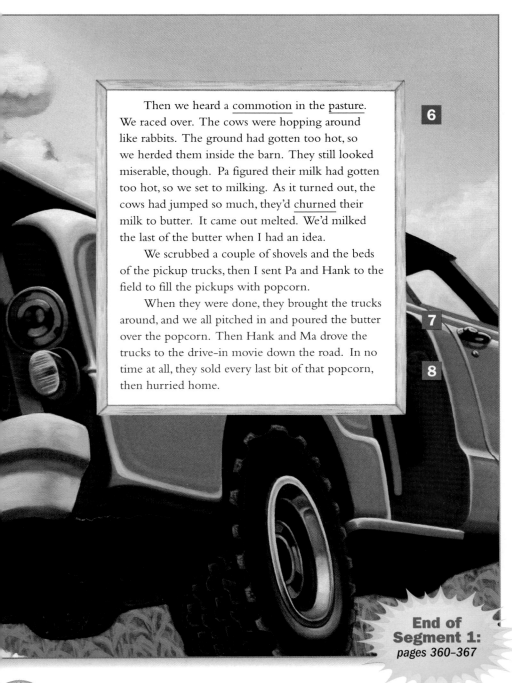

Then we heard a commotion in the pasture. We raced over. The cows were hopping around like rabbits. The ground had gotten too hot, so we herded them inside the barn. They still looked miserable, though. Pa figured their milk had gotten too hot, so we set to milking. As it turned out, the cows had jumped so much, they'd churned their milk to butter. It came out melted. We'd milked the last of the butter when I had an idea.

We scrubbed a couple of shovels and the beds of the pickup trucks, then I sent Pa and Hank to the field to fill the pickups with popcorn.

When they were done, they brought the trucks around, and we all pitched in and poured the butter over the popcorn. Then Hank and Ma drove the trucks to the drive-in movie down the road. In no time at all, they sold every last bit of that popcorn, then hurried home.

End of Segment 1:
pages 360–367

Reaching All Students

English Language Learners

English language learners may be unfamiliar with the cultural reference to selling buttered popcorn at the *drive-in movie* (p. 367). Find out if anyone in the class has seen a movie at a drive-in, and ask volunteers to share what they know. Explain that in the past drive-in movie theaters were common.

Wrapping Up Segment 1
pages 360–367

First, provide Extra Support for students who need it (page 366). Then bring all students together.

- **Review Predictions/Purpose** Discuss ways in which the text and illustrations made for a humorous story.

- **Model Strategies** Refer students to the **Strategies Poster** and have them take turns modeling Evaluate and other strategies they used as they read. Provide models if needed (page 363).

- **Share Group Discussions** Have students share their questions and literature discussions.

- **Summarize** Have students use the transparency and their Fantasy/Realism Chart to summarize the events in the story so far.

Comprehension/Critical Thinking

1 How do you think Hank feels about his sister's quick thinking? (Possible answers: He's jealous because he hasn't come up with any ideas. He's happy because it's helping. He admires it.) **Making Inferences**

2 What is the order of the main events in the story so far? (Geese get cooked in the Heat Wave, Heat Wave gets snagged and hits the farm, the corn pops, the dog freezes and thaws, the hot cows are herded into the barn and "milked," the popcorn is loaded onto the trucks, the butter is poured over it, the popcorn is sold.) Could any of the main events be left out without wrecking the story? (Probably the geese could be left out.) **Sequence of Events**

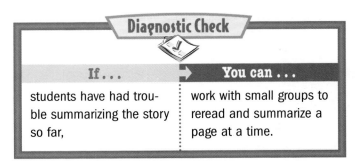

Diagnostic Check

If . . .	You can . . .
students have had trouble summarizing the story so far,	work with small groups to reread and summarize a page at a time.

Reading

Beginning of Segment 2:
pages 368–377

Reading Segment 2

pages 368–377

Purpose Setting Have students summarize the story to this point and evaluate how they feel about it so far. Then have students read pages 368–376.

 Journal Writing Students can record their feelings about the story and if and how those feelings change as they continue reading.

Vocabulary *(page 368)*

dog-paddled: swam holding head above water, paddling with arms in front, and kicking

whiff: slight wind, especially one carrying a smell

singe: burn slightly

We still had plenty of worries. We hurried to the field where we had oats planted. Sure enough, they had dried out. I tried wetting them down, but that didn't turn out to be such a good idea.

Soon I felt something slimy and thick rising up around my ankles. In another minute, it was waist high, and I could barely move. Turned out I'd created a whole field of oatmeal. It was lumpy, just like Ma's, and I about drowned in the stuff.

I dog-paddled to the edge and crawled out. Whoo-ee! That oatmeal was sticky! I told Pa we should bottle it, which we did later. It made fine glue.

It was then that I caught a whiff of something burning. I followed my nose to the barn and hurried inside. The cows were steaming, and their coats were starting to singe. Those poor critters were about to cook! We hosed them down and turned fans on them. It helped, but not enough. Pa always said I was the quickest thinker in the family, and I knew it was up to me to think of something else.

368

 Reaching All Students

Extra Support: Previewing the Text

Before reading Segment 2, preview the text, using the notes below. **While** reading, model strategies (pages 372 and 375). **After** reading, review the segment (page 377) before students join the Wrapping Up discussion.

pages 368–369 Another problem arises with wet, sticky oatmeal. What do you think the narrator will do?

pages 370–373 What happens to make the narrator's plans for the bread and the crows backfire?

pages 374–375 The narrator plants lettuce to cool the air.

page 376 The narrator explains planting lettuce worked because it was iceberg lettuce. How does this probably tie in to the early snowfall?

369

Spiral Review

Comprehension Skill Lesson
Compare and Contrast

OBJECTIVES

Students compare and contrast story details within a selection.

Remind students that to understand the relationships between two or more events, characters, or other details, they can use the skill of Compare and Contrast. Tell them that comparing is finding similarities and contrasting is finding differences.

Explain that a useful organizer with the Compare and Contrast skill is a Venn diagram. This consists of two circles or ovals that overlap in the middle. This overlap shows how two things are similar, while the parts of the circles that don't overlap show differences. Using a Venn diagram, take students through an example of comparing and contrasting the popcorn and the oatmeal scenes from the story.

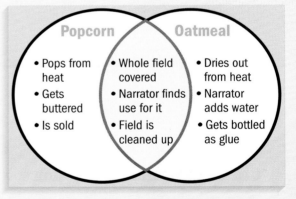

Popcorn — Oatmeal

Popcorn:
- Pops from heat
- Gets buttered
- Is sold

Both (overlap):
- Whole field covered
- Narrator finds use for it
- Field is cleaned up

Oatmeal:
- Dries out from heat
- Narrator adds water
- Gets bottled as glue

Have students make a Venn diagram to compare and contrast the effect of the Heat Wave on two types of animal on the farm or two events.

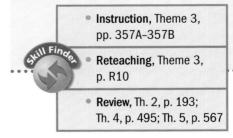

Skill Finder

- **Instruction,** Theme 3, pp. 357A–357B
- **Reteaching,** Theme 3, p. R10
- **Review,** Th. 2, p. 193; Th. 4, p. 495; Th. 5, p. 567

Reading

▶ **Supporting Comprehension**

9 What does the narrator mean when she says *"I figured it was time to take on the Heat Wave"*? (She is going to try to get rid of it. Until now, she has been dealing with the problems the Heat Wave has caused.)

10 How does the narrator's idea to attract crows compare with the usual farming practice? (Farmers usually want to chase crows away.)

11 Why do you think the author has the dough roll over chickens and pick up the tractor and the mule? (to build up both the suspense and the humor)

Vocabulary *(page 371)*

yeast: a substance that is used to make bread dough rise.

trough: a long, narrow container that holds water or food for animals

---

 Cross-Curricular Connection

Science How hot does it really get in Kansas? The highest recorded temperature in Kansas is 121 degrees Fahrenheit. That's about 22 degrees higher than your body temperature and is a temperature that 44 other states have never reached! In real life, 121 degrees is not hot enough to do the things in this story. Bread usually bakes at 350 degrees or higher. Geese roast in the oven at around 450 degrees. And popcorn pops at 475 degrees.

 Reaching All Students
English Language Learners

The elliptical, colloquial speech of the narrator will confuse many English language learners. Ask students to explain what the girl means when she says *"I about drowned in the stuff"* on page 368. In the sentence *Ended up big as the barn* on page 371, help students use context to identify the subject and to complete the simile by adding a second *as*.

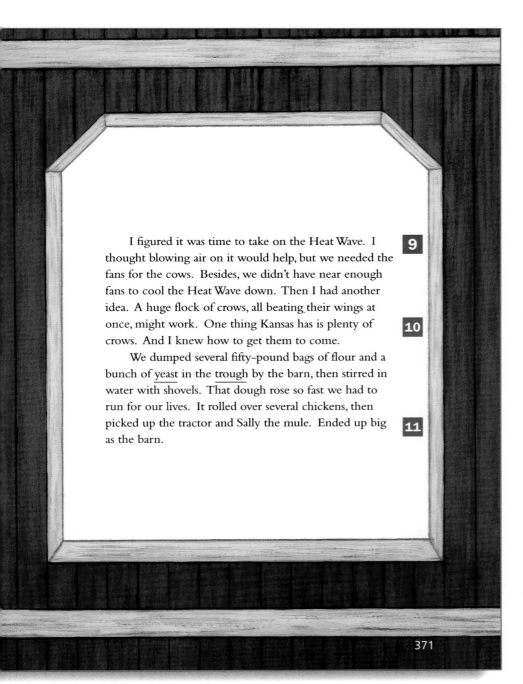

I figured it was time to take on the Heat Wave. I thought blowing air on it would help, but we needed the fans for the cows. Besides, we didn't have near enough fans to cool the Heat Wave down. Then I had another idea. A huge flock of crows, all beating their wings at once, might work. One thing Kansas has is plenty of crows. And I knew how to get them to come.

We dumped several fifty-pound bags of flour and a bunch of yeast in the trough by the barn, then stirred in water with shovels. That dough rose so fast we had to run for our lives. It rolled over several chickens, then picked up the tractor and Sally the mule. Ended up big as the barn.

9

10

11

371

Reaching All Students

English Language Learners

Understanding Similes

Review that a simile is a comparison using *like* or *as.* As they read, ask students to look for similes in this story. These include *like a rocket* (p. 363), *hopping around like rabbits* (p. 367), *big as the barn* (p. 371), and *like a bucking bronco* (p. 375). Ask volunteers to make up some similes of their own to share aloud.

Revisiting the Text

Spiral Review

Comprehension Skill Lesson
Story Structure

OBJECTIVES

Students

- identify characters, setting, and plot

- describe how a change in story structure can alter a story

Review the definitions for characters (main people or animals around whom the story events revolve), setting (the time and place a story occurs), and plot (the sequence of story events, which usually includes a problem and solution).

Divide the class into three groups and have each group identify either the characters, setting, or plot of *Heat Wave!* Reconvene the class to discuss their findings. (characters: narrator, Ma, Pa, Hank; setting: summer, a farm in Kansas; plot: A heat wave hits the narrator's family's farm and some unusual things happen. The narrator uses her quick thinking to turn bad things into good and breaks the heat wave.) Have the groups meet again to discuss what might change in the story if these elements were changed:

- a blizzard strikes instead

- the narrator isn't quick thinking

- the heat wave doesn't break

Skill Finder

• **Instruction,** Th. 1; pp. 57A–57B; Th. 4
• **Reteaching,** Theme 1, p. R10; Theme 4, p. R16
• **Review,** Theme 5, p. 543

▶ Strategy Focus: Evaluate

Student Modeling Ask students to model their evaluations of why the author allows the narrator to fail in her attempt to defeat the Heat Wave. If necessary, use the following prompt:

How would it have changed the feel of the story if the narrator had been immediately successful?

▶ Supporting Comprehension

12 What part of the text does the illustration on pages 372–373 represent? (The narrator and her family purposely tie themselves to a tree trunk so the crows' wings don't blow them away.)

Vocabulary *(page 373)*
resist: fight the urge for

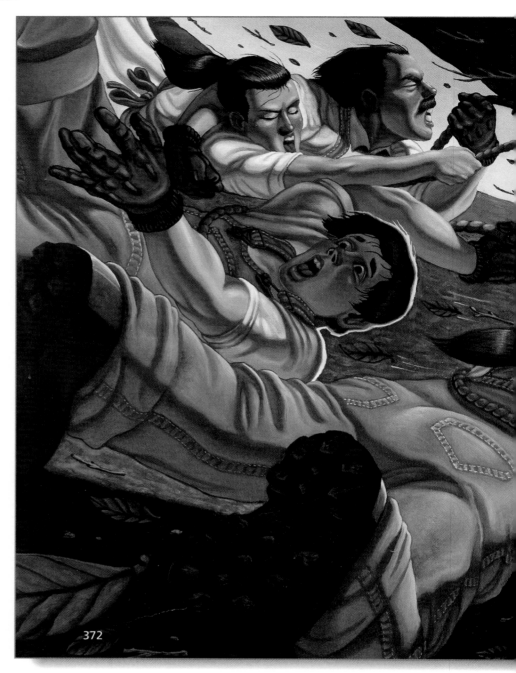

372

Reaching All Students

Extra Support

Strategy Modeling

Evaluate If students need help modeling the strategy, use this example to model it for them.

As the reader I can evaluate the usefulness of the exaggerated illustrations to add to the story's fun. Seeing the family hanging onto the ropes as if I were standing right next to them makes me laugh and feel like I have to hang on with them!

A few minutes later, the dough started baking in the heat. Smelled awful good, and that's what I was counting on. Crows can't resist the smell of baking bread, and soon every crow in Kansas came flocking to the farm. Their wings made so much wind, we had to tie ourselves around a giant tree trunk to keep from being blown away. It felt cooler already.

12

373

Reading Fluency

- **Rereading for Fluency:** After finishing the story, have students choose either Segment 1 or Segment 2 to reread to a partner. Encourage students to read with feeling and expression.

- **Assessing Fluency:** See guidelines in the Theme Assessment Wrap-Up, pages 382–383A.

Reading

▶ Supporting Comprehension

13 What does the author mean when she writes that *all that yeast had caused their spirits to rise?* (It's a joke: If yeast causes bread to rise, then it should help lift a mood.)

14 Are you surprised that the narrator comes up with another idea? Why or why not? (No, because it has been set up since the beginning that she saves the day.)

15 The author doesn't give any reason yet for the lettuce cooling the air. Based on what has come before, do you think the reason will be scientific? (No, it's likely to be another joke.)

Vocabulary *(page 375)*

lit: landed

temperature: measure of heat or coldness

licked: beaten

frisky: lively and playful

spirits: mood

sprouted: sent out new growth

 Cross-Curricular Connection

Art Landscape has been an important fixture in American art, as it has been around the world. Thomas Hart Benton, Grant Wood, and Grandma Moses were twentieth-century artists who painted scenes of America's heartland. They each had a distinct style that interpreted their ideas about the world they were painting, much the same as this artist has interpreted the ideas of the author. Try to bring in some examples of their work.

 Reaching All Students
English Language Learners

Idioms

English language learners may be unfamiliar with idiomatic expressions such as *changed his tune* on page 361; *take on (the Heat Wave)* on page 371; and *lit on the (bread), be licked,* and *worse for wear* on page 375.

The trouble was, those crows didn't keep flying. They lit on the bread and started eating. The temperature shot right back up, and I figured we might be licked.

The crows pecked at the bread until they freed Sally and the chickens. None of them were a bit worse for wear. In fact, they were right frisky. I figured all that yeast had caused their spirits to rise. **13**

Seeing Sally gave me one more idea. I told Pa to hitch her to the plow, and she plowed up a section of land in record time. While Pa was plowing, I found what I needed. I gave everyone lettuce seeds, and we started planting. Those seeds sprouted as soon as they hit the dirt. **14**

The bigger the lettuce grew, the cooler the air got. That Heat Wave put up a fight, all right. It rippled and twisted and squirmed like a bucking bronco. But as the lettuce cooled the air more, the Heat Wave started shrinking, until it finally disappeared altogether. **15**

375

Revisiting the Text

Visual Literacy Lesson
Artist's Style

OBJECTIVES

Students identify features of the artist's style of illustration.

Explain that in his illustrations the artist uses a style that complements the text for this story.

- The artist's style might be called surrealistic. It has the unreal feeling of a dream—or a tall tale. Common objects are put in unusual situations.

- Have students look at Anthology pages 362–363. There is a strong central image. The perspective—the visual point of view—is often exaggerated. In this case the viewer is down on the ground, looking up past the flowers to the narrator.

- Ask students to give their thoughts on what the artist's ideas might be of the relationship between the people and the landscape.

Have students work individually or in pairs. Ask them to go through the selection and for each spread list the central event being shown. For each illustration have them list details the artist has used to capture the spirit of the text.

Reaching All Students
Extra Support

Strategy Modeling

Phonics/Decoding Use this example to model the strategy.

When I read the letters in the word squirmed *from left to right, I notice the e-d ending. I know the q-u spelling usually sounds like /kw/. The i-r spelling sounds like /ur/. When I blend all the sounds together, I say /skwurm•ed/. Squirming is twisting and turning. Maybe the Heat Wave is twisting and turning.*

Reaching All Students
Challenge

Reading Card 9

Double-Meaning Words

Some words on this page have more than one meaning. Ask students to find the word *licked* in the first paragraph and reread the sentence. Have students give the meaning of *licked* as it is used in the sentence. Then have students provide another meaning for *licked* and use it in a sentence.

Have students look for other examples in the selection of words that can have more than one meaning.

Reading

▶ Supporting Comprehension

16 Has the author surprised you by the reason the lettuce worked? (Possible answers: Yes, because it was a joke, I couldn't figure it out. No, because I guessed the kind of lettuce.)

17 How might the narrator have fixed her mistake of planting too much lettuce? (She could have pulled some up or thought of something else, much the way she came up with other ideas.)

18 Do you think the author had the idea for the ending in mind all along or thought of it after most of the rest of the story was in place? Give reasons. (Answers will vary.)

> **Vocabulary** *(page 376)*
>
> **affected:** caused a change in
>
> **miscalculated:** planned or figured incorrectly

The weather vane and the barn cooled down, and the cows stopped steaming, too. They didn't seem much affected, except the fuzz on their hides never grew back. Ma had to knit them all sweaters for the winter.

So that's how I saved the farm, by planting lettuce. In case you're wondering how lettuce could cool the air, it wasn't just any kind of lettuce, you see. It was iceberg lettuce. I did make one mistake, though. I miscalculated the amount of lettuce I needed and planted too much.

Kansas had an awful early snowfall that year, but none of us ever let on why.

376

Meet the Author
HELEN KETTEMAN

What would you do if you didn't have a television in your house? That's just how Helen Ketteman grew up in a small Georgia town. Believe it or not, she says she is glad about that now. Instead of watching TV, she turned to books for entertainment.

She also invented stories for her sisters, and acted out plays for her neighbors. "I know that the reason I'm a writer today is because I read so much as a child," she says.

Other books: *Luck with Potatoes, The Year of No More Corn, Bubba the Cowboy Prince*

Meet the Illustrator
SCOTT GOTO

Scott Goto is certainly no stranger to heat waves. He lives in Hawaii, where hot weather is common. So it is no surprise that he did not have to do any weather research for his work on *Heat Wave!*

When Goto creates art for a children's book, he pretends he is the age of the reader. "This isn't very hard since a big part of me never grew up," says Goto. "I still love playing video games, watching cartoons, and buying toys."

To find out more about Helen Ketteman and Scott Goto, log on to Education Place.

www.eduplace.com/kids

End of Segment 2:
pages 368–377

Wrapping Up Segment 2
pages 368–377

Provide Extra Support for students who need it (page 376). Then bring all students together.

- **Review Predictions/Purpose** Have students evaluate whether the author succeeded in her attempt to entertain and whether they like the story and why.

- **Model Strategies** Have students tell how they used the Evaluate strategy, and then have them take turns modeling it. Ask what other strategies they found helpful while reading.

- **Share Group Discussions** Have students discuss how they feel about the story as a whole, now that they have finished reading it.

- **Summarize** Have students use their Fantasy/Realism Charts to summarize the story. Ask them how the charts helped them with their reading.

Comprehension/Critical Thinking

1. What would you expect to happen to geese, corn, cows, and oats, in a real heat wave? (Answers will vary.) What effect would planting iceberg lettuce have? (none) **Fantasy and Realism**

2. What would you expect Hank's attitude to be toward his sister now? (Answers will vary.) **Predicting Outcomes**

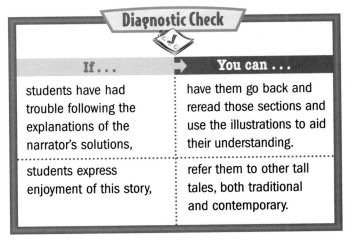

Diagnostic Check

If . . .	You can . . .
students have had trouble following the explanations of the narrator's solutions,	have them go back and reread those sections and use the illustrations to aid their understanding.
students express enjoyment of this story,	refer them to other tall tales, both traditional and contemporary.

Responding

▶ Think About the Selection

Discuss or Write Have students discuss or write their answers. Sample answers are provided; accept reasonable responses that are supported with evidence from the story.

1 **Making Inferences** She is a quick-thinker who can come up with creative strategies to solve problems, no matter how ridiculous or far-fetched.

2 **Story Structure** The heat wave is like the villain of the story. At the end of the story, it even "puts up a fight." Student answers may vary as to what a heat wave would say.

3 **Noting Details** Answers will vary, may include when the Heat Wave appears as a visible cloud, or when the flock of geese flies in one side and comes out the other side "plucked, stuffed, and roasted," or when the corn starts popping.

4 **Problem Solving** Answers will vary.

5 **Predicting Outcomes** He probably thinks his sister is pretty terrific and smart enough to do anything.

⭐ 6 **Connecting/Comparing** **Making Generalizations** Students might suggest that since the stranger brings cool temperatures with him, he might be able to conquer the Heat Wave by simply blowing on it.

Responding

Think About the Selection

1. What qualities make the girl so good at fighting the heat wave?

2. How is the heat wave like a character in the story? If the heat wave could speak, what would it say?

3. Many scenes in this selection exaggerate an ordinary event until it becomes amazing. Give three examples.

4. If the farm had been out of lettuce seeds, how else could the girl have defeated the heat wave?

5. Before the heat wave, the girl's brother teased her that girls couldn't be farmers. What do you think he says about her now?

6. Connecting/Comparing What do you think would happen if the stranger from Chris Van Allsburg's story were at the farm during the heat wave attack?

Narrating

Write a Sequel

Think about what would happen if the cool weather caused by the iceberg lettuce became a cold wave. Write a scene involving the girl doing battle with a cold wave that's just as amazing as the heat wave.

> **Tips**
> - Continue the tall-tale style of the story by using exaggeration and puns.
> - Include dialogue. Remember to use quotation marks.

378

Reaching All Students

English Language Learners

Beginning/Preproduction Fluency Bring in packages or examples of some of the foods mentioned in the story. These include *butter, flour, yeast, dough, oatmeal, (iceberg) lettuce.* Help students learn the names.

Early Production and Speech Emergence Working in mixed groups, students can create a word web that describes the girl. Help students with vocabulary.

Intermediate and Advanced Fluency Have students work in pairs to imagine other creative ways to fight the heat wave.

Science

Make a Fact File

Without the sun, there couldn't be heat waves. Using an encyclopedia or your science book, create a fact file about the sun. How does it heat the earth? How hot is it? How far away is it? Use illustrations to help support the facts you include.

Bonus Make and label a diagram showing how the earth's revolution around the sun affects the seasons.

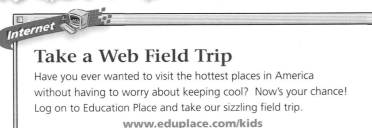

The Sun

Average Distance from Earth:

Age:

What it is made of:

Temperature:

Listening and Speaking

Tell a Tall Tale

Sit in a circle with a group and tell a story that will become more and more amazing as you go along. One person starts the story by telling about a realistic event. After one or two sentences, the next person continues the story by adding an exaggerated event. As the plot grows, each storyteller will make the tale stranger and stranger.

Tips

- Start with a sentence about something ordinary, such as "One day, on my way home from school, it started to rain."
- Review this theme to help you think of some wacky ideas.

Internet

Take a Web Field Trip

Have you ever wanted to visit the hottest places in America without having to worry about keeping cool? Now's your chance! Log on to Education Place and take our sizzling field trip.

www.eduplace.com/kids

379

Personal Response

Invite students to share their personal responses to *Heat Wave!* As an alternative, ask students to write in their journals about how they coped with a recent very hot or very cold wave.

Comprehension Check

Assign **Practice Book** page 192 to assess students' understanding of the selection.

Practice Book page 192

Heat Wave!
Comprehension Check
Interview Time

Name

Interview Time

You're the narrator being interviewed by reporters after you defeat the Heat Wave. Answer the reporters' questions.

What is your name?
I don't have one in the story. (2 points)

What happened here?
A Heat Wave got snagged on our weather vane. (Students can tell as many of the other main events as they wish.) (2)

Why is your ma knitting?
She's knitting sweaters for the cows whose coats got singed. (2)

Who beat the Heat Wave?
We all worked together to deal with the mess. Sally, our mule, gave me the idea that worked. (2)

How did you beat the Heat Wave?
We planted iceberg lettuce, and it cooled off the air. (2)

192   Theme 3: **That's Amazing!**   Assessment Tip: Total **10** Points

---

Reaching All Students

English Language Learners

Create a brainstorming list on the board of things that could happen if a cold wave hit the farm. Assist with vocabulary.

End-of-Selection Assessment

Selection Test Use the test in the **Teacher's Resource Blackline Masters** to assess selection comprehension and vocabulary.

Student Self-Assessment Have students assess their reading with additional questions such as

- What parts of this selection were difficult for me? Why?

- What strategies helped me understand the story?

- Would I recommend this story to my friends? Why?

Science Link

pages 380–381

▶ Skill: How to Read a Diagram

Read aloud the title of the link. Point out that a diagram is a labeled drawing that shows how something works, how something is put together, or how something happened. Ask students to name instances when a diagram could be helpful, such as following instructions in a technical manual. Here, students will look at a diagram that accompanies instructions for making and using a straw thermometer. Review the tips in the left column on page 380.

- Before reading the article, have students **identify** what the diagram is explaining and **predict** how it will be useful to them.

- Instruct them to **read** the individual **labels** so that they clearly understand how the text and graphic elements correspond.

- While students read the article, they should **look back** to the diagram periodically to help them.

Strategies to use might include Summarize and Monitor/Clarify.

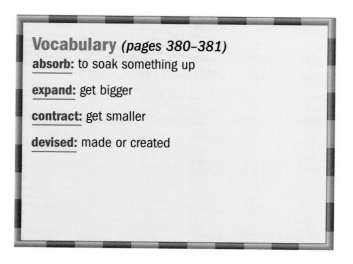

Vocabulary *(pages 380–381)*

absorb: to soak something up

expand: get bigger

contract: get smaller

devised: made or created

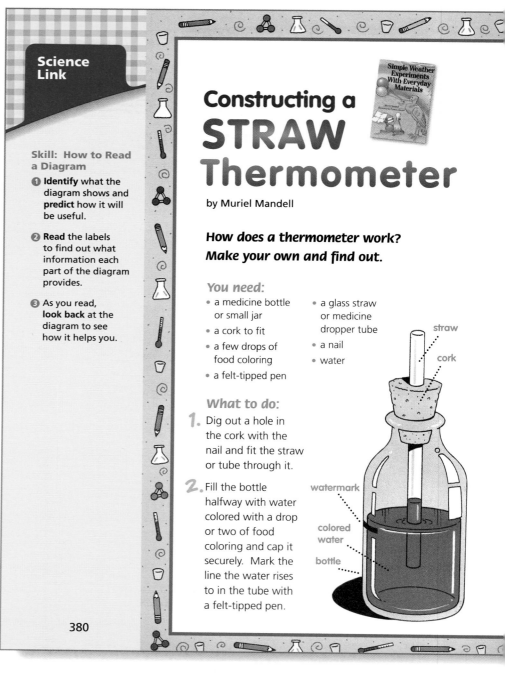

Science Link

Skill: How to Read a Diagram

❶ **Identify** what the diagram shows and **predict** how it will be useful.

❷ **Read** the labels to find out what information each part of the diagram provides.

❸ As you read, **look back** at the diagram to see how it helps you.

380

Simple Weather Experiments With Everyday Materials

Constructing a STRAW Thermometer

by Muriel Mandell

***How does a thermometer work?
Make your own and find out.***

You need:
- a medicine bottle or small jar
- a cork to fit
- a few drops of food coloring
- a felt-tipped pen
- a glass straw or medicine dropper tube
- a nail
- water

What to do:

1. Dig out a hole in the cork with the nail and fit the straw or tube through it.

2. Fill the bottle halfway with water colored with a drop or two of food coloring and cap it securely. Mark the line the water rises to in the tube with a felt-tipped pen.

straw

cork

watermark

colored water

bottle

Reaching All Students

Classroom Management

All Students

Reading the Diagram Have students study the diagram on the page. Then have them read the list of supplies and acquire the items. Next, direct them to read the steps and refer to parts of the diagram. Depending on the availability of supplies, you may wish to construct the thermometer as a class, or else assign student teams. Encourage students to keep detailed logs recording experiment results. You may choose to have students read the Why explanation at the end, prior to, or following the assembly of the thermometer.

3. Note the height of the water in the straw at room temperature, and also at different times and places —

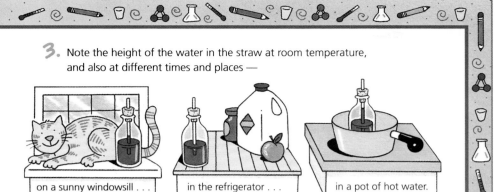

on a sunny windowsill . . .   in the refrigerator . . .   in a pot of hot water.

What happens:
The water goes up the tube when the temperature is warm and goes down when it is cold.

Why:
We measure temperature by the changes made. Temperature is really a measure of whether one object absorbs heat from or loses heat to another object.

Liquids expand when heated and contract when cooled. The liquid of the thermometer absorbs heat. It expands when it contacts anything warmer than itself, and contracts when contacting something cooler. Mercury and colored alcohol are usually used as the liquid in thermometers because they react so quickly.

Makers of commercial weather thermometers use a sealed glass tube that has a little bulb blown out at one end. They mark the thermometer's scale by placing its bulb in contact with melting ice.

The point at which the liquid contracts is 32° for a Fahrenheit scale and 0° for a centigrade scale. Then the bulb is placed in the steam from boiling water. The point at which it expands is marked 212°F or 100°C.

You can make a scale for your straw thermometer by comparing its levels with a commercial weather thermometer.

Gabriel Fahrenheit, a German physicist, devised the first commonly used scale in 1714. About thirty years later, a Swedish astronomer, Anders Celsius, established the centigrade scale, also known as the Celsius scale.

The first thermometer was invented in 1593 by the Italian physicist Galileo.

▶ Comprehension Check

Ask students to discuss these questions.

1 What will happen to the water level in the tube if a cat curls up against the bottle placed on a sunny windowsill? (The cat's body heat will probably make the level rise.) **Predicting Outcomes**

2 How might the data obtained from a straw thermometer compare with the data you might get from an oral thermometer? (Straw thermometers measure a wider range of temperature changes whereas an oral thermometer measures temperature change over very few degrees.) **Compare and Contrast**

3 In what ways might using the diagram help make constructing the thermometer easier? (It shows exactly what the thermometer should look like and how the individual pieces fit together.) **Problem Solving**

4 **Connecting/Comparing** Based on what you've learned about straw thermometers, do you think it could ever really get as hot as it did in *Heat Wave!*? Explain. (No. Based on both the tall tale genre of the story and the temperature readings obtained from the experiments, the extreme temperatures illustrated in *Heat Wave!* are clearly greatly exaggerated.) **Drawing Conclusions**

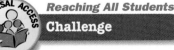

Reaching All Students

Challenge

Math

Have interested students use their science textbooks, the encyclopedia, or other reference materials to research the Fahrenheit/Centigrade conversion scale or formula. Using the scale, have them convert their experiment results into Centigrade readings and share their results with the class.

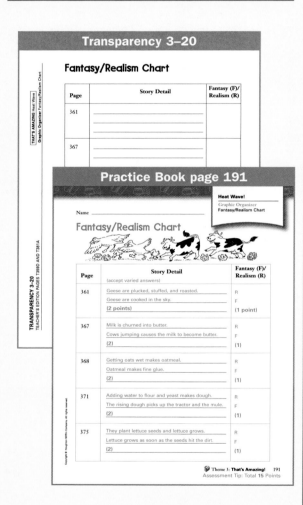

Transparency 3–20

Fantasy/Realism Chart

Practice Book page 191

Comprehension Skills

✓ Fantasy and Realism

▶ Teach

Review fantasy and realism in *Heat Wave!* Use **Transparency 3–20** to discuss

■ fantastic and realistic details in the story

■ how well the author succeeds in creating a funny and incredible story

■ how the author blends the fantastic with the real to make the story more believable

Students can refer to the selection and to **Practice Book** page 191.

Page	Story Detail (accept varied answers)	Fantasy (F)/Realism (R)
371	Adding water to flour and yeast makes dough.	R
	The rising dough picks up the tractor and the mule.	F
375	They plant lettuce seeds and lettuce grows.	R
	Lettuce grows as soon as the seeds hit the dirt.	F

Modeling Tell students that an author will blend fantasy with realism to make the reader believe, if only for a moment, that events in the story can truly happen. How well the author does this is determined by evaluating the author's use of fantastic and realistic details. Ask students to read along as you read aloud the final two paragraphs on page 376. Have students consider how well the author blends fantasy and realism in those paragraphs as you think aloud.

💭 Think Aloud

The author ends the story by saying that Kansas had an early snowfall that year. I can believe that. I've heard of it snowing in September in some places. But in the paragraph before, I see that the early snowfall was caused by the girl planting so much iceberg lettuce that she made the air cold enough for snow. Now that's unbelievable. The author almost made me believe it really snowed early that year. She's done a very good job of using fantasy and realism in this part of the story.

Explain to students that when details of fantasy and realism appear close together in a story, their effects on readers are stronger.

▶ Practice

Write the following page numbers on the board: 363, 365, 367, and 372. Tell students that they will work in pairs or small groups to decide how well the author uses fantasy and realism on those pages. Instruct them to use different examples than those already chosen. Have students record their answers on a chart similar to the one below and have them answer the questions that follow.

Fantasy	Page	Realism
Mercury blasts from the thermometer like a rocket. Flowers crawl under the porch.	363	none
Dog freezes though it's hot outside.	365	Wrapping a dog in a blanket will keep it warm.
They filled trucks with popcorn.	367	They sold popcorn at the movies.
The wind made by the crows' wings almost blew everyone away.	372	Crows like the smell of bread.

How well does the author use fantasy and realism? How did you decide?

▶ Apply

Use **Practice Book** pages 193–194 to diagnose whether students need Reteaching. Students who do not need Reteaching may work on Challenge/Extension Activities, page R13. Students who need easier text to apply the skill can use the **Reader's Library** selection "The Big Gust" and its Responding activity.

Skill Finder	• **Revisiting**, p. 365	• **Review**, Th. 3, p. 347; Th. 4, p. 399	• **Reteaching**, p. R12

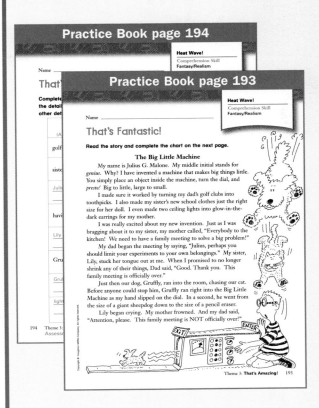

Practice Book page 194

Practice Book page 193

Heat Wave!
Comprehension Skill
Fantasy/Realism

Name _____

That's Fantastic!

Read the story and complete the chart on the next page.

The Big Little Machine

My name is Julius G. Malone. My middle initial stands for *genius*. Why? I have invented a machine that makes big things little. You simply place an object inside the machine, turn the dial, and *presto!* Big to little, large to small.

I made sure it worked by turning my dad's golf clubs into toothpicks. I also made my sister's new school clothes just the right size for her doll. I even made two ceiling lights into glow-in-the-dark earrings for my mother.

I was really excited about my new invention. Just as I was bragging about it to my sister, my mother called, "Everybody to the kitchen! We need to have a family meeting to solve a big problem!"

My dad began the meeting by saying, "Julius, perhaps you should limit your experiments to your own belongings." My sister, Lily, stuck her tongue out at me. When I promised to no longer shrink any of their things, Dad said, "Good. Thank you. This family meeting is officially over."

Just then our dog, Gruffly, ran into the room, chasing our cat. Before anyone could stop him, Gruffly ran right into the Big Little Machine as my hand slipped on the dial. In a second, he went from the size of a giant sheepdog down to the size of a pencil eraser.

Lily began crying. My mother frowned. And my dad said, "Attention, please. This family meeting is NOT officially over!"

Theme 3: **That's Amazing!** 193

Reaching All Students

Extra Support

- Reteaching, page R12
- **Reader's Library:** *That's Amazing!* Selection 3, "The Big Gust"

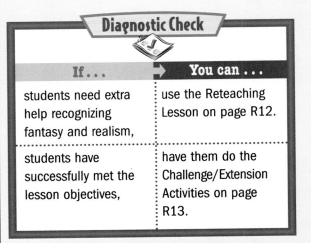

Diagnostic Check

If...	You can...
students need extra help recognizing fantasy and realism,	use the Reteaching Lesson on page R12.
students have successfully met the lesson objectives,	have them do the Challenge/Extension Activities on page R13.

Information & Study Skills

 Real-life Reading

Transparency 3–21

Weather Forecasts

Local 5-Day Weather Forecast

Today	Thursday	Friday	Saturday	Sunday
Partly cloudy and cold	Windy with a chance of snow	Mostly cloudy, chance of snow showers	Partly cloudy and cold	Mostly cloudy, chance of snow
High 24, Low 10.	High 27, Low 15.	High 24, Low 12.	High 25, Low 17.	High 30, Low 20.

▶ Teach

Real-life Reading Materials Remind students that they read other material every day in addition to their textbooks and reading for pleasure. This other kind of reading helps them in their daily lives. Offer a few examples, such as signs and menus, and ask students to provide others. Compile a list on the board. You might include the following: ads, TV and movie listings, calendars, and telephone books.

Weather Forecasts Explain that a weather forecast tells what the weather will probably be like today or over the next few days. Display **Transparency 3–21**. Point to the five day weather forecast at the top of the transparency. Have students read aloud the title and the heading for each day.

Modeling Demonstrate how to read and interpret a five day weather forecast using the transparency.

Think Aloud

The title and the headings tell me that this is a weather forecast for five days: today and the next four days. To find today's weather, I look in the first box. There it says "Partly cloudy and cold." It says it will be cold, but how cold? On the next line, I find the highest temperature of the day will be 24 degrees. That's cold! The lowest temperature will be 10 degrees. That's very, very cold. But the lowest temperature is late at night. Most of the day will be warmer. Now I know that I need to wear very warm clothes when I go outside.

▶ Practice

Have students demonstrate how to read and interpret a weather forecast. Invite volunteers to read aloud the forecasts on **Transparency 3–21** for Thursday through Sunday. Then ask questions such as:

- **On which days might it snow?** (Thursday, Friday, Sunday)

- **Which days will be partly cloudy with a little sunshine?** (Today, Saturday)

- **What does "high 27" mean?** (The highest temperature predicted for that day is 27 degrees.)

- **What does "low 12" mean?** (The lowest temperature predicted for that day is 12 degrees.)

▶ Apply

Point out that weather forecasts can be found in newspapers, on TV, and on the Internet as well.

Ask students to keep track of the different kinds of reading they do in one day. Have them write down what they have read and share their lists with their classmates.

Word Work Instructions

DAY 1	• Spelling Pretest • Spelling Instruction
DAY 2	• Structural Analysis Instruction • Spelling Practice
DAY 3	• Phonics Instruction • Spelling Practice
DAY 4	• Structural Analysis Reteaching • Vocabulary Skill Instruction • Spelling Game
DAY 5	• Expanding Your Vocabulary • Spelling Test

OBJECTIVES

Students

- read words with -ed or -ing endings
- read words with consonant digraphs
- use the Phonics/Decoding strategy to decode longer words
- learn academic language: **digraph**

Teacher's Note

Tell students that

- when a base word ends with e, the e is dropped before -ed or -ing is added (change/changed/changing)
- when a base word ends with one vowel followed by a single consonant, the consonant is usually doubled before adding -ed or -ing (wrap/wrapped/wrapping)

▶ Teach

Write these sentences on the board:

Tell students that -ed and -ing usually appear at the end of verbs. An -ing ending such as in the word hopping usually means that the action is continuing. The cows continued to hop. (Note that the spelling of the base word hop changes when the ending is added—the final p is doubled.) An -ed ending such as in the word herded usually means that the action happened in the past. Have students review the Phonics/Decoding strategy.

> The cows were <u>hopping</u> around like rabbits.
> We <u>herded</u> them inside the barn.

Modeling Display the following sentence and model how to decode baking: A few minutes later, the dough started <u>baking</u> in the heat.

Think Aloud

I see the -ing at the end of this word. When I remove it, I see b-a-k. That's not a word I recognize. However, I know that if the base word is bake, the letter e would have been dropped when the -ing ending was added to form the word baking. Baking is a way of cooking. It was so hot that the dough started cooking.

▶ Practice

Write these phrases on the board and have students copy the underlined words: <u>wetting</u> them down; <u>rising</u> up around my ankles; <u>stirred</u> in water; <u>pecked</u> at the bread; <u>stopped steaming</u>; <u>saved</u> the farm; in case you're <u>wondering</u>. Tell students to circle the -ed or -ing ending in each word and identify the base word. Have students decode the words and give their meanings.

▶ Apply

Have students complete **Practice Book** page 195.

Skill Finder	• Strategy Review: Phonics/Decoding, p. 299B	• Reteaching, p. R18

Phonics
Consonant Digraphs

• SELECTION •

Heat Wave!

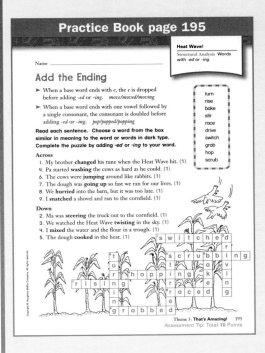

Teach

Tell students that understanding consonant digraphs can help them use the Phonics/Decoding strategy to decode unfamiliar words. Explain that

- A digraph is two letters which together make one sound.

- Some examples of consonant digraph spellings are *th, ch, sh, wh, ph, gh,* and *ng.*

Modeling Display this sentence and model how to decode *shovels:*
We scrubbed a couple of <u>shovels</u> and the beds of the pickup truck.

Think Aloud

I see the s-h digraph at the beginning of this word. Instead of the s and h each making its own sound, together they make one sound, /sh/. The first part of this word probably sounds like /shuhv/. Next I see the e-l spelling of the final /uhl/ sound and an s ending. When I put it all together, I say /SHUHV•uhlz/. A shovel is a tool used for scooping things up. That makes sense because they used the shovels to scoop up the popcorn.

Practice

Write these sentences on the board and have students copy the underlined words: *I wrapped him in a blanket, and he <u>thawed</u> out okay. The cows <u>churned</u> their milk to butter. I caught a <u>whiff</u> of something burning.*

Have students circle the consonant digraph in each word, pronounce the word, and then check to see it makes sense in the sentence.

Apply

Tell students to decode the following words and discuss their meanings: *weather, choose, shallow, whimper, enough, photograph, bring.* You may also want to have students brainstorm lists of other words containing consonant digraphs.

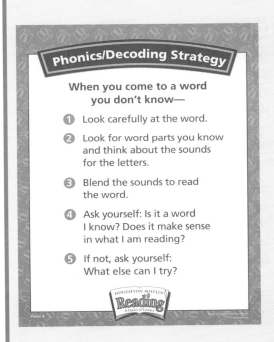

Phonics/Decoding Strategy

When you come to a word you don't know—

1. Look carefully at the word.
2. Look for word parts you know and think about the sounds for the letters.
3. Blend the sounds to read the word.
4. Ask yourself: Is it a word I know? Does it make sense in what I am reading?
5. If not, ask yourself: What else can I try?

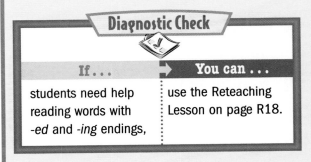

Diagnostic Check

If...	You can...
students need help reading words with -*ed* and -*ing* endings,	use the Reteaching Lesson on page R18.

OBJECTIVES

Students will write spelling words that end with -ed or -ing.

Spelling Words

Basic Words

dancing	dimmed
skipped	rubbing
hiking	striped
flipped	wasting
snapping	traced
raced*	stripped
landed	tanning
pleasing	smelling*
checking	phoning
dared	fainted

Review Words	Challenge Words
cared	breathing
joking	tiring
tapping	urged
wrapped*	scrubbed*
fixing	striving

*Forms of these words appear in the literature.

Reaching All Students
Extra Support

Basic Word List You may want to use only the left column of Basic Words with students who need extra support.

Spelling

✓ Words Ending with -ed or -ing

Day 1 — Teaching the Principle

Pretest Use the Day 5 Test sentences. Say each underlined word, read the sentence, and then repeat the word. Have students write only the underlined word.

Teach Write the following word equations on the board:

race + ed = raced
land + ed = landed
snap + ing = snapping

Say each inflected word *(raced, landed, snapping)* and have students repeat it. Explain that each word was made by adding the ending *-ed* or *-ing* to a base word, a word to which a beginning or an ending can be added. Then use the word equations to explain the following principles.

(race + ed = raced) If a base word ends with *e,* the *e* is dropped before adding *-ed* or *-ing.* (land + ed = landed) If a base word ends with two consonants, no spelling change is needed before adding *-ed* or *-ing.* (snap + ing = snapping) If a one-syllable word ends with a vowel followed by a single consonant, double the consonant before adding *-ed* or *-ing.*

Say each remaining Basic Word as you write it on the board, and have students repeat it. Ask students what happened when *-ed* or *-ing* was added.

Practice/Homework Assign **Practice Book** page 419. Tell students to use this Take-Home Word List to study the words they missed on the Pretest.

Day 2 — Reviewing the Principle

Practice/Homework Review the spelling principle and assign **Practice Book** page 196.

Day 3 — Vocabulary

Context Sentences List the Basic Words on the board. Tell students to write sentences for three words, leaving a blank for the Basic Word but including word clues to help a reader guess the missing word. Have students supply the missing words. (Sentences will vary.) Next, have students use each Basic Word from the board orally in a sentence. (Sentences will vary.)

Practice/Homework For spelling practice, assign **Practice Book** page 197.

Day 4 Grab Bag Spelling

Have partners make 25 word cards, one for each Basic and Review Word's base word. Also have them make 13 *-ing* cards and 12 *-ed* cards. Ask pairs to place the two groups of cards in separate paper bags and shake the bags. Then explain these rules:

Player 1 picks a card from each bag and displays them. Both players must put the word and ending together to form a new word, and write that word on a piece of paper. Player 2 then picks a card from each bag, and again both players write the new word. After every card has been played, players check their lists (against a spelling word list or in a dictionary) to determine who spelled more words correctly. The player with more correctly spelled words wins.

Practice/Homework For proofreading and writing practice, assign **Practice Book** page 198.

Day 5 Spelling Assessment

Test Say each underlined word, read the sentence, and then repeat the word. Have students write only the underlined word.

Basic Words

1. They are <u>dancing</u> slowly to the music.
2. We <u>skipped</u> with joy to the beat.
3. They are <u>hiking</u> on a mountain trail.
4. Has she <u>flipped</u> the eggs over?
5. I am <u>snapping</u> my fingers to the song.
6. The runner <u>raced</u> to the finish line.
7. The boats <u>landed</u> at the dock.
8. My good report card is <u>pleasing</u> to Dad.
9. The teacher is <u>checking</u> our papers.
10. Who <u>dared</u> to jump so high?
11. The lights in the room <u>dimmed</u>.
12. I am <u>rubbing</u> butter on an ear of corn.
13. The <u>striped</u> shirt is red, blue, and white.

14. Is she <u>wasting</u> time by waiting in line?
15. My sister <u>traced</u> the rose with her pen.
16. He <u>stripped</u> the paper off his gift box.
17. The sun is <u>tanning</u> his skin slowly.
18. The cook is <u>smelling</u> the soup.
19. I am <u>phoning</u> Mom to ask for a ride.
20. The last runner <u>fainted</u> from the heat.

Challenge Words

21. We can hear him <u>breathing</u>.
22. The game was <u>tiring</u>.
23. Mother <u>urged</u> me to smile.
24. I <u>scrubbed</u> the dirt off my face.
25. I am <u>striving</u> to win the race.

Spelling Spree!™

Students may use the **Spelling Spree!™** for extra practice with the spelling principles taught in this lesson.

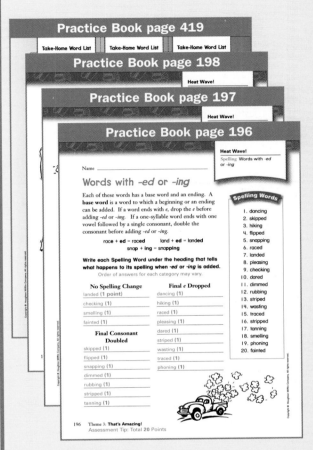

Practice Book page 419

Practice Book page 198

Practice Book page 197

Practice Book page 196

Heat Wave!
Spelling Words with *-ed* or *-ing*

Name _____

Words with *-ed* or *-ing*

Each of these words has a base word and an ending. A **base word** is a word to which a beginning or an ending can be added. If a word ends with *e*, drop the *e* before adding *-ed* or *-ing*. If a one-syllable word ends with one vowel followed by a single consonant, double the consonant before adding *-ed* or *-ing*.

race + ed = raced   land + ed = landed
snap + ing = snapping

Write each Spelling Word under the heading that tells what happens to its spelling when *-ed* or *-ing* is added.
Order of answers for each category may vary.

Spelling Words
1. dancing
2. skipped
3. hiking
4. flipped
5. snapping
6. raced
7. landed
8. pleasing
9. checking
10. dared
11. dimmed
12. rubbing
13. striped
14. wasting
15. traced
16. stripped
17. tanning
18. smelling
19. phoning
20. fainted

No Spelling Change	Final *e* Dropped
landed (1 point)	dancing (1)
checking (1)	hiking (1)
smelling (1)	raced (1)
fainted (1)	pleasing (1)
Final Consonant Doubled	dared (1)
skipped (1)	striped (1)
flipped (1)	wasting (1)
snapping (1)	traced (1)
dimmed (1)	phoning (1)
rubbing (1)	
stripped (1)	
tanning (1)	

196 Theme 3: **That's Amazing!**
Assessment Tip: Total 20 Points

··· Houghton Mifflin Spelling and Vocabulary ···
Correlated instruction and practice, p. 102

Reaching All Students
Challenge

Challenge Word Practice Have students use each Challenge Word in a different silly sentence that might have come from a tall tale. (Example: I <u>urged</u> that pig to take a bath.) Students can share their sentences with the class.

Word Work

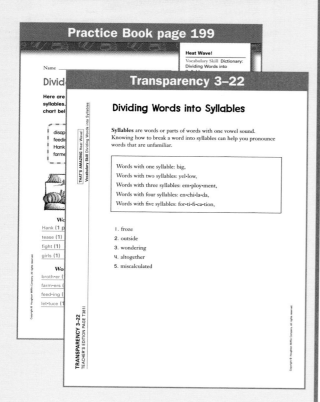

Vocabulary Skills

Dictionary: Dividing Words into Syllables

OBJECTIVES

Students

- recognize syllables
- understand how to divide words into syllables
- learn academic language: **syllable**

Practice Book page 199

Heat Wave!
Vocabulary Skill Dictionary: Dividing Words into

Transparency 3–22

Dividing Words into Syllables

Syllables are words or parts of words with one vowel sound. Knowing how to break a word into syllables can help you pronounce words that are unfamiliar.

Words with one syllable: big,
Words with two syllables: yel•low,
Words with three syllables: em•ploy•ment,
Words with four syllables: en•chi•la•da,
Words with five syllables: for•ti•fi•ca•tion,

1. froze
2. outside
3. wondering
4. altogether
5. miscalculated

THAT'S AMAZING Heat Wave! Vocabulary Skill Dividing Words into Syllables

TRANSPARENCY 3–22 TEACHER'S EDITION PAGE T381I

Teach

Display **Transparency 3–22,** blocking out all but the definition of *syllable.* Read the definition to the class. Point out that a syllable is a word or word part that contains a single vowel sound. If two vowels stand for one sound, they will be part of the same syllable. Explain to students that knowing how to divide a word into syllables makes it easier for them to sound out an unfamiliar word.

On the transparency, uncover the word box containing sample words broken into syllables. Explain that dots are placed between the syllables to show where the syllable breaks are. Read aloud each of the examples. Have the class repeat each word out loud, breaking it into distinct syllables. Suggest other words that fit into each number of syllables and write them on the transparency.

Modeling Display the last portion of the transparency, showing words 1 through 5. Model for students how to determine the number of syllables in a word, using words 1 and 2, *froze* and *outside.*

Think Aloud

When I say froze, *I hear only one vowel sound,* ō. *Since a syllable has only one vowel sound, I know that the word* froze *has one syllable. When I say* outside, *I hear two vowel sounds. I hear the first vowel sound,* ou, *in the first part of the word* out. *Even though* o *and* u *are two different vowels, they make one vowel sound in* out. *The second vowel sound,* ī, *is in the second half of the word,* side. *So the word* outside *has two syllables.*

▶ Practice

In pairs or small groups, have students answer questions 3 through 5 on the transparency. Have students share their work with the class and explain how they divided the words into syllables.

▶ Apply

Have students complete **Practice Book** page 199.

Expanding Your Vocabulary
Scientific Terms: Climate Words

Explain that climate plays an important role in this selection. Have students look through the selection to find words about climate, such as *heat wave* and *blizzard.* Then begin a word web that shows terms associated with climate, similar to the following:

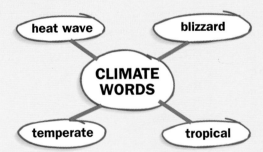

Have students work with partners to find additional climate words. Add these words to the web.

• Challenge/Extension
Activities, p. R19

··· **Houghton Mifflin Spelling and Vocabulary** ···
Correlated instruction and practice, pp. 138, 144

Reaching All Students

English Language Learners

Have students work with English-speaking partners to define the following: *affected, horizon, miscalculated, singe, temperature, weather vane, clump, harvest, commotion, pasture, whiff, yeast, trough.* Have students use the text and illustrations to help them establish definitions. They may use dictionaries if they wish.

OBJECTIVES

Students

- identify the tense of a verb as present, past, or future

- spell forms of past tense verbs correctly

- proofread and correct sentences with grammar and spelling errors

- use the correct tenses of verbs to improve writing

- learn academic language: **present tense, past tense, future tense**

Technology

Wacky Web Tales

Students may use the **Wacky Web Tales** floppy disk to create humorous stories and review parts of speech.

Grammar Skills

 Present, Past, and Future Tenses

Day 1

Display the chart at the top of **Transparency 3–23**, along with the three sentences that follow the chart.

Then ask students to look at *Heat Wave!* to find examples of present, past, and future tenses of verbs and to share the examples they find. For each sentence, have students identify the verb and give its tense. Then go over the following definitions and rules:

- The tense of a verb tells when something happens.

- A present tense verb shows action that is happening now.

- A past tense verb shows action that has already happened.

- Add *ed* to most verbs to form the past tense.

- Remember the rules for spelling the past tense of verbs.

- A future tense verb shows action that is going to happen. Verbs in the future tense use the helping verb *will*.

Now display the chart of rules for forming the past tense of verbs. Tell students to copy the numbered sentences at the bottom of **Transparency 3–23** on a separate sheet of paper. Have students rewrite each sentence, using the correct spelling of the past tense form of the verb named in parentheses. Then have students correct the Day 1 Daily Language Practice sentences on **Transparency 3–25**.

Day 2

Practice/Homework Have students correct the Day 2 Daily Language Practice sentences. Then assign **Practice Book** page 200.

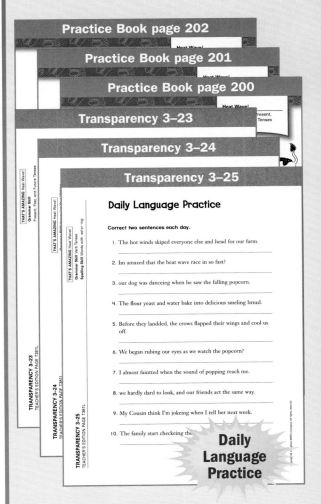

Day 3 — Tense Times

Write on separate cards these verbs: *plant, hurry, grab, help, snag, try, tease, pull, tie, slip.* Divide the class into three teams: Present Tense, Past Tense, and Future Tense. A member of the Present Tense team picks a verb card, goes to the chalkboard and writes a sentence using the present tense form of the verb. Then a member of the Past Tense team goes to the board and writes the same sentence in the past tense. Finally, a member of the Future Tense team writes the sentence in the future tense. For each sentence with a correctly spelled tense form, a team gets one point. Play continues until all the verb cards have been used. You may wish to have students switch teams to gain practice using all three verb tenses. Then have students correct the Day 3 Daily Language Practice sentences.

Day 4

Practice/Homework Have students correct the Day 4 Daily Language Practice sentences. Assign **Practice Book** page 201.

Day 5 — Improving Your Writing

Using the Correct Tense: Remind students that good writers make sure to use the verb tense that correctly shows the time of the action described. Point out that the tense of a verb tells when events take place: in the past, the present, or the future. Writers often use one verb tense to make the time of the events clear. Display the paragraph on **Transparency 3–24** and have students read it aloud.

Ask volunteers to suggest why the paragraph is confusing. Students should see that the paragraph contains all three tenses, past, present, and future, to describe events that took place in the past. Have students suggest changes in tense forms of verbs to show that the action has already taken place. Then have a volunteer read the corrected paragraph aloud. Discuss why the corrected paragraph is better than the original one. Then have students review a piece of their own writing to see if they can improve it by using correct tense forms.

Practice/Homework Have students correct the Day 5 Daily Language Practice sentences. Then assign **Practice Book** page 202.

············· **Houghton Mifflin English** ·············
Correlated instruction and practice, pp. 100–101

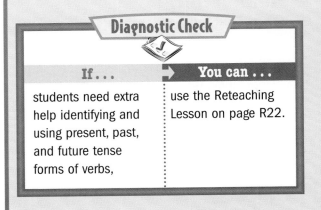

Diagnostic Check	
If . . .	**You can . . .**
students need extra help identifying and using present, past, and future tense forms of verbs,	use the Reteaching Lesson on page R22.

Writing Skills
Writing a Summary

Transparency 3–26

Writing a Summary

Summary: What Is a Heat ⟶ What Is a Heat Wave?

Transparency 3–27

Paraphrasing

"Sometimes the temperature soars so high, it feels as if the sun could singe the hair on top of your head."

Which paraphrasing does not change the author's meaning?

A. When the temperature goes that high, it feels like the sun is baking the hair on your head.

B. The temperature goes way, way up, and it feels as if the sun is burning your hair.

1. Heat waves can last for a few days, or for as long as several weeks.

2. They are caused when large masses of hot air get stuck over a particular region — and don't budge.

3. These hot spells can send the thermometer to over 100 degrees.

4. For example, too much heat can make you sick by forcing your body to work extra hard.

5. During a heat wave, be sure to drink lots of water even if you're not thirsty.

Penmanship

Teacher's Resource Disk: Penmanship Blackline Masters

Use these masters to model correct letter formation, size, and spacing and to give students practice writing legibly in cursive.

▷ Teach

Explain to students that a summary takes a longer piece of writing and shortens it. To summarize *Heat Wave!*, you would include just the main idea and the most important details or events, in your own words. The main idea tells what the story is about. Important details answer questions such as *who? what? when? where? why?* and *how?* about the main idea.

Read the summary of *Heat Wave!* from Get Set to Read on page 359 of the student anthology: *In the story you are about to read, one Kansas farm-girl tries to save her farm from a heat wave that may prove just too hot to handle.* Then model how to identify the main idea and the most important events. Ask: *What is the story about?* (a very hot heat wave) *Who is the story about?* (a farm-girl) *Where does the story take place?* (on a farm in Kansas)

▷ Practice

Display **Transparency 3–26.** Have students read "What Is a Heat Wave?" and the summary sentences next to the paragraphs. Ask:

- **What is the summary about?** (what a heat wave is)

- **Which sentence in the summary states the main idea?** (A heat wave occurs when a large mass of unusually hot, sticky air sits over a region for a period time.)

- **Which sentences in the summary are details about the main idea?** (Temperatures can reach more than 100° F. Heat waves can damage crops. Extreme hot weather can cause illness and death.)

You might use a graphic organizer like the following one to record student responses. Then model how to use the graphic organizer to summarize the passage.

Main Idea

Detail:

↓

Detail:

↓

Detail:

► Apply

Students can use **Practice Book** page 203 to help them plan and organize their writing. Tell students to use the graphic organizer to write a summary for the first three pages of *Heat Wave!* in the student anthology, pages 361–363. Remind them to begin their summaries with the main idea. The sentences that follow the main idea should include details that tell who, what, where, when, why, and how.

Improving Your Writing
Paraphrasing

Teach Tell students that they are paraphrasing when they write a summary or when they take notes for a report. Explain that paraphrasing is restating, or using your own words, without changing the author's meaning. Remind students that any time they relate what someone else has said, unless they are quoting directly, they are paraphrasing.

Practice To model how to paraphrase, display **Transparency 3–27.**

Have students read the examples at the top of the transparency. Ask them to identify the sentence, A or B, that restates the same idea in different words without changing the author's meaning. Discuss the two sentences. Help students identify which is the better paraphrase and why. Have the class practice paraphrasing the other sentences on the transparency.

Apply Assign **Practice Book** page 204. Then have students review their paraphrasing of pages 361–363 to check that they have not changed the author's meaning.

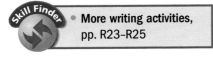

• More writing activities, pp. R23–R25

The Writer's Resource Library

Students may use this set of reference tools as they work on their own writing.

©Sunburst Technology Corporation, a Houghton Mifflin Company. All Rights Reserved.

Type to Learn™

Students may use **Type to Learn™** to learn proper keyboarding technique.

©Sunburst Technology Corporation, a Houghton Mifflin Company. All Rights Reserved.

Portfolio Opportunity

Save students' summaries as samples of their writing development.

········· **Houghton Mifflin English** ·········
Correlated instruction and practice, pp. H29–H30

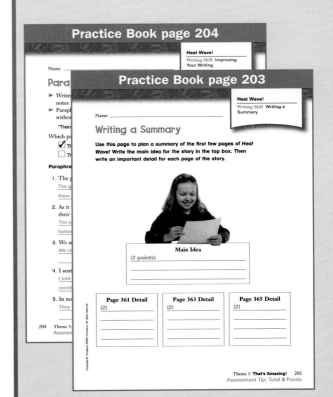

Practice Book page 204

Practice Book page 203

Heat Wave!
Writing Skill **Writing a Summary**

Name

Writing a Summary

Use this page to plan a summary of the first few pages of *Heat Wave!* Write the main idea for the story in the top box. Then write an important detail for each page of the story.

Main Idea
(2 points)

| Page 361 Detail (2) | Page 363 Detail (2) | Page 365 Detail (2) |

Theme 3: **That's Amazing!** 203
Assessment Tip: Total 8 Points

Listening/Speaking/Viewing

Listen to and Make an Announcement

▶ **Teach**

Invite students to think about an assembly program they attended or a television program they watched that included a master of ceremonies, or host. Tell them that the master of ceremonies is in charge of announcing what the spectators will see or hear next. Ask them what they think it takes to be a good master of ceremonies. Ask students to help you generate a list of guidelines for making effective announcements. Make sure that the following guidelines are mentioned:

- Think about the purpose of what you are saying.

- Put stress, or special emphasis, on the words that are important.

- Use pauses to separate ideas.

- Speak clearly and loudly enough to be heard, but do not shout.

Then point out to students that there are also important things to know about listening to announcements. Work with students to brainstorm a list of guidelines for listeners. Make sure that the following guidelines are included:

- Listen carefully for important information such as names, places, and times.

- Pay special attention to any instructions that you may be expected to follow.

Reaching All Students

English Language Learners

Have English language learners work in mixed groups to brainstorm ideas for an announcement advising their community of a forecasted heat wave. Announcements must include the key vocabulary *singe, temperature,* and *affected,* as well as ways people can protect themselves from the heat. Allow students to work with a partner and refer to this list as they write the announcement.

▶ Practice

In small groups, have students copy the following announcement onto cards: *Tonight on our stage we present the greatest talent on seven continents. The person you are about to meet has played before packed houses in Europe and Asia, won rave reviews in Africa and Australia, broken records for attendance in North and South America, and received a standing ovation from the penguins in Antarctica! Please give a warm welcome to—[name of their favorite performer]!* Have students practice saying the announcement. Ask them to evaluate each others' presentations in terms of the guidelines.

▶ Apply

Have students work individually, in pairs, or in groups together to write their own announcement that instructs students to do something. For example, students might ask listeners to assemble in the hallway on a certain day at a certain time for a given purpose such as a fire drill. Have students take turns presenting their announcements to the class. Evaluate their work in terms of the guidelines that have been established. Also, monitor listening comprehension by asking student listeners to repeat the instructions presented in the announcement.

Improving Speaking Skills

Share with students the following additional tips for making announcements:

- If you are making an announcement, try to think ahead about questions you might be asked by your listeners. Do not refer to names or places that your listeners are unlikely to know without including an explanation.

- If you are making an announcement that includes instructions, be sure to name the people whom you expect to follow the instructions. Do not leave your listeners wondering whether or not the instructions apply to them or to others.

Spiral Review

Comprehension: *Author's Viewpoint*

▶ Review

Review what students have learned about author's viewpoint.

- Author's viewpoint reflects his or her attitude, values, and purpose for writing.

- The language used, the information given and left out, and the illustrations or photographs all help to reveal the author's feelings.

- It is up to the reader to infer the author's viewpoint by using various story clues.

Tell students that one way to determine an author's viewpoint is by the words he or she uses. Show and discuss the following word web based on page 368. Ask students: Does the author think children like or dislike oatmeal?

▶ Apply

Have pairs of students create a word web like the one on the chalkboard to find out the author's viewpoint about farm animals. Tell pairs to write this in the center oval of their word webs: "Things the Girl Did for the Farm Animals." Ask them to find specific phrases about the girl's actions to write in the other ovals. If they need help, direct them to the last line of page 365 for an example. When they have finished, tell them to write a sentence telling what they infer about the author's feelings about animals. Have students share their word webs with the class. (Examples: got the cows in the barn, hosed the cows down, turned fans on cows, helps free Sally and the chickens; Possible answers for author's viewpoint include: farm animals need lots of care; farm animals are important and must be protected)

 Author's Viewpoint Grade 4, Theme 1, p. 79A

Dictionary: *Entry Words and Their Meanings*
Vocabulary: *Multiple-Meaning Words*
Dictionary: *Multiple-Meaning Words*

▶ Review

Review what students have learned about dictionary entries and multiple-meaning words.

- An entry word is a word that is entered and defined in a dictionary. Entry words are in alphabetical order. For example, *popcorn* comes before *potato*.

- An entry shows the base form of a word with its syllable breaks, pronunciation, part of speech, one or more definitions with sample sentences, and word forms with different endings for different uses.

- Certain word forms are not entry words. These include plurals of nouns, *-ed* and *-ing* forms of verbs, and *-er* and *-est* forms of adjectives and adverbs.

- For words with multiple meanings, the most commonly used meaning appears as the first definition in a dictionary. A boldfaced number precedes each definition.

Write the sample entry below on the board and use it to point out the features of a dictionary entry and to review the meanings of *fine* used as an adjective:

fine *adjective* **1.** Consisting of small particles: *The sand was as fine as powder.* **2.** Very small or thin: *Can you read the fine print?* **3.** Very good in quality or appearance: *The oatmeal made fine glue.*

▶ Apply

Have pairs use a student dictionary to look up and copy the entry for one of these multiple-meaning words from *Heat Wave!*: *tune* (p. 361), *wave* (p. 361), *hound* (p. 365), *bed* (p. 367), *field* (p. 368), *coats* (p. 368), *fans* (p. 371), *wear* (p. 375), *hides* (p. 376). Assign a different word to each pair. When they have finished copying their entries, have pairs read the sentence from the selection containing their word to the class. Have them tell which meaning best fits the context of the sentence.

- **Entry Words and Their Meanings** Grade 4, Theme 2, p. 215I
- **Multiple-Meaning Words** Grade 4, Theme 1, p. 57I; Theme 2, p. 275I

Skill Reminder

Subjects and Predicates; Writing Complete Sentences

Remind students that a complete sentence has both a subject and a predicate. The main word in a complete subject is the simple subject. The main word in a complete predicate is the simple predicate. Write these sentences from *Heat Wave!* on the board. Ask students to underline the complete subject once and the complete predicate twice.

The mercury blasted out of the porch thermometer like a rocket.

Those poor critters were hot!

Then have students circle and label the simple subject and simple predicate in each sentence. (subjects: mercury, critters; predicates: blasted, were)

Taught: *Grade 4, Theme 1*
Reviewed: *Grade 4, Theme 2*

Theme Assessment Wrap-Up

▶ Preparing for Testing

Remind students that they can use test-taking strategies to help them do well on important tests.

Writing a Personal Response Tell students that today they will learn strategies for writing a response about a topic. Have them read Taking Tests on Anthology pages 382–383.

Discuss the tips on Anthology page 382 with students. Mention these points:

■ Remind students to organize their ideas before they begin writing. Tell them to make notes about their answer to the question(s) and their reasons or examples.

■ Remind students to tell about the topic throughout their response. They may want to review their notes and cross out reasons or examples that do not relate to the topic.

More Practice The **Practice Book,** pages 205–206, contains additional writing prompts for more practice.

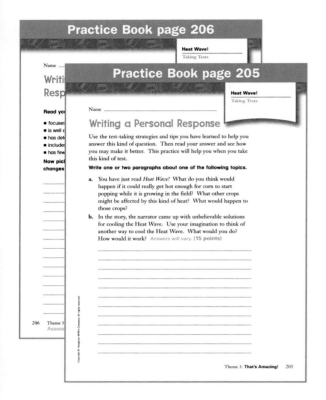

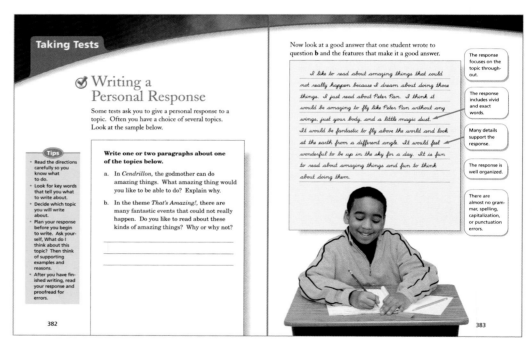

► Assessing Student Progress

Formal Assessment The **Integrated Theme Test** and the **Theme Skills Test** are formal group assessments used to evaluate student performance on theme objectives. The **Theme Skills Test** may be used as a pretest or may be administered following the theme.

The **Integrated Theme Test** assesses students' progress as readers and writers in a format that reflects instruction. Authentic literary passages test reading skills in context.

The **Theme Skills Test** assesses students' mastery of specific reading and language art skills taught in the theme. Individual skill subtests can be administered separately.

■ Integrated test of reading and writing skills: Comprehension strategies and skills, word skills, spelling, grammar, and writing

■ Tests discrete skills: Comprehension skills, word skills, spelling, grammar, writing, and information and study skills

Spelling Review/Assessment

Review with students the Spelling Words and, if appropriate, the Challenge Words from the spelling lessons on pages 323G, 357G, and 381G. Have volunteers summarize each spelling principle and explain how the words in each lesson illustrate the principle.

Practice Book

Practice Book: pp. 207–209
Take-Home Word Lists: Practice Book Handbook

5-Day Spelling Plan

See p. 323G

Pretest/Test

1. In a <u>make-believe</u> story, <u>anything</u> can seem true.
2. Jack <u>raced</u> across the pond to see the <u>snapping</u> turtle.
3. They called the <u>doctor</u> after the announcer <u>fainted</u>.
4. Christina got <u>homesick</u> after <u>ninety-nine</u> days.
5. To get to the <u>railroad</u>, don't go to the <u>airport</u>!
6. It was <u>pleasing</u> when the lights <u>dimmed</u>.
7. The army lost the war during the <u>final</u> <u>battle</u>.
8. He drinks lots of water <u>whenever</u> the <u>weather</u> is hot.
9. Was it <u>all right</u> if she <u>skipped</u> her piano class?
10. Don't go <u>hiking</u> without first <u>checking</u> your supplies.
11. The <u>uncle</u> of the king in the story was a poor <u>beggar</u>.
12. He won the gold <u>medal</u> in the <u>smelling</u> contest.
13. My dog is trying to <u>understand</u> what is <u>proper</u> behavior.
14. Avoid <u>trouble</u> by wearing your <u>seat belt</u>.
15. My <u>towel</u> is <u>striped</u>, but yours has dots.

Challenge Words

16. In a <u>postscript</u>, he described his new <u>motorcycle</u>.
17. In case of fire, try <u>breathing</u> through a wet <u>handkerchief</u>.
18. My mom <u>urged</u> us to keep the kitchen <u>scrubbed</u>.
19. Did you <u>cancel</u> because of your hurt <u>shoulder</u>?
20. We are <u>striving</u> to remember where the <u>decimal</u> point goes.

UNIVERSAL ACCESS *Reaching All Students*
Challenge

Challenge Words Practice Have students use the Challenge Words from the Take-Home Word List to write a story about something amazing.

Oral Reading Fluency

Early Grade 4	99–125 words per min.
Mid-Grade 4	112–133 words per min.
Late Grade 4	118–145 words per min.

For some students in Grade 4, you may want to check the oral fluency rate three times during the year. Students can check their own fluency by timing themselves reading easier text. The rates above are approximate.

Decoding and comprehension should be considered together in evaluating students' reading development. For information on how to select appropriate text, administer fluency checks, and interpret results, see the **Teacher's Assessment Handbook.**

For more information on assessing fluency, also see the Back to School section of this **Teacher's Edition.**

▶ Assessing Student Progress (continued)

Assessing Fluency Oral reading fluency is a useful measure of a student's development of rapid automatic word recognition. Students who are reading on level in Grade 4 should be able to read, accurately and with expression, in appropriate level text at the approximate rates shown in the table to the left. In this theme, an appropriate selection to be used with most students is *Heat Wave!*

Using Multiple Measures Student progress is best evaluated through multiple measures, which can be collected in a portfolio. The portfolio provides a record of student progress over time and can be useful in conferencing with the student, parents, or other educators. In addition to the tests mentioned on page 383, portfolios might include the following:

- Observation Checklist from this theme
- Story writing from the Reading-Writing Workshop
- Other writing, projects, or artwork
- One or more items selected by the student

Using Assessment for Planning Instruction You can use the results of theme assessments to evaluate individual students' needs and to modify instruction during the next theme. For more detail, see the test manuals or the **Teacher's Assessment Handbook.**

Customizing Instruction

Student Performance Shows:	Modifications to Consider:
Difficulty with Decoding or Word Skills	**Emphasis:** Word skills, phonics, reading for fluency; check for phonemic awareness **Resources:** Teacher's Edition: *Phonics Review, Structural Analysis Reteaching lessons;* Phonics Screening Test; Lexia Quick Phonics Assessment CD-ROM; Lexia Phonics CD-ROM: Intermediate Intervention
Difficulty with Oral Fluency	**Emphasis:** Reading and rereading of independent level text; vocabulary development **Resources:** Teacher's Edition: *Leveled Books;* Reader's Library; Theme Paperbacks; Literature Resources; Book Adventure Website
Difficulty with Comprehension	**Emphasis:** Oral comprehension; strategy development; story comprehension; vocabulary development **Resources:** Teacher's Edition: *Extra Support notes, Comprehension Reteaching lessons;* Get Set for Reading CD-ROM
Overall High Performance	**Emphasis:** Independent reading and writing; vocabulary development; critical thinking **Resources:** Teacher's Edition: *Think About the Selection questions, Challenge notes;* Theme Paperbacks; Literature Resources; Book Adventure Website; Education Place Website; Challenge Handbook

Theme Resources

Resources *for* That's Amazing!

Contents

One Day in May
Reader's Library for The Stranger

One Day in May
by Kitty Colton

Selection Summary
Transplanted from the country, Lin can't find spring in the gray city in *One Day in May*. An odd woman with bird's-nest hair and mossy clothes points out signs that Lin had missed— a budding twig, a falcon's nest. The woman then agrees there has been too much rain, and the sun bursts forth. Lin brightens up, only to find the odd woman gone and a patch of tulips in her place, leaving the reader to wonder "Who *was* that unusual woman?"

Key Vocabulary
grates: bars covering openings on the street where subway steam can escape

stoop: steps that lead to the front door

scowl: to frown in an angry way

stubbornly: in an unwilling way

contented: peaceful and pleased

▶ Preparing to Read

Building Background Ask students to think about spring: What signs show that spring is coming? What colors do students associate with spring? What weather? How does spring make them feel? Do they think there's a difference between spring in the country and spring in the city? If so, what?

Developing Key Vocabulary Make sure students understand the meanings of the Key Vocabulary words listed at the left. Remind them to use the Phonics/Decoding Strategy when they come to a word they don't know. For students who need more help with decoding, use the review on the next page.

▶ Strategy/Skill Focus

Refer students to the Strategy Poster. Review when and how to use the Monitor/Clarify Strategy.

Noting Details Connect looking for signs of spring to looking for story details that tell more about important story ideas or events. Invite students to monitor their reading to see what interesting or unusual details they notice about this day in May. Remind them to stop if they are confused to try to clarify the problem.

On the board, write this sentence from the story.

> The woman jumped to her feet and pointed down. A branch *had* sprouted up where she was sitting. "Sometimes you don't notice what's right in front of your nose," she said.

Help students see how the woman's comment to Lin encourages Lin to note details around her. Then invite volunteers to identify the story details in this passage: *the woman jumped up and pointed down; a branch had sprouted.*

▶ Previewing the Text

Have a volunteer read the title and introduction. Then encourage students to browse through the illustrations and describe what they see. Point out the odd details about the woman. Invite predictions about how she will be involved in the story.

▶ Supporting the Reading

Have students read silently or with a partner. If needed, use these prompts:

pages 4–9

- *What does Lin wish she could see out her window on this spring day?*

- *What does she see instead? How does this make her feel?*

- *Describe the woman who appears. What do you think she might do?*

pages 10–15

- *What strange thing does Cleo do? How does the woman react?*

- *How does the woman seem to feel about animals? about trees?*

- *Do you think the branch was there before the woman sat down? Explain.*

pages 16–20

- *What bit of nature does the woman point out on the building?*

- *What happens at the end? Who might this unusual woman be?*

▶ Responding

After students have finished *One Day in May,* begin a discussion of the story by helping them answer the questions on page 21. Then have students think about how details support important story ideas by filling in the web on page 21.

Sample Answers 1) gray 2) She loves everything about nature, including gray rainy days that help things grow. 3) She has twigs and leaves in her hair and a spider hanging from her ear. She understands the pigeon. Wherever she sits, things grow. **Details Web:** possible entries: walls, roofs, streets, steam, sky, buildings, stoop.

Reaching All Students
English Language Learners

Building Background Draw on any personifications of the seasons from students' cultures such as Jack Frost. Help students understand the western concept of Mother Nature, so students will have a schema for the unusual women in the story.

Key Vocabulary Students may have difficulty with the various similies on pages 8, 9, and 16. Help them understand what two things are being compared in each simile.

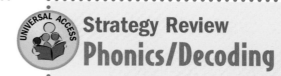

Strategy Review
Phonics/Decoding

Model using the Phonics/Decoding Strategy. Write this sentence on the board and point to the word *agreement:*

> Cleo poked her head out and meowed her <u>agreement</u>.

Think Aloud

When I look at the letters of this word from left to right, I see the base word /agree/. I know that word. Next, I see that /m-e-n-t/ has been added. I know this is a suffix that can be added to the end of a base word to make a new word, such as "basement" or "movement." So the word is /agree + ment/. Agreement. That means Cleo is meowing to show that she agrees with someone.

Diagnostic Check

If . . .	You can . . .
students need help with decoding	use the lesson above to review the Phonics/Decoding Strategy.
students have difficulty noting details	use the Reteaching lesson on page R8.

Tattercoat
by Susan DeLaney

Selection Summary

In *Tattercoat*, a goat herder tells a Cinderella story of the orphaned girl Tattercoat—so-called because of her raggedy coat. The herder meets her, wandering the hills, and becomes her one true friend. The herder's beautiful flute music makes all who look at Tattercoat see the goodness in her heart. When a prince meets Tattercoat, walking with the herder, he is immediately captivated with her and invites her to a ball. Tattercoat and the Prince dance all night, are soon married, and live happily ever after.

Key Vocabulary

surrounding: close-by, neighboring

lord: man who has a high rank or position

rind: tough outer layer

lag: to stay behind

Tattercoat
Reader's Library for Cendrillon

▶ Preparing to Read

Building Background Make sure that students are familiar with the story of Cinderella. Call on volunteers to summarize that story. Use several volunteers, each summarizing one section, such as Cinderella's being treated as a servant in the home of her wicked stepmother and stepsisters.

Developing Key Vocabulary Make sure students understand the meanings of the Key Vocabulary words listed at the left. Remind them to use the Phonics/Decoding Strategy when they come to a word that they do not know. For students who need more help with decoding, use the review on the next page.

▶ Strategy/Skill Focus

Refer students to the Strategy Poster. Review when and how to use the Question Strategy.

Compare/Contrast To better understand changes in the story, encourage students to pose questions that involve comparing and contrasting. On the board, write this sentence from *Tattercoat:*

> *Her rags had changed to a deep blue gown, and on her once-bare feet were sparkling silver shoes.*

Lead students to compare and contrast Tattercoat before and after the change that the sentence describes. (She is the same person, but her appearance is different. Before, her clothes were threadbare. After, she is dressed elegantly.)

▶ Previewing the Text

Lead students through the pages of *Tattercoat*. Discuss the illustrations, using words from the story as often as possible. Draw students' attention to the picture on page 26. Discuss with them what the woman in the baby's eyes might mean and who the woman might be.

▶ Supporting the Reading

Have students read silently or with a partner. If needed use these prompts:

pages 22–27

- *How is the family's life different before and after the daughter marries?*

- *What action makes the young lord sad as he goes to war? What thought makes him glad?*

- *What does it mean when the narrator says that the grandparents no longer have room in their hearts for love? Why do they feel this way?*

pages 28–34

- *How does Tattercoat get her name?*

- *Describe Tattercoat's life when she meets the goat herder.*

- *Why do you think the goat herder lags behind as the stranger and Tattercoat talk and laugh? Who is the stranger?*

pages 35–38

- *What problem does Tattercoat identify as soon as the prince is gone?*

- *What secret does the goat herder know that can solve Tattercoat's problem?*

- *What do you think that the goat herder means when he says, "I wouldn't have it any other way"?*

Strategy Review
Phonics/Decoding

Model using the Phonics/Decoding Strategy. Write this excerpt on the board and point to the word *galloped*:

> The prince <u>galloped</u> off on his horse.

Think Aloud

I know how to divide this word between the /l/s, which gives me /g–a–l/, and /l–o–p–e–d/. I think the first part rhymes with "pal," and "Sal," like in the story Blueberries for Sal. I try saying the second part with a long /o/ like in "roped". My guess doesn't sound right, so I'll check the dictionary. I find that the word is pronounced: /GAL lə ped/.

▶ Responding

After students have finished reading *Tattercoat*, begin a discussion of the story by helping them answer the comprehension questions on page 39. The have students refer to their completed charts as they compare and contrast different versions of the Cinderella story.

Sample Answers Questions **1)** The goat herder **2)** Her father and grandparents are too absorbed in their grief to care for her, and the servants are too busy. **3)** Before: Sad and neglected, but for her friendship with the goat herder; After: A happy princess **Chart:** Same, Same, Different, Same

Reaching All Students
English Language Learners

Building Background Some students may be familiar with another version of the Cinderella story. Invite volunteers to share any such stories from other cultures.

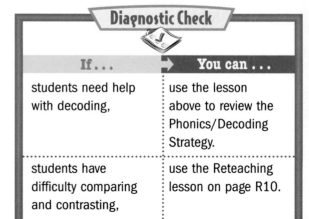

Diagnostic Check

If . . .	You can . . .
students need help with decoding,	use the lesson above to review the Phonics/Decoding Strategy.
students have difficulty comparing and contrasting,	use the Reteaching lesson on page R10.

The Big Gust

Reader's Library for Heat Wave!

The Big Gust
by Andrew Clements

Selection Summary

The Big Gust is a tall tale about why each person from Mayville will always remember what he or she was doing the day the big gust came. Jean Adams' dog inflated like a balloon. Tommy James's dragon kite took him on a wild ride. A vegetable garden was carried onto a roof. A duck pond blew into a school gym. A sport shop's stock of tennis balls bounced all the way to Chestertown. Although strange things have since happened in Mayville, nothing has been as wild as that one big gust.

Key Vocabulary

gust: sudden, brief rush of wind

hail: small balls of ice and snow that fall to Earth as precipitation

picket: pointed post

jumble: mass of things all mingled together

Preparing to Read

Building Background Ask students if they have ever heard a story that gets more and more amazing—and less and less believable—with each retelling, such as a tall tale. After volunteers offer answers, inform students that *The Big Gust* is mostly about things that could not really happen. Point out that the story is, however, set in a realistic place.

Developing Key Vocabulary Make sure students understand the meanings of the Key Vocabulary words listed at the left. Remind them to use the Phonics/Decoding Strategy when they come to a word that they do not know. For students who need more help with decoding, use the review on the next page.

Strategy/Skill Focus

Refer students to the Strategy Poster. Review when and how to use the Evaluate Strategy.

Fantasy/Realism Encourage students, as they read the story, to distinguish between things that could happen and things that could not happen in real life. On the board, write this excerpt from *The Big Gust*:

> *Gary Jones was all set to fix his picket fence. When the big gust came, every single picket and a whole box of nails went up in a jumble. But when they came down, Gary had a new fence. And he'd never even picked up his hammer!*

Lead students in differentiating the make-believe (the fence's building itself) and real (the picket fence, pickets, nails, and hammer) parts of the passage.

Previewing the Text

Lead students through the pages of *The Big Gust*. Discuss the illustrations, using words from the story as often as possible. As you leaf through the book, point out the true-to-life characters engaged in make believe scenes. Call on volunteers to identify scenes that look fun to read.

▶ Supporting the Reading

Have students read silently or with a partner. If needed use these prompts:

pages 40–45

- *What is the setting of the story?*

- *How did Clipper get her name?*

- *At what point in the part about Clipper can you tell that the author is writing make-believe?*

pages 46–51

- *How does the big gust help Elsie Chen win first prize for her tomatoes?*

- *How does the big gust affect what game the kids play in the school gym?*

- *Do you think the kids enjoy reading their library books more or less after the big gust comes? Explain your answer.*

pages 52–56

- *How is Chestertown affected by the big gust?*

- *How does Gary Jones' life change after the big gust?*

- *Tell how the story would be different if it were about a real gust.*

▶ Responding

After students have finished reading *The Big Gust*, begin a discussion about the story by helping them answer the comprehension questions on page 57. Then have students complete their charts.

Sample Answers Questions **1)** Elsie Chen **2)** That the caller is being chased by a barking balloon with hair ribbons **3)** Jean Adams' dog, Clipper; she got that way by yawning—and being blown up—when the big gust came **Chart:** What Could Happen: Tomatoes grow better closer to the sun; kids play kickball in the school gym. What Could Not Happen: Garden blows away and lands in one piece on a roof; pond with animals and lily pads in place blows into a gym.

Reaching All Students
English Language Learners

Building Background Invite students to share with the class any unforgettable weather events that they have experienced in their countries of origin.

Strategy Review
Phonics/Decoding

Model using the Phonics/Decoding Strategy. Write this excerpt on the board and point to the word *tomatoes*:

> *"Oh, good," thought Elsie. "Now my <u>tomatoes</u> are closer to the sun."*

Think Aloud

As I look at the letters of this word from left to right, I see that there are three parts that look like words I know: /t-o/, /m-a/, and /t-o-e-s/. The words are "to," "Ma," and "toes." I'll try to put these three words together: /TOO//ma//toes/. That doesn't sound quite right, but it does sound like another word I know: /tuh MAY toes/ — tomatoes. Tomatoes taste good in spaghetti.

Diagnostic Check

If . . .	You can . . .
students need help with decoding,	use the lesson above to review the Phonics/Decoding Strategy.
students have difficulty differentiating fantasy and realism	use the Reteaching lesson on page R12.

Comprehension Skills: Noting Details

Reteaching

OBJECTIVES

Students

- use details to explain a character's feelings
- use details to visualize events
- use details to infer important ideas

Teach

Write the following sentence on the board: *This place has a bed, a dresser, and a closet with clothes.*

Ask students, *What place usually has these things?*

Ask students to identify the place and to explain how they knew. Encourage students to use the following strategy for noting details as they read.

1. Notice important details.
2. Think about what they mean.
3. Use details to visualize events.

Practice

Have students follow in their books as you read aloud pages 306–308. Work with students to select the details that can be used to learn who the stranger is. Model the thinking.

Think Aloud

Who is this stranger? On page 306 I learn that the mercury is stuck at the bottom when the doctor takes the stranger's temperature.

On page 308 I read that when the man eats with the Baileys, he is fascinated by the steam that rises from the hot food. Also, Mrs. Bailey shivers. So somehow, this man is connected to things being cold. I have some good clues, but I'll have to read more before I can figure out who the stranger is.

With students, skim the rest of the story. Help them identify other details that might help solve the mystery. (p. 310, fascinated by geese flying south; p. 312, seasons don't change; p. 314, stranger departs and weather gets cold, leaves turn; p. 316, every autumn, "See you next fall" appears on farmhouse window)

Remind students that these details describe what happens when autumn comes. Help them see that the author provided details to help readers identify the stranger as Autumn.

Apply

Have students keep track of details and use them to understand the story better as they read the **Reader's Library** selection *One Day in May* by Kitty Colton. Have students complete the questions and activity on the Responding Page.

Skill Finder • Noting Details, pp. 323A–323B

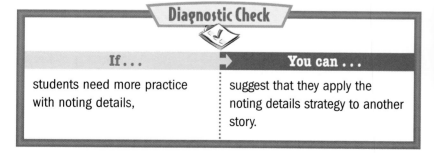

Diagnostic Check

If...	You can ...
students need more practice with noting details,	suggest that they apply the noting details strategy to another story.

Comprehension Skills: Noting Details
Challenge/Extension

Science
Explore Autumn Changes

Small Group Activity Ask a group of students to make an illustrated chart showing details of the many different changes associated with autumn: animal migration and hibernation, climate changes, responses of various trees and plants, and so on. Students can use encyclopedias and science books to do their research. Have the group present and explain the chart to the class.

Listening/Speaking
Use Details to Guess Places

Partner Activity Have students work in pairs to play this "detail" guessing game. One student gives three details about a place, which the other student must then guess. If the second student cannot guess, the first student should provide another three details, then another three, and so on, until the second student either guesses or gives up. Have each student take two or three turns providing clues and guessing.

Challenge
Writing
Write Character Sketches

Independent Activity Ask students to describe a real or imaginary person, using at least six details about how that person looks, sounds, and acts. Have students share their character sketches with the rest of the class.

Reader's Library

Comprehension Skills: Compare and Contrast

Reteaching

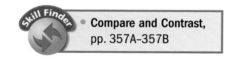

OBJECTIVES

Students

- distinguish between comparison and contrast
- infer comparison and contrast
- compare and contrast details, characters, and events in a story

Teach

Draw a Venn diagram, such as the one shown here, on the chalkboard.

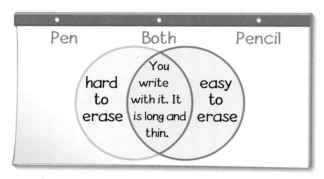

Pen   Both   Pencil

hard to erase | You write with it. It is long and thin. | easy to erase

Show students a pen and a pencil. Ask how the two items are alike. Write students' responses in the overlapping section of the two circles. Explain to students that they have just made a comparison.

Now ask students how a pen and a pencil are different. Write responses in the appropriate outer sections of the Venn diagram. Explain to students that when they think about how two people, places, things, or events are different, they are contrasting them.

Practice

With students, go through *Cendrillon* and identify differences between characters and events. (p. 335, Mamma and Vitaline eat well, while Cendrillon does not; Vitaline and Mamma can go to the ball, but Cendrillon cannot; p. 339, Cendrillon's "poor calico dress" becomes a fancy gown; p. 340, the narrator's "shift" becomes "a fine red dress"; p. 350, Cendrillon's clothes change from poor to rich to poor again)

Then go through the story looking for examples of things that are similar. (p. 331, Cendrillon and the narrator are both loving and kind; p. 345, Cendrillon and the narrator are both happy; p. 347, Cendrillon and the narrator are both dressed like washerwomen; p. 349, Mamma and Vitaline both say Cendrillon is lazy)

Jot student responses on a Venn diagram or other graphic organizer.

Apply

Have students compare and contrast the characters in the **Reader's Library** selection *Tattercoat* by Susan Delaney. Ask students to complete the questions and activity on the Responding Page.

Skill Finder
- **Compare and Contrast,** pp. 357A–357B

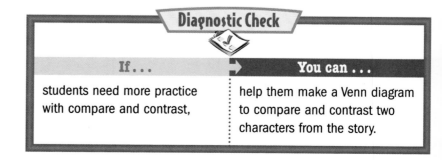

Diagnostic Check

If . . .	You can . . .
students need more practice with compare and contrast,	help them make a Venn diagram to compare and contrast two characters from the story.

Comprehension Skills: Compare and Contrast
Challenge/Extension

Art/Science
Create Contrasting Pictures

 Small Group Activity Ask students to think about how the same place can look different during different seasons or different weather. Then have each group choose two contrasting views of a familiar place, for example, the school playground on a sunny day and on a rainy day, or the view from the classroom window in winter and in spring. Invite students to create two pictures illustrating these contrasts, and have them present their pictures to the class.

 ## Challenge
Listening/Speaking
Compare and Contrast Two Stories

Partner Activity Have students recall the story of Cinderella, or give them a copy of the story. Then invite them to work in pairs to make a chart comparing and contrasting the original version of this fairy tale to *Cendrillon*. Invite students to present their charts to the class.

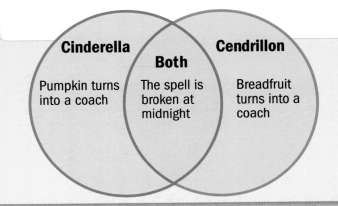

Cinderella — Pumpkin turns into a coach

Both — The spell is broken at midnight

Cendrillon — Breadfruit turns into a coach

Writing
Write Comparison/Contrast Paragraphs

Independent Activity Show students two contrasting images of comparable items, for example, two different kinds of parties, two different meals, or two different images of stormy weather. Invite students to write one paragraph, telling how the two images are alike, and another, telling how they are different.

Reader's Library

Comprehension Skills: Fantasy and Realism

Reteaching

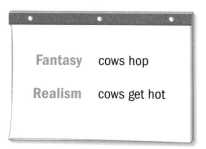

OBJECTIVES

Students

- recognize the difference between fantasy and reality in a fantasy story
- identify fantastic and realistic details in a fantasy story

Teach

Tell students the following stories:

Story 1 *Today, I got to school, took off my coat, and sat down at my desk. Then the principal came into the room and began to talk to me.*

Story 2 *Today, I rode my dinosaur to get to school. I took off my coat and stood on the ceiling, waiting for the class to arrive. Then a glowing, green giant started to talk to me.*

Ask students how the stories are alike and how they are different. Help students see that the second story is a *fantasy*, even though it has some elements of reality. On a chart, make two lists: *Fantasy* and *Realism*. Have students identify the different types of details in the two stories.

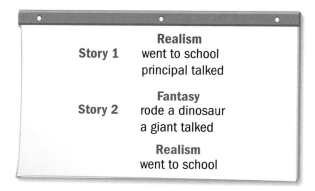

Story 1	**Realism** went to school principal talked
Story 2	**Fantasy** rode a dinosaur a giant talked
	Realism went to school

Point out that in *Heat Wave!*, the author mixes fantastic and realistic details. Good readers need to keep them sorted out. Read the second paragraph on page 361 aloud with students. Then model distinguishing between fantasy and reality:

Think Aloud

The narrator is feeding the chickens—that's something she could really do. But then she sees "a big old clump of crinkled, yellow air rolling across the sky." That's not real! You can't see air like that! I can see that this author is mixing fantasy and realism in this fantasy story.

Practice

With students, go through *Heat Wave!* and list details under *Fantasy* or *Realism*.

Fantasy	cows hop
Realism	cows get hot

Apply

Have students keep track of fantasy and reality in the **Reader's Library** selection *The Big Gust* by Andrew Clements. Ask students to complete the questions and activity on the Responding Page.

Skill Finder
- Fantasy and Realism, pp. 381A–381B

Diagnostic Check

If . . .	You can . . .
students need more practice with fantasy and realism,	have them read another fantasy story and work with them to identify each detail of fantasy.

Comprehension Skills: Fantasy and Realism
Challenge/Extension

Art
Create Fantastic and Realistic Pictures

 Partner Activity Ask students to think of a real place that they are familiar with. It might be a place in or near their homes, a location in the school, or a place in their community. Have them make two pictures: one showing something that could really happen in that place, and another showing a fantasy. The fantasy picture might include absurd happenings, such as snowing marshmallows, or it might feature fantastic characters, such as dragons. Invite students to share their work with their partners, who can identify the fantastic elements in the second picture.

 ## Challenge
Listening/Speaking
Tell a Group Story that Mixes Fantasy and Realism

Small Group Activity Have groups of four to six students tell a collective fantasy story. Tell students to go around a circle, each student adding a spoken sentence until the story is done. Then ask students to list at least three things in their story that were fantasy and three that were real. Students might also enjoy making a group illustration of their stories.

Writing
Begin a Fantasy Story

Independent Activity Invite students to write one or two paragraphs beginning a story that mixes fantasy with reality. Give students highlighters of contrasting colors. Ask them to highlight the fantasy details in one color and the things that could really happen in another.

Structural Analysis Skills: Compound Words

Reteaching

OBJECTIVES

Students

- read words that are compound words

- identify the two words that make up a compound word

- identify the meaning of compound words

Teach

Write the following sentence on the board: *Katy watched from her bedroom window.*

Ask students to read the underlined word. Explain that two base words have been combined to form a new word. Draw a line between the two base words so that students can see its parts.

Write another sentence on the board: *He left his skateboard in the driveway this afternoon.*

Draw a line under the three compound words and then discuss the following steps for decoding compound words:

1. Find the two small words.
2. Think about the meaning of each small word.
3. Put the two small words together.

Students can refer to the **Phonics/Decoding Strategy Poster** for more tips.

Practice

Help students practice identifying visual patterns of compound words. Display the following list, and read each word aloud with students.

basketball   pancake
airplane   notebook
postcard   backyard

Discuss the meaning of each word. Ask students to come to the board, draw a line between the two base words, say each one, and then say the whole word and use it in a sentence.

Apply

Display the following compound words:

downstairs   toothbrush
flashlight   rowboat
newspaper   popcorn

Write the compound words from the list on index cards. Cut the cards into two parts. Have students work together to match parts. Ask pairs to write a sentence using the compound word formed from their word parts. Have students read their sentences aloud.

Skill Finder · Compound Words, p. 323E

Diagnostic Check

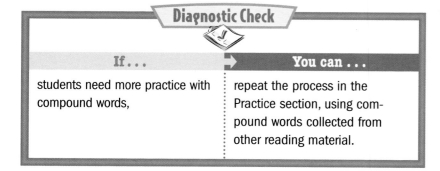

If...	You can ...
students need more practice with compound words,	repeat the process in the Practice section, using compound words collected from other reading material.

That's Amazing!
Vocabulary Activities

Synonyms

Partner Activity Display these words from the first page of the story: *cool, breeze.* Ask students if there are other words that mean the same or almost the same as *cool.* (cold, icy, chilly, freezing). Repeat the question for breeze. (wind) Remind students that two or more similar words are called *synonyms.*

Have students write synonyms for the following words from the story:

Story Word	Synonyms
road	street, highway
terror	fear, horror
hot	burning, sizzling
shyly	timidly
happy	cheerful, content
upset	worried, nervous
dashed	rushed, hurried, ran

Challenge
Vocabulary Expansion

Small Group Activity Invite students to look at the description of the stranger's clothes on page 306. Help students identify the specific adjectives that Van Allsburg uses: *odd, rough, leather.*

Ask students how using precise words helps make the story more exciting. (The words are so specific that you can picture exactly what the stranger is wearing and how unusual his clothing is.)

Work with students to find some other precise adjectives to describe the stranger. (timid, shy, awkward, curious, friendly, puzzled, confused)

Have students work together in small groups to create a character sketch of a mysterious person, using as many specific adjectives as they can. Then have the groups present their sketches to the class, reading them aloud in dramatic, mysterious voices.

Structural Analysis Skills: The Suffix -able

Reteaching

OBJECTIVES

Students

- recognize when words have the suffix *-able*
- decode words with the suffix *-able*

Teach

Write the following sentences on the board:

> The shoe was small, and Vitaline's large toes were <u>breakable</u>.
> Her new dress was <u>washable</u>.

Ask students what is similar about the underlined words. Call attention to the suffix *-able*. Explain that it means "having the ability to do something."

Using the first sample sentence, model how you would decode words with with the suffix *-able*.

Think Aloud

I start to read this sentence, "The shoe was small, and Vitaline's large toes were _____." I can't read this word right away. Sometimes it helps to break a word into parts. Do I recognize any parts of this word? Yes. Here is the suffix -able. The first part of this word is break. When I put the parts together, I get breakable. It makes sense in this sentence.

Review the following strategy for decoding words with suffixes.

1. Divide the word into a base word and a suffix.
2. Think about the meaning of the base word.
3. Think about the suffix and its meaning.
4. Put the base word and suffix together and say the word.
5. Check that it makes sense in the sentence.

Students can refer to the **Phonics/Decoding Strategy Poster** for more tips.

Practice

Display the following words with the suffix *-able:*

> curable
>
> reachable
>
> likable
>
> manageable

Read each word aloud with students. Then have a volunteer draw a line between the base word and the suffix. Invite students to read each part aloud, then read the whole word and use it in a sentence.

Apply

Display more words with *-able*: *believable, imaginable, available, portable*. Have students draw a line between the suffix and the rest of the word, read each word part, and then read the entire word.

Skill Finder
- **The Suffix -able,** p. 357E

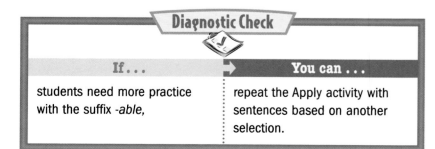

Diagnostic Check

If . . .	You can . . .
students need more practice with the suffix *-able*,	repeat the Apply activity with sentences based on another selection.

That's Amazing!
Vocabulary Activities

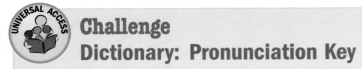

Challenge
Dictionary: Pronunciation Key

Small Group Activity Write on the board these words from page 331: *mahogany, struggled, christening.*

Ask students what they would do if they wanted to say these words but didn't know how to pronounce them. Remind students that they can look up pronunciations in the dictionary.

Pronunciations are written in a special code, called *phonetic spelling.* The guide to this code, the *pronunciation key,* is found at the bottom of each dictionary page.

Review a sample dictionary page with students. Then have partners look up *mahogany, struggled,* and *christening* and copy the words onto flash cards—regular spelling on one side, phonetic spelling on the other. Encourage them to find three other difficult words from the story and make phonetic flash cards for them too. Then have partners take turns showing each other flash cards and pronouncing the words.

Vocabulary Expansion

Partner Activity Invite students to look at the description of the fine ladies' clothes on page 332. Help students identify the specific words used: *satin, velvet.*

Help students see how these specific nouns help readers picture the clothes more easily.

With students, find other specific nouns and adjectives used to describe clothing in the story. (p. 339, calico, velvet, turban, silk, slippers, embroidered; p. 340, shift; p. 350, shawl.)

Have students work in pairs to write a description of someone else at the ball—Vitaline, Mamma, Paul, or another character—using as many specific nouns and adjectives as they can. Then have partners illustrate their sketches and present them to the class.

Structural Analysis Skills: Words with *-ed* or *-ing*

 Reteaching

Theme Resources

Word Work

Teach

Display the following sentences and ask students to read them aloud with you:

> He <u>changed</u> his tune that day.
> I <u>looked</u> out across the horizon.
> The geese were <u>plucked</u>, <u>stuffed</u>, and <u>roasted</u>.
> I was <u>feeding</u> the chickens.
> The Heat Wave came <u>rolling</u> across the sky.

Ask students what is similar about each set of underlined words. Mask the first half of each word to help students focus on the suffixes.

Model for students how to decode *crinkled* in this story sentence: *I looked out across the horizon and saw a big old clump of crinkled, yellow air rolling across the sky.*

Think Aloud

I looked out across the horizon and saw a big old clump of _____ ." I can't read this word right away. But I'll look for a part I know. Do I recognize any parts of this word? Yes. Here is the suffix, -ed. The first part of this word is crinkle. *When I put the parts together, I get* crinkled. *It makes sense in this sentence.*

Remind students that sometimes when *-ed* is added to a word, the first part of the word drops an *e: change + ed = changed.* Sometimes when *-ing* is added to a word, an extra letter is added: *pop + ing = popping.*

Practice

Display the following sets of base words and inflected forms, and read the words aloud with students.

holler	hollered	hollering
pop	popped	popping
blast	blasted	blasting
pull	pulled	pulling

Read each word aloud with students.

Students can refer to the **Phonics/Decoding Strategy Poster** for more tips.

Apply

Have pairs of students choose four of the words ending in *-ed* or *-ing* from the Practice list. Ask them to use the words in sentences. Have partners exchange papers and take turns reading the sentences aloud.

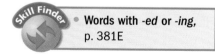

Skill Finder
- Words with *-ed* or *-ing*, p. 381E

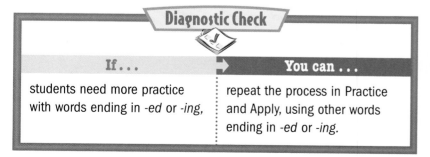

Diagnostic Check

If . . .	You can . . .
students need more practice with words ending in *-ed* or *-ing*,	repeat the process in Practice and Apply, using other words ending in *-ed* or *-ing*.

That's Amazing!
Vocabulary Activities

Challenge
Using Adjectives

Partner Activity Invite students to look at the description of the oatmeal on page 368. Help students identify the vivid adjectives that make this description come to life: *slimy, thick, lumpy, sticky.* Point out that these adjectives describe how things feel. Encourage students to suggest some other words that describe touch. (smooth, rough, silky, scratchy, crinkly, mushy)

Have students work in pairs to play a guessing game. One student gives two clues about an object. The other student has to guess the object. Then students switch roles. Continue to play until each student has had two or three turns.

Vocabulary Expansion

Small Group Activity Work with students to list on the board the various farm animals named in *Heat Wave!*: chickens, geese, hound dog, cows, crows, mule.

Invite students to add other farm animals to the list, such as *ducks, turkeys, horses, pigs,* and *cats.* Then work with students to complete a semantic features chart like this one:

Type of Animal	Flies	Swims	Walks on Land	Works	Produces Food	Eaten as Food
chickens			X		X	X
geese	X	X	X			X
hound dog			X			
crows	X					
mule			X	X		

Grammar Skills: Action Verbs

Reteaching

OBJECTIVES

Students
- identify action verbs
- use action verbs in sentences

Teach

Write the following sentences about *The Stranger* on the chalkboard:

> Mr. Bailey drove home.
>
> The man fell down.
>
> Katy peeked into the room.

Remind students that most verbs are words that show action. Ask students to identify the verb in each sentence on the board. (drove, fell, peeked)

Help students identify some of the action verbs that appear on the first page of the story, for example, *liked, whistled, blew, jammed.* Then ask students to read the sentences in which those verbs appear.

Practice

Work with students to identify some more action verbs from page 304: *found, knelt, opened, looked, jumped, tried, fell, took.* Write these words on the board. Ask students to read the sentences in which those verbs appear.

Encourage students to add words to the list: *run, walk, hop, skip, lift, clap, shake* [head], *nod.*

Invite volunteers to come up and mime actions for their classmates to identify. Add those action verbs to the list. Have students use each verb in a sentence.

Apply

Ask students to think about how they would respond to this stranger, if he had visited them. Have students work in small groups to write sentences describing what might happen. Each sentence should include an action verb. Have each group share their sentences with the class.

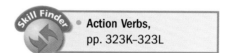
Skill Finder • Action Verbs, pp. 323K–323L

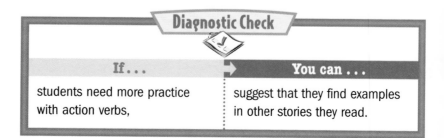

Diagnostic Check

If . . .	You can . . .
students need more practice with action verbs,	suggest that they find examples in other stories they read.

Writing & Language | Theme Resources

Grammar Skills: Main Verbs and Helping Verbs

Reteaching

Teach

Display the following sentences:

> I <u>live</u> on a green island.
> I <u>have lived</u> on a green island.

Ask students to compare the two sets of underlined words. (One is in the present; the other, in the past. One verb has one word; the other, two.) Put a double line under the main verb, and circle the helping verb in the second sentence above. Then review these concepts:

- When a verb has more than one word, the main verb shows the action.
- A helping verb works with the main verb. The verbs *am, is,* and *are* help other verbs show action that is happening now. Display this example: *Cendrillon <u>is going</u> to the ball.*
- The verbs *was, were, have, has,* and *had* help other verbs show action that happened in the past. Display these examples:

The Prince <u>has</u> <u>looked</u> everywhere for the slipper's owner.
Madame and Vitaline <u>have</u> <u>acted</u> rudely.

Practice

Help students underline main verbs and circle helping verbs in sentences about the story:

Paul is dancing with Cendrillon.
I have found a way to help Cendrillon.
Paul has placed the slipper on her foot.
We had found ourselves on the dusty road beside a smashed breadfruit.

Ask students to supply some original, story-based sentences, using main and helping verbs. Continue to underline main verbs and circle helping verbs.

Apply

Have students suggest a list of ten action verbs that act as main verbs. Tell students to get into small groups that have an even number of members. Ask half the group to name one of the action verbs, and the other half to add a helping verb. Then the group as a whole creates an original sentence, using the main verb and helping verb.

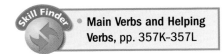

Skill Finder • **Main Verbs and Helping Verbs,** pp. 357K–357L

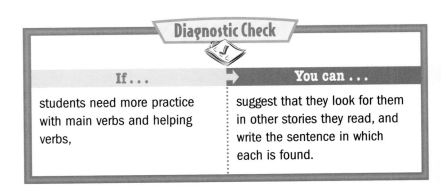

Diagnostic Check

If . . .	You can . . .
students need more practice with main verbs and helping verbs,	suggest that they look for them in other stories they read, and write the sentence in which each is found.

Grammar Skills: Present, Past, and Future Tenses

Reteaching

OBJECTIVES

Students identify the tense of a verb as present, past, or future.

Teach

Display the following sentences:

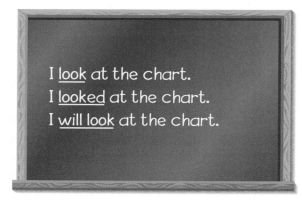

I <u>look</u> at the chart.
I <u>looked</u> at the chart.
I <u>will look</u> at the chart.

Remind students that the tense of a verb tells when something happens.

- *Present tense* shows action that is happening now.
- *Past tense* shows action that has already happened.
- *Future tense* shows action that is going to happen.

Discuss the examples.

Practice

Write the following sentences on the board. Ask students to identify the tenses.

> *I take my sister to school.* (present)
> *She dropped her books.* (past)
> *We will find a new backpack for her.* (future)

Then write the following words on the board: *look, help, crawl.* Have students write the past and future tense of each word.

Apply

Have students look back at the story *Heat Wave!* and choose three verbs. Ask them to write the present and future tenses of each word.

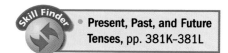
Skill Finder • **Present, Past, and Future Tenses, pp. 381K–381L**

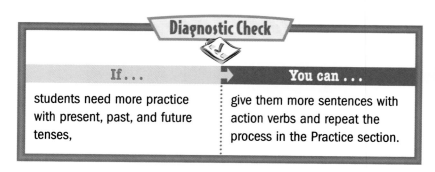

Diagnostic Check

If . . .	You can . . .
students need more practice with present, past, and future tenses,	give them more sentences with action verbs and repeat the process in the Practice section.

Theme Resources

Writing & Language

That's Amazing!
Writing Activities

Challenge
Write an Amazing Story

Encourage students to think of something amazing that they would enjoy writing about. They might create a myth of a supernatural tale like *The Stranger,* adapt a fairy tale like *Cendrillon,* tell a tall tale like *Heat Wave!* Students might also enjoy mixing elements of fantasy with reality, as these stories do.

Write a Newspaper Story

Invite students to imagine that they are news reporters sent to cover an amazing event. They might be covering the events of one of the three stories or reporting on some other suprising event, whether real or imaginary. Remind students that a good news story includes "the 5 *W*s and *H*"—*who, what, when, where, why,* and *how*—and that it gives the most important information first. Encourage students to include quotes from experts, participants, or witnesses, and have students write headlines for their stories.

That's Amazing!
Writing Activities

Write a Friendly Letter

Ask students to suppose they could write a letter to one of the characters in these amazing stories. What questions would they ask? What message would they like to communicate? Invite students to write their letters and then share them with a writing partner, who creates a response.

Write an Autobiography

Some students may feel that something amazing has happened to them—perhaps not in the fantastic manner of these stories, but still deserving of the title "amazing." If so, encourage students to write a few paragraphs telling what happened to them and why they consider it amazing.

That's Amazing!
Writing Activities

Challenge
Write a Business Letter

Ask students to imagine that they are applying for a job at the newly created "Amazing Events Bureau." Their job will be to create amazing events that will surprise, puzzle, and amaze the general public. Tell students that in their letters they should explain why they would be good at this job and suggest one or two amazing events that they would stage if they got the job, for example, a cotton candy blizzard or a mule that can fly.

Amazing Events Bureau

Write a Diary Entry

Invite students to write journal entries about amazing things they imagine could happen at school or in their neighborhood.

Technology

Students can use the **Student Writing Center** for all their writing activities.

Portfolio Opportunity

Save responses to activities on these three pages for writing samples.

That's Amazing!
Cross-Curricular Activities

Challenge
Math
Converting Temperatures

 Both *The Stranger* and *Heat Wave!* feature unusual temperatures: one very cold, the other very hot.

- First, explain to students that there are two ways of measuring temperature: Fahrenheit (used in England and the United States) and centigrade/Celsius (used in most of the rest of the world and in scientific experiments).
- Show students how to convert one type of temperature to the other (Fahrenheit to Celsius: subtract 32 and multiply by 5/9; Celsius to Fahrenheit, multiply by 9/5 and add 32).
- Invite students to imagine the temperature of the stranger (tell them that water freezes at 32 degrees Fahrenheit and 0 degrees Celsius) and of the Heat Wave (tell them that water boils at 212 degrees Fahrenheit and 100 degrees Celsius).
- Share other key temperatures: normal body temperature (98.6 degrees Fahrenheit), local average and record-breaking temperatures in winter and summer.

- Encourage students to plot all of these temperatures on a chart, from coldest to hottest, in both Fahrenheit and Celsius.

Music/Dance
Amazing Dances

Students might enjoy working independently, in pairs, or in small groups to create a dance version of *Cendrillon, The Stranger,* or a story of their own creation.

- Encourage students to choose or create live music, recorded music, or a rhythm accompaniment that conveys a sense of amazement and wonder as background to the dance.
- Students might also create costumes for their dances.
- Have students present their dances to the class.

That's Amazing
Cross-Curricular Activities

Drama/Speaking
"Believe It or Not" Stories

Share Ripley's *Believe It or Not* with a small group of students.

- Invite each of them to choose one of the characters in that collection and prepare to play him or her on an "amazing" talk show.
- Some students may prefer to create their own characters and invent their own amazing feats to share.
- Suggest that the group choose a talk show host as well. Have the group members work together to come up with some questions that the host might ask.
- Students can rehearse their talk show, then present it to the class, who might enjoy asking questions from the audience.

Science
Natural Wonders

 Invite students to do some research into the stories behind such real-life amazing phenomena as the following:

- Old Faithful, the geyser at Yellowstone National Park that erupts every hour;
- chameleons, who can change color to match their backgrounds;
- homing pigeons, who can find their way "home" across enormous distances.

Help students find science books or encyclopedias that can help them learn about the amazing phenomenon they have chosen. Encourage students to prepare a brief oral report with a visual aid and to share their "wonders" with the class.

Technology Resources

American Melody
P. O. Box 270
Guilford, CT 06437
800-220-5557

Audio Bookshelf
174 Prescott Hill Road
Northport, ME 04849
800-234-1713

Baker & Taylor
100 Business Court Drive
Pittsburgh, PA 15205
800-775-2600

BDD Audio
1540 Broadway
New York, NY 10036
800-223-6834

Big Kids Productions
1606 Dwyer Ave.
Austin, TX 78704
800-477-7811
www.bigkidsvideo.com

Blackboard Entertainment
2647 International
Boulevard
Suite 853
Oakland, CA 94601
800-968-2261
www.blackboardkids.com

Books on Tape
P.O. Box 7900
Newport Beach, CA 92658
800-626-3333

Filmic Archives
The Cinema Center
Botsford, CT 06404
800-366-1920
www.filmicarchives.com

Great White Dog Picture Company
10 Toon Lane
Lee, NH 03824
800-397-7641
www.greatwhitedog.com

HarperAudio
10 E. 53rd St.
New York, NY 10022
800-242-7737

Houghton Mifflin Company
222 Berkeley St.
Boston, MA 02116
800-225-3362

Informed Democracy
P.O. Box 67
Santa Cruz, CA 95063
831-426-3921

JEF Films
143 Hickory Hill Circle
Osterville, MA 02655
508-428-7198

Kimbo Educational
P. O. Box 477
Long Branch, NJ 07740
900-631-2187

The Learning Company
(dist. for Broderbund)
1 Athenaeum St.
Cambridge, MA 02142
800-716-8506
www.learningcompa-
nyschool.com

Library Video Co.
P. O. Box 580
Wynnewood, PA 19096
800-843-3620

Listening Library
One Park Avenue
Old Greenwich, CT 06870
800-243-4504

Live Oak Media
P. O. Box 652
Pine Plains, NY 12567
800-788-1121
liveoak@taconic.net

Media Basics
Lighthouse Square
P.O. Box 449
Guilford, CT 06437
800-542-2505
www.mediabasicsvideo.com

Microsoft Corp.
One Microsoft Way
Redmond, WA 98052
800-426-9400
www.microsoft.com

National Geographic Society
1145 17th Street N. W.
Washington, D. C. 20036
800-368-2728
www.nationalgeographic.com

New Kid Home Video
1364 Palisades Beach Road
Santa Monica, CA 90401
310-451-5164

Puffin Books
345 Hudson Street
New York, NY 10014
212-366-2000

Rainbow Educational Media
4540 Preslyn Drive
Raleigh, NC 27616
800-331-4047

Random House Home Video
201 E. 50th St.
New York, NY 10022
212-940-7620

Recorded Books
270 Skipjack Road
Prince Frederick, MD 20678
800-638-1304
www.recordedbooks.com

Sony Wonder
Dist. by Professional Media
Service
19122 S. Vermont Ave.
Gardena, CA 90248
800-223-7672

Spoken Arts
8 Lawn Avenue
P. O. Box 100
New Rochelle, NY 10802
800-326-4090

SRA Media
220 E. Danieldale Rd.
DeSoto, TX 75115
800-843-8855

Sunburst Communications
101 Castleton St.
P. O. Box 100
Pleasantville, NY 10570
800-321-7511
www.sunburst.com

SVE & Churchill Media
6677 North Northwest
Highway
Chicago, IL 60631
800-829-1900

Tom Snyder Productions
80 Coolidge Hill Road
Watertown, MA 02472
800-342-0236
www.tomsnyder.com

Troll Communications
100 Corporate Drive
Mahwah, NJ 07430
800-526-5289

Weston Woods
12 Oakwood Avenue
Norwalk, CT 06850-1318
800-243-5020
www.scholastic.com

Lesson Planning Support

Top Left Worksheet

Name _____

Make It Amazing!

Change the underlined words in the paragraph below to make it amazing. The first one is done for you. Accept reasonable answers, sample answers provided.

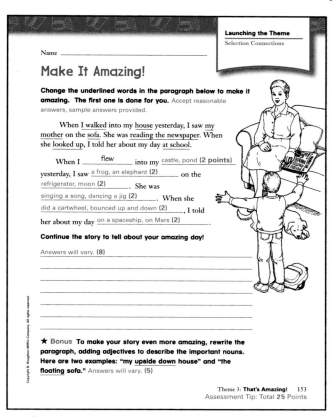

When I walked into my house yesterday, I saw my mother on the sofa. She was reading the newspaper. When she looked up, I told her about my day at school.

When I ___flew___ into my castle, pond (2 points) yesterday, I saw a frog, an elephant (2) on the refrigerator, moon (2). She was singing a song, dancing a jig (2). When she did a cartwheel, bounced up and down (2), I told her about my day on a spaceship, on Mars (2)

Continue the story to tell about your amazing day!

Answers will vary. (8)
_____
_____
_____
_____
_____

★ **Bonus** To make your story even more amazing, rewrite the paragraph, adding adjectives to describe the important nouns. Here are two examples: "my upside down house" and "the floating sofa." Answers will vary. (5)

Theme 3: **That's Amazing!** 153
Assessment Tip: Total **25** Points

Teacher's Book, page 293B

Top Right Worksheet

Name _____

That's Amazing!

	What in the story was realistic?	What amazing things happened in the story?
The Stranger	Most things from the story are realistic: the family, their house, their activities, and some of the stranger's behavior. **(4 points)**	The stranger has many odd traits: his low temperature breaks the thermometer; the rabbits are not afraid of him; leaves have stopped changing color.**(4)**
Cendrillon	People lead everyday lives; they have realistic attitudes; the island of Martinique is described realistically. **(4)**	Nannin's wand changes everyday items into special things. Things miraculously change back. **(4)**
Heat Wave!	The family lives on a farm, and the surroundings and possessions are all realistic at first: geese, cows, flowers, corn, crows. **(4)**	Everything that happens to these normal items is fantastic: geese are cooked by the heat wave, flowers walk, cow's milk turns to butter, lettuce cools air. **(4)**

Which of these stories was most amazing to you? Put a mark on the line for each story, labeled with the story's title, to show how realistic you think each one was! Answers will vary. **(2)**

```
0               5               10
Realistic                   Fantastic
```

154   Theme 3: **That's Amazing!**
Assessment Tip: Total **26** Points

Teacher's Book, page 293B

Bottom Left Worksheet

Name _____

Chilly Crossword

Complete the puzzle using words from the vocabulary list. Write the word that fits each clue.

Vocabulary
autumn
draft
etched
frost
mercury
peculiar
thermometer
timid

Across
2. season of year between summer and winter (1 point)
4. very thin covering of ice (1)
6. an instrument that measures temperature (1)
8. a flow of air (1)

Down
1. strange, odd (1)
3. silvery metal used in thermometers (1)
5. made a design by cutting lines (1)
7. shy; easily frightened (1)

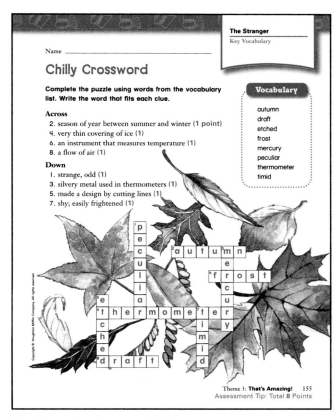

Theme 3: **That's Amazing!** 155
Assessment Tip: Total **8** Points

Teacher's Book, page 299B

Bottom Right Worksheet

Falling Words

```
autumn  draft   etched   frost
mercury  peculiar  thermometer  timid
```

1. As ___autumn___ approaches, leaves begin to turn color, farmers harvest their crops, and the temperature drops.
2. To keep out the cold ___draft___, Dad puts up the storm windows and seals the cracks around the doors.
3. This morning, we saw icy, white ___frost___ on our windows.
4. I ___etched___ my name in the frost with my fingernail.
5. I asked Mom to look at the ___thermometer___ and tell me how cold it was.
6. She said that the silvery line of ___mercury___ stopped at 25 degrees.
7. I thought it was ___peculiar___ when a robin landed on my windowsill; robins should have flown south weeks ago.
8. The ___timid___ bird flapped away in fear as I waved to it.

Teacher's Book, page 299B

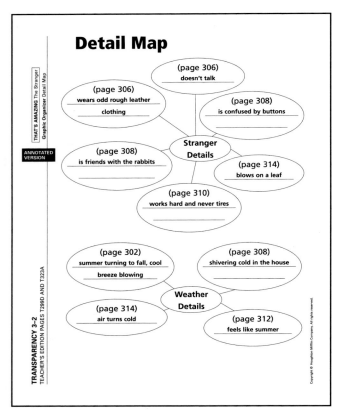

Teacher's Book, pages 299D and 323A

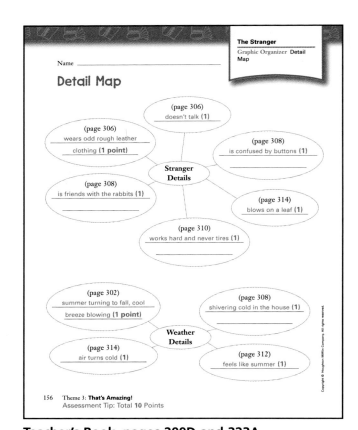

Teacher's Book, pages 299D and 323A

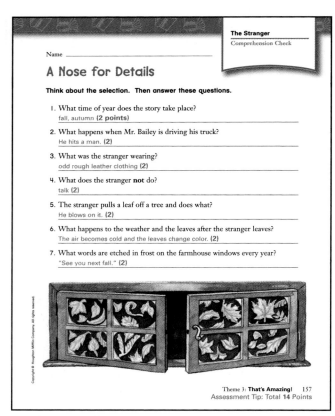

Teacher's Book, page 319

Teacher's Book, page 323B

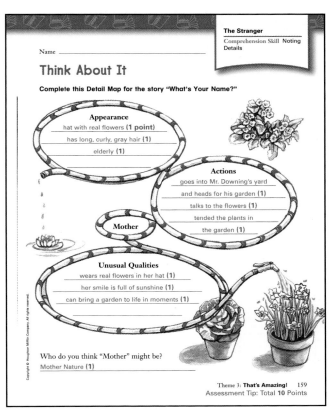

Teacher's Book, page 323B

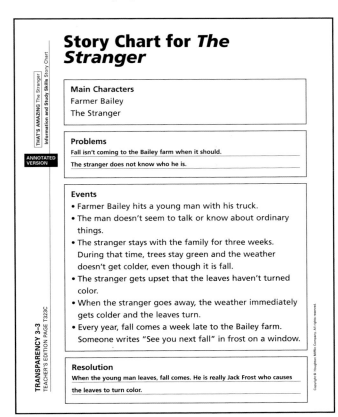

Teacher's Book, page 323C

Teacher's Book, page 323F

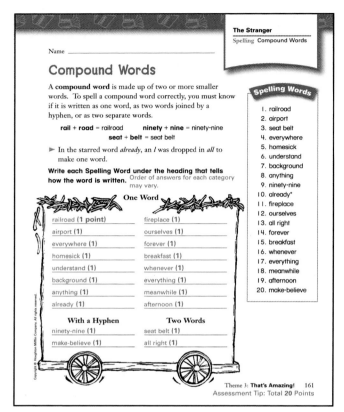

Compound Words

The Stranger
Spelling **Compound Words**

Name _____

A **compound word** is made up of two or more smaller words. To spell a compound word correctly, you must know if it is written as one word, as two words joined by a hyphen, or as two separate words.

rail + road = railroad   **ninety + nine** = ninety-nine
seat + belt = seat belt

▶ In the starred word *already*, an *l* was dropped in *all* to make one word.

Write each Spelling Word under the heading that tells how the word is written. Order of answers for each category may vary.

One Word

railroad (**1 point**)	fireplace (1)
airport (1)	ourselves (1)
everywhere (1)	forever (1)
homesick (1)	breakfast (1)
understand (1)	whenever (1)
background (1)	everything (1)
anything (1)	meanwhile (1)
already (1)	afternoon (1)

With a Hyphen   **Two Words**

ninety-nine (1)   seat belt (1)
make-believe (1)   all right (1)

Spelling Words
1. railroad
2. airport
3. seat belt
4. everywhere
5. homesick
6. understand
7. background
8. anything
9. ninety-nine
10. already*
11. fireplace
12. ourselves
13. all right
14. forever
15. breakfast
16. whenever
17. everything
18. meanwhile
19. afternoon
20. make-believe

Theme 3: **That's Amazing!**   161
Assessment Tip: Total **20** Points

Teacher's Book, page 323H

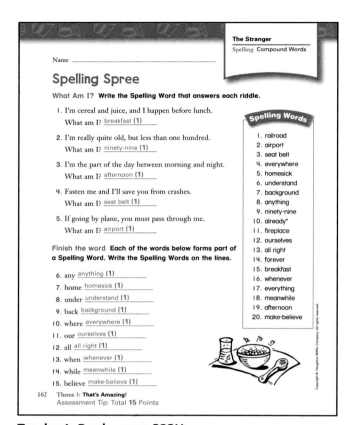

Spelling Spree

The Stranger
Spelling **Compound Words**

Name _____

What Am I? **Write the Spelling Word that answers each riddle.**

1. I'm cereal and juice, and I happen before lunch.
   What am I? breakfast (1)

2. I'm really quite old, but less than one hundred.
   What am I? ninety-nine (1)

3. I'm the part of the day between morning and night.
   What am I? afternoon (1)

4. Fasten me and I'll save you from crashes.
   What am I? seat belt (1)

5. If going by plane, you must pass through me.
   What am I? airport (1)

Finish the word **Each of the words below forms part of a Spelling Word. Write the Spelling Words on the lines.**

6. any anything (1)
7. home homesick (1)
8. under understand (1)
9. back background (1)
10. where everywhere (1)
11. our ourselves (1)
12. all all right (1)
13. when whenever (1)
14. while meanwhile (1)
15. believe make-believe (1)

Spelling Words
1. railroad
2. airport
3. seat belt
4. everywhere
5. homesick
6. understand
7. background
8. anything
9. ninety-nine
10. already*
11. fireplace
12. ourselves
13. all right
14. forever
15. breakfast
16. whenever
17. everything
18. meanwhile
19. afternoon
20. make-believe

162   Theme 3: **That's Amazing!**
Assessment Tip: Total **15** Points

Teacher's Book, page 323H

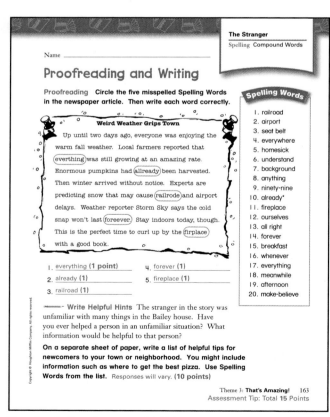

Proofreading and Writing

The Stranger
Spelling **Compound Words**

Name _____

Proofreading   Circle the five misspelled Spelling Words in the newspaper article. Then write each word correctly.

Weird Weather Grips Town

Up until two days ago, everyone was enjoying the warm fall weather. Local farmers reported that *everthing* was still growing at an amazing rate. Enormous pumpkins had *allready* been harvested. Then winter arrived without notice. Experts are predicting snow that may cause *railrode* and airport delays. Weather reporter Storm Sky says the cold snap won't last *foreever*. Stay indoors today, though. This is the perfect time to curl up by the *firplace* with a good book.

1. everything (**1 point**)   4. forever (1)
2. already (1)   5. fireplace (1)
3. railroad (1)

Spelling Words
1. railroad
2. airport
3. seat belt
4. everywhere
5. homesick
6. understand
7. background
8. anything
9. ninety-nine
10. already*
11. fireplace
12. ourselves
13. all right
14. forever
15. breakfast
16. whenever
17. everything
18. meanwhile
19. afternoon
20. make-believe

_____ **Write Helpful Hints** The stranger in the story was unfamiliar with many things in the Bailey house. Have you ever helped a person in an unfamiliar situation? What information would be helpful to that person?

On a separate sheet of paper, write a list of helpful tips for newcomers to your town or neighborhood. You might include information such as where to get the best pizza. Use Spelling Words from the list. Responses will vary. (10 points)

Theme 3: **That's Amazing!**   163
Assessment Tip: Total **15** Points

Teacher's Book, page 323H

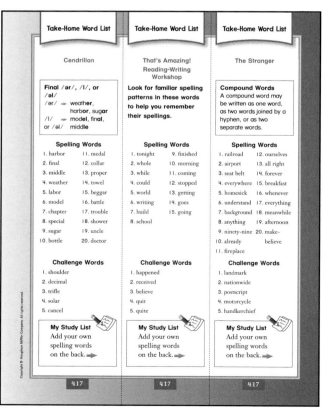

Take-Home Word List	Take-Home Word List	Take-Home Word List
Cendrillon	**That's Amazing!** Reading-Writing Workshop	**The Stranger**

Cendrillon

Final /ər/, /l/, or /əl/
/ər/ → weather, harbor, sugar
/l/ → model, final, or /əl/ → middle

Spelling Words
1. harbor   11. medal
2. final   12. collar
3. middle   13. proper
4. weather   14. towel
5. labor   15. beggar
6. model   16. battle
7. chapter   17. trouble
8. special   18. shower
9. sugar   19. uncle
10. bottle   20. doctor

Challenge Words
1. shoulder
2. decimal
3. trifle
4. solar
5. cancel

That's Amazing! Reading-Writing Workshop

Look for familiar spelling patterns in these words to help you remember their spellings.

Spelling Words
1. tonight   9. finished
2. whole   10. morning
3. while   11. coming
4. could   12. stopped
5. world   13. getting
6. writing   14. goes
7. build   15. going
8. school

Challenge Words
1. happened
2. received
3. believe
4. quit
5. quite

The Stranger

Compound Words A compound word may be written as one word, as two words joined by a hyphen, or as two separate words.

Spelling Words
1. railroad   13. all right
2. airport   14. forever
3. seat belt   15. breakfast
4. everywhere   16. whenever
5. homesick   17. everything
6. understand   18. meanwhile
7. background   19. afternoon
8. anything   20. make-
9. ninety-nine   believe
10. already
11. fireplace

Challenge Words
1. landmark
2. nationwide
3. postscript
4. motorcycle
5. handkerchief

My Study List Add your own spelling words on the back.→

My Study List Add your own spelling words on the back.→

My Study List Add your own spelling words on the back.→

417   417   417

Teacher's Book, page 323H

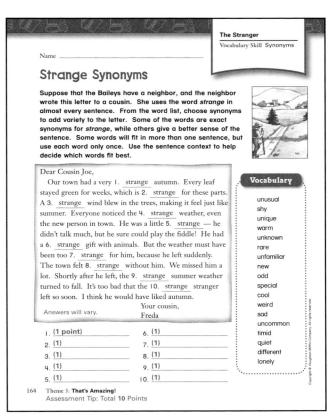

Strange Synonyms

The Stranger
Vocabulary Skill Synonyms

Name _____

Suppose that the Baileys have a neighbor, and the neighbor wrote this letter to a cousin. She uses the word *strange* in almost every sentence. From the word list, choose synonyms to add variety to the letter. Some of the words are exact synonyms for *strange*, while others give a better sense of the sentence. Some words will fit in more than one sentence, but use each word only once. Use the sentence context to help decide which words fit best.

Dear Cousin Joe,
    Our town had a very 1. __strange__ autumn. Every leaf stayed green for weeks, which is 2. __strange__ for these parts. A 3. __strange__ wind blew in the trees, making it feel just like summer. Everyone noticed the 4. __strange__ weather, even the new person in town. He was a little 5. __strange__ — he didn't talk much, but he sure could play the fiddle! He had a 6. __strange__ gift with animals. But the weather must have been too 7. __strange__ for him, because he left suddenly. The town felt 8. __strange__ without him. We missed him a lot. Shortly after he left, the 9. __strange__ summer weather turned to fall. It's too bad that the 10. __strange__ stranger left so soon. I think he would have liked autumn.

Answers will vary.

Your cousin,
Freda

Vocabulary

unusual
shy
unique
warm
unknown
rare
unfamiliar
new
odd
special
cool
weird
sad
uncommon
timid
quiet
different
lonely

1. __(1 point)__   6. __(1)__
2. __(1)__   7. __(1)__
3. __(1)__   8. __(1)__
4. __(1)__   9. __(1)__
5. __(1)__   10. __(1)__

164   Theme 3: **That's Amazing!**
    Assessment Tip: Total **10** Points

Teacher's Book, page 323I

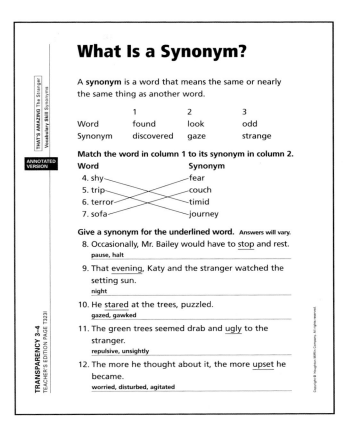

What Is a Synonym?

THAT'S AMAZING The Stranger
Vocabulary Skill Synonyms

ANNOTATED
VERSION

A **synonym** is a word that means the same or nearly the same thing as another word.

	1	2	3
Word	found	look	odd
Synonym	discovered	gaze	strange

Match the word in column 1 to its synonym in column 2.

Word	Synonym
4. shy	fear
5. trip	couch
6. terror	timid
7. sofa	journey

Give a synonym for the underlined word. Answers will vary.

8. Occasionally, Mr. Bailey would have to <u>stop</u> and rest.
   pause, halt

9. That <u>evening</u>, Katy and the stranger watched the setting sun.
   night

10. He <u>stared</u> at the trees, puzzled.
    gazed, gawked

11. The green trees seemed drab and <u>ugly</u> to the stranger.
    repulsive, unsightly

12. The more he thought about it, the more <u>upset</u> he became.
    worried, disturbed, agitated

TRANSPARENCY 3–4
TEACHER'S EDITION PAGE T323I

Teacher's Book, page 323I

Letter with Action Verbs

The Stranger
Grammar Skill Action Verbs

Name _____

What if Katy Bailey had a cousin and she wrote a letter to him? Read the letter. Circle each action verb and write it on the lines below.

Dear Cousin,
    We (have) a new guest at our house. I (think) he (lives) in the forest near us. He (wears) a leather shirt and pants. His breath (makes) things cold. I (call) him "Jack Frost." He (likes) my mother's cooking, though. He especially (enjoys) her homemade vegetable soup. I (hope) you (meet) him soon.
Love,
Katy

have **(1 point)**   think **(1)**
lives **(1)**   wears **(1)**
makes **(1)**   call **(1)**
likes **(1)**   enjoys **(1)**
hope **(1)**   meet **(1)**

Theme 3: **That's Amazing!**   165
Assessment Tip: Total **10** Points

Teacher's Book, page 323L

Take Action!

The Stranger
Grammar Skill Action Verbs

Name _____

Suppose Katy tells her class about the stranger who came to stay with her family. Complete Katy's story by filling each blank with an action verb. Choose verbs from the box or use action verbs of your own.
(1 point for each answer.)

    One fall day as my father __drives (1 point)__ his truck along the road, he __hears (1)__ a loud thump. He __jams (1)__ on the brakes and __jumps (1)__ out of the truck. Father __helps (1)__ the stranger into his truck.
    The doctor __listens (1)__ to the stranger's heart. The stranger __grows (1)__ stronger and __works (1)__ with Father on the farm. When the stranger __disappears (1)__, the leaves __change (1)__ color and the weather turns cold.

change
disappears
drives
grows
hears
jams
helps
jumps
listens
works

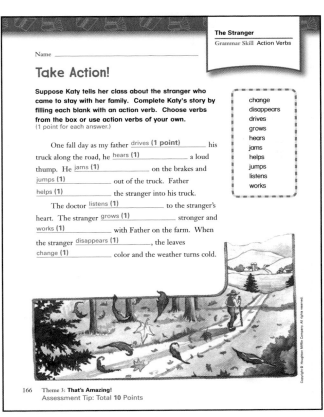

166   Theme 3: **That's Amazing!**
    Assessment Tip: Total **10** Points

Teacher's Book, page 323L

Lesson Planning Support *(Continued)*

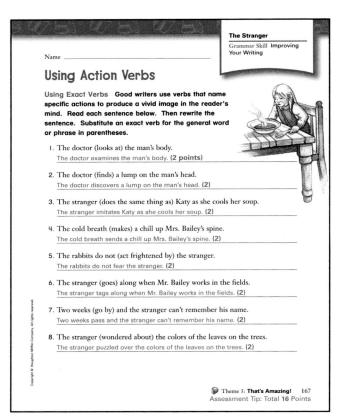

Teacher's Book, page 323L

Action Verbs

ANNOTATED VERSION

- An **action verb** is a word that shows action.

  A cool breeze blows across Farmer Bailey's face.
  The truck hits the stranger.
  The man opens his eyes.

1. The man <u>wears</u> leather clothes.
2. Mr. Bailey <u>speaks</u> to the man.
3. The doctor <u>listens</u> to the man's heart.
4. The man <u>eats</u> the delicious hot food.
5. The two rabbits <u>hop</u> toward the man.
6. They <u>look</u> back at the man.
7. The man <u>pitches</u> hay very well.
8. He never <u>rests</u> from the work.
9. A flock of geese <u>flies</u> overhead.
10. The stranger <u>watches</u> the geese in the sky.

Teacher's Book, page 323L

Using Exact Verbs

ANNOTATED VERSION

Good writers use exact verbs that give the reader an exact visual image.

1. The man (moves his hand back and forth on) the little rabbit's ears.
2. The flock of geese (moves through the air) in perfect V formation.
3. The stranger (looks hard) at the geese in flight.
4. The man could not (bring to mind) his name.
5. The man (goes up) the highest hill on the farm.

1. **The man strokes the rabbit's ears.**
2. **The flock of geese flies in perfect V formation.**
3. **The stranger stares at the geese in flight.**
4. **The man could not remember (or recall) his name.**
5. **The man climbs the highest hill on the farm.**

Teacher's Book, page 323L

Daily Language Practice

ANNOTATED VERSION

Correct two sentences each day.

1. Almost every where the leaves change color in the autumn.
   Almost everywhere the leaves change color in the autumn.
2. Outsid, the air is cold, but in side, the kitchen is warm.
   Outside, the air is cold, but inside, the kitchen is warm.
3. The family gathers by the fire place in the evening?
   The family gathers by the fireplace in the evening.
4. When ever the stranger breathed, the whole room grew cold.
   Whenever the stranger breathed, the whole room grew cold.
5. Menewhile, the rabbits hopped up into the mans arms.
   Meanwhile, the rabbits hopped up into the man's arms.
6. While the stranger was there, every thing went well?
   While the stranger was there, everything went well.
7. Sum times the stranger have looked sad.
   Sometimes the stranger has looked sad.
8. Everyday at brekfast the stranger eat well.
   Every day at breakfast the stranger eats well.
9. he was happy to eat any thing for lunch?
   He was happy to eat anything for lunch.
10. The Children think he is getting home sick.
    The children think he is getting homesick.

Teacher's Book, page 323L

THEME 3: That's Amazing!

Writing an Explanation

Title — **Green Leaves Turn Yellow, Orange, and Red**

Topic Sentence —
    The green leaves of summer turn yellow, orange, and red in autumn. Leaves are green because of a substance called chlorophyll. Chlorophyll makes food for the tree. Two-thirds of the color of leaves comes from green chlorophyll. There is so much green chlorophyll in summer leaves that we cannot see the other colors in them until fall. As the weather grows colder, trees draw the food stored in their leaves back into the branches and trunk. The green chlorophyll breaks down. Now we can see the other colors that were overshadowed by green chlorophyll. About 23 percent of leaf color is a substance called xanthophyll. It is yellow. About ten percent of leaf color is carotin. Carotin gives leaves (and carrots) their orange color. Sugar maples and scarlet oaks turn bright red because of anthocyanim, which is red. When the green chlorophyll retires, yellow, orange, and red get to show their colors.

Supporting Reasons/ Facts —

Teacher's Book, page 323M

Audience

Writers are always aware of their audience.

• Formal writing is for reports, presentations, and other school assignments.

  Formal: Leaves are green because of a substance called chlorophyll. Chlorophyll makes food for the tree. Two-thirds of the color of leaves comes from chlorophyll.

• Informal writing is for friendly letters, postcards, or e-mails between friends.

  Informal: I love how green everything is in May. When I look out my window, I can see green for miles!

Look at each of the following topics. Make a formal statement about each topic, as if you were reporting it to a group of people you didn't know. Then make an informal statement as if you were sending an e-mail to a friend.

fall colors
frost on the window
heating the house in the winter
ice melting
spring buds on trees

Teacher's Book, page 323M

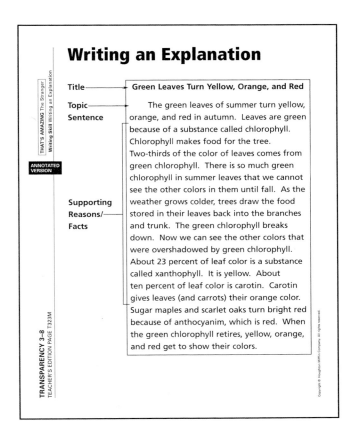

The Stranger
Writing Skill Writing an Explanation

Name _____

Writing an Explanation

Use this page to plan your explanation. You can explain why something happens or how something happens. Then number your reasons or facts in the order you will use them.

| Topic: (1 point) |
| Title: (1) |

| Topic Sentence: (2) |

Reason / Fact: (2)	Reason / Fact: (2)

Reason / Fact: (2)	Reason / Fact: (2)

168   Theme 3: **That's Amazing!**
Assessment Tip: Total **12** Points

Teacher's Book, page 323N

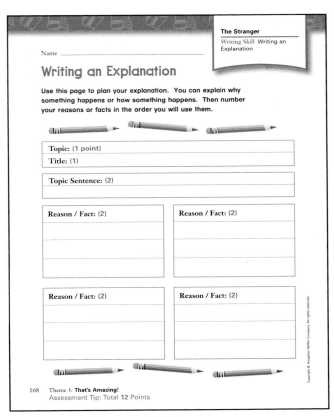

The Stranger
Writing Skill Improving Your Writing

Name _____

Audience

Writers are always aware of their audience. A good writer will adapt the style of writing to fit the reader.
▶ Formal writing is used for reports, presentations, many school assignments, and business letters.

  Formal: Deer can be found in almost all regions of the United States. Although they are wild animals, they can become quite used to the presence of human beings.

▶ Informal writing is for friendly letters, postcards, or e-mails between friends.

  Informal: We saw the most incredible deer today. I was careful to walk up to it really slowly. I stretched out my hand, and it sniffed my palm. It felt really funny!

Write two short paragraphs about the change of seasons. Make the first one formal, as if you were giving a report. Make the second one informal, as if you were writing a postcard to a good friend.

The Change of Seasons

Formal:
Responses will vary. **(6 points)**
_____
_____
_____

Informal:
Responses will vary. **(6)**
_____
_____
_____

Theme 3: **That's Amazing!**   169
Assessment Tip: Total **12** Points

Teacher's Book, page 323N

Story Elements

Beginning
Characters: _____

Setting: _____

Problem: _____

Middle
Details about problem: _____

Efforts to solve problem: _____

Ending
Resolution of problem: _____

How characters grew or learned: _____
_____

Teacher's Book, page 325B

Developing Plot, Characters, and Setting

Plot
Problem or conflict: _____

Efforts to resolve problem: _____

Final resolution of problem: _____

Main Character
Appearance: _____

Likes and dislikes: _____

Behavior: _____

Feelings and thoughts: _____

Setting
Country or state: _____
City or town: _____
Time period: _____
Local sights and sounds: _____

Teacher's Book, page 325C

Writing Dialogue

No Dialogue Version	Dialogue Version
Molly asked her brother if he planned on going to the Fall Fiesta. Simon said he planned to go. Molly felt something was wrong. Finally Simon told her he didn't know how to dance.	"Are you going to the Fall Fiesta?" Molly asked. "I suppose so," Simon said. "What's wrong?" Molly asked. "Oh nothing," he said. "It's just that I don't know how to dance."

No Dialogue Version	Dialogue Version
Molly suggested that she teach Simon how to dance. But Simon thought that was ridiculous. She didn't know how to dance either. So Molly suggested that they teach each other how to dance.	Paragraphs will vary.

No Dialogue Version	Dialogue Version
Molly found a "How to Dance" book. It was not so hard after all, Simon felt. Molly was proud of him; he had taught himself to dance well. Simon agreed. But he said that he never could have done it without Molly's help.	Paragraphs will vary.

Teacher's Book, page 325D

Using Possessives

A **possessive** shows ownership.
• Add **'s** to make nouns possessive.
• For plurals that end in **s**, add an apostrophe.

1. A. The offer of the scorpion was: "I promise I won't sting you, crocodile, if you give me a ride across the river."
   B. The scorpion's offer was: "I promise I won't sting you, crocodile, if you give me a ride across the river."

2. A. Scorpions are natural enemies of crocodiles.
   B. Scorpions are crocodiles' natural enemies.

3. To the surprise of the crocodile, the scorpion stung it halfway across the river.
   To the crocodile's surprise, the scorpion stung it halfway across the river.

4. The cry of the victim was, "Why did you do this?"
   The victim's cry was, "Why did you do this?"

5. "The nature of scorpions is to sting," said the scorpion.
   "Scorpions' nature is to sting," said the scorpion.

6. The moral of the storyteller is, "Nature is not always nice."
   The storyteller's moral is, "Nature is not always nice."

Teacher's Book, page 325E

Name _____

Revising Your Story

Reread your story. What do you need to make it better? Use this page to help you decide. Put a checkmark in the box for each sentence that describes your story.

Rings the Bell!

☐ The setting and characters are well defined.

☐ My story has an interesting beginning, middle, and end.

☐ I made good use of dialogue in my story.

☐ The main character solves the story's problem in an interesting way.

☐ There are almost no mistakes.

Getting Stronger

☐ The setting and characters are described in a general way.

☐ The plot could be more interesting.

☐ I could add more details and dialogue to the story.

☐ The main character's solution to the problem could be more interesting.

☐ There are a few mistakes.

Try Harder

☐ The plot is not interesting.

☐ There is no clear problem.

☐ I haven't included details or dialogue.

☐ There are a lot of mistakes.

170   Theme 3: **That's Amazing!**

Teacher's Book, page 325E

Name _____

Using Possessives

A **possessive** shows ownership.
▶ Add 's to make nouns possessive.
▶ For plurals that end in s, add an apostrophe.

Rewrite each phrase, using a possessive noun. Then use the new phrase in a sentence of your own.

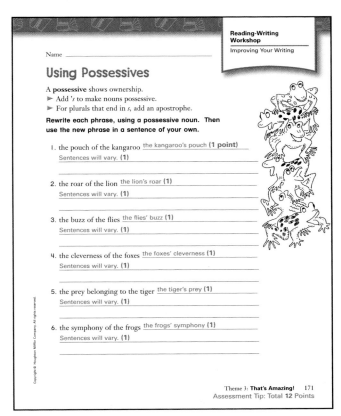

1. the pouch of the kangaroo the kangaroo's pouch **(1 point)**
   Sentences will vary. **(1)**

2. the roar of the lion the lion's roar **(1)**
   Sentences will vary. **(1)**

3. the buzz of the flies the flies' buzz **(1)**
   Sentences will vary. **(1)**

4. the cleverness of the foxes the foxes' cleverness **(1)**
   Sentences will vary. **(1)**

5. the prey belonging to the tiger the tiger's prey **(1)**
   Sentences will vary. **(1)**

6. the symphony of the frogs the frogs' symphony **(1)**
   Sentences will vary. **(1)**

Theme 3: **That's Amazing!**   171
Assessment Tip: Total **12** Points

Teacher's Book, page 325E

Name _____

Spelling Words

Words Often Misspelled Look for familiar spelling patterns to help you remember how to spell the Spelling Words on this page. Think carefully about the parts that you find hard to spell in each word.

Write the missing letters in the Spelling Words below.

1. ton i g h t **(1 point)**
2. w h ole **(1)**
3. w h ile **(1)**
4. c o u l d **(1)**
5. w o r ld **(1)**
6. w r iting **(1)**
7. b u i ld **(1)**
8. s c h ool **(1)**
9. fini s h ed **(1)**
10. mo r n ing **(1)**
11. c o m ing **(1)**
12. sto p p ed **(1)**
13. ge t t ing **(1)**
14. g o e s **(1)**
15. g o ing **(1)**

Study List On a separate piece of paper, write each Spelling Word. Check your spelling against the words on the list. Order of words may vary. **(5 points)**

Spelling Words

1. tonight
2. whole
3. while
4. could
5. world
6. writing
7. build
8. school
9. finished
10. morning
11. coming
12. stopped
13. getting
14. goes
15. going

172   Theme 3: **That's Amazing!**
Assessment Tip: Total **20** Points

Teacher's Book, page 325F

Name _____

Spelling Spree

Write a Spelling Word to fit each clue.

1. a word meaning "at the same time as" while **(1 point)**
2. a two-syllable synonym for done finished **(1)**
3. the opposite of going coming **(1)**
4. a pencil helps you with this writing **(1)**
5. what the car did at the red light stopped **(1)**
6. the whole wide world **(1)**
7. a synonym for leaving going **(1)**
8. what carpenters do build **(1)**
9. a place for learning school **(1)**
10. not broken into smaller pieces whole **(1)**

Word Addition Combine the first part of the first word with the second part of the second word to write a Spelling Word.

11. goat + sees goes **(1)**
12. couch + mold could **(1)**
13. tons + light tonight **(1)**
14. more + inning morning **(1)**
15. germ + sitting getting **(1)**

Spelling Words

1. tonight
2. whole
3. while
4. could
5. world
6. writing
7. build
8. school
9. finished
10. morning
11. coming
12. stopped
13. getting
14. goes
15. going

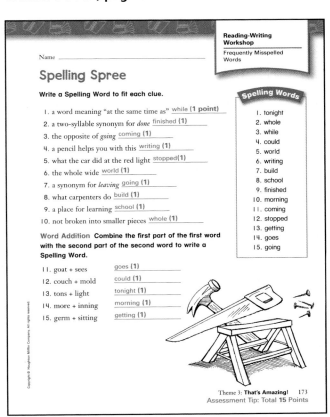

Theme 3: **That's Amazing!**   173
Assessment Tip: Total **15** Points

Teacher's Book, page 325F

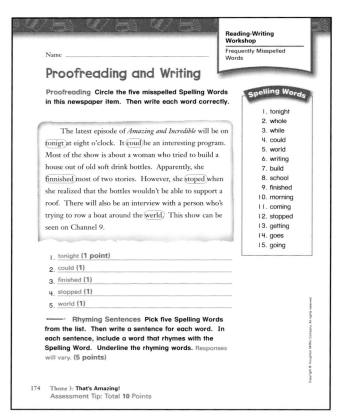

Teacher's Book, page 325F

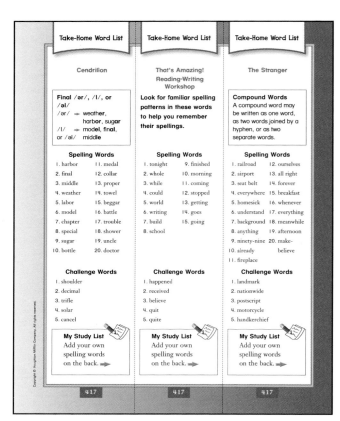

Teacher's Book, page 325F

Teacher's Book, page 327B

Fairy-Tale Words

d	crossly	a. a woman who acts as a child's parent
e	elegant	b. thinking highly of oneself
a	godmother	c. a child whose parents have died
c	orphan	d. in a grumpy way
f	peasant	e. graceful, stylish
b	proud	f. describing a poor farm worker

1. The boy felt so ___proud___ after the last test that he didn't study for this one, and he failed.
2. The girl looked ___crossly___ at her dog because he ate her dinner.
3. When I was six, my parents died, and I became an ___orphan___.
4. I was very happy when my ___godmother___ took me in to her family after my parents died.
5. My bedroom is very ___elegant___ It's decorated with stylish things.
6. My grandfather lived a ___peasant___ life, never having much and always working very hard.

Teacher's Book, page 327B

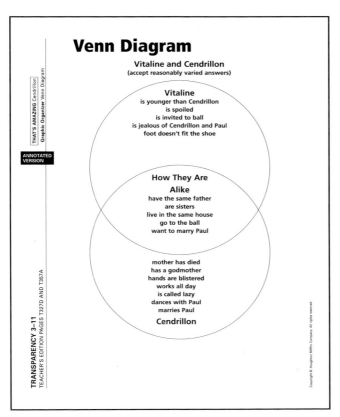

Teacher's Book, pages 327D and 357A

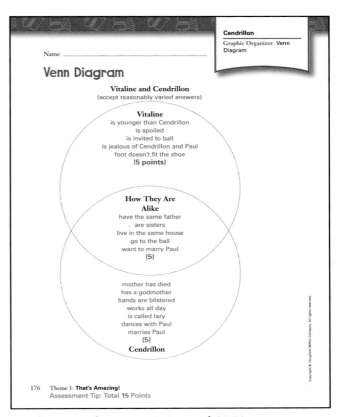

Teacher's Book, pages 327D and 357A

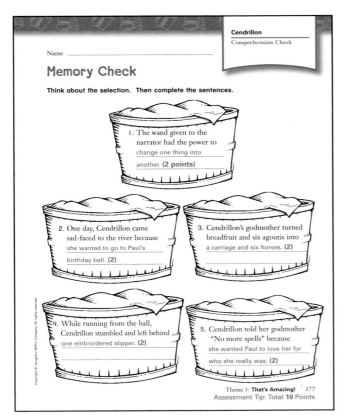

Teacher's Book, page 355

Cendrillon
Comprehension Skill
Compare/Contrast

Name _____

A Resourceful Parent

Read the story. Then complete the Venn diagram on the following page.

A Costume for the Carnival

It was carnival time and everyone was hurrying to make or find the most original costume to win the grand prize. Pantaloon, a rich boy, and Harlequin, a poor boy, both wanted to win.

Pantaloon's rich father ordered a costume from a famous tailor. When completed, the costume was spectacular. It was made of gold cloth, trimmed with yellow diamonds, complete with purple gloves and a hat with feathers.

Since Harlequin was poor, he didn't know what to do. His mother suggested, "Why don't you ask if you can borrow an extra costume from one of your friends?"

Harlequin ran to the house of every one of his friends, but at every house it was the same. "I'm sorry, Harlequin, I don't have an extra costume. But I have these scraps of cloth left over. You may have them—if they will help."

Sadly, Harlequin brought the scraps to his mother. His mother had an idea and sent him off to bed. Harlequin did as he was told. The next morning there, at the foot of his bed, lay the most beautiful costume he had ever seen! His mother had used the scraps and cut them into diamond shapes. Then she had sewn all the shapes together to create a costume with every color of the rainbow! She had sewn on sequins so the costume caught the light and shined and sparkled. He even had a matching hat with feathers!

Harlequin pulled on his costume and hurried to the Square. Did his costume win the prize for the most original? Well, what do you think?

178   Theme 3: **That's Amazing!**

Teacher's Book, page 357B

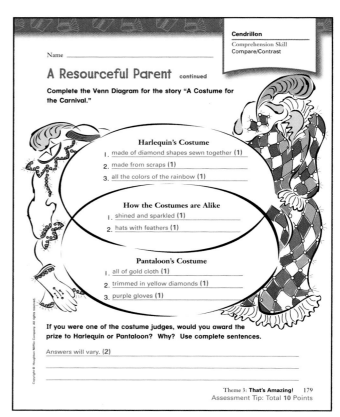

Cendrillon
Comprehension Skill
Compare/Contrast

Name _____

A Resourceful Parent   *continued*

Complete the Venn Diagram for the story "A Costume for the Carnival."

Harlequin's Costume
1. made of diamond shapes sewn together **(1)**
2. made from scraps **(1)**
3. all the colors of the rainbow **(1)**

How the Costumes are Alike
1. shined and sparkled **(1)**
2. hats with feathers **(1)**

Pantaloon's Costume
1. all of gold cloth **(1)**
2. trimmed in yellow diamonds **(1)**
3. purple gloves **(1)**

If you were one of the costume judges, would you award the prize to Harlequin or Pantaloon? Why? Use complete sentences.

Answers will vary. **(2)**

_____

_____

Theme 3: **That's Amazing!**   179
Assessment Tip: Total **10** Points

Teacher's Book, page 357B

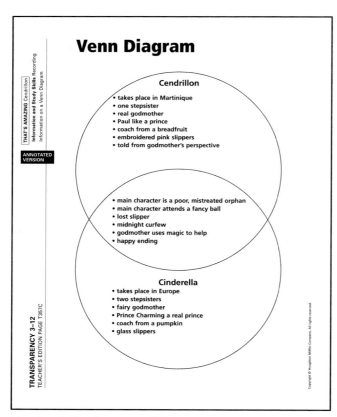

Venn Diagram

Cendrillon
- takes place in Martinique
- one stepsister
- real godmother
- Paul like a prince
- coach from a breadfruit
- embroidered pink slippers
- told from godmother's perspective

- main character is a poor, mistreated orphan
- main character attends a fancy ball
- lost slipper
- midnight curfew
- godmother uses magic to help
- happy ending

Cinderella
- takes place in Europe
- two stepsisters
- fairy godmother
- Prince Charming a real prince
- coach from a pumpkin
- glass slippers

Teacher's Book, page 357C

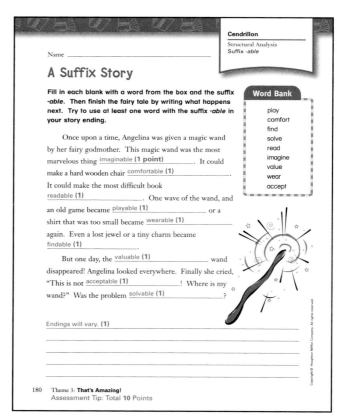

Cendrillon
Structural Analysis
Suffix *-able*

Name _____

A Suffix Story

Fill in each blank with a word from the box and the suffix *-able*. Then finish the fairy tale by writing what happens next. Try to use at least one word with the suffix *-able* in your story ending.

Word Bank

play
comfort
find
solve
read
imagine
value
wear
accept

Once upon a time, Angelina was given a magic wand by her fairy godmother. This magic wand was the most marvelous thing imaginable **(1 point)**. It could make a hard wooden chair comfortable **(1)**. It could make the most difficult book readable **(1)**. One wave of the wand, and an old game became playable **(1)** or a shirt that was too small became wearable **(1)** again. Even a lost jewel or a tiny charm became findable **(1)**.

But one day, the valuable **(1)** wand disappeared! Angelina looked everywhere. Finally she cried, "This is not acceptable **(1)**! Where is my wand?" Was the problem solvable **(1)**?

Endings will vary. **(1)**

_____

_____

_____

180   Theme 3: **That's Amazing!**
Assessment Tip: Total **10** Points

Teacher's Book, page 357F

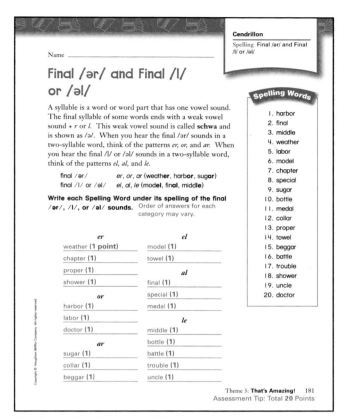

Top-left worksheet:

Name _____

Cendrillon
Spelling Final /ər/ and Final /l/ or /əl/

Final /ər/ and Final /l/ or /əl/

A syllable is a word or word part that has one vowel sound. The final syllable of some words ends with a weak vowel sound + *r* or *l*. This weak vowel sound is called **schwa** and is shown as /əl/. When you hear the final /ər/ sounds in a two-syllable word, think of the patterns *er*, *or*, and *ar*. When you hear the final /l/ or /əl/ sounds in a two-syllable word, think of the patterns *el*, *al*, and *le*.

final /ər/ → *er, or, ar* (weather, harbor, sugar)
final /l/ or /əl/ → *el, al, le* (model, final, middle)

Write each Spelling Word under its spelling of the final /ər/, /l/, or /əl/ sounds. Order of answers for each category may vary.

er
weather **(1 point)**
chapter **(1)**
proper **(1)**
shower **(1)**

or
harbor **(1)**
labor **(1)**
doctor **(1)**

ar
sugar **(1)**
collar **(1)**
beggar **(1)**

el
model **(1)**
towel **(1)**

al
final **(1)**
special **(1)**
medal **(1)**

le
middle **(1)**
bottle **(1)**
battle **(1)**
trouble **(1)**
uncle **(1)**

Spelling Words
1. harbor
2. final
3. middle
4. weather
5. labor
6. model
7. chapter
8. special
9. sugar
10. bottle
11. medal
12. collar
13. proper
14. towel
15. beggar
16. battle
17. trouble
18. shower
19. uncle
20. doctor

Theme 3: **That's Amazing!** 181
Assessment Tip: Total **20** Points

Teacher's Book, page 357H

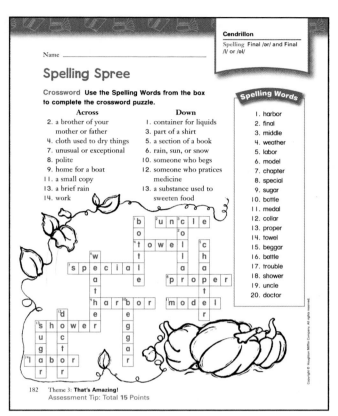

Top-right worksheet:

Name _____

Cendrillon
Spelling Final /ər/ and Final /l/ or /əl/

Spelling Spree

Crossword Use the Spelling Words from the box to complete the crossword puzzle.

Across
2. a brother of your mother or father
4. cloth used to dry things
7. unusual or exceptional
8. polite
9. home for a boat
11. a small copy
13. a brief rain
14. work

Down
1. container for liquids
3. part of a shirt
5. a section of a book
6. rain, sun, or snow
10. someone who begs
12. someone who practices medicine
13. a substance used to sweeten food

Spelling Words
1. harbor
2. final
3. middle
4. weather
5. labor
6. model
7. chapter
8. special
9. sugar
10. bottle
11. medal
12. collar
13. proper
14. towel
15. beggar
16. battle
17. trouble
18. shower
19. uncle
20. doctor

182 Theme 3: **That's Amazing!**
Assessment Tip: Total **15** Points

Teacher's Book, page 357H

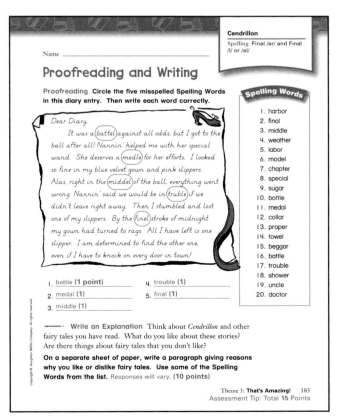

Bottom-left worksheet:

Name _____

Cendrillon
Spelling Final /ər/ and Final /l/ or /əl/

Proofreading and Writing

Proofreading Circle the five misspelled Spelling Words in this diary entry. Then write each word correctly.

Dear Diary,
It was a (battel) against all odds, but I got to the ball after all! Nannin' helped me with her special wand. She deserves a (medle) for her efforts. I looked so fine in my blue velvet gown and pink slippers. Alas, right in the (middel) of the ball, everything went wrong. Nannin' said we would be in (truble) if we didn't leave right away. Then I stumbled and lost one of my slippers. By the (finel) stroke of midnight my gown had turned to rags. All I have left is one slipper. I am determined to find the other one, even if I have to knock on every door in town!

1. battle **(1 point)**
2. medal **(1)**
3. middle **(1)**
4. trouble **(1)**
5. final **(1)**

Spelling Words
1. harbor
2. final
3. middle
4. weather
5. labor
6. model
7. chapter
8. special
9. sugar
10. bottle
11. medal
12. collar
13. proper
14. towel
15. beggar
16. battle
17. trouble
18. shower
19. uncle
20. doctor

Write an Explanation Think about *Cendrillon* and other fairy tales you have read. What do you like about these stories? Are there things about fairy tales that you don't like?

On a separate sheet of paper, write a paragraph giving reasons why you like or dislike fairy tales. Use some of the Spelling Words from the list. Responses will vary. **(10 points)**

Theme 3: **That's Amazing!** 183
Assessment Tip: Total **15** Points

Teacher's Book, page 357H

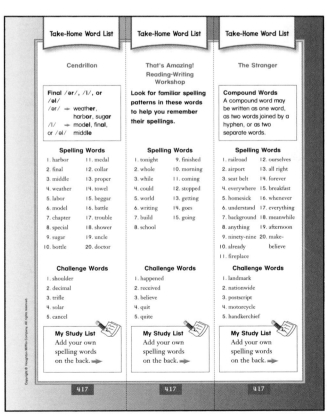

Bottom-right worksheet:

Take-Home Word List | **Take-Home Word List** | **Take-Home Word List**

Cendrillon

Final /ər/, /l/, or /əl/
/ər/ → weather, harbor, sugar
/l/ or /əl/ → model, final, middle

Spelling Words
1. tonight
2. final
3. middle
4. weather
5. labor
6. model
7. chapter
8. special
9. sugar
10. bottle
11. medal
12. collar
13. proper
14. towel
15. beggar
16. battle
17. trouble
18. shower
19. uncle
20. doctor

Challenge Words
1. shoulder
2. decimal
3. trifle
4. solar
5. cancel

My Study List
Add your own spelling words on the back. →

That's Amazing!
Reading-Writing Workshop

Look for familiar spelling patterns in these words to help you remember their spellings.

Spelling Words
1. tonight
2. whole
3. while
4. could
5. world
6. writing
7. build
8. school
9. finished
10. morning
11. coming
12. stopped
13. getting
14. goes
15. going

Challenge Words
1. happened
2. received
3. believe
4. quit
5. quite

My Study List
Add your own spelling words on the back. →

The Stranger

Compound Words
A compound word may be written as one word, as two words joined by a hyphen, or as two separate words.

Spelling Words
1. railroad
2. airport
3. seat belt
4. everywhere
5. homesick
6. understand
7. background
8. anything
9. ninety-nine
10. already
11. fireplace
12. ourselves
13. all right
14. forever
15. breakfast
16. whenever
17. everything
18. meanwhile
19. afternoon
20. make-believe

Challenge Words
1. landmark
2. nationwide
3. postscript
4. motorcycle
5. handkerchief

My Study List
Add your own spelling words on the back. →

417 | 417 | 417

Teacher's Book, page 357H

Lesson Planning Support *(Continued)*

Teacher's Book, page 357I

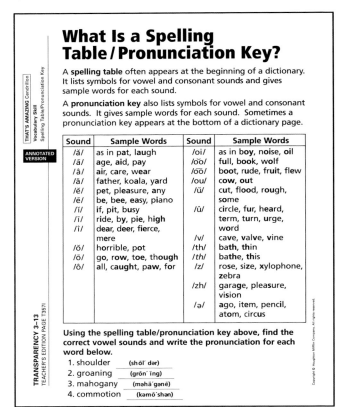

Teacher's Book, page 357I

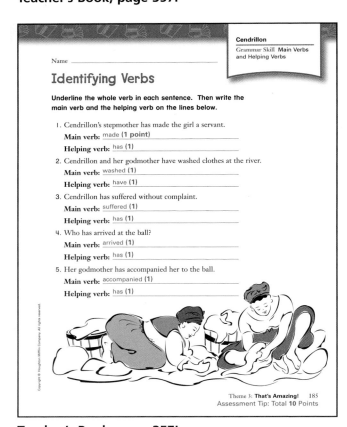

Teacher's Book, page 357L

Teacher's Book, page 357L

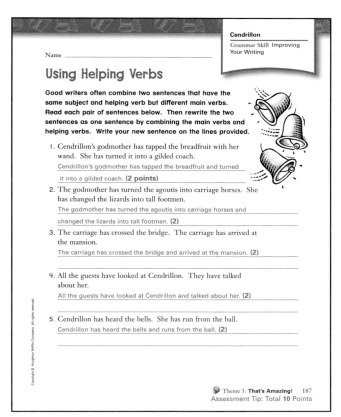

Cendrillon

Grammar Skill Improving Your Writing

Name _____

Using Helping Verbs

Good writers often combine two sentences that have the same subject and helping verb but different main verbs. Read each pair of sentences below. Then rewrite the two sentences as one sentence by combining the main verbs and helping verbs. Write your new sentence on the lines provided.

1. Cendrillon's godmother has tapped the breadfruit with her wand. She has turned it into a gilded coach.
   Cendrillon's godmother has tapped the breadfruit and turned it into a gilded coach. **(2 points)**

2. The godmother has turned the agoutis into carriage horses. She has changed the lizards into tall footmen.
   The godmother has turned the agoutis into carriage horses and changed the lizards into tall footmen. **(2)**

3. The carriage has crossed the bridge. The carriage has arrived at the mansion.
   The carriage has crossed the bridge and arrived at the mansion. **(2)**

4. All the guests have looked at Cendrillon. They have talked about her.
   All the guests have looked at Cendrillon and talked about her. **(2)**

5. Cendrillon has heard the bells. She has run from the ball.
   Cendrillon has heard the bells and runs from the ball. **(2)**

Theme 3: **That's Amazing!**   187
Assessment Tip: Total **10** Points

Teacher's Book, page 357L

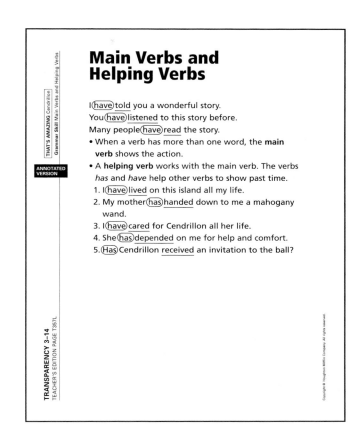

ANNOTATED VERSION

Main Verbs and Helping Verbs

I have told you a wonderful story.
You have listened to this story before.
Many people have read the story.

- When a verb has more than one word, the **main verb** shows the action.
- A **helping verb** works with the main verb. The verbs *has* and *have* help other verbs to show past time.

1. I have lived on this island all my life.
2. My mother has handed down to me a mahogany wand.
3. I have cared for Cendrillon all her life.
4. She has depended on me for help and comfort.
5. Has Cendrillon received an invitation to the ball?

Teacher's Book, page 357L

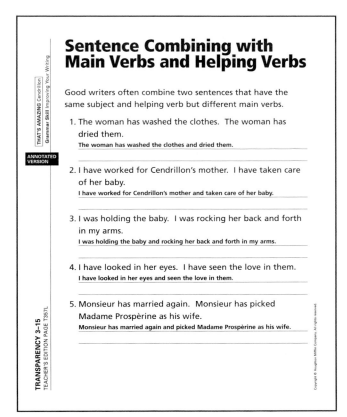

ANNOTATED VERSION

Sentence Combining with Main Verbs and Helping Verbs

Good writers often combine two sentences that have the same subject and helping verb but different main verbs.

1. The woman has washed the clothes. The woman has dried them.
   The woman has washed the clothes and dried them.

2. I have worked for Cendrillon's mother. I have taken care of her baby.
   I have worked for Cendrillon's mother and taken care of her baby.

3. I was holding the baby. I was rocking her back and forth in my arms.
   I was holding the baby and rocking her back and forth in my arms.

4. I have looked in her eyes. I have seen the love in them.
   I have looked in her eyes and seen the love in them.

5. Monsieur has married again. Monsieur has picked Madame Prospèrine as his wife.
   Monsieur has married again and picked Madame Prospèrine as his wife.

Teacher's Book, page 357L

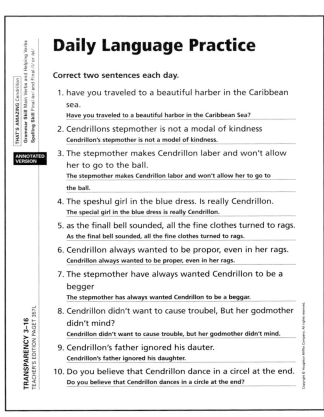

ANNOTATED VERSION

Daily Language Practice

Correct two sentences each day.

1. have you traveled to a beautiful harber in the Caribbean sea.
   Have you traveled to a beautiful harbor in the Caribbean Sea?

2. Cendrillons stepmother is not a modal of kindness
   Cendrillon's stepmother is not a model of kindness.

3. The stepmother makes Cendrillon laber and won't allow her to go to the ball.
   The stepmother makes Cendrillon labor and won't allow her to go to the ball.

4. The speshul girl in the blue dress. Is really Cendrillon.
   The special girl in the blue dress is really Cendrillon.

5. as the finall bell sounded, all the fine clothes turned to rags.
   As the final bell sounded, all the fine clothes turned to rags.

6. Cendrillon always wanted to be propor, even in her rags.
   Cendrillon always wanted to be proper, even in her rags.

7. The stepmother have always wanted Cendrillon to be a begger
   The stepmother has always wanted Cendrillon to be a beggar.

8. Cendrillon didn't want to cause troubel, But her godmother didn't mind?
   Cendrillon didn't want to cause trouble, but her godmother didn't mind.

9. Cendrillon's father ignored his dauter.
   Cendrillon's father ignored his daughter.

10. Do you believe that Cendrillon dance in a circel at the end?
    Do you believe that Cendrillon dances in a circle at the end?

Teacher's Book, page 357L

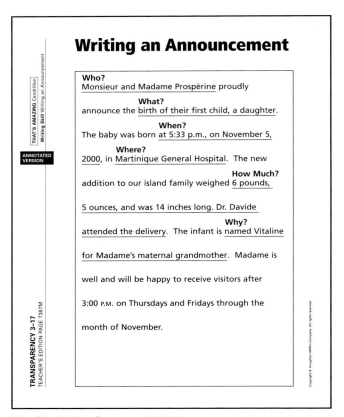

Writing an Announcement

THAT'S AMAZING Cendrillon
Writing Skill Writing an Announcement

ANNOTATED VERSION

Who?
Monsieur and Madame Prospèrine proudly

What?
announce the birth of their first child, a daughter.

When?
The baby was born at 5:33 p.m., on November 5,

Where?
2000, in Martinique General Hospital. The new

How Much?
addition to our island family weighed 6 pounds,

5 ounces, and was 14 inches long. Dr. Davide

Why?
attended the delivery. The infant is named Vitaline

for Madame's maternal grandmother. Madame is

well and will be happy to receive visitors after

3:00 P.M. on Thursdays and Fridays through the

month of November.

TRANSPARENCY 3-17
TEACHER'S EDITION PAGE T357M

Teacher's Book, page 357M

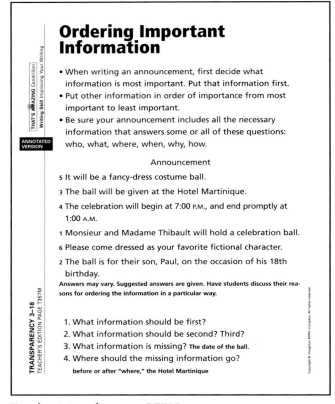

Ordering Important Information

THAT'S AMAZING Cendrillon
Writing Skill Improving Your Writing

ANNOTATED VERSION

- When writing an announcement, first decide what information is most important. Put that information first.
- Put other information in order of importance from most important to least important.
- Be sure your announcement includes all the necessary information that answers some or all of these questions: who, what, where, when, why, how.

Announcement

5 It will be a fancy-dress costume ball.

3 The ball will be given at the Hotel Martinique.

4 The celebration will begin at 7:00 P.M., and end promptly at 1:00 A.M.

1 Monsieur and Madame Thibault will hold a celebration ball.

6 Please come dressed as your favorite fictional character.

2 The ball is for their son, Paul, on the occasion of his 18th birthday.

Answers may vary. Suggested answers are given. Have students discuss their reasons for ordering the information in a particular way.

1. What information should be first?
2. What information should be second? Third?
3. What information is missing? The date of the ball.
4. Where should the missing information go?
   before or after "where," the Hotel Martinique

TRANSPARENCY 3-18
TEACHER'S EDITION PAGE T357M

Teacher's Book, page 357M

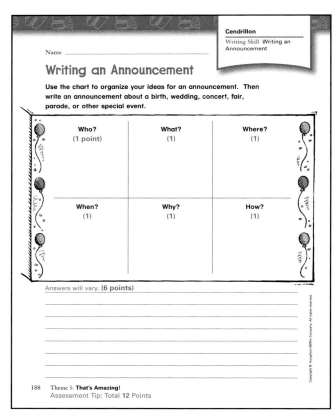

Name _____

Cendrillon
Writing Skill Writing an Announcement

Writing an Announcement

Use the chart to organize your ideas for an announcement. Then write an announcement about a birth, wedding, concert, fair, parade, or other special event.

Who? (1 point)	What? (1)	Where? (1)
When? (1)	Why? (1)	How? (1)

Answers will vary. (6 points)

_____

_____

_____

_____

_____

188   Theme 3: **That's Amazing!**
        Assessment Tip: Total **12** Points

Teacher's Book, page 357N

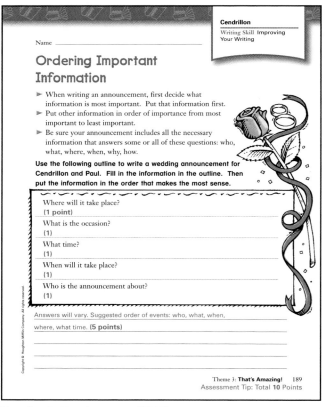

Name _____

Cendrillon
Writing Skill Improving Your Writing

Ordering Important Information

► When writing an announcement, first decide what information is most important. Put that information first.
► Put other information in order of importance from most important to least important.
► Be sure your announcement includes all the necessary information that answers some or all of these questions: who, what, where, when, why, how.

Use the following outline to write a wedding announcement for Cendrillon and Paul. Fill in the information in the outline. Then put the information in the order that makes the most sense.

Where will it take place? (1 point)

What is the occasion? (1)

What time? (1)

When will it take place? (1)

Who is the announcement about? (1)

Answers will vary. Suggested order of events: who, what, when, where, what time. (5 points)

_____

_____

_____

Theme 3: **That's Amazing!**   189
Assessment Tip: Total **10** Points

Teacher's Book, page 357N

Lesson Planning Support   Theme Resources

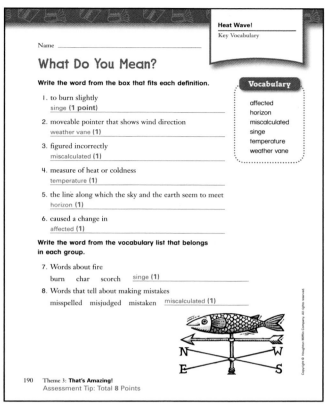

Heat Wave!
Key Vocabulary

Name _____

What Do You Mean?

Write the word from the box that fits each definition.

Vocabulary
affected
horizon
miscalculated
singe
temperature
weather vane

1. to burn slightly
   singe **(1 point)**

2. moveable pointer that shows wind direction
   weather vane **(1)**

3. figured incorrectly
   miscalculated **(1)**

4. measure of heat or coldness
   temperature **(1)**

5. the line along which the sky and the earth seem to meet
   horizon **(1)**

6. caused a change in
   affected **(1)**

Write the word from the vocabulary list that belongs in each group.

7. Words about fire
   burn   char   scorch   singe **(1)**

8. Words that tell about making mistakes
   misspelled   misjudged   mistaken   miscalculated **(1)**

190   Theme 3: **That's Amazing!**
Assessment Tip: Total **8** Points

Teacher's Book, page 359B

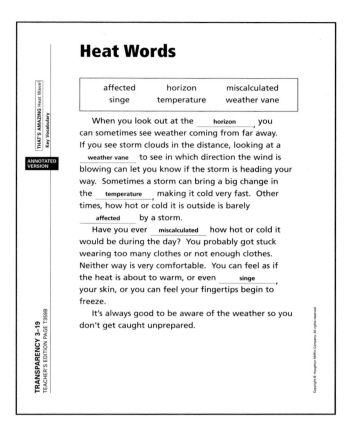

THAT'S AMAZING Heat Wave!
Key Vocabulary

ANNOTATED VERSION

Heat Words

| affected | horizon | miscalculated |
| singe | temperature | weather vane |

When you look out at the ___horizon___, you can sometimes see weather coming from far away. If you see storm clouds in the distance, looking at a ___weather vane___ to see in which direction the wind is blowing can let you know if the storm is heading your way. Sometimes a storm can bring a big change in the ___temperature___, making it cold very fast. Other times, how hot or cold it is outside is barely ___affected___ by a storm.

Have you ever ___miscalculated___ how hot or cold it would be during the day? You probably got stuck wearing too many clothes or not enough clothes. Neither way is very comfortable. You can feel as if the heat is about to warm, or even ___singe___ your skin, or you can feel your fingertips begin to freeze.

It's always good to be aware of the weather so you don't get caught unprepared.

TRANSPARENCY 3-19
TEACHER'S EDITION PAGE T359B

Teacher's Book, page 359B

THAT'S AMAZING Heat Wave
Graphic Organizer Fantasy/Realism Chart

ANNOTATED VERSION

Fantasy/Realism Chart

Page	Story Detail (accept varied answers)	Fantasy (F)/ Realism (R)
361	Geese are plucked, stuffed, and roasted.	R
	Geese are cooked in the sky.	F
367	Milk is churned into butter.	R
	Cows' jumping causes the milk to become butter.	F
368	Getting oats wet makes oatmeal.	R
	Oatmeal makes fine glue.	F
371	Adding water to flour and yeast makes dough.	R
	The rising dough picks up the tractor and the mule.	F
375	They plant lettuce seeds and lettuce grows.	R
	Lettuce grows as soon as the seeds hit the dirt.	F

TRANSPARENCY 3-20
TEACHER'S EDITION PAGES T359D AND T381A

Teacher's Book, pages 359D and 381A

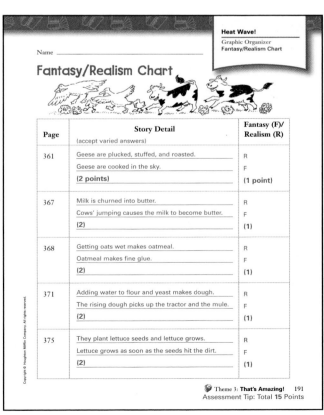

Heat Wave!
Graphic Organizer
Fantasy/Realism Chart

Name _____

Fantasy/Realism Chart

Page	Story Detail (accept varied answers)	Fantasy (F)/ Realism (R)
361	Geese are plucked, stuffed, and roasted.	R
	Geese are cooked in the sky.	F
	(2 points)	(1 point)
367	Milk is churned into butter.	R
	Cows' jumping causes the milk to become butter.	F
	(2)	(1)
368	Getting oats wet makes oatmeal.	R
	Oatmeal makes fine glue.	F
	(2)	(1)
371	Adding water to flour and yeast makes dough.	R
	The rising dough picks up the tractor and the mule.	F
	(2)	(1)
375	They plant lettuce seeds and lettuce grows.	R
	Lettuce grows as soon as the seeds hit the dirt.	F
	(2)	(1)

Theme 3: **That's Amazing!**   191
Assessment Tip: Total **15** Points

Teacher's Book, pages 359D and 381A

Lesson Planning Support (Continued)

Teacher's Book, page 379

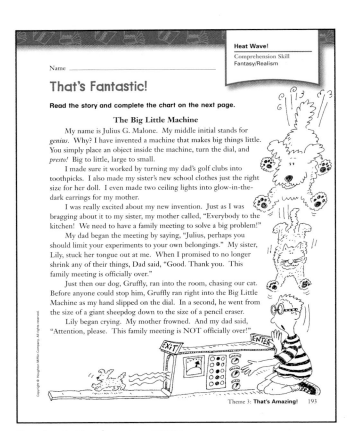

Teacher's Book, page 381B

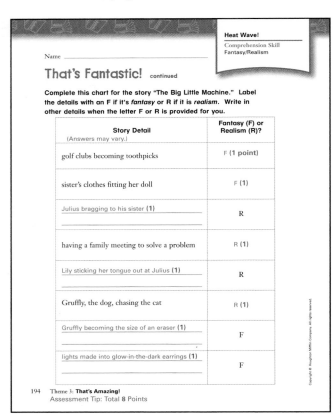

Teacher's Book, page 381B

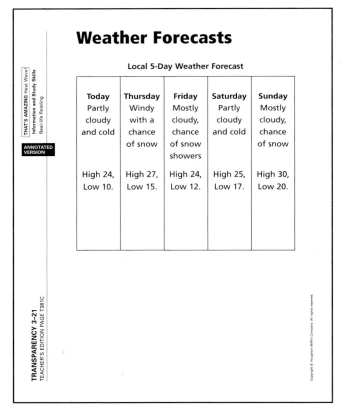

Teacher's Book, page 381C

Panel 1 (top left)

Name _____

Add the Ending

▶ When a base word ends with *e*, the *e* is dropped before adding *-ed* or *-ing*. *move/moved/moving*

▶ When a base word ends with one vowel followed by a single consonant, the consonant is doubled before adding *-ed* or *-ing*. *pop/popped/popping*

Read each sentence. Choose a word from the box similar in meaning to the word or words in dark type. Complete the puzzle by adding *-ed* or *-ing* to your word.

turn
rise
bake
stir
race
drive
switch
grab
hop
scrub

Across
1. My brother **changed** his tune when the Heat Wave hit. (1)
4. Pa started **washing** the cows as hard as he could. (1)
6. The cows were **jumping** around like rabbits. (1)
7. The dough was **going up** so fast we ran for our lives. (1)
8. We **hurried** into the barn, but it was too late. (1)
9. I **snatched** a shovel and ran to the cornfield. (1)

Down
2. Ma was **steering** the truck out to the cornfield. (1)
3. We watched the Heat Wave **twisting** in the sky. (1)
4. I **mixed** the water and the flour in a trough. (1)
5. The dough **cooked** in the heat. (1)

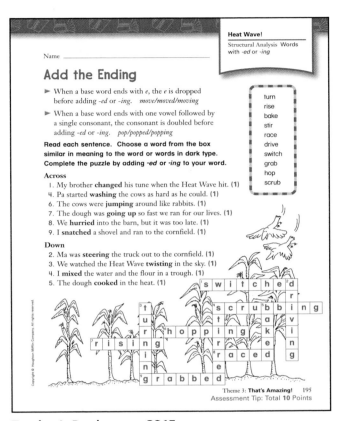

Theme 3: **That's Amazing!**   195
Assessment Tip: Total **10** Points

Teacher's Book, page 381F

Panel 2 (top right)

Name _____

Words with *-ed* or *-ing*

Each of these words has a base word and an ending. A **base word** is a word to which a beginning or an ending can be added. If a word ends with *e*, drop the *e* before adding *-ed* or *-ing*. If a one-syllable word ends with one vowel followed by a single consonant, double the consonant before adding *-ed* or *-ing*.

race + ed = raced   land + ed = landed
snap + ing = snapping

Write each Spelling Word under the heading that tells what happens to its spelling when *-ed* or *-ing* is added.
Order of answers for each category may vary.

No Spelling Change	Final *e* Dropped
landed **(1 point)**	dancing (1)
checking (1)	hiking (1)
smelling (1)	raced (1)
fainted (1)	pleasing (1)
	dared (1)
Final Consonant Doubled	striped (1)
skipped (1)	wasting (1)
flipped (1)	traced (1)
snapping (1)	phoning (1)
dimmed (1)	
rubbing (1)	
stripped (1)	
tanning (1)	

Spelling Words

1. dancing
2. skipped
3. hiking
4. flipped
5. snapping
6. raced
7. landed
8. pleasing
9. checking
10. dared
11. dimmed
12. rubbing
13. striped
14. wasting
15. traced
16. stripped
17. tanning
18. smelling
19. phoning
20. fainted

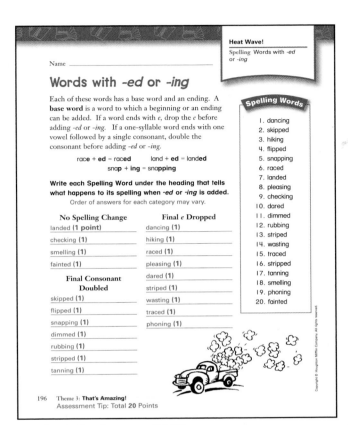

196   Theme 3: **That's Amazing!**
Assessment Tip: Total **20** Points

Teacher's Book, page 381H

Panel 3 (bottom left)

Name _____

Spelling Spree

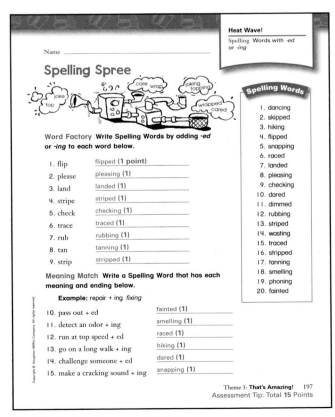

Word Factory Write Spelling Words by adding *-ed* or *-ing* to each word below.

1. flip   flipped **(1 point)**
2. please pleasing (1)
3. land   landed (1)
4. stripe striped (1)
5. check   checking (1)
6. trace   traced (1)
7. rub   rubbing (1)
8. tan   tanning (1)
9. strip   stripped (1)

Meaning Match Write a Spelling Word that has each meaning and ending below.

Example: repair + ing *fixing*

10. pass out + ed   fainted (1)
11. detect an odor + ing   smelling (1)
12. run at top speed + ed raced (1)
13. go on a long walk + ing hiking (1)
14. challenge someone + ed dared (1)
15. make a cracking sound + ing snapping (1)

Spelling Words

1. dancing
2. skipped
3. hiking
4. flipped
5. snapping
6. raced
7. landed
8. pleasing
9. checking
10. dared
11. dimmed
12. rubbing
13. striped
14. wasting
15. traced
16. stripped
17. tanning
18. smelling
19. phoning
20. fainted

Theme 3: **That's Amazing!**   197
Assessment Tip: Total **15** Points

Teacher's Book, page 381H

Panel 4 (bottom right)

Name _____

Proofreading and Writing

Proofreading Circle the five misspelled Spelling Words in the following memo. Then write each word correctly.

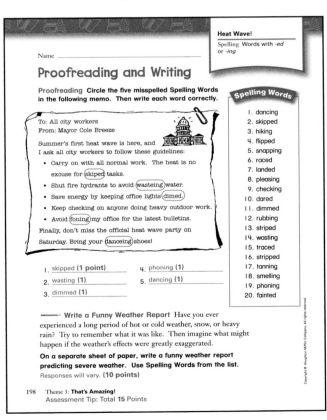

To: All city workers
From: Mayor Cole Breeze

Summer's first heat wave is here, and I ask all city workers to follow these guidelines:
• Carry on with all normal work. The heat is no excuse for (skiped) tasks.
• Shut fire hydrants to avoid (wasteing) water.
• Save energy by keeping office lights (dimed.)
• Keep checking on anyone doing heavy outdoor work.
• Avoid (foning) my office for the latest bulletins.
Finally, don't miss the official heat wave party on Saturday. Bring your (danceing) shoes!

1. skipped **(1 point)**   4. phoning (1)
2. wasting (1)   5. dancing (1)
3. dimmed (1)

Spelling Words

1. dancing
2. skipped
3. hiking
4. flipped
5. snapping
6. raced
7. landed
8. pleasing
9. checking
10. dared
11. dimmed
12. rubbing
13. striped
14. wasting
15. traced
16. stripped
17. tanning
18. smelling
19. phoning
20. fainted

——— Write a Funny Weather Report Have you ever experienced a long period of hot or cold weather, snow, or heavy rain? Try to remember what it was like. Then imagine what might happen if the weather's effects were greatly exaggerated.

On a separate sheet of paper, write a funny weather report predicting severe weather. Use Spelling Words from the list.
Responses will vary. **(10 points)**

198   Theme 3: **That's Amazing!**
Assessment Tip: Total **15** Points

Teacher's Book, page 381H

Lesson Planning Support *(Continued)*

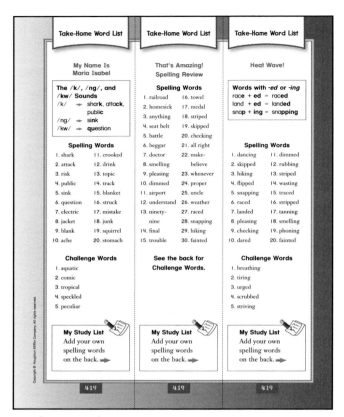

Teacher's Book, page 381H

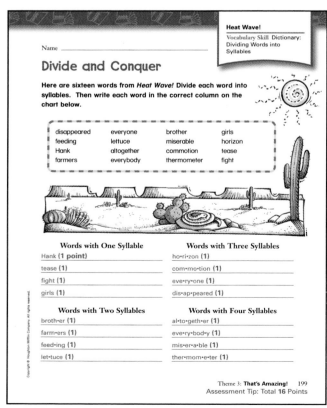

Teacher's Book, page 381I

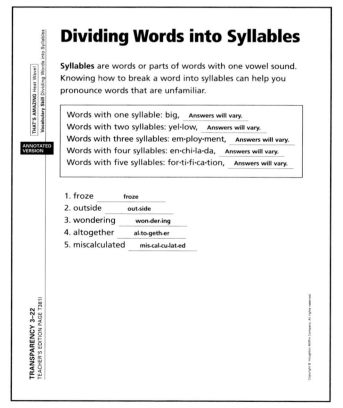

Teacher's Book, page 381I

Name _____

Grammar Skill Present, Past, and Future Tenses

Getting the Tense

Underline the verb in each sentence. Then write each verb in the correct column, under *Present Tense*, *Past Tense*, or *Future Tense*.

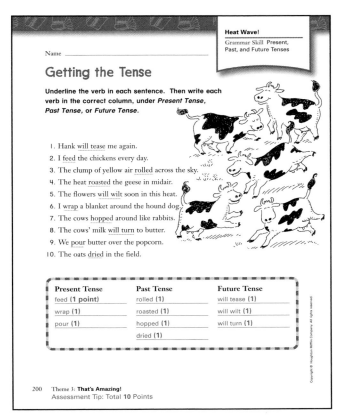

1. Hank will tease me again.
2. I feed the chickens every day.
3. The clump of yellow air rolled across the sky.
4. The heat roasted the geese in midair.
5. The flowers will wilt soon in this heat.
6. I wrap a blanket around the hound dog.
7. The cows hopped around like rabbits.
8. The cows' milk will turn to butter.
9. We pour butter over the popcorn.
10. The oats dried in the field.

Present Tense	Past Tense	Future Tense
feed **(1 point)**	rolled **(1)**	will tease **(1)**
wrap **(1)**	roasted **(1)**	will wilt **(1)**
pour **(1)**	hopped **(1)**	will turn **(1)**
	dried **(1)**	

200 Theme 3: **That's Amazing!**
Assessment Tip: Total **10** Points

Teacher's Book, page 381L

Name _____

Grammar Skill Present, Past and Future Tenses

Reporting in the Past Tense

Help the reporter complete the news story by writing the correct past-tense forms of the verbs in parentheses.

Last week an unusual thing happened **(1 point)** (happen) We suffered **(1)** _____ a very sudden heat wave. (suffer) No one quite believed **(1)** _____ the temperature. (believe) The mercury just blasted **(1)** _____ out of the thermometer at one farm here. (blast) The ground was so hot, cows jumped **(1)** _____ up and down. (jump) Their movements turned **(1)** _____ their milk to butter. (turn) The farmer's daughter hosed **(1)** _____ the hot cows down and cooled **(1)** _____ them. (hose) (cool) She tried **(1)** _____ wetting down the oats but she only created **(1)** _____ a huge, lumpy field of oatmeal. (try) (create) If you have any other stories about the heat wave, call the newspaper immediately.

Write three sentences of your own about the heat wave, using past tense verbs.

Responses will vary. **(2 points each)**

_____

_____

_____

Theme 3: **That's Amazing!** 201
Assessment Tip: Total **16** Points

Teacher's Book, page 381L

Name _____

Grammar Skill Improving Your Writing

Using the Correct Tense

Good writers make sure to choose the verb tense that correctly shows the time of the action described. Read the diary entry that the girl in the story might have written. Rewrite it so that all of the verbs show that the events have already happened.

Dear Diary,
Yesterday begins like a normal day. It turns out to be a strange day. It will start with a hot wind blowing in. The wind sounds like the roar of a lion. The wind quickly heats up everything.
This wind created lots of trouble. It nearly burns all the crops. We save the popcorn, though. At one point, I almost will drown in oatmeal. Finally, some crows flap their wings and cool us off.

Yesterday **began (1 point)** like a normal day. It **turned (1)** out to be a strange day. It **started (1)** with a hot wind blowing in. The wind **sounded (1)** like the roar of a lion. The wind quickly **heated (1)** up everything.

This wind created lots of trouble. It nearly **burned (1)** all the crops. We **saved (1)** the popcorn, though. At one point, I almost **drowned (1)** in oatmeal. Finally, some crows **flapped (1)** their wings and **cooled (1)** us off.

_____

_____

_____

202 Theme 3: **That's Amazing!**
Assessment Tip: Total **10** Points

Teacher's Book, page 381L

Present, Past, and Future Tenses

Verb Tenses

Present	Past	Future
listen, listens	listened	will listen
She listens.	She listened.	She will listen.
They listen.		

The boy hears a loud roar.   present tense
The flowers crawled under the porch.   past tense
The corn will pop soon.   future tense

Rules for Forming the Past Tense

Most Verbs: Add -ed	turn + ed = turned
Verbs ending in e: Drop the e and add -ed	race + ed = raced
Verbs ending with a consonant and y: Change the y to i and add -ed	hurry + ed = hurried
Verbs ending with a single vowel and a consonant: Double the consonant and add -ed	wrap + ed = wrapped

We   herded   the cows inside the barn. (herd)
The oats   dried   out. (dry)
I   hosed   the cows down. (hose)
We   stirred   water into the flour. (stir)

Teacher's Book, page 381L

Using the Correct Tense

Good writers make sure to choose the verb tense that correctly shows the time of the action described. Remember to use the correct tense of verbs in your writing.

Yesterday I visit my friend's farm. Strange things will happen that day. The weather will seem really hot. I never will experience a heat wave before. The flowers by the front porch actually pull themselves out of the ground and look for shade. Some of the crops actually will cook right in the field. In the middle of the day, we saw a blizzard in the cornfield. But it wasn't snow at all. The corn pop, and popcorn swirl all around.

Yesterday I visited my friend's farm. Strange things happened that day. The weather seemed really hot. I never experienced a heat wave before. The flowers by the front porch actually pulled themselves out of the ground and looked for shade. Some of the crops actually cooked right in the field. In the middle of the day, we saw a blizzard in the cornfield. But it wasn't snow at all. The corn popped, and popcorn swirled all around.

Teacher's Book, page 381L

Daily Language Practice

Correct two sentences each day.

1. The hot winds skiped everyone else and head for our farm.
   The hot winds skipped everyone else and headed for our farm.

2. Im amazed that the heat wave race in so fast?
   I'm amazed that the heat wave raced in so fast.

3. our dog was danceing when he saw the falling popcorn.
   Our dog was dancing when he saw the falling popcorn.

4. The flour yeast and water bake into delicious smeling bread.
   The flour, yeast, and water baked into delicious smelling bread.

5. Before they landded, the crows flapped their wings and cool us off.
   Before they landed, the crows flapped their wings and cooled us off.

6. We began rubing our eyes as we watch the popcorn?
   We began rubbing our eyes as we watched the popcorn.

7. I almost faintted when the sound of popping reach me.
   I almost fainted when the sound of popping reached me.

8. we hardly dard to look, and our friends act the same way.
   We hardly dared to look, and our friends acted the same way.

9. My Cousin think I'm jokeing when I tell her next week.
   My cousin will think I'm joking when I tell her next week.

10. The family start checkeing the farm in a few days.
    The family will start checking the farm in a few days.

Teacher's Book, page 381L

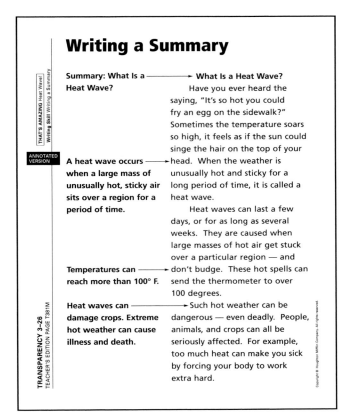

Writing a Summary

Summary: What Is a Heat Wave?

A heat wave occurs when a large mass of unusually hot, sticky air sits over a region for a period of time.

Temperatures can reach more than 100° F.

Heat waves can damage crops. Extreme hot weather can cause illness and death.

What Is a Heat Wave?

Have you ever heard the saying, "It's so hot you could fry an egg on the sidewalk?" Sometimes the temperature soars so high, it feels as if the sun could singe the hair on the top of your head. When the weather is unusually hot and sticky for a long period of time, it is called a heat wave.

Heat waves can last a few days, or for as long as several weeks. They are caused when large masses of hot air get stuck over a particular region — and don't budge. These hot spells can send the thermometer to over 100 degrees.

Such hot weather can be dangerous — even deadly. People, animals, and crops can all be seriously affected. For example, too much heat can make you sick by forcing your body to work extra hard.

Teacher's Book, page 381M

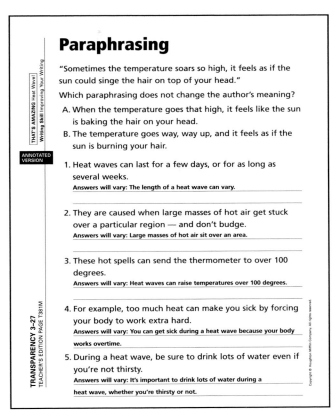

Paraphrasing

"Sometimes the temperature soars so high, it feels as if the sun could singe the hair on top of your head."

Which paraphrasing does not change the author's meaning?

A. When the temperature goes that high, it feels like the sun is baking the hair on your head.

B. The temperature goes way, way up, and it feels as if the sun is burning your hair.

1. Heat waves can last for a few days, or for as long as several weeks.
   Answers will vary: The length of a heat wave can vary.

2. They are caused when large masses of hot air get stuck over a particular region — and don't budge.
   Answers will vary: Large masses of hot air sit over an area.

3. These hot spells can send the thermometer to over 100 degrees.
   Answers will vary: Heat waves can raise temperatures over 100 degrees.

4. For example, too much heat can make you sick by forcing your body to work extra hard.
   Answers will vary: You can get sick during a heat wave because your body works overtime.

5. During a heat wave, be sure to drink lots of water even if you're not thirsty.
   Answers will vary: It's important to drink lots of water during a heat wave, whether you're thirsty or not.

Teacher's Book, page 381M

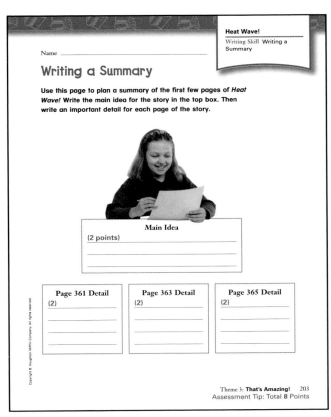

Name _____

Heat Wave!

Writing Skill Writing a Summary

Writing a Summary

Use this page to plan a summary of the first few pages of *Heat Wave!* Write the main idea for the story in the top box. Then write an important detail for each page of the story.

Main Idea

(2 points)

Page 361 Detail	Page 363 Detail	Page 365 Detail
(2)	(2)	(2)

Theme 3: **That's Amazing!**   203
Assessment Tip: Total **8** Points

Teacher's Book, page 381N

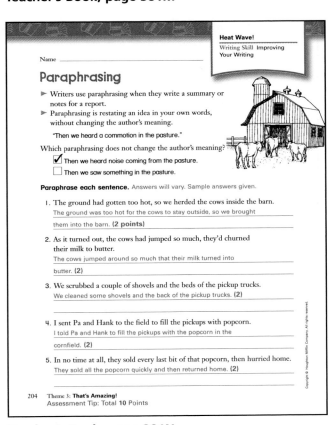

Name _____

Heat Wave!

Writing Skill Improving Your Writing

Paraphrasing

► Writers use paraphrasing when they write a summary or notes for a report.

► Paraphrasing is restating an idea in your own words, without changing the author's meaning.

"Then we heard a commotion in the pasture."

Which paraphrasing does not change the author's meaning?

☑ Then we heard noise coming from the pasture.

☐ Then we saw something in the pasture.

Paraphrase each sentence. Answers will vary. Sample answers given.

1. The ground had gotten too hot, so we herded the cows inside the barn.
   The ground was too hot for the cows to stay outside, so we brought them into the barn. **(2 points)**

2. As it turned out, the cows had jumped so much, they'd churned their milk to butter.
   The cows jumped around so much that their milk turned into butter. **(2)**

3. We scrubbed a couple of shovels and the beds of the pickup trucks.
   We cleaned some shovels and the back of the pickup trucks. **(2)**

4. I sent Pa and Hank to the field to fill the pickups with popcorn.
   I told Pa and Hank to fill the pickups with the popcorn in the cornfield. **(2)**

5. In no time at all, they sold every last bit of that popcorn, then hurried home.
   They sold all the popcorn quickly and then returned home. **(2)**

204   Theme 3: **That's Amazing!**
Assessment Tip: Total **10** Points

Teacher's Book, page 381N

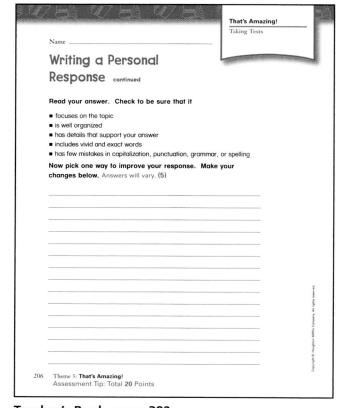

That's Amazing!
Taking Tests

Name _____

Writing a Personal Response

Use the test-taking strategies and tips you have learned to help you answer this kind of question. Then read your answer and see how you may make it better. This practice will help you when you take this kind of test.

Write one or two paragraphs about one of the following topics.

a. You have just read *Heat Wave!* What do you think would happen if it could really get hot enough for corn to start popping while it is growing in the field? What other crops might be affected by this kind of heat? What would happen to those crops?

b. In the story, the narrator came up with unbelievable solutions for cooling the Heat Wave. Use your imagination to think of another way to cool the Heat Wave. What would you do? How would it work? Answers will vary. **(15 points)**

Theme 3: **That's Amazing!** 205

Teacher's Book, page 382

That's Amazing!
Taking Tests

Name _____

Writing a Personal Response *continued*

Read your answer. Check to be sure that it

- focuses on the topic
- is well organized
- has details that support your answer
- includes vivid and exact words
- has few mistakes in capitalization, punctuation, grammar, or spelling

Now pick one way to improve your response. Make your changes below. Answers will vary. **(5)**

206 Theme 3: **That's Amazing!**
Assessment Tip: Total **20** Points

Teacher's Book, page 382

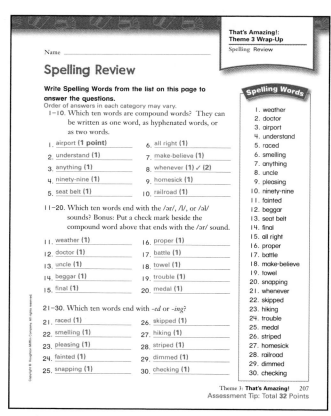

That's Amazing!:
Theme 3 Wrap-Up
Spelling Review

Name _____

Spelling Review

Write Spelling Words from the list on this page to answer the questions.
Order of answers in each category may vary.

1–10. Which ten words are compound words? They can be written as one word, as hyphenated words, or as two words.

1. airport **(1 point)**
2. understand **(1)**
3. anything **(1)**
4. ninety-nine **(1)**
5. seat belt **(1)**
6. all right **(1)**
7. make-believe **(1)**
8. whenever **(1)** ✓ **(2)**
9. homesick **(1)**
10. railroad **(1)**

11–20. Which ten words end with the /ər/, /l/, or /əl/ sounds? Bonus: Put a check mark beside the compound word above that ends with the /ər/ sound.

11. weather **(1)**
12. doctor **(1)**
13. uncle **(1)**
14. beggar **(1)**
15. final **(1)**
16. proper **(1)**
17. battle **(1)**
18. towel **(1)**
19. trouble **(1)**
20. medal **(1)**

21–30. Which ten words end with *-ed* or *-ing*?

21. raced **(1)**
22. smelling **(1)**
23. pleasing **(1)**
24. fainted **(1)**
25. snapping **(1)**
26. skipped **(1)**
27. hiking **(1)**
28. striped **(1)**
29. dimmed **(1)**
30. checking **(1)**

Spelling Words

1. weather
2. doctor
3. airport
4. understand
5. raced
6. smelling
7. anything
8. uncle
9. pleasing
10. ninety-nine
11. fainted
12. beggar
13. seat belt
14. final
15. all right
16. proper
17. battle
18. make-believe
19. towel
20. snapping
21. whenever
22. skipped
23. hiking
24. trouble
25. medal
26. striped
27. homesick
28. railroad
29. dimmed
30. checking

Theme 3: **That's Amazing!** 207
Assessment Tip: Total **32** Points

Teacher's Book, page 383

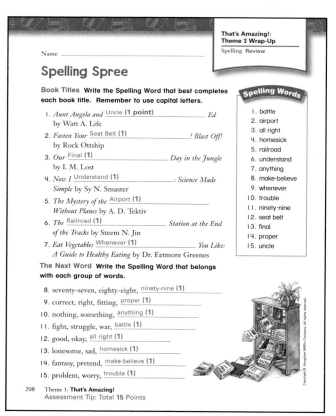

That's Amazing!:
Theme 3 Wrap-Up
Spelling Review

Name _____

Spelling Spree

Book Titles Write the Spelling Word that best completes each book title. Remember to use capital letters.

1. *Aunt Angela and* Uncle **(1 point)** _____ *Ed* by Watt A. Life
2. *Fasten Your* Seat Belt **(1)** _____ *! Blast Off!* by Rock Ottship
3. *Our* Final **(1)** _____ *Day in the Jungle* by I. M. Lost
4. *Now I* Understand **(1)** _____ *: Science Made Simple* by Sy N. Smaster
5. *The Mystery of the* Airport **(1)** _____ *Without Planes* by A. D. Tektiv
6. *The* Railroad **(1)** _____ *Station at the End of the Tracks* by Steem N. Jin
7. *Eat Vegetables* Whenever **(1)** _____ *You Like: A Guide to Healthy Eating* by Dr. Eetmore Greenes

The Next Word Write the Spelling Word that belongs with each group of words.

8. seventy-seven, eighty-eight, ninety-nine **(1)**
9. correct, right, fitting, proper **(1)**
10. nothing, something, anything **(1)**
11. fight, struggle, war, battle **(1)**
12. good, okay, all right **(1)**
13. lonesome, sad, homesick **(1)**
14. fantasy, pretend, make-believe **(1)**
15. problem, worry, trouble **(1)**

Spelling Words

1. battle
2. airport
3. all right
4. homesick
5. railroad
6. understand
7. anything
8. make-believe
9. whenever
10. trouble
11. ninety-nine
12. seat belt
13. final
14. proper
15. uncle

208 Theme 3: **That's Amazing!**
Assessment Tip: Total **15** Points

Teacher's Book, page 383

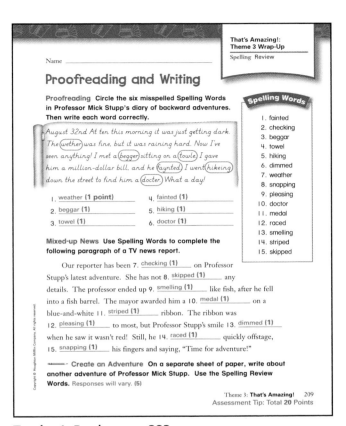

Teacher's Book, page 383

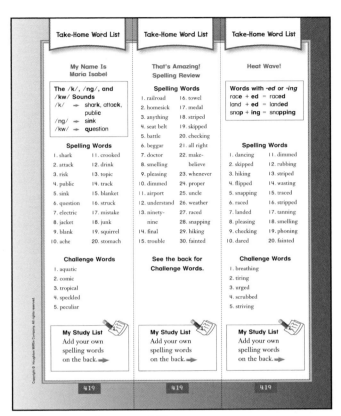

Teacher's Book, page 383

Glossary

This glossary contains meanings and pronunciations for some of the words in this book. The Full Pronunciation Key shows how to pronounce each consonant and vowel in a special spelling. At the bottom of the glossary pages is a shortened form of the full key.

Full Pronunciation Key

Consonant Sounds

b	**bib, ca**bb**age**	kw	**choir, quick**	t	**tight, stopped**
ch	**church, stitch**	l	**lid, needle, tall**	th	**bath, thin**
d	**deed, mailed, puddle**	m	**am, man, dumb**	th	**bathe, this**
		n	**no, sudden**	v	**cave, valve, vine**
f	**fast, fife, off, phrase, rough**	ng	**thing, ink**	w	**with, wolf**
		p	**pop, happy**	y	**yes, yolk, onion**
g	**gag, get, finger**	r	**roar, rhyme**	z	**rose, size, xylophone, zebra**
h	**hat, who**	s	**miss, sauce, scene, see**		
hw	**which, where**			zh	**garage, pleasure, vision**
j	**judge, gem**	sh	**dish, ship, sugar, tissue**		
k	**cat, kick, school**				

Vowel Sounds

ă	**pat, laugh**	ô	**horrible, pot**	û	**cut, flood, rough, some**
ā	**ape, aid, pay**	ō	**go, row, toe, though**		
â	**air, care, wear**	ô	**all, caught, for, paw**	û	**circle, fur, heard, term, turn, urge, word**
ä	**father, koala, yard**	oi	**boy, noise, oil**		
ĕ	**pet, pleasure, any**	ou	**cow, out**	yōō	**cure**
ē	**be, bee, easy, piano**	ōō	**full, book, wolf**	yōō	**abuse, use**
ĭ	**if, pit, busy**	ōō	**boot, rude, fruit, flew**	ə	**ago, silent, pencil, lemon, circus**
ī	**ride, by, pie, high**				
î	**dear, deer, fierce, mere**				

Stress Marks

Primary Stress ´: bi·ol·o·gy [bī **ŏl´** ə jē]
Secondary Stress ´: bi·o·log·i·cal [bī´ ə **lŏj´** ĭ kəl]

Pronunciation key and definitions © 1998 by Houghton Mifflin Company. Adapted and reprinted by permission from *The American Heritage Children's Dictionary*.

710

A

a·blaze (ə **blāz´**) *adj.* On fire: *One match set the fire **ablaze**.*

a·bun·dance (ə **bŭn´** dəns) *n.* A large amount: *The hikers saw an **abundance** of wildlife in the forest.*

ad·ven·tur·er (ad **vĕn´** chər ər) *n.* A person who takes part in bold, dangerous, or risky activities: *The **adventurers** were the first to reach the mountaintop.*

af·fect (ə **fĕkt´**) *v.* To cause a change in; have an effect on: *Hot, dry weather **affected** the crops.*

ag·gres·sive·ly (ə **grĕs´** ĭv lē) *adv.* Very actively and forcefully: *She worked **aggressively** to get elected.*

al·le·giance (ə **lē´** jəns) *n.* Loyalty to one's country, a person, or a cause: *The player showed her **allegiance** to the team by playing her best.*

am·pli·fi·er (ăm´ plə fī´ ər) *n.* An electronic device that makes sound stronger or louder: *The **amplifiers** allowed everyone in the large room to hear the speech.*

an·ces·tor (ăn´ sĕs´ tər) *n.* A person in one's family who lived many years ago.

ar·range·ment (ə **rānj´** mənt) *n.* Planning done beforehand; preparation: *The family made **arrangements** for their vacation.*

at·ten·tive·ly (ə **tĕn´** tĭv lē) *adv.* With attention or alertness: *We listen **attentively** to our teacher.*

au·tumn (ô´ təm) *n.* The season of the year between summer and winter.

B

be·wil·der (bĭ **wĭl´** dər) *v.* To puzzle greatly: *The city's busy streets **bewildered** the young boy.*

blare (blâr) *v.* To make a loud harsh noise, as of a horn: *The car horn was **blaring** in the street.*

bliz·zard (blĭz´ ərd) *n.* A very long, heavy snowstorm with strong winds.

bor·row (bŏr´ ō) *v.* To take something with the understanding that it will be returned: *Matt let his friend **borrow** his book.*

boy·cott (boi´ kŏt´) *n.* A refusal to use, buy from, or deal with a store, company, person, or nation: *Many people joined the **boycott** against the store's unfair policy.*

bunk·house (bŭngk´ hous´) *n.* A building in a ranch or camp where a group of people sleeps: *The **bunkhouse** had twenty beds.*

C

ca·reer (kə **rîr´**) *n.* A profession or occupation that a person follows as a life's work: *Raul chose a **career** as a teacher.*

cham·ber (chăm´ bər) *n.* A hall or room used by a group of lawmakers or judges: *The mayor spoke in the crowded **chamber**.*

blizzard

chamber
Chamber comes from the Latin word for "room." Now it can refer to a room, like a bedroom, or to a small space, like the chamber of a heart.

ōō **boot** / ou **out** / ū **cut** / û **fur** / hw **which** / th **thin** / th **this** / zh **vision** / ə **ago, silent, pencil, lemon, circus**

711

---

char·ac·ter (kăr´ ĭk tər) *n.* A symbol, such as a letter or number, used in printing or writing: *Joe painted red **characters** on a sign for the Chinese New Year.*

charred (chärd) *adj.* Burned or scorched by fire: *Only a few **charred** walls were left after the house fire.*

check out (chĕk out) *v.* To sign out and take: *You can **check out** books from the library.*

check·point (chĕk´ point´) *n.* A place along a route where a check or count is made: *The runners were counted at each **checkpoint**.*

cit·i·zen (sĭt´ ĭ zən) *n.* A person who is an official member of a country: *American **citizens** vote for a president every four years.*

cit·i·zen·ship (sĭt´ ĭ zən shĭp´) *n.* The legal position of a citizen of a country, with the duties, rights, and privileges of this position: *The judge granted **citizenship** to all the people at the ceremony.*

civ·il rights (sĭv´ əl rīts) *adj.* Relating to the legal privileges of a citizen, as in the civil rights movement: *The **civil rights** movement supported fairness for all.*

clas·si·cal (klăs´ ĭ kəl) *adj.* Of or relating to a musical style developed in Europe in the 1700s: *The orchestra played **classical** music.*

con·duc·tor (kən **dŭk´** tər) *n.* The person in charge of a railroad train or subway: *The **conductor** collected our tickets on the train.*

con·sec·u·tive (kən sĕk´ yə tĭv) *adj.* Following one right after the other: *Chad hit a home run in three **consecutive** games.*

con·sume (kən **sōōm´**) *v.* To destroy by burning: *The house was **consumed** by the fire.*

con·tract (kŏn´ trăkt´) *n.* A written agreement that the law can enforce: *The band signed a **contract** to record two CDs.*

cord (kôrd) *n.* A measure for a stack of cut wood. A cord is eight feet long, four feet wide, and four feet high: *The men cut and stacked two **cords** of wood.*

cor·ral (kə **răl´**) *n.* A fenced-in area for cattle or horses.

cou·ra·geous (kə **rā´** jəs) *adj.* Having or showing courage; brave: *The **courageous** policeman saved the child from drowning.*

coy·o·te (kī ō´ tē) *or* (kī´ ōt´) *n.* An animal similar to a wolf that lives in western North America.

crest (krĕst) *n.* Something that grows out of an animal's head, such as a cluster of feathers: *There was a **crest** of bright blue feathers on the bird's head.*

cross·ly (krôs´ lē) *adv.* In a grumpy or grouchy way: *Evie looked **crossly** at Gabe when he sat in her favorite chair.*

cy·cle (sī´ kəl) *n.* A series of events that is regularly repeated in the same order: *The **cycles** of seasons are the same each year.*

corral
Corral is a Spanish word that means a "an enclosed area for cattle." It comes from an old Latin word for "circle" or "ring."

conductor

ă **rat** / ā **pay** / â **care** / ä **father** / ĕ **pet** / ē **be** / ĭ **pit** / ī **pie** / î **fierce** / ŏ **pot** / ō **go** / ô **paw, for** / oi **oil** / ōō **book**

712

D

de·but (dā´ byōō´) *or* (dā **byōō´**) *n.* A first performance in public: *Rosa made her musical **debut** at the school concert.*

dem·on·strate (dĕm´ ən strāt´) *v.* To show clearly; reveal: *This race **demonstrated** his speed.*

de·pot (dē´ pō) *or* (dĕp´ ō) *n.* A railroad or bus station.

de·ter·mined (dĭ **tûr´** mĭnd) *adj.* Having or showing firmness in sticking to a goal: *Dave was **determined** to become a doctor.*

dis·ap·point·ed (dĭs´ ə point´ əd) *adj.* Made unhappy because hopes or wishes were not satisfied: *Chris was **disappointed** that she wasn't picked for the soccer team.*

draft (drăft) *n.* A flow of air: *A cold **draft** made the boy shiver.*

drought (drout) *n.* A period of little or no rain: *The **drought** dried up the farmer's crops.*

E

ea·ger (ē´ gər) *adj.* Full of strong desire; excited: *Ramón was **eager** to learn to swim.*

el·e·gant (ĕl´ ĭ gənt) *adj.* Marked by good taste; stylish and graceful: *The people at the fancy party looked very **elegant**.*

em·ber (ĕm´ bər) *n.* A piece of glowing coal or wood in the ashes of a fire: *The log burned until only an **ember** remained.*

en·rich (ĕn **rĭch´**) *v.* To improve the quality of by adding certain parts, qualities, or ingredients: *Music can **enrich** your life.*

etch (ĕch) *v.* To make a drawing or design by cutting lines: *Lynn **etched** her name in the soft clay.*

e·ven·tu·al·ly (ĭ vĕn´ chōō əl lē) *adv.* At the end; finally: *After a long delay, the train **eventually** arrived at the station.*

ex·pe·ri·enced (ĭk spîr´ ē ənst) *adj.* Possessing skill or knowledge from having done a particular thing in the past: *The **experienced** workers solved the problem quickly.*

F

fare (fâr) *n.* The money a person must pay to travel, as on a plane, train, or bus: *The bus driver collected my **fare**.*

field (fēld) *v.* In baseball, to catch or pick up a ball and throw it to the correct player: *The outfielder had difficulty **fielding** the ball.*

fierce (fîrs) *adj.* Wild and mean; dangerous: *The lion sounded **fierce** when it roared.*

first base·man (fûrst bās´ mən) *n.* The baseball player who fields from a position near first base.

flam·ma·ble (flăm´ ə bəl) *adj.* Easy to set fire to and able to burn rapidly: *Old wooden buildings are very **flammable**.*

fare

ōō **boot** / ou **out** / ū **cut** / û **fur** / hw **which** / th **thin** / th **this** / zh **vision** / ə **ago, silent, pencil, lemon, circus**

713

frost

G

H

front·ier (frŭn tîr´) *n.* A remote or distant area beyond which few or no people live: *The family went west and settled on the frontier.* ♦ *adj.* Relating to the frontier: *Frontier life was difficult.*

frost (frôst) *n.* A very thin covering of ice: *The cold weather coated the windows with frost.*

gath·er·ing (gă̆th´ ər ing) *n.* A coming together of people: *The party was a family gathering.*

gear (gîr) *n.* Equipment, such as tools or clothing, used for a particular activity: *We bought camping gear for our hike.*

glare (glâr) *v.* To stare angrily: *After the argument, Mark was glaring at his brother.*

god·moth·er (gŏd´ mŭth´ ər) *n.* A woman or girl who acts as parent or guardian of a child, in the event that the child's parents are unable to: *Leah was asked to be the baby's godmother.*

hom·age (hŏm´ ĭj) *n.* Special public honor or respect: *The crowd paid homage to the famous artist at the awards ceremony.*

home·land (hōm´ lănd) *n.* The country in which one was born or has lived for a long time: *Seema returned to her homeland after many years in a foreign country.*

home·stead (hōm´ stĕd´) *n.* A house with the land and buildings belonging to it: *The homestead has belonged to his family for generations.* ♦ *In the 1800s, land given by the government to a person who settled on and farmed it: Finally, the covered wagon reached the family's homestead.*

hon·or (ŏn´ ər) *v.* To show special respect for: *People came to honor the heroes at the parade.*

ho·ri·zon (hə rī´ zən) *n.* The line along which the earth and the sky appear to meet: *I watched the sun rise over the horizon.*

I

im·mense (ĭ mĕns´) *adj.* Of great size, scale, or degree: *The immense building seemed to touch the clouds.*

J

jazz (jăz) *n.* A type of music with a strong rhythm which developed in the United States from work songs, hymns, and spirituals: *When the pianist plays jazz, she sometimes invents the song as she goes along.*

jolt (jōlt) *v.* To move, ride, or cause to move in a jerky way: *The bus was jolting along the bumpy road.*

ă rat / ā pay / â care / ä father / ĕ pet / ē be / ĭ pit / ī pie / î fierce / ŏ pot / ō go / ô paw, for / oi oil / ōo book

714

L

landscape

land·scape (lănd´ skāp´) *n.* A stretch of land: *Emily admired the landscape of rolling hills.*

lap (lăp) *v.* To take up with the tip of the tongue: *Have you ever watched a cat lap up water?* ♦ *n.* The front part of a sitting person's body from the waist to the knees: *The cat slept on Yoshi's lap.*

long (lông) *v.* To wish or want very much: *My mother longed to see her childhood home again.*

lum·ber·jack (lŭm´ bər jăk´) *n.* A person who chops down trees and hauls the logs to a sawmill.

lurch·ing (lûrch´ ing) *adj.* Sudden, heavy, unsteady movements to one side or forward: *The lurching boat made Roslyn sway back and forth.*

lure (lŏŏr) *n.* Fake bait used to attract and catch fish: *The fisherman tied a silver lure to his line.*

M

mar·vel (mär´ vəl) *v.* To be filled with surprise, amazement, or wonder: *Don marveled at the beautiful waterfall.*

mer·cu·ry (mûr´ kyə rē) *n.* A silvery-white metal that is a liquid at room temperature; used in thermometers.

mis·cal·cu·late (mĭs kăl´ kyə lāt´) *v.* To plan or figure incorrectly; make a mistake: *Amy miscalculated how much money she needed.*

mis·un·der·stand·ing (mĭs´ ŭn dər stăn´ dĭng) *n.* A failure to understand: *Carl's feelings were hurt because of a misunderstanding over whose turn it was.*

mod·est (mŏd´ ĭst) *adj.* Having a quiet, humble view of one's own talents, abilities, or accomplishments; not boastful: *The piano player was modest even though he was very talented.*

mur·mur (mûr´ mər) *n.* A low, constant sound: *We often hear the murmur of running water from the nearby stream.*

mush·er (mŭsh´ ər) *n.* The driver of a dog sled team.

N

ner·vous·ly (nûr´ vəs lē) *adv.* With concern, worry, or fear: *He nervously walked onto the stage to deliver his speech.*

O

oath (ōth) *n.* A pledge or promise to act in a certain way: *The new citizens pledged an oath to obey the laws of the United States.*

op·por·tu·ni·ty (ŏp´ ər tōō´ nĭ tē) *or* (ŏp´ ar tyōō´ nĭ tē) *n.* A good chance to advance oneself: *Joining the school band was an opportunity to make new friends.*

or·phan (ôr´ fən) *n.* A child whose parents are dead.

lumberjack
Lumberjack is a compound word made up of *lumber,* meaning trees used for wood, and *jack,* meaning "man." *Jack* originally comes from the Hebrew name for Jacob.

P

phonograph

pioneer
Pioneer comes from the Italian word for "foot soldier," the first kind of soldier to go into battle. Today, *pioneer* refers to the settlers of the American West or to anyone who leads the way for others.

peas·ant (pĕz´ ənt) *adj.* Of or relating to a poor farmer or farm worker: *The couple lived a simple peasant life in the country.*

pe·cu·liar (pĭ kyōōl´ yər) *adj.* Unusual; strange or odd: *The warm weather was peculiar for January.*

per·sist (pər sĭst´) *v.* To continue repeatedly to say or do something: *My sister persisted in asking me to read to her.*

pho·no·graph (fō´ nə grăf´) *n.* An old-fashioned record player: *Jenna danced to a happy song playing on the phonograph.*

pi·o·neer (pī´ ə nîr´) *n.* A person who settles in an unknown, unclaimed region: *The pioneers made their new homes in the valley.*

pitch in (pĭch ĭn) *v.* To start working with other people to get a job done: *Everyone on the farm pitches in to finish the work.*

plaque (plăk) *n.* A flat piece of wood, metal, or stone with writing on it that usually honors a person or event: *Plaques on the sunken ship honor the people who lost their lives.*

plat·form (plăt´ fôrm) *n.* A raised floor or surface, for example, by a track at a train station: *They stood on the platform, waiting for the train.*

prai·rie (prâr´ ē) *adj.* Of the plains, a wide area of flat or rolling land with tall grass and few trees: *The prairie winds covered everything with dust.*

pro·test (prə tĕst´) *or* (prō´ tĕst´) *v.* To express strong objections to something: *Many people came to protest the plan to build a new airport.*

proud (proud) *adj.* **1.** Thinking too highly of oneself: *The boy was proud because he thought he was better than anyone else.* **2.** Full of self-respect: *Li felt proud to be marching in the parade.*

R

re·mind (rĭ mīnd´) *v.* To make someone remember something: *The song reminded him of home.*

re·new (rĭ nōō´) *or* (rĭ nyōō´) *v.* To make new again; bring new life to: *Each spring the forest renews itself with green leaves.*

re·un·ion (rē yōōn´ yən) *n.* A gathering of members of a group who have not seen each other for a while: *The school holds its yearly reunions in the gym.*

rhythm (rĭth´ əm) *n.* **1.** A movement, action, or condition that repeats in a regular pattern: *Everyone's walk has a special rhythm.* **2.** A musical pattern with a series of regularly accented beats: *We sang songs with many different rhythms.*

rug·ged (rŭg´ ĭd) *adj.* Having a rough, uneven surface: *The rugged trail was hard to climb.*

ă rat / ā pay / â care / ä father / ĕ pet / ē be / ĭ pit / ī pie / î fierce / ŏ pot / ō go / ô paw, for / oi oil / ōo book

716

S

scale
Scale comes from the Old Norse word for "bowl," or a drinking vessel made from a shell. Scales used to have two plates or bowls to hold the objects that were being weighed.

satch·el (săch´ əl) *n.* A small bag used for carrying books, clothing, or other small items: *The two satchels held all she owned.*

sat·is·fac·tion (săt´ ĭs făk´ shən) *n.* The condition of being pleased and contented: *Her satisfaction with her family showed in her big smile.*

scale (skāl) *n.* **1.** One of the small, thin, flat parts that cover a fish or reptile: *The lizard was covered with shiny green scales.* **2.** An instrument used for weighing: *Anton weighed a bunch of bananas on the scale.*

scav·en·ger (skăv´ ĭn jər) *n.* An animal that feeds on dead animals or plants: *Scavengers often eat dead fish.*

set·tler (sĕt´ lər) *n.* A person who settles, or makes a home, in a new region: *The settlers traveled west to find a better life.*

ship·wreck (shĭp´ rĕk´) *n.* **1.** A wrecked ship: *The Titanic is the most famous of all shipwrecks.* **2.** The destruction of a ship, in a collision or because of a storm: *A shipwreck may happen during a storm at sea.*

short·stop (shôrt´ stŏp´) *n.* The baseball player who plays the position between second and third bases.

singe (sĭnj) *v.* To burn slightly; scorch: *Celia saw that the fire was about to singe her sweater.*

slump (slŭmp) *v.* **1.** To sink down suddenly: *The woman slumped to the ground and cried.* **2.** To experience a period of poor performance, especially in a sport: *Our best hitter always slumps in hot weather.*

snake (snāk) *v.* To move like a snake: *The line of children snaked through the playground.*

snow·shoe (snō´ shōō´) *n.* A rounded wooden frame with leather strips stretched across it, attached to the shoe; used for walking on top of the snow.

spawn (spôn) *v.* To lay eggs and reproduce, as fish and some other water animals do: *Salmon return to spawn in the same river where they were born.*

spe·cial·ize (spĕsh´ ə līz) *v.* To be involved in a particular activity or branch of study: *This bookstore specializes in children's books.*

sports·man·ship (spôrts´ mən ship´) *n.* The quality of someone who acts with dignity in difficult situations, especially used with people who play sports: *It was good sportsmanship to clap for the other team.*

sto·ry·tel·ler (stôr´ ē tĕl´ ər) *n.* A person who tells stories.

stride (strīd) *v.* To walk with long steps: *The boy strides quickly down the street.*

stu·pen·dous (stōō pĕn´ dəs) *adj.* Amazing; marvelous: *The falling star was a stupendous sight.*

G2   **Glossary**

thermometer
Thermometer comes from two Greek words: *thermē*, meaning "heat," and *metron*, meaning "measure." A thermometer measures heat.

weathervane

sur·round (sə **round´**) *v.* To put all around: *He **surrounded** his desk with pictures of his family.*

sur·vi·vor (sər **vī´** vər) *n.* Someone or something that has stayed alive: *The rescue ship picked up the **survivors** from the lifeboats.*

T

teem·ing (**tēm´** ĭng) *adj.* Full; crowded: *The parade moved through the **teeming** city streets.*

tem·per·a·ture (**tĕm´** pər ə chŏor) *n.* Hotness or coldness as measured on a standard scale: *The **temperature** outside was low, so we put on our warmest clothes.*

ther·mom·e·ter (thər **mŏm´** ĭ tər) *n.* An instrument that measures temperature, usually by the height of a liquid that expands or contracts inside a slender glass tube.

tim·ber (**tĭm´** bər) *n.* **1.** Trees that can be used as wood: *They used **timber** from their own land to build their house.* **2.** A long, heavy piece of wood for building; a beam: *Only a few blackened **timbers** of the barn remained after the fire.*

tim·id (**tĭm´** ĭd) *adj.* Easily frightened; shy: *The **timid** squirrel sat still until everyone had left.*

tire·less (**tīr´** lĭs) *adj.* Capable of working a long time without getting tired: *She was a **tireless** worker who always stayed late.*

trou·ble·some (**trŭb´** əl səm) *adj.* Causing trouble or difficulty: *Ben felt he was in a **troublesome** situation when he couldn't find the movie tickets.*

U

un·sink·a·ble (ŭn **singk´** ə bəl) *adj.* Not capable of being sunk: *The ship was so big that people thought it was **unsinkable**.*

V

voy·age (**voi´** ĭj) *n.* A long journey to a distant place, usually made by ship or airplane.

W

weath·er·vane (**wĕth´** ər vān´) *n.* A moveable pointer that shows which way the wind is blowing: *The **weathervane** on top of the barn pointed north.*

woods·man (**wŏŏdz´** mən) *n.* A person who works or lives in the forest: *The young **woodsman** walked to the forest every day.*

world·wide (**wûrld´ wīd´**) *adj.* Extending or spreading throughout the world: *Several songs became **worldwide** hits.*

wreck·age (**rĕk´** ĭj) *n.* The remains of something that has been damaged or destroyed: *The **wreckage** of the ship was found on the ocean floor.*

ă rat / ā pay / â care / ä father / ĕ pet / ē be / ĭ pit / ī pie / î fierce / ŏ pot / ō go / ô paw, for / oi oil / ŏŏ book

Acknowledgments

A Very Important Day, by Maggie Rugg Herold, illustrated by Catherine Stock. Text copyright © 1995 by Maggie Rugg Herold. Illustrations copyright © 1995 by Catherine Stock. Reprinted by permission of HarperCollins Publishers.
Akiak: A Tale from the Iditarod, by Robert J. Blake. Text and illustrations copyright © 1997 by Robert J. Blake. All rights reserved. Reprinted by permission of Philomel Books, a division of Penguin Putnam, Inc.
Boss of the Plains: The Hat That Won The West, by Laurie Carlson, illustrated by Holly Meade. Text copyright © 1998 by Laurie Carlson. Illustrations copyright © 1998 by Holly Meade. Reprinted by permission of Dorling Kindersley Publishing, Inc.
Selection from *By the Shores of Silver Lake*, by Laura Ingalls Wilder. Copyright © 1939 by Laura Ingalls Wilder. Copyright renewed © 1967 by Roger L. MacBride. Reprinted by permission of HarperCollins Publishers.
Cendrillon: A Caribbean Cinderella, by Robert D. San Souci, illustrated by Brian Pinkney. Text copyright © 1998 by Robert D. San Souci. Illustrations copyright © 1998 by Brian Pinkney. All rights reserved. Reprinted by permission of Simon & Schuster Books for Young Readers, an imprint of Simon & Schuster Children's Publishing Division.
Finding the Titanic, by Robert D. Ballard, illustrated by Ken Marschall. Published by Cartwheel Books, a division of Scholastic, Inc. Copyright © 1993 by Madison Press, Ltd. Reprinted by permission of Scholastic, Inc. and Madison Press, Ltd.
Gloria Estefan: A Real-Life Biography, by Susan Boulais. Copyright © 1998 by Mitchell Lane Publishers, Inc. Reprinted by permission.
Grandfather's Journey, by Allen Say. Copyright © 1993 by Allen Say. Reprinted by permission of Houghton Mifflin Company.
Happy Birthday, Dr. King!, by Kathryn Jones, illustrated by Floyd Cooper. Copyright © 1994 by The Children's Museum, Boston. Published by Modern Curriculum Press, Inc., an imprint of Pearson Learning. Reprinted by permission.
Heat Wave!, by Helen Ketteman, illustrated by Scott Goto. Text copyright © 1998 by Helen Ketteman. Illustrations copyright © 1998 by Scott Goto. Reprinted by permission of Walker & Company. All rights reserved.
The Last Dragon, by Susan Miho Nunes, illustrated by Chris K. Soentpiet. Text copyright © 1995 by Susan Miho Nunes. Illustrations copyright © 1995 by Chris K. Soentpiet. Reprinted by permission of Houghton Mifflin Company.
Lou Gehrig: The Luckiest Man, by David A. Adler, illustrated by Terry Widener. Text copyright © 1997 by David A. Adler. Illustrations copyright © 1997 by Terry Widener. Reprinted by permission of Harcourt, Inc.
Marven of the Great North Woods, by Kathryn Lasky, illustrated by Kevin Hawkes. Text copyright © 1997 by Kathryn Lasky Knight. Illustrations copyright © 1997 by Kevin Hawkes. Reprinted by permission of Harcourt, Inc.
Selection from *My Name Is María Isabel*, by Alma Flor Ada, illustrated by K. Dyble Thompson. Text copyright © 1993 by Alma Flor Ada. Jacket illustration copyright © 1993 by K. Dyble Thompson. Reprinted by permission of Atheneum Books for Young Readers, an imprint of Simon & Schuster Children's Publishing Division.
Salmon Summer, written and photo-illustrated by Bruce McMillan. Copyright © 1998 by Bruce McMillan. Reprinted by permission of Houghton Mifflin Company.
Sing to the Stars, by Mary Brigid Barrett. Copyright © 1994 by Mary Brigid Barrett-Groth. Published by Little Brown & Company. Reprinted by permission of Curtis Brown, Ltd.
Selection from *Skylark*, by Patricia MacLachlan. Copyright © 1994 by Patricia MacLachlan. Reprinted by permission of HarperCollins Publishers.
The Stranger, by Chris Van Allsburg. Copyright © 1986 by Chris Van Allsburg. Reprinted by permission of Houghton Mifflin Company.
Tanya's Reunion, by Valerie Flournoy, illustrated by Jerry Pinkney. Text copyright © 1995 by Valerie Flournoy. Illustrations copyright © 1995 by Jerry Pinkney. Reprinted by arrangement with Dial Books for Young Readers, a division of Penguin Putnam, Inc.
Tomás and the Library Lady, by Pat Mora, illustrated by Raul Colón. Text copyright © 1997 by Pat Mora. Illustrations copyright © 1997 by Raul Colón. Reprinted by permission of Alfred A. Knopf, a division of Random House, Inc.
Wildfires, by Seymour Simon. Copyright © 1996 by Seymour Simon. Reprinted by permission of HarperCollins Publishers.

Focus Selections

"The Anteater," from *Beast Feast*, by Douglas Florian. Copyright © 1994 by Douglas Florian. Reprinted by permission of Harcourt, Inc.
"By Myself," from *Honey, I Love and Other Poems*, by Eloise Greenfield, pictures by Diane and Leo Dillon. Text copyright © 1978 by Eloise Greenfield. Reprinted by permission of HarperCollins Publishers.
"The Case of the Earthenware Pig," from *Encyclopedia Brown Solves Them All*, by Donald J. Sobol. Copyright © 1968 by Donald J. Sobol. Reprinted by permission of Dutton Children's Books, a division of Penguin Putnam, Inc.
"How Turtle Flew South for the Winter," reprinted by permission from *Native American Stories*, told by Joseph Bruchac from Keepers of the Earth, by Michael J. Caduto and Joseph Bruchac, © 1991 Fulcrum Publishing, Golden, CO www.fulcrum-books.com. All rights reserved.
"I Watched an Eagle Soar," from *Dancing Teepees: Poems of American Indian Youth*, by Virginia Driving Hawk Sneve. Copyright © 1989 by Virginia Driving Hawk Sneve. All rights reserved. Reprinted by permission of Holiday House, Inc.
"Oda a mis zapatos/Ode to My Shoes," from *Bellybutton of the Moon* and Other Summer Poems, by Francisco X. Alarcón. Copyright © 1998 by Francisco X. Alarcón. Reprinted by permission of Children's Book Press, San Francisco, CA.
"The Panther," from *Custard and Company*, by Ogden Nash. Copyright © 1940 by Ogden Nash. First published in the Saturday Evening Post. Reprinted by permission of Little Brown and Company, Inc.
"Pencils," from *Who Shrank My Grandmother's House? Poems of Discovery*, by Barbara Esbensen. Copyright © 1992 by Barbara Esbensen. Reprinted by permission of HarperCollins Publishers.
"Rabbit," from *The Llama Who Had No Pajama: 100 Favorite Poems*, by Mary Ann Hoberman. Copyright © 1973 by Mary Ann Hoberman. Reprinted by permission of Harcourt, Inc.
"The Seed," from *Always Wondering*, by Aileen Fisher. Copyright © 1991 by Aileen Fisher. Reprinted by permission of Marian Reiner for the author.
"Sky-Fish," from *Out in the Dark and Daylight*, by Aileen Fisher. Copyright © 1980 by Aileen Fisher. Reprinted by permission of Marian Reiner for the author.
"The Sticks of Truth," from *Stories to Solve: Folktales from Around the World*, retold by George Shannon. Copyright © 1985 by George W. B. Shannon. Reprinted by permission of HarperCollins Publishers.
Excerpt from the play *Tales of a Fourth Grade Nothing*, by Judy Blume, adapted by Bruce Mason. Copyright © by the Seattle Children's Theatre. Reprinted by permission.
"Tiger," from *How the Animals Got Their Colors*, by Michael Rosen, illustrated by John Clementson. Text copyright © 1992, 1991 by Michael Rosen. Illustrations copyright © 1991, 1992 by John Clementson. Reprinted by permission of Harcourt, Inc.
"Why the Sun and the Moon Live in the Sky," from *How Many Spots Does a Leopard Have? and Other Tales*, by Julius Lester, illustrated by David Shannon. Text copyright © 1989 by Julius Lester. Illustrations copyright © 1989 by David Shannon. Reprinted by permission of Scholastic, Inc.

Links and Theme Openers

"A Real Lesson in Democracy," from the March 10, 1999 *Fort Lauderdale Sun-Sentinel*. Copyright © 1999 by the Florida Sun-Sentinel. Reprinted by permission.
"The Art of Music," by Richard Mühlberger, adapted from February 1998 Highlights for Children. Copyright © 1998 by Highlights for Children, Inc. Reprinted by permission.
"Canada Geese," from *The Great Frog Race And Other Poems*, by Kristine O'Connell George. Text copyright © 1997 by Kristine O'Connell George. Reprinted by permission of Houghton Mifflin Company. All rights reserved.
"Children Cast Kids Voting Ballots," from the April 25, 1999 *El Paso Times*. Copyright © 1999 by the El Paso Times. Reprinted by permission.
"Constructing A Straw Thermometer," from *Simple Weather Experiments with Everyday Materials*, by Muriel Mandell. Copyright © 1990 by Muriel Mandell. Reprinted by permission of Sterling Publishing Company, Inc.
Selection from *Dear Mrs. Parks: A Dialogue with Today's Youth*, by Rosa Parks. Text copyright © 1996 by Rosa L. Parks. Jacket copyright © 1996 by Mark T. Kerrin. Reprinted by permission of Lee & Low Books, Inc., New York, NY.
"Even in Summer," originally titled "Weather Conditions" and untitled in *Cricket Never Does*, by Myra Cohn Livingston. Copyright © 1976, 1997 by Myra Cohn Livingston. Reprinted by permission of Marian Reiner.
"Fall Wind," from *Make Things Fly*, by Margaret Hillert. Copyright © by Margaret Hillert. Reprinted by permission of the author, who controls all rights.
"Falling Leaves," by Lucinda A. Cave from *Children's Playmate*. Copyright © 1996 by Children's Better Health Institute, Benjamin Franklin Literary & Medical Society, Inc. Reprinted by permission.
"Figuring It Out: Math, Baseball Statistics, and Keeping Score," from *The First Book of Baseball*, by Marty Appel. Copyright © 1988 by Marty Appel. Front cover photographs copyright © Chuck Solomon. Reprinted by permission of Crown Children's Books, a division of Random House, Inc.
"Finding Her Way," by Karen Crowe, adapted from January/February 1999 *American Girl*. Copyright © 1999 by Pleasant Company. Reprinted by permission.
"Firefly There," by M. L. Bittle-DeLapa. Copyright © 1985 by M. L. Bittle-DeLapa. First published in WoodNotes: Winter 1990, Number 4, and in Haiku Moment, 1993 by Charles E. Tuttle, Inc. Reprinted by permission of M. L. Bittle-DeLapa.
"Flame Busters," by R. G. Schmidt, adapted from June 1999 National Geographic World. Copyright © 1999 by the National Geographic Society. Reprinted by permission.
"Frog's Shadow," by Virginia Brady Young. Copyright © by Virginia Brady Young. Reprinted by permission.
Selection from *Fun & Games for Family Gatherings*, by Adrienne Anderson. Copyright © 1996 by Adrienne Anderson. Reprinted by permission of Reunion Research.
"Go, Team, Go!" by Judith E. Rinard from December 1996 National Geographic World. Copyright © 1996 by the National Geographic Society. Reprinted by permission.
"Going Out of My Way," from *Fresh Scent: Selected Haiku*, by Lee Gurga, first published by Brooks Books. Copyright © 1998 by Lee Gurga. Reprinted by permission.
"Happy New Year," from *Festivals*, by Meryl Doney. Text copyright © 1996 by Meryl Doney. Illustrations copyright © 1996 by Franklin Watts. Reprinted by permission of Franklin Watts, a division of Grolier Publishing.
"Iceberg Right Ahead!" by Gail Skroback Hennessey, adapted from March 1999 *Contact Kids*. Copyright © 1999 by Children's Television Workshop. Reprinted by permission.
"Kids Voting Results Match Adults' Tally," from the November 5, 1998 *Honolulu Advertiser*. Copyright © 1998 by the Honolulu Advertiser. Reprinted by permission.
Selection from *Making Books That Fly, Fold, Wrap, Hide, Pop Up, Twist, and Turn*, by Gwen Diehn. Copyright © 1998 by Gwen Diehn. Reprinted by permission of Lark Books, Asheville, NC. www.larkbooks.com.
"May Rains!" untitled haiku by Sanpu from *Talking to the Sun: An Illustrated Anthology of Poems for Young People*, edited by Kenneth Koch and Kate Farrell. Compilation copyright © 1985 by Kenneth Koch and Kate Farrell. Reprinted by permission of Henry Holt and Company LLC.
"Migrating Geese," by Charles Dickson. Copyright © 1993 by Charles Dickson. Reprinted by permission of Virginia Dickson.
"Moon of Falling Leaves," from *Thirteen Moons on a Turtle's Back*, by Joseph Bruchac and Jonathan Logan. Copyright © 1992 by Joseph Bruchac and Jonathan London. Reprinted by permission of Philomel Books, a division of Penguin Putnam, Inc.
"My Song," by Kimberly Eagle Bull, originally appeared in *When the Rain Sings: Poems by Young Native Americans*, Simon & Schuster/National Museum of the American Indian, Smithsonian Institution. Copyright © 1999 by Kimberly Eagle Bull. Reprinted by permission.
"The Name Game," adapted from *Do People Grow on Family Trees?*, by Ira Wolfman. Copyright © 1991 by Ira Wolfman and the Statue of Liberty – Ellis Island Foundation, Inc. Reprinted by permission of Workman Publishing Co., Inc. All rights reserved.
"Nature Is," from *The Random House Book of Poetry for Children*, selected and introduced by Jack Prelutsky. Copyright © 1983 by Jack Prelutsky. Reprinted by permission of Random House Children's Books, a division of Random House, Inc.
"Rain Sayings," from *It's Raining Cats and Dogs*, by Franklyn M. Branley. Copyright © 1987 by Franklyn M. Branley. Reprinted by permission of Houghton Mifflin Company. Cover of April 1989 Faces reprinted by permission of Cobblestone Publishing, Inc. Cover copyright

© 1989 by Cobblestone Publishing, Inc.
Recipe from *Larios on the Beach*. Copyright © Larios on the Beach Restaurant. Reprinted by permission.
"Seal Island Kids," by Yva Momatiuk and John Eastcott, adapted from May 1999 Ranger Rick. Copyright © 1999 by the National Wildlife Federation. Reprinted by permission.
"Snow Runners," by William G. Scheller from February 1999 National Geographic World. Copyright © 1999 by the National Geographic Society. Reprinted by permission.
"Summer Sky," by Shiki from *The Penguin Book of Zen Poetry*, edited and translated by Lucien Stryk and Takashi Ikemoto. Copyright © 1963, 1965, 1977 by Lucien Stryk and Takashi Ikemoto. Reprinted by permission of Lucien Stryk.
"Sunflakes," from *Country Pie*, by Frank Asch. Copyright © 1979 by Frank Asch. Reprinted by permission of HarperCollins Publishers.
"This Land Is Your Land," words and music by Woody Guthrie. TRO © Copyright 1956 (Renewed), 1958 (Renewed), 1970 (Renewed) Ludlow Music, Inc., New York, New York. Reprinted by permission.

Special thanks to the following teachers whose students' compositions appear as Student Writing Models: Cindy Cheatwood, Florida; Diana Davis, North Carolina; Kathy Driscoll, Massachusetts; Linda Evers, Florida; Heidi Harrison, Michigan; Eileen Hoffman, Massachusetts; Julia Kraftsow, Florida; Bonnie Lewison, Florida; Kanetha McCord, Michigan.

Credits

Photography

4 (tr) image Copyright ©2000 PhotoDisc, Inc. **16** (bl)National Baseball Hall of Fame Library, Cooperstown, NY. **19** (b) ©Richard Cooke/Corbis. **20–21** Rob Bossi/Outside Images/PNI. **26** (banner) image Copyright ©2000 PhotoDisc Inc. (inset)©Galen Rowell/Mountain Light. **26–7** (bkgd)©Jeff Schultz/Alaska Stock. **27**(inset) ©Jeff Schultz/Alaska Stock. **28** Jeanne Conover. **29** (bkgd) image Copyright ©2000 PhotoDisc, Inc. **53** (b) ©Jeff Schultz/Alaska Stock. **54–7** Richard Nowitz/NGS Image Collection. **60** (b) ©Christie's Images Inc. **61** (tl) Archive Pictures. (tr, br) Brown Brothers. **75** Houghton Mifflin Company. **76** (b) Japanese American National Museum. **80** (banner)image Copyright ©2000 PhotoDisc Inc. **80–1** The Titanic, 1911. Antonio Jacobsen (1850-1921) ©Christie's Images Inc. **82** Illustration by Ken Marschall ©1993 from FINDING THE TITANIC, a Scholastic/Madison Press Book. **83** The Titanic, 1911. Antonio Jacobsen (1850-1921) ©Christie's Images Inc. **84** (both) Emory Kristof/NGS Image Collection. **85** Don Lynch Collection. **86** (left inset) ©Underwood & Underwood/Corbis. (right inset) ©Ralph White/Corbis. **86–7** Illustration by Ken Marschall ©1993 from FINDING THE TITANIC, a Scholastic/Madison Press Book. **87** (left inset) ©Ralph White/Corbis. (right inset) The Illustrated London News Picture Library. **89** Illustration by Ken Marschall ©1993 from FINDING THE TITANIC, a Scholastic/Madison Press Book. **90–1** Illustration by Ken Marschall ©1993 from FINDING THE TITANIC, a Scholastic/Madison Press Book. **92–3** The Illustrated London News Picture Library. **94** Brown Brothers. **97** (tl) Perry Thorsvik/NGS Image Collection. (tr) Martin Bowen/Woods Hole Oceanographic Institution. (bl) ©Ralph White/Corbis. (br) Harland & Wolff Photographic Collection, ©National Museums and Galleries of Northern Ireland, Ulster Folk & Transport Museum negative no. H1455. **98** Illustration by Ken Marschall ©1993 from FINDING THE TITANIC, a Scholastic/Madison Press Book. **99** Hulton-Deutsch Collection/Corbis. **100** Emory Kristof/NGS Image Collection. **101** (bkgd) image Copyright ©2000 PhotoDisc, Inc. (inset) AP/Wide World/Lennox McLendon. **102** (b) Don Lynch Collection. **104–5** ©VCG/FPG International. **105** (all) Courtesy, International Ice Patrol, U.S. Coast Guard. **107** (top) Courtesy, International Ice Patrol, U.S. Coast Guard. **108** (banner) image Copyright ©2000 PhotoDisc, Inc. (l) Union Pacific Museum Collection. **109** Corbis Images. **110** (bkgd) image Copyright ©2000 PhotoDisc, Inc. **127** (bkgd) Artville. (top)Corbis/Bettmann. (b)Jim Rimi Photography. (picture frames)Image Farm. **127–8** Union Pacific Railroad Museum. **130–33** (all)©Ron Cortes. **148** (l) Hulton-Deutsch Collection/Corbis. (r)©1998 Viacom International. All Rights Reserved. **156** Courtesy, Special Collections Library, University of California Riverside/Rivera Library. **157** (tl) ©Al Key. (tr) Courtesy, Southwest Texas State University. (b) Courtesy, University of California Riverside Media Services. **158** (t) Courtesy, Random House. (b) Courtesy, Raúl Colón. **178** (b) Cary Wolinsky/Stock Boston. **179** Hereford Cathedral Library. Photo by Gordon W. Taylor L.R.P.S. **180** (t) Scala/Art Resource, NY. (b) Eric Lessing/Art Resource, NY. **181** Scott Goodwin Photography. "Old King Cole" Courtesy, Michael Canoso. **184** (bc) John Rubartsch for Reunions Magazine. (br) ©Ron Karten/Omni-Photo Communications, Inc. **185** (t) ©Bob Daemmrich/Stock Boston/PNI. (b) Patrick Robinson for Reunions Magazine. **186** (t) Courtesy, Valerie Flournoy. (b) Myles Pinkney. **216–17** (b) Church of Jesus Christ of Latter-Day Saints Archives Division #C-188. **217** (t) Used by Permission, Utah State Historical Society, All Rights Reserved. Photo no. 917.81. (c) Courtesy, John B. Stetson Company. **218** (t) ©Courtesy, DK Publishing. (b) ©Bill Franson Photography. **241** (cr) Paramount Pictures/Movie Still Archives. **242** Denver Public Library no. Z332. **245** (bl) The Kansas State Historical Society, Topeka, Kansas. **246** R. Kord/H. Armstrong Roberts. **247** (t) ©Henry T. Kaiser/The Picture Cube, Inc. (bl) Corbis/Patrick Ward. (br) ©James Marshall. **248** Courtesy, William Morrow. **272** (t) Courtesy, Kids Voting USA. (b) Dayton Daily News. **273–5** (bkgd) Donovan Reese/Tony Stone Images. **282** The Image Bank. **292** (banner) image Copyright ©2000 PhotoDisc, Inc. **292–3** "Olive Trees" (detail), 1889, Vincent van Gogh. The Minneapolis Institute of Arts. **298** (b) ©Zig Leszczynski/Animals Animals. **299** (l) ©Jose Azel/Aurora. (tr) ©Chase Smith/Corbis. (br) ©Ed Young/Corbis. **300** (cr) Scott Goodwin Photography. (bkgd) image Copyright ©2000 PhotoDisc, Inc. **318** image Copyright ©2000 PhotoDisc, Inc. **319** (tl) image Copyright ©2000 PhotoDisc, Inc. **326** (cr) ©Jake Rajs/Tony Stone Images. **327** (t) ©Chad Ehlers/Tony Stone Images. (border fish) ©Norbert Wu. (border red hibiscus) ©Amos Nachoum/Corbis. (border orange hibiscus) image Copyright ©2000 PhotoDisc, Inc. **328** (bkgd) image Copyright ©2000 PhotoDisc, Inc. (t) Dennis Gray/Mercury Pictures. (b) Michael Tamborrino/Mercury Pictures. **355** (l) image Copyright ©2000 PhotoDisc, Inc. (r) ©The Walt Disney Company/Courtesy, Kobal Collection. **356** (b) Culver Pictures. **357** (tl) North Wind Picture Archives. (tc) The New York Public Library for the Performing Arts (tr) ©Jack Vartoogian. **358** (banner) image Copyright ©2000 PhotoDisc, Inc. (c) ©Charles O'Rear/Corbis. **359** ©Miro Vintoniv/Stock Boston. **360** (bkgd) image Copyright ©2000 PhotoDisc, Inc. **377** (t) Courtesy, Helen Ketteman. (b) Courtesy, Scott Goto. **384–5** Index Stock. **390** (t) ©James Frank/Stock Connection/PNI. (b) ©Frank Siteman/Stock Boston/PNI. **391** (t) Bob Daemmrich/Stock Boston. (b) ©Frank Siteman/Stock Boston. **392** (t) Ann Duffy. (b) Courtesy, Melodye Rosales. **409** (l) image Copyright ©2000 PhotoDisc, Inc. (r) Ken Karp. **410** (b) ©Coco McCoy/Rainbow/PNI. **411** (t) ©David Lees/Corbis. (b) ©Roger Garwood & Trish Ainslie/Corbis. **412** (t) ©Minnesota Historical Society/Corbis. **413** (t) image Copyright ©2000 PhotoDisc, Inc. **415** (t) Photo Courtesy of Clearwater County Historical Society, Bagley, MN. (b) Minnesota Historical Society. **443** (t) Christopher Knight (b) Courtesy, Kevin Hawkes. **446–7** Scott S. Warren/NGS Image Collection. **447** (tr) image Copyright ©2000 PhotoDisc, Inc. (br) ©Scott S. Warren. **448** (cl) (cr) ©Scott S. Warren. (t) ©Scott S. Warren/NGS Image Collection. **449** (t) ©Tom Brakefield/Bruce Coleman Inc. NY. (b) Scott S. Warren/NGS Image Collection. **450** ©Robert Brenner/PhotoEdit. **451** (t) ©Barbara Alper/Stock Boston. (b) ©Gary A. Conner/PhotoEdit. **452** (bkgd) Neo Vision/Photonica. (t) Courtesy, Susan Miho Nunes. (b) Michael Tamborinno/Mercury Pictures. **453** (bkgd) Neo Vision/Photonica. **481** images Copyright ©2000 PhotoDisc, Inc. **482-3** ©A. Ramey/PhotoEdit. **486** (b) ©David Young-Wolff/PhotoEdit. **486–7** image Copyright ©2000 PhotoDisc, Inc. **487(t)** ©Carol and Mike Werner/Stock Boston. (b) ©Lawrence Migdale/Stock Boston. **488** (t) Mary Brigid Barrett. (b) Thor Swift/Mercury Pictures. **509** (r) image Copyright ©2000 PhotoDisc, Inc. **510** John Bigelow Taylor/Art Resource, NY. **511** (t) Erich Lessing/Art Resource, NY. (b) Green Violinist, 1923-24, Marc Chagall. Oil on canvas. Gift, Solomon R. Guggenheim, 1937. The Solomon R. Guggenheim Museum, New York. Photograph by David Heald ©The Solomon R. Guggenheim Foundation, New York. **514** image Copyright ©2000 PhotoDisc, Inc. **516** image Copyright ©2000 PhotoDisc, Inc. **517** ©James C. Amos/Photo Researchers. **520** ©Jeff Vanuga/Corbis. **521** ©Niall Benvie/Corbis. **522** ©William A. Bake/Corbis. **523** ©Jeff Vanuga/Corbis. **524** image Copyright ©2000 PhotoDisc, Inc. **526** (banner) image Copyright ©2000 PhotoDisc, Inc. (t) ©Mark Anderson/Rubber Ball Productions/PNI. **526–7** ©Tony Stone Images/Chris Shinn. **532** (b) ©Bettmann/Corbis. **531** ©Bettmann/Corbis. **534** (t) Courtesy, Kathryn Jones. (b) Velma Cooper. **539** ©Flip Schulke/Corbis. **542** AP/Wide World. **552** (inset) AP/Wide World. (frame) Image Farm. **554** AP/Wide World. **558** (b) ©Bob Kramer. **559** (t) ©Jack Vartoogian. (bl) ©Bob Kramer. (br) ©Susan Wilson. (CD) image Copyright ©2000 PhotoDisc, Inc. **561** (t) image Copyright ©2000 PhotoDisc, Inc. (b)Anthony Nesye/Liaison International. **562** (t) Randy Taylor/SYGMA. (b) AP/Wide World Photos. **563** Arnaldo Magnani/Liaison International. **564** (l) Govert De Roos/Sunshine/Retna. (r) image Copyright ©2000 PhotoDisc, Inc. **565** Gregory Kearney Lawson/Liaison International. **566** Les Stone/SYGMA. **567** (l) image Copyright ©2000 PhotoDisc, Inc. (r) Sherry Rayn Barnett/Michael Ochs Archives/Venice CA. **568** Joe Traver/Liaison International. **569** (l) image Copyright ©2000 PhotoDisc, Inc. (r) Murry H. Sill/Life Magazine ©Time, Inc. **570** Mitchell Gerber/CORBIS. **571** Dirck Halstead/Liaison International. **572** Ed Kennedy. **573** AP/Wide World Photos. **574** (l) Mitchell Gerber/Corbis. (r) AP/Wide World. **575** (t) Raul Demolina/SYGMA. (b) Allen Eveston/The Palm Beach Post. **576** (l) Gamma Liaison. (r) Gary Gershoff/Retna. **577** (l) Courtesy, Mitchell Lane Publishers. (r) image Copyright ©2000 PhotoDisc, Inc. **580** Photo by Maggie Rodriguez, Courtesy, Estefan Enterprises. **582** (t) National Baseball Hall of Fame Library, Cooperstown, NY. (b) National Baseball Hall of Fame Library, Cooperstown, NY. **582–3** (b) National Baseball Hall of Fame Library, Cooperstown, NY. **583** (b) AP/Wide World Photos. **603** (t) Michael Tamborrino/Mercury Pictures. (b) Paul Buck/Mercury Pictures. **604** image Copyright ©2000 PhotoDisc, Inc. **605** Corbis/Bettmann. **607** (t) National Baseball Hall of Fame Library, Cooperstown, NY. (b) ©Bettmann/Corbis. **624** image Copyright ©2000 PhotoDisc, Inc. (inset)©Tom Brakefield/The Stock Market. **626** (t) ©Tony Stone Images/Pat O'Hara. (banner) ©Thomas Wiewandt/Masterfile. **626–7** Corbis Royalty Free. **632** (banner) image Copyright ©2000 PhotoDisc, Inc. (t) ©Richard Cooke/CORBIS. (b) ©Wolfgang Kaehler/CORBIS. **633** (b)©Tom Bean/CORBIS. (cr) ©W. Perry Conway/CORBIS. **634** (t) John Henry Williams/Bruce Coleman, Inc. (inset) Photo by Benner McGee/©1995 Bruce McMillan. **635** (bkgd) image Copyright ©2000 PhotoDisc, Inc. **635–43** ©Bruce McMillan. **648** image Copyright ©2000 PhotoDisc, Inc. **649** image Copyright ©2000 PhotoDisc, Inc. **650** (b) ©Yva Momatuik & John Eastcott. **650–1** (bkgd) image Copyright ©2000 PhotoDisc, Inc. **651** (t) Map Courtesy of Ranger Rick™ Magazine. Copyright 1999 National Wildlife Federation. (b) ©Yva Momatuik & John Eastcott. **653–4** ©Yva Momatuik & John Eastcott. **656** ©Kevin Schafer/CORBIS. **657** ©Kevin Schafer/CORBIS. **659** (t) ©Raymond Gehman/CORBIS. (cl) ©Dennis Flaherty/Photo Researchers, Inc. (br) ©Dr. Edward S. Ross. **660** images Copyright ©2000 PhotoDisc, Inc. (inset) Courtesy, Seymour Simon. **662** (t) image Copyright ©2000 PhotoDisc, Inc. **663** Dan Morrison. **665** Seymour Simon. **667** Dan Morrison. **668–9** Alan and Sandy Carey. **671** Alan and Sandy Carey. **673** Alan and Sandy Carey. **675** Gary Braasch/Life. **677** Seymour Simon. **678–9** John J. Lopinot/Silver Image. **681** Alan and Sandy Carey. **682** image Copyright ©2000 PhotoDisc, Inc. **684–5** (all) ©Dan Helms. **686** (cl) ©Kevin Schafer/CORBIS. (cr) ©W. Perry Conway/CORBIS. **686-7** (bkgd) ©David Muench/CORBIS. **687** Nebraska State Historical Society, Solomon D. Butcher Collection. **688** (t) John MacLachlan. (b) Lisa Ratgeb. **705** Photofest. **711** ©Lowell Georgia/Corbis. **712** ©Wolfgang Kaehler/Corbis. **713** ©David Young-Wolff/PhotoEdit. **714** ©Richard Hamilton Smith/Corbis. **715** ©Adam Woolfitt/Corbis. **716** image Copyright ©2000 PhotoDisc, Inc. **717** image Copyright ©2000 PhotoDisc, Inc. **718** image Copyright ©2000 PhotoDisc, Inc.

Assignment Photography

8 (ml), **103** (r), **279, 289, 290, 150–1, 485** (b), **581** Joel Benjamin; **278, 280–1, 284, 286, 288, 409** (r), **509** (l) Ken Karp; **214, 215** Allan Landau; **135, 277, 383, 513, 609, 709** Tony Scarpetta.

Illustration

29 (i), **30–51** Robert Blake. **62** (i), **63–74** Allen Say. **78–79** Lark Carrier. **110** (i), Garth Williams. **111–126** Copyright, 2001 by Dorris Ettlinger. **136–137** Dave Kramer. **139–143** Michael Chesworth. **144–147** Linda S. Wingerter. **243, 244, 245** William Brinkley and Associates. **321** Pablo Torricella. **322–323** Linda Wingerter. **326** (maps) XNR Productions, Inc. **380–381** Chris Reed. **392, 394, 397–407, 408** (b) Copyright, 2001 by Melodye Benson Rosales. **489** (i), **490–507** Sandra Speidel. **519** nancy Gibson-Bash. **580–581** Francisco Mora. **610–611** Barry Rockwell. **615–619** Krystyna Stasiak. **613–614** Craig Spearing. **620–623** Fred Lynch. **633, 658** XNR Productions, Inc. **689** (i) Marcia Sewall. **690–703** David Soman. **706–707** George Schill.

Index

Boldface page references indicate formal strategy and skill instruction.

Comprehension skills

author's viewpoint, *353*

cause and effect, **305**

compare and contrast, *327C, 327D,* *329,* **333,** *354, 357,* **357A–357B,** **369,** *381, R4–R5*

conclusions, drawing, **315,** *317, 318,* *323, 354, 357, 381*

details, noting, *299C, 299D, 306,* **307,** *308, 312, 318, 323,* **323A–323B,** *330, 332, 340, 342,* *344,* **349,** *357, 378, R2–R3,* *R8–R9*

fantasy/realism, **347,** *354, 358G,* *359C, 359D,* **365,** *377,* **381A–381B,** *R6–R7, R12–R13*

generalizations, making, *378*

inferences. *See* Inferences, making.

judgments, making, *309, 318, 339,* *353*

main idea, supporting details, *309, 344*

predicting outcomes, *309, 317, 354,* *357, 377, 378, 381*

problem solving/decision making, *339, 378, 381*

sequence of events, *367*

story structure, **371,** *378*

See also Lessons; Picture clues; Spiral Review; Strategies, reading.

Comprehension strategies. *See* Strategies, reading.

Computer activities. *See* Technology resources.

Connections

between grammar and writing, *323E*

between literature and life experience, *357*

between reading and writing, *324,* *325, 325A*

between expository and narrative selections, *357, 381*

between narrative selections, *326J,* *354, 358J*

between strategies and skills, **299C,** **327C, 359C**

theme connections, *298A, 298D,* *299A, 318, 326G, 326J, 327A,* *354, 358G, 358J, 359A, 378,* *381*

Constructing meaning from text. *See* Comprehension skills; Decoding skills; Language; Phonics; Strategic reading.

Content areas, reading in the

multicultural, *298A–298D,* *325I–325J, 325K–325L*

music, *356–357*

science, *299A, 359A, 380–381*

social studies, *327A*

See also Cross-curricular activities.

Context clues. *See* Decoding skills; Vocabulary.

Conventions of language. *See* Grammar and usage; Mechanics, language; Speech, parts of.

Cooperative learning activities, *308,* *309, 315, 316, 317, 321, 323A, 323D,* *323E, 323H, 323J, 323P, 325A, 325J,* *338, 339, 352, 353, 356, 357B, 357E,* *357F, 357H, 357J, 357P, 366, 367, 371,* *376, 377, 381B, 381E, 381J, 381P, R9,* *R11, R11, R13, R15, R17*

Cooperative reading. *See* Reading modes.

Creative dramatics

dramatizing, *R27*

role-play, **323P**

Creative response. *See* Responding to literature.

Creative thinking, *298D, 318, 319,* *354, 355, 378, 379*

Critical thinking, *309, 317, 323, 339,* *353, 357, 367, 377, 381*

Cross-cultural connections. *See* Multicultural activities/information. Cross-curricular activities, *R26–R27*

Cross-curricular links

art, *374, R11, R13*

dance, *356–357, R26*

drama, *R27*

math, *381, R26*

multicultural. *See* Multicultural activities/information.

music, *357, R26*

science, *306, 312, 370, 380–381, R9,* *R11, R27*

social studies, *342*

Cue systems. *See* Decoding skills, context clues; Phonics; Structural analysis.

Cultural diversity. *See* Multicultural activities/information.

D

Daily language practice, *323K, 323L,* *357K, 357L, 381K, 381L*

Decoding skills

blending, **299B, 327B,** *345,* **381F**

chunking, *299B, 314,* **323E,** *345,* *359B*

context clues, **299B,** *314,* **323E, 323J,** *327B, 345, 359B,* **381F, 381G**

longer words, **323E–323F, 357E–357F,** **381E–381F**

multi-syllabic words, *314,* **357F,** **381I–381J**

phonics/decoding strategy, *299B,* *314,* **323E, 323F,** *327B, 345,* **357E, 357F,** *359B, 375,* **381E,** **381F,** *R2, R3, R4, R5, R6, R7*

See also Phonics; Spiral Review; Structural analysis; Vocabulary, selection.

Details, noting important, related, and sufficient. *See* Comprehension skills.

Diagrams. *See* Graphic information, interpreting; Graphic organizers.

Dialogue. *See* Language; Writing skills.

Diaries and journals. *See* Journal.

Dictionary skills

dividing words into syllables, **381I–381J**

for holding a conversation, **323O–323P**

for listening attentively, **323O, 323P, 381O, 381P**

for listening to an announcement, **381O–381P**

to encourage others, **323P**

in a writing conference. *See* Reading-Writing Workshop, conferencing.

prior knowledge for, *298A, 326G, 358G*

purpose

to analyze and evaluate. *See* Literature, analyzing; Literature, evaluating.

to compare/contrast, *298C, 326G, 326H, 326I, 326J*

to distinguish fantasy and realism, *358G, 358H, 358I, 358J*

to think aloud. *See* Modeling, think aloud.

to visualize. *See* Visualizing.

to a read aloud. *See* Reading modes.

to an audiotape. *See* Audiotapes.

to creative dramatics. *See* Creative dramatics.

to literature discussion. *See* Responding to literature.

to oral presentation. *See* Speaking activities.

to oral reading. *See* Reading modes; Rereading.

to poetry, *320–323*

to weather reports, **381C–381D**

Listening comprehension

compare and contrast, **326G–326J**

fantasy and realism, **358G–358J**

noting details, **298A–298D**

Literacy, expanding. *See* Skill links.

Literary analysis

classic literature, *326G–326J, 328–353, R4–R5*

common themes, *298A, 298D, 299A, 318, 326E, 326H, 327A, 354, 358G, 358J, 359A, 378, 381*

compare different versions of same story, **323C**, *329, 338, 339,* **357B, 357C, 357D, 357O–357P**

compare literature from different cultures, *329, 357B, 357C, 357D*

elements of fiction and nonfiction, *313, 331, 363*

ethnic diversity, *298A–298D,* **325I–325J,** *325K–325L*

gender diversity, *360–376*

lesson or moral, *315, 325M, 353*

literary language and terms, *313, 335*

stereotypes, recognizing, *342, 352*

See also Literary genres; Poetry.

Literary appreciation. *See* Literature, analyzing.

Literary devices

alliteration, *322*

analogies and similes, *R3*

characterization, *363*

descriptive language, *308, 325L, R19*

details, *306*

exaggeration/hyperbole, *360*

fairy tale objects, *344*

foreshadowing, *332*

imagery, *320, 321, 322*

narrator, *335, 344, 348, 362*

nonsense, *366*

omniscient narrator, *335*

passage of time, *316*

point of view, *308, 335, 336, 344, 365*

repetition, *316*

simile, *R3*

sound words, *325J*

suspense, *302, 304*

Literary genres, characteristics of

allegory, *315*

fairy tales, **331**

fantasy, **313**

poetry, **322**

tall tales, **363**

See also Expository text; Narrative text; Selections in Anthology.

Literary skills. *See* Literary analysis; Literary devices; Poetic devices; Story elements.

Literature

analyzing, **323C, 323D, 357C, 357D**

comparing. *See* Connections.

discussion. *See* Responding to literature.

evaluating, *298D, 316, 321, 359C, 361, 363, 364, 366, 367, 368, 372, 377*

interpreting, *298D, 308, 318, 326J, 338, 352, 354, 357B, 357C, 357D, 358J, 366, 376, 378*

linking. *See* Skills link.

responding to. *See* Responding to literature.

See also Literary devices; Story elements

Locating information. *See* Information skills.

M

Main idea and supporting details, identifying. *See* Comprehension skills.

Maps, using. *See* Graphic information, interpreting.

Mathematics activities. *See* Cross-curricular activities.

Meaning, constructing from text. *See* Comprehension skills; Decoding skills; Language; Phonics; Strategic reading.

Mechanics, language

capitalization

proofreading, **325F**

punctuation

hyphen, *323E*

possessives, **325E**

proofreading, **325F**

quotation marks, *325D*

Mental images. *See* Visualizing.

encyclopedia, *298C, 381, R27*
newspaper, *381D*
See also Graphic information.
study strategies
skimming and scanning, *327C*
test-taking strategies, *382*
See also Research activities; Spiral Review.

Rereading
cooperatively, *367, 373*
for comprehension, *309, 311, 323A, 323B, 367, 377*
orally, *311, 367*
to support answer, *318, 322, 354, 378*
with feeling and expression, *311, 341, 373*

Research activities, *298C, 380, 381, R27*

Responding to literature, options for
discussion, *298D, 308, 318, 325J, 325L, 325N, 326J, 338, 352, 354, 358J, 366, 376, 378, R3, R5, R7*
internet, *319, 355, 379*
personal response, *298D, 319, 326J, 355, 358G, 358J, 379*
writing, *318, 354, 378*

Reteaching. *See* Individual needs, reteaching.

Retelling
story, *298D, 323C, 325I, 325J*

Revising. *See* Reading-Writing Workshop, steps of.

Rhyme. *See* Poetic devices.

Rhythm. *See* Poetic devices.

Root words. *See* Structural analysis.

S

Science activities. *See* Cross-curricular activities.

Selecting books. *See* Independent and recreational reading.

Selections in Anthology
fairy tale
Cendrillon by Robert D. San Souci, *328–353*
fantasy
Stranger, The by Chris Van Allsburg, *300–317*
poetry. *See* Poems in Anthology.
nonfiction
"Let's Have a Ball!" *356–357*
science experiment
"Constructing a Straw Thermometer" from *Simple Weather Experiments with Everyday Materials* by Muriel Mandell, *380–381*
tall tale
Heat Wave! by Helen Ketteman, *360–376*

Self-assessment
reading, *319, 355, 379*
theme goals, *382–383*
writing project, *325G*

Self-correcting reading strategy. *See* Strategies, reading, monitor.

Semantic cues. *See* Decoding skills, context clues; Vocabulary skills.

Sentences. *See* Grammar and usage.

Sequence of events, noting. *See* Comprehension skills.

Setting. *See* Story elements.

Shared learning. *See* Cooperative learning activities.

Skill Reminder, *323Q–323R, 357Q–357R, 381Q–381R*

Skills links
diagram, how to read a, **380–381**
poem, how to read a, **320–323**
time line, how to read a, **356–357**

Skills, major
compare and contrast, *327D, 333,* **357A**
fantasy and realism, *359D, 365,* **381A**
noting details, *299D, 307,* **323A**

Skimming and scanning. *See* Adjusting reading rate.

Social studies activities. *See* Cross-curricular activities.

Sound-spelling patterns. *See* Phonics; Spelling.

Sounding out words. *See* Decoding skills, blending.

Speaking activities
announcements, **381O, 381P**
composing sentences, *323G, 323J, 357G, 381J*
conversations, **323O–323P**
describing, *298A, 299D, 308, 315*
discussion, *298D, 299A, 304, 309, 316, 317, 323D, 324, 325J, 325L, 325N, 326J, 327A, 339, 353, 358E, 358J, 359A, 367, 371, 377, 381N*
dramatics. *See* Creative dramatics.
explanation, *317*
express ideas, *298D, 308, 318, 326J, 338, 352, 354, 358J, 366, 376, 378*
guidelines
for anticipating questions or problems, *381P*
for appropriate communication behaviors, **323O–323P, 357O–357P, 381O–381P**
for asking clarifying questions, *323O*
for comparing and contrasting texts, **357O–357P**
for demonstrating understanding, *323O, 323P*
for encouraging others, *323P*
for making announcements, **381O–381P**
for self-questioning about a text, *357P*
for speaking loudly and clearly, **381O**
literature discussion. *See* Responding to literature.

"Yes, It Can Really Rain Frogs! Rain of All Sorts" by Spencer Christian and Antonia Felix, *358G–358J*

Teacher's Note, *298B, 298C, 299C, 323E, 326H, 327C, 357E, 357J, 359C, 381E*

Teaching across the curriculum. *See* Content areas, reading in the; Cross-curricular activities.

Teaching and management
managing assessment, *292G–292H*
managing instruction, *292E–292F, 296A–297A, 298A, 323E, 323K, 326C–326D, 326G, 357E, 357K, 358C–358D, 358G, 381E, 381K*
managing program materials, *292E–292F, 296A–297A, 326C–326D, 358C–358D*
parent conferences. *See* Home/Community Connections book.
special needs of students, meeting. *See* Individual needs, meeting; Individual needs, reteaching.

Technology resources, *R28*
Get Set for Reading CD-ROM, *299A, 327A, 359A*
Internet, *319, 355, 379*
Spelling Spree! ™, *323H, 357H, 381H*
Type to Learn™ Jr., *323N, 325A, 357N, 381N*
Wacky Web Tales, *323K, 357K, 381K*
The Writer's Resource Library, *323N, 325A, 357N, 381N*
www.eduplace.com, *319, 355, 379*

Test-taking skills. *See* Reference and study skills.

Text organization and structure
author notes, *325I*
captions, *356*
introductory paragraph, *356*
time line structure, *356–357*
See also Comprehension skills.

Theme. *See* Literary analysis, lesson or moral.

Theme Assessment wrap-up, *382, 383, N384*

Theme at a Glance, *292E–292F*

Theme concepts, *293A*

Theme Paperbacks
Little Oh by Laura Krauss Melmed, *325K–325L*
Real Thief, The by William Steig, *325M–325N*
Story of the Milky Way, The by Joseph Bruchac and Gayle Ross, *325I–325J*

Theme projects, *293B*

Theme, Launching the, *293A–293B*

Themes
That's Amazing!, *292A–383A*

Think Aloud. *See* Modeling.

Thinking
creatively. *See* Creative thinking.
critically. *See* Critical thinking.

Topics, selecting. *See* Research activities; Reading-Writing Workshop, prewriting.

Universal Access Plans, *297B–297C, 326E–326F, 358E–358F*
See also Individual needs, meeting.

Usage. *See* Grammar and usage.

V

Venn diagrams. *See* Graphic organizers.

Verbs. *See* Speech, parts of.

Videotapes, *292D*

Viewing activities
art, *375*
purpose
for comprehension, *375*
to access information, *375*
to analyze, *375*
to appreciate art, *375*
to distinguish realism and fantasy, *375*
to identify main idea, supporting details, *375*
to relate to real life, **381C, 381D**
television, **381C, 381D**
videotapes. *See* Videotapes.

Visual literacy
artist's style, **375**
point of view, **303**

Visualizing, *307, 320,* **381M**

Vocabulary, expanding
classifying/categorizing, **323K**
compound words. *See* Structural analysis.
context, using. *See* Decoding skills.
homophones, *323J*
multiple-meaning words, **357G**, *375*
root words, *334*
scientific terms:
weather words, **323J**
climate words, **381J**
technology words, **323G**
types of clothing, **357J**
word study, *334*
word webs. *See* Graphic organizers, word webs.
See also Language concepts and skills.

Vocabulary, selection
key words, *298C, 299B, 302, 306, 308, 314, 316, 320, 322, 325I, 325K, 325M, 327B, 330, 332, 334, 336, 338, 340, 342, 348, 350, 356, 359B, 362, 364, 366, 368, 370, 372, 374, 376, 380, R2, R4, R6*
See also Context, using; Daily Language Practice; Decoding skills.

Vocabulary skills
multiple-meaning words, **357G**, *375*
shades of meaning, **323I**
signal words for cause and effect, *305*
synonyms, **323I–323J**, *R15*
word origins, **323G**, *357J*

See also Dictionary skills; Spiral Review; Vocabulary, expanding; Vocabulary, selection.

Vowels. *See* Phonics; Spelling.

W

Word analysis. *See* Structural analysis; Vocabulary, expanding; Vocabulary, selection.

Word webs. *See* Graphic organizers.

Writer's craft
point of view: first-person, **335**

Writer's log. *See* Journal.

Writing activities and types
announcement, **357M–357N**
autobiography, *R24*
business letter, *R25*
compare/contrast paragraph, **357D**
cooperative writing. *See* Shared writing.
diary entry, *R25*
explanation, *315,* **323M–323N**
evaluation, *361*
friendly letter, *R24*
independent. *See* Independent writing.
information about story, *301, 310, 340*
newspaper story, *R23*
paragraph, *315*
poetry, *323*
questions, *327C, 329, 340*
reaction to story events, *319, 368, 379*
sentences, *357G*
story, *R23*
summary, **381M–381N.** *See also* Summaries, written.
tall tale sentences, *381H*
See also Reading-Writing Workshop, Writer's craft.

Writing as a process. *See* Reading-Writing Workshop.

Writing conferences. *See* Reading-Writing Workshop.

Writing modes
evaluative, *361*
expository, *315,* **323M–323N**
expressive, *323, R25. See also* Journal.
functional, **357M–357N,** *R24, R25*
informative, **381M–381N,** *R23*
narrative, *R23, R24*

Writing skills
computer tools, using. *See* Technology resources.
drafting skills
beginning, middle, and end, *324, 325,* **325B, 325C**
beginning with a topic sentence, **323M, 323N**
characters, *324, 325,* **325C**
conflict, resolving a story, *324, 325,* **325B**
details, using interesting, **357M, 357N**
dialogue, writing natural, *324, 325,* **325D**
facts and reasons, supporting the topic with, **323M, 323N**
five W's, including the, **381N**
friendly language, including, **357M, 357N**
main idea and details, **381M, 381N**
multiple characters, using, **325C**
organizing writing by time order or order of importance, **323M, 323N**
sequence of events, *324,* **325B**
setting, **325C**
voice, using an engaging, *324*
formats. *See* Writing, activities
prewriting skills
adapting a familiar story, **325A**
audience and purpose, **325A, 357M**
discussion, **325A**
organizing and planning, **325B, 381N**
process writing, steps of. *See* Reading-Writing Workshop.
proofreading skills

checking for missing information, **357N**
publishing skills
booklet, *325A*
bulletin board display, *323N, 325A, 325G*
read aloud festival, *325G*
submit story to magazine, *325G*
revising skills
audience, **323N**
correct tense, using the, **381L**
exact verbs, using, **323L**
formal and informal language, transforming, **323N**
ordering important information in an announcement, **357N**
paraphrasing, **381M, 381N**
possessives, singular and plural, **325E**
sentence combining with main verbs and helping verbs, **357L**
See also Reading-Writing Workshop; Spiral Review; Writer's craft.